APOCALYPTIC SHEEP AND GOATS
IN MATTHEW AND 1 ENOCH

EMORY STUDIES IN EARLY CHRISTIANITY

Vernon K. Robbins, General Editor
Roy R. Jeal, General Editor
Robert H. von Thaden Jr., Associate Editor
David B. Gowler, Associate Editor
Juan Hernández Jr.
Susan E. Hylen
Brigitte Kahl
Mikeal C. Parsons
Russell B. Sisson
Shively T. J. Smith
Elaine M. Wainwright

Number 24

APOCALYPTIC SHEEP AND GOATS IN MATTHEW AND 1 ENOCH

Elekosi F. Lafitaga

SBL PRESS

Atlanta

Copyright © 2022 by Elekosi F. Lafitaga

Publication of this volume was made possible by the generous support of the Pierce Program in Religion of Oxford College of Emory University.

The editors of this series express their sincere gratitude to David E. Orton and Deo Publishing for publication of this series 2009–2013.

All rights reserved. No part of this work may be reproduced or transmitted in any form or by any means, electronic or mechanical, including photocopying and recording, or by means of any information storage or retrieval system, except as may be expressly permitted by the 1976 Copyright Act or in writing from the publisher. Requests for permission should be addressed in writing to the Rights and Permissions Office, SBL Press, 825 Houston Mill Road, Atlanta, GA 30329 USA.

Library of Congress Control Number: 2022933681

Cover design is an adaptation by Bernard Madden of Rick A. Robbins, Mixed Media (19" x 24" pen and ink on paper, 1981). Cover design used by permission of Deo Publishing.

Contents

Abbreviations vii

1. Approaching Matthew's Apocalyptic Discourse 1
   1.1. Introduction   1
   1.2. Apocalyptic Literature and Apocalyptic   2
   1.3. Matthew and Apocalyptic   15
   1.4. The Scope, Thesis, and Significance   35

2. Metaphor and Rhetoric 41
   2.1. Introduction: Apocalyptic Discourse   41
   2.2. Metaphor Theory   44
   2.3. Sociorhetorical Interpretation   67
   2.4. Plan of Study   78

3. Animal Apocalypse: A Metaphorical Reading 81
   3.1. Introduction   81
   3.2. Animal Apocalypse   82
   3.3. The Animal Apocalypse as Allegory   92
   3.4. A Reading   95
   3.5. Sheep and the Lord of the Sheep   110
   3.6. Torah: Path of the Sheep   122
   3.7. Apocalyptic Communication   135
   3.8. Wisdom   155
   3.9. A Possible Social and Historical Scenario?   162
   3.10. Animal Apocalypse as Scripture   166

4. The Inner Textures of Matthew 25:31–46 173
   4.1. Introduction   173
   4.2. The Text of Matthew 25:31–46   175
   4.3. The Broader Narrative Context   185

4.4. The Immediate Literary Context	213

5. The Apocalyptic Discourse of Matthew 25:31–46 229
   5.1. Introduction 229
   5.2. A Metaphorical Reading 229
   5.3. Conclusion 243

Appendix A: Aristotle and Topos..247

Appendix B: Cicero and Quintilian on Metaphors.........................271

Bibliography...281

Ancient Sources Index..309
Modern Authors Index...321
Subject Index...325

Abbreviations

Primary Sources

1 En.	1 Enoch
2 Bar.	2 Baruch
3 Bar.	3 Baruch
3 Philip.	Demosthenes, *3 Philippic*
An. post.	Aristotle, *Analytica posteriora*
Ant.	Josephus, *Jewish Antiquities*
Apoc. Mos.	Apocalypse of Moses
b.	Babylonian Talmud
Brut.	Cicero, *Brutus*
Cat.	Aristotle, *Categoriae*
Crat.	Plato, *Cratylus*
Creation	Philo, *On the Creation of the World*
Criti.	Plato, *Critias*
De an.	Aristotle, *De anima*
De or.	Cicero, *De oratore*
Ep.	Seneca, *Epistulae morales*
Eq.	Aristophanes, *Equites*
Evag.	Isocrates, *Evagoras*
Fam.	Cicero, *Epistulae ad familiares*
Gen. Rab.	Genesis Rabbah
Gorg.	Plato, *Gorgias*
Hel.	Gorgias, *Helena*
Hist. an.	Aristotle, *Historia animalium*
Inst.	Quintilian, *Institutio oratoria*
Int.	Aristotle, *De interpretatione*
Jub.	Jubilees
LAE	Life of Adam and Eve
Leg.	Plato, *Leges*
LXX	Septuagint

viii   Abbreviations

Mem. rem.   Aristotle, *De memoria et reminiscentia*
Metaph.   Aristotle, *Metaphysica*
MT   Masoretic Text
Or. Brut.   Cicero, *Orator ad M. Brutum*
Paed.   Clement of Alexandria, *Paedagogus*
Pesah.   Pesahim
Phaedr.   Plato, *Phaedrus*
Phileb.   Plato, *Philebus*
Phys.   Aristotle, *Physica*
Poet.   Aristotle, *Poetica*
Praep. ev.   Eusebius of Caesarea, *Praeparatio evangelica*
Prot.   Plato, *Protagoras*
Pss. Sol.   Psalms of Solomon
Ran.   Aristophanes, *Ranae*
Rhet.   Aristotle, *Rhetorica*
Rhet. Her.   Rhetorica ad Herennium
Sib. Or.   Sibylline Oracles
T. Dan   Testament of Dan
T. Isaac   Testament of Isaac
T. Job   Testament of Job
Test. Ab.   Testament of Abraham
Theaet.   Plato, *Theaetetus*
Tim.   Plato, *Timaeus*
Top.   Aristotle, *Topica*

Secondary Sources

AB   Anchor Bible
ABD   *Anchor Bible Dictionary.* Edited by David Noel Freed-
                   man. 6 vols. New York Doubleday, 1992.
AJSR   *Association for Jewish Studies Review*
AnBib   Analecta biblica
AOS   American Oriental Series
BBR   *Bulletin for Biblical Research*
BDAG   Danker, Frederick W., Walter Bauer, William F. Arndt,
                   and F. Wilbur Gingrich. *Greek-English Lexicon of
                   the New Testament and Other Early Christian Litera-
                   ture.* 3rd ed. Chicago: University of Chicago Press,
                   2000.

Abbreviations

BDB	Brown, Francis, S. R. Driver, and Charles A. Briggs. *A Hebrew and English Lexicon of the Old Testament.* Oxford: Clarendon, 1907.
BETL	Bibliotheca Ephemeridum Theologicarum Lovaniensium
BibInt	Biblical Interpretation Series
BibNot	*Biblische Notizen*
BJS	Brown Judaic Studies
BR	*Biblical Research*
CBQ	*Catholic Biblical Quarterly*
CBQMS	Catholic Biblical Quarterly Monograph Series
ConBNT	Coniectanea Neotestamentica or Coniectanea Biblica: New Testament Series
ConBOT	Coniectanea Biblica: Old Testament Series
EJL	Early Judaism and Its Literature
ETS	Erfurter theologische Studien
ExpTim	*Expository Times*
FOTL	Forms of the Old Testament Literature
FRLANT	Forschungen zur Religion und Literatur des Alten und Neuen Testaments
HALOT	Koehler, Ludwig, Walter Baumgartner, and Johann J. Stamm. *The Hebrew and Aramaic Lexicon of the Old Testament.* Translated and edited under the supervision of Mervyn E. J. Richardson. 2 vols. Leiden: Brill, 2001.
HBT	*Horizons in Biblical Theology*
HSM	Harvard Semitic Monographs
HSS	Harvard Semitic Studies
HTR	*Harvard Theological Review*
HTSTSt	*HTS Teologiese Studies*
IBT	Interpreting Biblical Texts
ICC	International Critical Commentary
IDBSup	*Interpreter's Dictionary of the Bible: Supplementary Volume.* Edited by Keith Crim. Nashville: Abingdon, 1976.
Int	*Interpretation*
JBL	*Journal of Biblical Literature*
JCTCRS	Jewish and Christian Texts in Context and Related Studies

JSJ	*Journal for the Study of Judaism in the Persian, Hellenistic, and Roman Periods*
JSJSup	Supplements to the Journal for the Study of Judaism
JSNT	*Journal for the Study of the New Testament*
JSNTSup	Journal for the Study of the New Testament Supplement Series
JSOTSup	Journal for the Study of the Old Testament Supplement Series
JTC	*Journal for Theology and the Church*
JTS	*Journal of Theological Studies*
LCL	Loeb Classical Library
LNTS	The Library of New Testament Studies
LSJ	Liddell, Henry George, and Robert Scott, Henry Stuart Jones. *A Greek-English Lexicon*. 9th ed. with revised supplement. Oxford: Clarendon, 1996.
MSJ	*The Master's Seminary Journal*
NIGTC	New International Greek Testament Commentary
NovT	*Novum Testamentum*
NRSV	New Revised Standard Version
NTS	*New Testament Studies*
OEBI	*The Oxford Encyclopedia of Biblical Interpretation*. Edited by Steven L. McKenzie. 2 vols. Oxford: Oxford University Press, 2013.
OTL	Old Testament Library
OTP	*Old Testament Pseudepigrapha*. Edited by James H. Charlesworth. 2 vols. New York: Doubleday, 1983–1985.
PTMS	Pittsburgh Theological Monograph Series
PVTG	Pseudepigrapha Veteris Testamenti Graece
QJS	*Quarterly Journal of Speech*
RPP	*Religion Past and Present: Encyclopedia of Theology and Religion*. Edited by Hans Dieter Betz et al. 14 vols. Leiden: Brill, 2007–2013.
RSV	Revised Standard Version
SBLDS	Society of Biblical Literature Dissertation Series
SBLSymS	Society of Biblical Literature Symposium Series
SBT	Studies in Biblical Theology
SBTS	Sources for Biblical Theological Study
SNTSMS	Society for New Testament Studies Monograph Series

STDJ	Studies on the Texts of the Desert of Judah
StZ	*Stimmen der Zeit*
SVTP	Studia in Veteris Testamenti Pseudepigrapha
TDNT	*Theological Dictionary of the New Testament.* Edited by Gerhard Kittel and Gerhard Friedrich. Translated by Geoffrey W. Bromiley. 10 vols. Grand Rapids, 1964–1976.
TS	*Theological Studies*
TSAJ	Texte und Studien zum antiken Judentum
TynBul	*Tyndale Bulletin*
USQR	*Union Seminary Quarterly Review*
VTSup	Supplements to Vetus Testamentum
WBC	Word Biblical Commentary
ZTK	*Zeitschrift für Theologie und Kirche*

1

Approaching Matthew's Apocalyptic Discourse

1.1. Introduction

For many readers, apocalyptic and eschatological judgment have long characterized the Gospel of Matthew.[1] For example, it is from his study of the Gospel of Matthew that Ernst Käsemann coined the dictum, "apocalyptic is the mother of all Christian theology."[2] Matthew's eschatological imageries of judgment are often identified as apocalyptic and referred to as Matthew's apocalyptic discourses (e.g., Matt 25:31–46). However, it is not clear what exactly that apocalyptic identity entails. In the past, scholars who have read Matthew's eschatological judgment in light of Jewish apocalyptic literature assigned a specific function to its apocalyptic character. For example, David C. Sim perceives the apocalyptic material in Matthew to reflect an ideology that some scholars of Jewish apocalyptic literature call "apocalyptic eschatology." For Sim, that clearly indicates Matthew's intentions about an imminent parousia and judgment.[3]

A recent turn by scholarship on apocalyptic literature recognizes apocalyptic as a cultural phenomenon distinct from eschatology, a phenomenon that points toward the literary and intellectual creativity of Jewish scribes. This suggests that apocalyptic and eschatology are distinc-

---

1. For convenience, I will refer to the text of the Gospel of Matthew as Matthew. If in places it seems I may be referring to the author, I refer to the implied author, which may stand also as editors. I may also utilize *Matthean* in modifying texts that are products of redacting/editing sources, which I perceive as intertexts of inner-Synoptic and intertextual dialogue in the texts. I will refer also to the implied audience when speaking of the text's intended audience.

2. Ernst Käsemann, "Die Anfänge christlicher Theologie," *ZTK* 57 (1960): 162–85, ET Käsemann, "The Beginnings of Christian Theology," *JTC* 6 (1969): 17–46.

3. I will return to David C. Sim's work below.

-1-

2   Apocalyptic Sheep and Goats in Matthew and 1 Enoch

tive and should not be conflated. If this is true, then in contrast to what Sim and others say,[4] apocalyptic in the Gospel of Matthew may not equate with an ideology or social movement. That allows for a reassessment of the relations between apocalyptic in Matthew and possible notions of an imminent parousia and judgment. Thus, it is important that this study on the function of Matthew's apocalyptic discourse of judgment imagery establishes at the outset a working definition of *apocalyptic*.

1.2. Apocalyptic Literature and Apocalyptic

Scholars have long explored the nature of apocalyptic literature and attempted to define the extent to which we can refer to a text as apocalyptic.[5] Ancient authors did not understand ἀποκάλυψις the way modern scholarship interprets *apocalypse*, that is, as identifying forms of literary works, nor did they use the adjective ἀποκαλυπτικός to describe the contents of these works.[6] The need to distinguish between apocalyptic and

---

4. I will return below with a survey of literature of those who equate apocalyptic material of Matthew with the imminent coming judgment.

5. With reference to Rev 1:1, Friedrich Luecke is credited for first using *apocalypsis* in a generic sense for Jewish and Christian texts that were similar in form and content to the Revelation of John. See Friedrich Luecke, *Versuch einer vollstaendigen Einleitung in die Offenbarung Johannis und in die gesammte apokalyptische Literatur* (Bonn: Eduard Weber, 1832). By the mid-1900s, *apocalyptic(ally)* as verb, noun, and adjective were often used interchangeably by scholars and theologians alike, and the overlap of categories created confusion to the point that many abandoned the term. David Hellholm, like many others, recognizes that the generic designation *apocalypse* was influenced by the self-reference in the prologue of Revelation, which should be seen not only as a title but also as a reference to a genre. See David Hellholm, "Apocalypse," *RPP*, 1:297. See also Klaus Koch, *The Rediscovery of Apocalyptic*, SBT 2/22 (Naperville, IL: Allenson, 1972), 18.

6. Morton Smith, "On the History of ΑΠΟΚΑΛΥΠΤΩ and ΑΠΟΚΑΛΥΨΙΣ," in *Apocalypticism in the Mediterranean World and the Near East: Proceedings of the International Colloquium on Apocalypticism Uppsala, August 12–17, 1979*, ed. David Hellholm, 2nd ed. (Tübingen: Mohr Siebeck, 1983), 9–20. The Greek verb ἀποκαλύπτω, "to reveal, disclose, uncover," was in use as far back as Plato (*Prot.* 352a; *Gorg.* 455d). The noun ἀποκάλυψις appeared in Philodemus to mean "revelation" in the literal sense (Περί κακίον 22.15). Both refer to things related to humans. Plato uses the verb figuratively, for example when Socrates asks Protagoras to reveal his opinion. In addition, Gorgias informs Socrates that he will reveal his opinions concerning oratory. Philodemus speaks in the above instance about uncovering the head. Smith argues that the LXX never uses ἀποκάλυψις to refer to things relating to the divine, but that

1. Approaching Matthew's Apocalyptic Discourse   3

eschatology has been on the minds of scholars.[7] Instead of acknowledging the past for exacting use of the terms, scholars recently have been mobilizing for a resolution.[8] This includes identifying the origins of apocalyptic

---

it does use the verb ἀποκαλύπτω to refer to things relating to humans. The adjective ἀποκαλυπτικός is regularly cited as first coming from Clement of Alexandria (*Paed.* 1.1), describing the divine Word as "revealing" when taught, which is not necessarily what scholars today call apocalypse (see Smith, "On the History," 10–11). Smith conjectures that, in the final centuries BCE, a rise in belief among the "lower-middle-class" that the gods had secrets to reveal took hold in the eastern Mediterranean (Smith, "On the History," 12–14). By extension, this would culminate in the use of ἀποκάλυψις in Rev 1:1: "The revelation [ἀποκάλυψις] of Jesus Christ which God gave to him to show his servants what must soon come to pass." Smith points out that both the noun and verb appear in the LXX but more often refer to matters being revealed among humans (Smith, "On the History," 10–11).

7. H. H. Rowley, *The Relevance of Apocalyptic: A Study of Jewish and Christian Apocalypses from Daniel to the Revelation* (London: Lutterworth, 1944), 49. In noticing the absence of eschatology in some Jewish Apocalypses, Rowley already suggested in a work published in 1944 that the distinction between apocalyptic and eschatology must be made: "Just because so much eschatology enters into all apocalyptic, the two terms are commonly confused."

8. Koch, *Rediscovery of Apocalyptic*, 13–15. The interest in distinguishing between the terms follows the concern for the lack of clarity as to the relationship between the Old Testament and New Testament. According to Koch, theologians have provided excessive and unfounded answers that are due to the lack of studies by scholars of the historical aspects of apocalypses. Koch's call for a resolution became a turning point to rejuvenate the studies of apocalyptic literature as scholars began to (re)define the relevant terminologies. This may have been the point at which apocalyptic as a literary genre became more defined, for in the last decade of the twentieth century, scholarship on apocalyptic literature began to choose between two approaches to apocalyptic: apocalyptic as a literary genre and apocalyptic as a theological concept. In distinguishing between form, content, and function, Koch designated *apocalypse* as a literary genre, *apocalyptic* as describing the literary contents found in the apocalypses, and *apocalypticism* as an intellectual movement (Koch, *Rediscovery of Apocalyptic*, 18–33). Koch went on to list six characterizing entities. These were visions (discourse cycles with *angelus interpres*), spiritual turmoil, paraenetical discourses, pseudonym, mythical images rich in symbolism, and composite character. Koch notes that "the generic characteristics of the *paraenetic* sections, as well as the origins of the form, are still uninvestigated" (Koch, *Rediscovery of Apocalyptic*, 25). He asks whether these came from either the wisdom or the prophetic traditions. His recognition of symbolism will be significant later in this study as I explore apocalyptic language. For a survey of studies on apocalyptic literature up to the second half of the twentieth century in light of the term/concept of apocalyptic, see Richard E. Sturm, "Defining the Word 'Apocalyptic,'" in *Apocalyptic and the New Testament: Essays in Honor of J. Louis Martyn*, ed.

4 Apocalyptic Sheep and Goats in Matthew and 1 Enoch

phenomena and establishing a definition that defines the phenomena in terms of form, content, and function.

John J. Collins led a group of scholars in establishing a definition of apocalypse at the Society of Biblical Literature meeting in 1979, the proceedings of which were published in *Semeia* 14.[9] Many scholars today have accepted this definition as a heuristic paradigm. Collins wrote,

> Apocalypse is a genre of revelatory literature with a narrative framework, in which a revelation is mediated by an otherworldly being to a human recipient, disclosing a transcendent reality that is both temporal, insofar as it envisages an eschatological salvation, and spatial, insofar as it involves another super natural world.

Collins classifies two types of apocalypses: historical and otherworldly journeys.[10] He finds the adjective *apocalyptic* more useful if it refers to works identified as apocalypses and suggests that it can be extended legitimately to other literature insofar as that literature resembles the apocalypses. For Collins, apocalyptic contents consist of a worldview that perceives the world as mysterious.[11] He states, "If we say that a work is apocalyptic we encourage the reader to expect that it frames its message within the view of the world that is characteristic of the genre."[12] Collins goes on to list those characteristic elements. He favors prophetic origins of the apocalypses, while acknowledging wisdom material of the wider Mesopotamian and Hellenistic world.[13] We might ask at this point: If a

---

Joel Marcus and Marion L. Soards (Sheffield: JSOT Press, 1989). Sturm in this essay conveniently places the history of scholarship before the mid–nineteen hundreds in two broad approaches to the term apocalyptic: apocalyptic as a literary genre and as a theological concept.

9. John J. Collins, ed., "Introduction: Towards the Morphology of a Genre," *Semeia* 14 (1979): 1–20.

10. Collins, "Introduction," 13. See also John J. Collins, *The Apocalyptic Imagination: An Introduction to Jewish Apocalyptic Literature*, 2nd ed. (Grand Rapids: Eerdmans, 1998), 6.

11. Collins, "Introduction," 8. For example, "human life [that] is bounded in the present by the supernatural world of angels and demons and in the future by the inevitability of a final judgment."

12. Collins, *Apocalyptic Imagination*, 9.

13. Collins, "The Jewish Apocalypses," *Semeia* 14 (1979): 28. Reproduced in Collins, *Apocalyptic Imagination*, 7. He lists cosmogony, primordial events, recollection of past, *ex eventu* prophecy, persecution, other eschatological upheavals, judgment/

1. Approaching Matthew's Apocalyptic Discourse

particular worldview underlies apocalyptic literature, what prevents the gospel writers from sharing the same worldview? Why is such a worldview linked a priori with apocalypse as a genre?

Assuming a prophetic origin and function to the phenomenon of apocalyptic, some scholars attribute to apocalyptic literature a social movement of a suffering and marginalized group.[14] In taking considerable care not to link function too closely with content, Collins perceives an apocalyptic movement to exist "if it shared the conceptual framework of the genre, endorsing a worldview in which supernatural revelation, the heavenly world, and eschatological judgment played essential parts."[15] The problem is that not all Jewish apocalypses, such as 1 Enoch, contain a developed eschatology. There may also be as many different types of apocalyptic movements as there are different kinds of apocalypses. For Collins,

---

destruction of wicked, judgment/destruction of world, judgment/destruction of otherworldly beings, cosmic transformation, resurrection, and other forms of afterlife.

14. Paul D. Hanson, *The Dawn of Apocalyptic: The Historical and Sociological Roots of Early Jewish Apocalyptic Eschatology* (Philadelphia: Fortress, 1979). Hanson clearly delineates the apocalyptic phenomenon into form, content, and function. In the power structures of the hierocracy, as Hanson argues, visionary successors of the prophets felt helpless under these conditions and doubtful of prophetic visions like Second Isaiah; hence, they were inclined toward eschatological perceptions of the sort found in apocalyptic literature. For Hanson, the dominant feature of Jewish apocalypse is "apocalyptic eschatology," since it would be "mindful of the historical dimension behind its [apocalyptic] development" (Hanson, *Dawn of Apocalyptic*, 10). Hanson defines apocalyptic eschatology as "the disclosure (usually esoteric in nature) to the elect of the prophetic vision of Yahweh's sovereignty (including his future dealings with his people, the inner secrets of the cosmos, etc.) which vision the visionaries have ceased to translate into terms of plain history, real politics and human instrumentality because of a pessimistic view of reality growing out of the bleak postexilic conditions in which the visionary group found itself." In a later work, Hanson describes apocalyptic as follows: "Apocalyptic is commonly the mode of thought adopted by people who have grown deeply disillusioned with the realities of this world. They feel that the normal channels of power have passed them by. They feel cut off from their own societies, victimized and abandoned." See Paul D. Hanson, *Old Testament Apocalyptic*, IBT (Nashville: Abingdon, 1987), 34. See also Paul D. Hanson, "Apocalypses and Apocalypticism," *ABD* 1:279–82. There he repeats his definition of the word *apocalyptic* as designating a phenomenon of disclosure, namely, that of "heavenly secrets in visionary form to a seer for the benefit of a religious community experiencing suffering or perceiving itself victimized by some form of deprivation." These, however, I argue here to be problematic.

15. Collins, *Apocalyptic Imagination*, 12–13.

6   Apocalyptic Sheep and Goats in Matthew and 1 Enoch

movements differ in context and cannot be assumed to be universal. He contends that social setting does not seem to be inferred from the literary genre and that it varies through time and space.[16] How then can we say that social movement is apocalyptic?

Paolo Sacchi and Gabriele Boccaccini offer an interesting alternative to the relations of content (apocalyptic) and genre (apocalypse).[17] For these Italian scholars, the adjective *apocalyptic* designates a tradition of thought, whose cornerstone is the conception of evil as the cause of sin and of corrupted creation. This tradition of thought, they insist, should be understood apart from the genre. They state that "the 'apocalyptic' tradition cannot be defined as the [distinct] tradition of thought of the Apocalypses,"[18] because,

---

16. John J. Collins, "Genre, Ideology and Social Movements," in *Mysteries and Revelations: Apocalyptic Studies since the Uppsala Colloquium*, ed. John J. Collins and James H. Charlesworth (Sheffield: Sheffield Academic, 1991), 19–20.

17. Sacchi sees apocalyptic as a single tradition built upon the origin of evil pervasive in the book of 1 Enoch. See Paolo Sacchi, *Jewish Apocalyptic and Its History*, trans. William J. Short (Sheffield: Sheffield Academic, 1990). Boccaccini, in a scholarly discussion demarcating a decade since the Uppsala Colloquium, briefly summarizes Italian scholarship on apocalyptic studies and suggests that we can speak of an apocalyptic tradition of thought apart from the apocalypses themselves. See Gabrielle Boccaccini, "The Contribution of Italian Scholarship," in Collins and Charlesworth, *Mysteries and Revelations*, 33–50. Following the lead of Paolo Sacchi, Italian scholars chart the apocalyptic tradition, which spans seven periods from the fifth century BCE to the second century CE, that is, from 1 Enoch (which constitutes the first five periods) to 2 Baruch and 4 Ezra (which constitute the seventh period in the second century CE). It is now commonly understood that these writings may span from the third century BCE to the second century CE instead.

18. Boccaccini, "Contribution of Italian Scholarship," 48. Boccaccini repeats this notion in a separate work. See Gabrielle Boccaccini, *Middle Judaism: Jewish Thought, 300 BCE to 200 CE* (Minneapolis: Fortress, 1991). There he links this tradition of thought to wisdom literature, namely, to Job and Qoheleth, and the question of divine knowledge and human freedom (or the lack thereof). A counterpart to this apocalyptic tradition, according to Boccaccini, can be found in the book of Ben Sira and Daniel, where there is a different ideological tradition. However, in a later essay, "The Covenantal Theology of the Apocalyptic Book of Daniel," in *Enoch and Qumran Origins: New Light on a Forgotten Connection*, ed. Gabriele Boccaccini (Grand Rapids: Eerdmans, 2005), he explains that the paradox is solved, and Daniel can be considered as apocalyptic. He bases this change of conviction on Collins's statement: "the Jewish apocalypses were not produced by a single apocalyptic movement but constituted a genre that could be utilized by different groups in various situations" (Collins, Apocalyptic Imagination, 280).

1. Approaching Matthew's Apocalyptic Discourse 7

as Boccaccini suggests, "the documents belonging to the apocalyptic tradition are neither all nor only Apocalypses."[19] As such, insofar as it denotes an ideology, apocalyptic can occur in more than one genre. This allows Boccaccini and others to suggest that similar traditions of thought found in other genres can be described as apocalyptic as well. This transference of ideology from one genre to another may be the key reason why so many people have applied thoughts gleaned from apocalypses to other literary genres, like the gospels. However, an ideology can just as easily be speculative as identifying a social movement. The thought that apocalyptic can be found in other genres is an appealing idea, but why is it that the articulation of the problem of evil or eschatology in some apocalypses must be labeled apocalyptic in genres that are not actually apocalypses?

The International Colloquium at Uppsala in 1979 offered significant and critical insights for the study and definition of the apocalyptic phenomenon, as well as relevant terms.[20] We find in its proceedings astute challenges to Collins's generic definition.[21] One notable contribution is by Jean Carmignac, who articulates undeniable features of apocalyptic literature in his definition. Carmignac's essay seeks a definition broad enough to

---

19. Boccaccini, *Middle Judaism*, 130.

20. David Hellholm, ed., *Apocalypticism in the Mediterranean World and the Near East: Proceedings of the International Colloquium on Apocalypticism Uppsala, August 12–17, 1979*, 2nd ed. (Tübingen: Mohr Siebeck, 1989). This international meeting was held in Uppsala in 1979 on the topic of apocalypticism within the wider Mediterranean and Near Eastern context. The papers from this conference were published several years later in 1983. The committee for that conference turned down the attempts for a definition by a select group, and so the contributors each provided their own. The editor, David Hellholm, later commented that this was fortunate, as it may have been too early for an overall definition. See David Hellholm, "Methodological Reflections on the Problem of Definition of Generic Texts," in Collins and Charlesworth, *Mysteries and Revelations*, 135.

21. E. P. Sanders, who is most critical of Collins, finds the classification of an apocalypse and its characteristic elements problematic. For Sanders, those classified as apocalypses lack most of the listed traits, while those literary works containing the traits are not classified as apocalypses. See E. P. Sanders, "The Genre of Palestinian Jewish Apocalypses," in Hellholm, *Apocalypticism in the Mediterranean World*, 449. In adopting an essentialist approach, Sanders proposes that Jewish Palestinian apocalypses are more distinctive in their emphasis on the themes of revelation and reversal (Sanders, Genre of Palestinian Jewish Apocalypses," 456). He identifies Palestinian Jewish works as including Dan 7–12, 1 Enoch, Jub. 23, 4 Ezra, 2 Baruch, Testament of Abraham, and Testament of Levi.

include all possible prospective literary works.[22] He designates *apocalyptic* as a term that describes the literary genre, and calls those works that utilize this genre *apocalypse*.[23] He defines apocalypse as "a literary genre that describes the celestial revelations through symbols."[24] Carmignac defines the genre based solely on its spatial content,[25] while emphasizing language found in apocalypses. Such a definition foregrounds literary descriptions of contents within apocalypses.[26] Unlike Collins and others, eschatology plays no necessary role in Carmignac's paradigm. Of crucial importance in this study is that, as for Carmignac so for Klaus Koch, symbolic language forms an integral part of apocalyptic studies.[27]

Although discerning the origins of apocalyptic is beyond the scope of this study, it is an overstatement to locate apocalypses in either prophetic or wisdom traditions;[28] however, expanding apocalyptic's roots beyond the confines of the Hebrew Bible would certainly help to avoid such simplification. Scholars have now generally accepted the roots of Jewish apocalypses as lying ultimately in traditions of Near Eastern and

---

22. Jean Carmignac, "Description du phenomene de l'Apocalyptique dans l'Ancient Testament," in Hellholm, *Apocalypticism in the Mediterranean World*, 163–70.

23. See P. Vielhauer, "Apocalypses and Related Subjects: Introduction," in *New Testament Apocrypha*, ed. E. Hennecke and W. Schneemelcher (Philadelphia: Lutterworth, 1965), 2:581–607, esp. 582. Vielhauer states: "By means of the word 'Apocalyptic' we designate first of all the literary genre of the Apocalypses, i.e., revelatory writings which disclose the secrets of the beyond and especially of the end of time, and then secondly, the realm of ideas from which this literature originates."

24. Carmignac, "Description," 165.

25. Christopher Rowland later emphasizes this spatial content, saying that "apocalyptic seems essentially to be about the revelation of the divine mysteries." See Christopher Rowland, *The Open Heaven: A Study of Apocalyptic in Judaism and Early Christianity* (New York: Crossroad, 1982), 70–72.

26. See also Koch, *Rediscovery of Apocalyptic*, 18–33, and Lars Hartman, "Survey of the Problem of Apocalyptic Genre," in Hellholm, *Apocalypticism in the Mediterranean World*, 329–44.

27. One of Koch's defining characteristics of apocalyptic is "mythical images rich in symbolism."

28. E. P. Sanders represents a view that finds significance in both the prophetic and wisdom traditions in apocalypses. He strives to incorporate eschatology and the mediation of revelation on equal terms. This view is also shared by Ithamar Gruenwald, *From Apocalypticism to Gnosticism: Studies in Apocalypticism, Merkavah Mysticism and Gnosticism* (New York: Lang, 1988), 76; Gruenwald, *Apocalyptic and Merkavah Mysticism* (Leiden: Brill, 1980). See also John Barton, *Oracles of God: Perceptions of Ancient Prophecy in Israel after the Exile* (London: Darton, Longman & Todd, 1986).

1. Approaching Matthew's Apocalyptic Discourse

Mediterranean mythologies and literature.[29] Daniel Boyarin insists that "one does not need to search for the origins of 'apocalypticism,' for the connections with the Babylonian scribal wisdom are sufficient to explain the tradition."[30] Such roots affirm past arguments of Gerhard von Rad, Michael E. Stone, Jonathan Z. Smith, and Hans Dieter Betz in emphasizing the association of apocalypses with wisdom traditions of the ancient Near East and the wider Hellenistic world. These perspectives present a more promising path for appreciating the literary and intellectual creativity evident within apocalyptic literature.[31] Smith states that the apocalyptic

---

29. Richard J. Clifford, S.J., "The Roots of Apocalypticism in Near Eastern Myth," in *The Continuum History of Apocalypticism*, ed. Bernard McGinn, John J. Collins, and Stephen J. Stein (New York: Continuum, 2003), 3–29. See also Anders Hultgard, "Persian Apocalpyticism," 30–63, in the same volume. See also Martin Hengel, *Judaism and Hellenism: Studies in Their Encounter in Palestine during the Early Hellenistic Period*, trans. John Bowden, 2 vols. (Minneapolis: Fortress, 1991).

30. Boyarin's expertise in the Babylonian Talmud and cultural affinities of Jewish-Christian relations in late antiquity is insightful. For example, see Daniel Boyarin, *A Traveling Homeland: The Babylonian Talmud as Diaspora* (Philadelphia: University of Pennsylvania, 2015); Boyarin, *The Jewish Gospels: The Story of the Jewish Christ* (New York: New Press, 2012); Boyarin, *A Radical Jew: Paul and the Politics of Identity* (Berkeley: University of California, 1994). The above quotation is taken from a chapter discussion on Jewish apocalypse by Boyarin, "Rethinking Apocalypse; or, Apocalypse Then" (unpublished manuscript). The ways in which I have taken up my views of apocalyptic in this study are indebted to his insights.

31. Gerhard von Rad, *Old Testament Theology: The Theology of Israel's Prophetic Tradition*, trans. D. Stalker, vol. 2 (New York: Harper & Row, 1965). Von Rad makes the argument that *Apokalyptik* springs not from Israelite prophecy but from Israelite wisdom. The close link he makes between *Apokalyptik* and wisdom leads him to link the literary conventions in apocalypses to "figurative discourses" or *meshalim* typical of wisdom traditions (2:306). For him, the interpretation of oracles and dreams is the task of the wise man; here he draws a parallel with the Joseph story (2:324–26). Among others, occurrences of paraenetical material in the apocalyptic writings, theodicy, and stylistic devices (i.e., the use of a question-and-answer method) are significant links with wisdom (2:326–27). See Michael E. Stone, "Lists of Revealed Things in the Apocalyptic Literature," in *Magnalia Dei: The Mighty Acts of God; Essays on the Bible and Archaeology in Memory of G. Ernest Wright*, ed. Frank Moore Cross, Werner E. LeMarke, and Patrick D. Miller (Garden City, NY: Doubleday, 1976), 426; Jonathan Z. Smith, "Wisdom and Apocalyptic," in *Religious Syncretism in Antiquity: Essays in Conversation with Geo Widengren*, ed. Birger A. Pearson (Missoula: Scholars Press, 1975), 131–56. Smith argues for continuity between apocalyptists and ancient Babylonian scribalism, which is the beginning of the relationship between wisdom and apocalypses. See also Hans Dieter Betz, "On the Problem of the Religio-historical

phenomenon is "wisdom lacking a royal patron," a definition with which Smith rightly questions the "lachrymose theory" of apocalypticism. Smith insists that the phenomenon is not a response to religious persecution but an *expression* of it.[32] He further states that the apocalyptic phenomenon is "a learned rather than a popular religious phenomenon."

Defining the apocalyptic phenomenon in terms of form, content, and function has not held up to scrutiny. Apocalyptic as denoting worldview, social movement, and ideology raises more questions than it offers solutions. Recently, Lester L. Grabbe, Philip R. Davies, and Daniel Boyarin have suggested we redefine our approach.[33] These scholars place more emphasis upon seeing Jewish apocalypses as reflecting a mode of Jewish thinking and literary creativity in the midst of the Near Eastern world of ancient intellectuals than reflecting an ideology or a movement confined to groups of Jews located at the margins of society. Davies defines apocalypse as "a literary communication of esoteric knowledge, purportedly mediated by a heavenly figure to (usually so, but not in the book of Revelation) a renowned figure of the past."[34] He states,

> This definition ... permits us to divide the subject-matter of the knowledge into political, historical futuristic, astronomical, halakhic, *listenwissenschaftlich*. It is also broad enough to contain both Jewish and non-Jewish apocalypses. The content of an apocalypse is therefore *esoteric* knowledge of a kind that could be acquired not by human

---

Understanding of Apocalypticism," *JTC* 6 (1969): 134–54; Hengel, *Judaism and Hellenism*, esp. 1:210–18.

32. Smith, "Wisdom and Apocalyptic," 149, 154–55. Smith sees this as an expression of "the trauma of the cessation of native kingship."

33. Phillip R. Davies, *On the Origins of Judaism*, Bible World (Oakville, CT: Equinox, 2008); Lester L. Grabbe, "Prophetic and Apocalyptic: Time for New Definitions—and New Thinking," in *Knowing the End from the Beginning: The Prophetic, the Apocalyptic and Their Relationships*, ed. Lester L. Grabbe and Robert D. Haak (New York: T&T Clark, 2003): 107–33. Grabbe sees both prophetic and apocalyptic literature as scribal products. To distinguish between the two is misplaced: "With regard to both prophecy and apocalyptic, however, the product before us is a scribal creation which may have little or nothing to do with an actual prophet or visionary" (132). See also G. G. Xeravits, "Wisdom Traits of the Eschatological Prophet," in *Wisdom and Apocalypticism in the Dead Sea Scrolls and in the Biblical Tradition*, ed. F. Garcia Martinez (Leuven: Leuven University Press, 2003): 183–92. Boyarin finds traces of the origins in Babylonian scribal wisdom. See n. 30 above.

34. Davies, *On the Origins of Judaism*, 103.

observation or reason but by revelation. The supernatural origin of the revelation and the pseudonymous attribution of the literary report to a venerable figure of the past imply to the recipient that the knowledge is both irrefutable and powerful. Certain additional features can indicate the purpose and background of a particular apocalypse; for example, many Jewish apocalypses contain exhortation and consolation. The purpose of the revealed knowledge in these cases is to give assurance in the face of crisis or calamity (e.g., Daniel, 4 Ezra). If the content of the apocalypse is halakhic or quasi-historical (e.g., Jubilees, despite its historiographical guise), we may suppose that it represents a claim to the cosmic correctness of a certain way of behaving.[35]

Here Davies identifies the content with esoteric knowledge that is broad but limited only to the esoteric nature defined by the genre, and that it is mediated by a heavenly being to a renowned figure of the past. The revelatory and communicative essence of this definition is certainly not unique to Davies and perhaps unobjectionable.[36] However, Davies's emphasis on the literary creativity of apocalyptic and his association of this literary phenomenon with Jewish scribes and sages is especially significant.[37] Davies

---

35. Davies, *On the Origins of Judaism*, 103. See also Rowland, *Open Heaven*, 14: "To speak of apocalyptic, therefore, is to concentrate on the theme of the direct communication of the heavenly mysteries in all their diversity."

36. E.g., Rowland, *Open Heaven*, 21. In response to Rowland, Collins states, "Such a definition is unobjectionable as far as it goes" (*Apocalyptic Imagination*, 10).

37. Davies pinpoints Babylonian manticism as what likely influenced the scribes who wrote apocalypses. For example, Mesopotamian manticism includes "the perception of all human experience as forming an 'interlocking totality,' which makes the associations of phenomena significant and potentially predictive," and "irregularities" within an ordered world that hint at the involvement of gods in human history (Davies, *On the Origins of Judaism*, 109). From this involvement, we can derive inferences for human virtue and ethics. The association between the doings of the gods and human behavior (ethical wisdom), as Davies suggests, is the very subject of mantic lore. He states, "Mantic lore is thus empirical, based on observation, as is instructional or 'ethical' wisdom, the one concerned with the doings and decisions of the gods, the other with human behavior" (Davies, *On the Origins of Judaism*, 110). Indeed, manticism is not confined to Babylonian practices, as it is also found in Egyptian and Hellenistic literature, but Babylonian Jewry may have been instrumental (Collins, *Apocalyptic Imagination*, 28). Although Collins points out that manticism is found in Egyptian and Hellenistic literature, he does not deny influences of Babylonian dream interpretation in Jewish apocalypses. See, for example, John J. Collins, *Seers, Sibyls and Sages in Hellenistic-Roman Judaism* (Leiden: Brill, 2001), 35. In fact, Collins finds the work of

12   Apocalyptic Sheep and Goats in Matthew and 1 Enoch

notes that in Jewish apocalyptic literature such practices are attributed especially to the wise. He hesitates to label the contents as apocalyptic, not because they are not but because that label is unnecessary, for the revelation of heavenly secrets has been "a long-established and well-embedded scribal convention" that can be traced back to scribes of ancient Babylonia.[38]

1.2.1. A Working Definition of Apocalypse and Apocalyptic

In defining the genre apocalypse, therefore, the first part of Collins's definition cited above remains helpful: "Apocalypse is a genre of revelatory literature with a narrative framework, in which a revelation is mediated by an otherworldly being to a human recipient." Davies defines the nature of this revelation and its contents further, seeing apocalypse as "a literary communication of esoteric knowledge." This knowledge is acquired only *through heavenly revelation* and not through human observation and reason. It may or may not include eschatology. Carmignac characterizes the contents in terms of the salient features of that heavenly communication, suggesting that the literary genre "describes the celestial revelations *through symbols*," which Davies suggests stem from wisdom traditions of both Jewish and the Near East—namely, Babylonian—origins.[39] Apocalyptic then *is the adjective that describes the literary communication of*

VanderKam and Kvanvig plausible, who argue for literary influences and connections between Babylonian material and Enoch and Daniel. See James C. VanderKam, *Enoch and the Growth of an Apocalyptic Tradition*, CBQMS 16 (Washington, DC: Catholic Biblical Association of America, 1984); Helge S. Kvanvig, *Roots of Apocalyptic: The Mesopotamian Background of the Enoch figure and of the Son of Man* (Neukirchen-Vluyn: Neukirchener Verlag, 1988).

38. Davies, *On the Origins of Judaism*, 112. He explains this hesitance by saying, "Anyone might write an apocalypse, just as anyone might write a biography, compose an oracle, write a letter, or make a speech. It is part of a repertoire of literary forms." But then he asks, "Why should we take that classification further, when we do not for any other genre?" (Davies, *On the Origins of Judaism*, 101). Davies argues that classifying an apocalypse as a genre is one thing, but classifying the contents of that genre under the same definition is another.

39. Davies, *On the Origins of Judaism*, 112. He states, "Certainly, the symbolic vision represents a mantic device, whereby something observed is imbued with an esoteric meaning. This may involve a simple wordplay ... or a more developed perception, as in a dream ... and can be stretched into a quite elaborate 'historical' review from the mouth of an angelic intermediary." Here I integrate definitions of Carmignac, "Description," 163–70, and Davies, *On the Origins of Judaism*, 103.

1. Approaching Matthew's Apocalyptic Discourse 13

esoteric knowledge through heavenly revelation and symbols, which may take the form of dreams, visions, or angelic pronouncements.[40] This definition sees apocalypses and apocalyptic primarily as a literary and scribal phenomenon.

Yet Collins rightly suggests that apocalyptic is not simply conceptual "but is generated by social and historical circumstances."[41] In this regard, Davies looks to the activities of Jewish scribes of wisdom traditions. These scribes were among the social elite. He states,

> The social background of "apocalyptic" writing thus furnished is more fully described and precisely documented by the activity of political "established" and cultural cosmopolitan scribes than of visionary "counter-establishment" conventicles.[42]

Indeed, on this basis, apocalyptic literature would not have been a product of a marginal, alienated, or oppressed group.[43] Boyarin agrees but suggests that the best way to flesh out this idea is to consider the distinct views in apocalyptic literature along a broader continuum of both space and time of intellectual exchanges among Jewish scribes.[44] This study takes seriously this insight as it attempts to chart possible influences from the Book of Dreams on the Gospel of Matthew and as it considers them as literary and scribal activities. As such, these influences and activities are inseparable from cultural knowledge (memories and traditions) and historical experiences.

Our working definition of apocalypse does not depart altogether from Collins's, which delineates the significant elements of apocalypses

---

40. Rowland, *Open Heaven*, 9–10.

41. Collins, *Apocalyptic Imagination*, 22.

42. Davies, *On the Origins of Judaism*, 112.

43. Contra Hanson, who states, as noted above, "Apocalyptic is commonly the mode of thought adopted by people who have grown deeply disillusioned with the realities of this world. They feel that the normal channels of power have passed them by. They feel cut off from their own societies, victimized and abandoned" (*Old Testament Apocalyptic*, 34).

44. Boyarin, "Rethinking Apocalypse; or, Apocalypse Then." On this point, Boyarin cites Annette Yoshiko Reed, "From Scribalism to Sectarianism: The Angelic Descent Myth and the Social Settings of Enochic Pseudepigraphy," chapter 2 in *Fallen Angels and the History of Judaism and Christianity: The Reception of Enochic Literature* (Cambridge: Cambridge University Press, 2005). In this chapter Reed responds positively to Davies's proposition and concludes that the scribes were among the elites rather than separatists (Reed, *Fallen Angels*, 69).

14   Apocalyptic Sheep and Goats in Matthew and 1 Enoch

as being a revelation (message), a heavenly mediator, and a recipient. It is obviously a paradigm of communicating an esoteric message for which a divine being or an angelic interpreter is needed. The designation *apocalyptic* extends to the literary expressions and tools of that communication, that is, metaphors, allegory, intertextual allusions, motifs, themes, and so on. Therefore, one may also refer to the persuasive and argumentative features of the communication as apocalyptic rhetoric. This literary description of apocalyptic enables its exploration in other genres such as epistles and the gospels.[45]

This stance departs from Collins's and others' definition by perceiving eschatology as distinct from apocalyptic, though they are not mutually exclusive. Apocalyptic refers to the literary contents of Jewish apocalypses that communicate esoteric knowledge via heavenly beings. Eschatology refers to ideas and beliefs of the end time (i.e., the coming end, end-time judgment, eternal death, eternal life, etc.). These ideologies are found in some Jewish apocalyptic texts (e.g., Daniel, the Book of Dreams, 1 En. 83–90, the Epistle of Enoch 92–105, Revelation) but not all. In speaking of eschatology, Christopher Rowland identifies it as including

> the critical nature of human decisions, the fate of the individual believer's soul after death, the termination of this world order and a setting up of another, events like the last judgment and the resurrection of the dead, and a convenient way of *referring to future hopes about the coming of God's kingdom on earth, irrespective of whether in fact it involves an ending of the historical process.*[46]

------

45. The formal categories that Collins have adopted, following Hanson—apocalypse, apocalyptic eschatology, and apocalypticism—do not account for the many different possibilities of apocalyptic, some of which are found in the Pauline corpus, where inter alia, although apocalyptic features are evident, they are not considered apocalypses. See, for example, Greg Carey, *Ultimate Things: An Introduction to Jewish and Christian Apocalyptic Literature* (Saint Louis: Chalice, 2005), 6. To account for those instances, Carey introduces the addition of "apocalyptic discourse." See also Greg Carey, "Introduction," in *Vision and Persuasion: Rhetorical Dimensions of Apocalyptic Discourse*, ed. Greg Carey and L. Gregory Bloomquist (Saint Louis: Chalice, 1999), 1–15. The addition of "apocalyptic discourse" to the formal categories would account for those discourses that do not have the generic framework of an apocalypse. This is where the generic definition seems to break down.

46. Christopher Rowland, "The Eschatology of the New Testament Church," in *The Oxford Handbook of Eschatology*, ed. Jerry L. Walls, (Oxford: Oxford University Press, 2008), 56 (italics mine).

1. Approaching Matthew's Apocalyptic Discourse

It is the last part (in italics) that Rowland, and thus this study, adopts as a working definition for eschatology, since it is, as he states, "an important feature of many texts from the Second Temple period."

Features of eschatology are simply features within apocalypses that are not part of the genre's definition.[47] Davies's clarification about the relationship between eschatology and apocalyptic is worth remembering at this point: "If we need to explain the introduction of eschatology between ben Sira and Daniel (a gap of forty years), the events in Judah are sufficient. The Antiochean crisis did provoke the creation of the book of Daniel, and of one or two of the Enochic apocalypses. But it [did] not create 'apocalyptic.' "[48] It would also be an error to overemphasize eschatological judgment or the last judgment as a governing theme, within the apocalyptic discourses of Matthew, that projects fear. Such theological reading is a thing of the past that has taken the back seat to readings that resonate more of God's mercy and righteousness, as within more recent theological inquiry.[49] Following this stance, this study will highlight God's mercy and righteousness rather than focus on fear of the last judgment. This reading, as I will argue, is more in line with textual evidence within the apocalyptic discourses of the Gospel of Matthew.

1.3. Matthew and Apocalyptic

Scholarship on the Gospel of Matthew and apocalyptic has not been extensive in the last fifty years. For much of that time, the treatment of apocalyptic in scholarship about the Gospel of Matthew has been predominantly in terms of eschatological ideology to the extent that apocalyptic becomes its primary force.[50] For many, apocalyptic in the Gospel of Matthew under-

---

47. Christopher Rowland and John Barton, eds., "Introduction," in *Apocalyptic in History and Tradition* (Sheffield: Sheffield Academic, 2002), 3.

48. Davies, *On the Origins of Judaism*, 114.

49. For example, see the discussion in Olaf Rölver, *Christliche Existenz zwischen den Gerichten Gottes* (V&R unipress, 2010), 15–16. This study admits that it would do better if it would have engaged more fully with current European scholarship on theological trends that pertain to apocalypticism and the New Testament. It would find that the acquisition of theological perception is more historically and scientifically grounded and less lofty and radical, as witnessed in past theological endeavors of the twentieth century. For a work on a more scientific reading of Jesus and judgment in the gospels, see Christian Riniker, *Die Gerichtsverkündigung Jesus* (Bern: Lang, 1999).

50. Leopold Sabourin, "Apocalyptic Traits in Matthew's Gospel," *Religious Studies Bulletin* 3 (1983): 19–36; D. A. Hagner, "Apocalyptic Motifs in the Gospel of Matthew:

16   Apocalyptic Sheep and Goats in Matthew and 1 Enoch

scores the idea behind thoughts of the end of days or strong notions of the parousia (second coming) of the Son of Man and final judgment. As such, they conflate apocalyptic with an ideology or religious perspective of eschatology born out of an alienated group.[51] From the discussion above, the works of P. Hanson and P. Sacchi linger behind these conflations. As a result, the literary and intellectual creativity of using and reusing cultural traditions evident in the expressions of the heaven and earth connection is neglected. Studies on the treatment of apocalyptic in Matthew since 2000 have made strides in realizing and identifying this distinction. These studies, though few, examine metaphorical language and closer literary connections to Jewish apocalyptic literature. I will survey them briefly here.

1.3.1. Matthew and Apocalyptic in the Past

Without a doubt, the Gospel of Matthew contains features commonly found in Jewish apocalypses. In the late nineteenth and early twentieth centuries,

---

Continuity and Discontinuity," *HBT* 7 (1985): 53–82; Hagner, "Imminence and Parousia in the Gospel of Matthew," in *Texts and Contexts: Biblical Texts in Their Textual and Situational Contexts*, ed. Tord Fornberg and David Hellholm (Oslo: Scandinavian University Press, 1995), 77–92; O. L. Cope, "'To the Close of the Age': The Role of Apocalyptic Thought in the Gospel of Matthew," in Marcus and Soards, *Apocalyptic and the New Testament*, 113–24; Graham N. Stanton, *A Gospel for a New People: Studies in Matthew* (Louisville: Westminster John Knox, 1992), esp. chapter 9: "Once More: Matthew 25:31–46"; David C. Sim, *Apocalyptic Eschatology in the Gospel of Matthew* (Cambridge: Cambridge University Press, 1996).

51. This is best expressed by Paul D. Hanson, who sees apocalyptic eschatology as the dominating feature of Jewish apocalypses. For him, apocalyptic eschatology was a religious perspective, which "focuses on the disclosure (usually esoteric in nature) to the elect of the cosmic vision of Yhwh's sovereignty" that emerges from a pessimistic view of reality in postexilic conditions. See Hanson, *Dawn of Apocalyptic*, 10. In his essay in the *Anchor Bible Dictionary*, he repeats his definition of the word *apocalyptic* as designating a phenomenon of disclosure, namely, that of "heavenly secrets in visionary form to a seer for the benefit of a religious community experiencing suffering or perceiving itself victimized by some form of deprivation" (See Hanson, "Apocalypses and Apocalypticism," *ABD* 1:279–82). Elsewhere, Hanson describes further this pessimistic view of reality. He states, "Apocalyptic is commonly the mode of thought adopted by people who have grown deeply disillusioned with the realities of this world. They feel that the normal channels of power have passed them by. They feel cut off from their own societies, victimized and abandoned" (See Hanson, "Apocalypticism," *IDBSup*, 30).

1. Approaching Matthew's Apocalyptic Discourse   17

Johannes Weiss and Albert Schweitzer had already recognized the presence of apocalyptic features in the Gospel of Matthew within the speeches of the historical Jesus.[52] Historical Jesus aside, it was B. H. Streeter who saw the importance of apocalyptic for the *author* of the Gospel of Matthew.

B. H. Streeter

Already in the early twentieth century, B. H. Streeter was taking seriously apocalyptic material as additions and editions of the author of the Gospel of Matthew.[53] For him, Matthew's apocalyptic material functions to describe the imminent coming end and parousia, a perspective that continues up until the ending of the twentieth century in the works of David C. Sim.

In the context of the first century, Streeter makes the following generalization:

> The whole history of Jewish literature during the three preceding centuries shows that, whenever there was a period of acute persecution, the fact that older writers had foretold a great tribulation as a necessary prelude to a catastrophic intervention of God to deliver His people from their oppressors, led to a revival of Apocalyptic expectation, accompanied by a republication of older Apocalypses and the composition of new ones.[54]

Two presuppositions here define for Streeter what he means by apocalyptic. First, apocalyptic is an expectation of the end time. As such, apocalyptic denotes an ideology of the end time in which God will intervene to deliver his people from persecution. Second, apocalyptic describes a literary genre, that is, a type of literature called apocalypse.[55] Streeter uses the adjective substantively to denote both ideology and literature.

---

52. For example, Johannes Weiss, *Jesus' Proclamation of the Kingdom of God*, trans. Richard Hyde Hiers and David Larrimore Holland (Philadelphia: Fortress, 1971); Albert Schweitzer, *The Quest of the Historical Jesus: A Critical Study of Its Progress from Reimarus to Wrede* (New York: Macmillan, 1968).

53. B. H. Streeter, *The Four Gospels: A Study of Origins*, rev. ed. (London: Macmillan, 1930), 496. See also Sim, *Apocalyptic Eschatology*, 3.

54. Streeter, *Four Gospels*, 475.

55. Streeter states elsewhere that apocalyptic is a literary genre, that is, a type of literature with literary conventions (Streeter, *Four Gospels*, 491).

Leopold Sabourin

Leopold Sabourin points out themes and traits throughout the Gospel of Matthew (chs. 6–28) that are found in apocalypses and affirms that Matthew is the most apocalyptic of all the gospels.[56] Sabourin further states, "The revelation is made through images and symbols, which is appropriate for visions and suits the supernatural and mysterious character of the message to be transmitted."[57] However, he leaves these important details aside and focuses on his understanding of apocalyptic as a religious thought or perspective, in the center of which lies the interpretation of history.[58] Sabourin interprets apocalyptic traits in terms of religious thought, framed by what Paul D. Hanson calls "apocalyptic eschatology." Pronouncements about the salvation of the righteous and condemnation of the wicked in the gospels presuppose apocalyptic ethics. For Sabourin, this was the message of John the Baptist (Matt 3:1–12); he hoped that a coming judgment would provoke repentance. Yet in this passage, the message of John the Baptist is of a Davidic Messiah. Nonetheless, Sabourin in general acknowledges a mysterious character in a revelatory message that is transmitted through images and symbols. However, he perceives apocalyptic strictly as eschatological thought and according to eschatological functions that for him resemble Jewish apocalyptic literature.

O. L. Cope

Cope's essay on the role of apocalyptic thought in the Gospel of Matthew is relevant partly for the proposition identified in its title, and partly for the attention it receives from those who are interested in the relationship between Matthew and apocalyptic. Drawing upon Günther Bornkamm's essay "End-Expectation and Church in Matthew" as a starting point, Cope attempts to argue for the role of "apocalyptic thought" in Matthew. After listing four main points of Bornkamm's thesis, he praises the essay

---

56. He cites Jewish apocalypses such as Daniel, Jubilees, Testaments of the Twelve Patriarchs, Sibylline Oracles, Assumption of Moses, 4 Ezra, Syriac and Greek Apocalypses of Baruch, 1 Enoch (1–71), and the Greek translation of 2 Enoch (Sabourin, "Apocalyptic Traits in Matthew's Gospel," 19 n. 1).

57. Sabourin, "Apocalyptic Traits in Matthew's Gospel," 19.

58. Following influential studies of D. S. Russell, *Apocalyptic: Ancient and Modern* (Philadelphia: Fortress, 1978), and Hanson, *Dawn of Apocalyptic*, to name several.

for pointing out the importance of eschatological judgment to Matthew's ecclesiology, ethics, and Christology. The main critique Cope makes of Bornkamm's essay in light of eschatological judgment in Matthew is that Bornkamm understates his case. Cope highlights the pervasiveness of the judgment theme in the Gospel of Matthew. Yet nowhere in the essay does he explain what he means by apocalyptic, only that he uses *apocalyptic* synonymously with *eschatological judgment*. For example, when referring to apocalyptic in Matthew, three times he uses *apocalyptic/judgment*—to refer to an "apocalyptic/judgment backdrop," "apocalyptic/judgment language," and an "apocalyptic/judgment motif."[59] He concludes his essay by referring to the important roles "apocalyptic/eschatological thought" plays in early Christianity. Following Ernst Käsemann's famous dictum, "apocalyptic is the mother of all Christian theology," Cope defines apocalyptic thought in terms of eschatological judgment.

Graham N. Stanton

Both Graham N. Stanton and Donald A. Hagner acknowledge apocalyptic traditions behind Matthew's eschatology and turn to the social setting as a functional explanation.[60] Stanton calls Matt 25:31–46 apocalyptic discourse. He states, "Since apocalyptic writings usually function as a consolation to groups of God's people who perceive themselves to be under threat or alienated from the society in which they live, this is likely to be the central thrust of Matt 25:31–46."[61] In short, apocalyptic fulfills the needs of a social group that has parted ways with and been alienated by the larger Jewish community. For Stanton, apocalyptic as religious ideology inevitably becomes a defining characteristic of a social group, one that is alienated and marginal. I find this problematic, but will reserve my comments till later, for Hagner and Sim adopt this stance as well.

Donald A. Hagner

In one of two articles on apocalyptic and the Gospel of Matthew, Hagner, like Stanton before him, suggests that "alienation and the experience of hostility and persecution have been shown to be the key sociological factors that

---

59. Cope, "To the Close of the Age," 114, 115, 116, 120.
60. See also Sim, *Apocalyptic Eschatology*, 11.
61. Stanton, *Gospel for a New People*, 222.

20   Apocalyptic Sheep and Goats in Matthew and 1 Enoch

stimulate apocalyptic thought and form apocalyptic movements."[62] Hagner rightly felt the need first to provide a working definition of apocalyptic, something previous Matthean scholarship on apocalyptic had failed to do.[63] After discussing briefly the work of Hanson, Hagner proposes that the Gospel of Matthew is not an apocalypse but has an apocalyptic perspective, a point he shares with Sabourin: "Central to apocalyptic is the disclosure that in the near future God will demonstrate his faithfulness to the promises of scripture by the final transformation of the present order into a radically new age wherein the righteous will finally be blessed and the wicked judged."[64] Ironically, while he aims to define apocalyptic, he actually conflates apocalyptic with eschatology. In fact, he equates apocalyptic proper with future eschatology, that is, the hope that God will bring about judgment and transformation in the future.

Hagner's article focuses on "apocalyptic motifs" (meaning motifs like those typically found in apocalypses) that make the Gospel of Matthew "apocalyptic-like," and he limits "apocalyptic proper" to future aspects of Matthew's eschatology.[65] However, these motifs are made to fit his definition of apocalyptic above, and so he seems to find himself, as did Streeter, in a dilemma when dealing with exhortations regarding the present. He concludes that while apocalyptic events may be present, their full consummation lies in the future. For Hagner, everything about Matthew that makes it apocalyptic-like (i.e., dream-visions, angelic mediators and their revelations, its astronomical phenomena, its stress on the unusual, its expression of the coming salvation, and the activity of the Holy Spirit) is made to mean eschatology. By conflating a conjectured perspective of

---

62. Hagner, "Apocalyptic Motifs," 58. He seems to be unaware of Stanton's work cited above. He cites G. W. E. Nickelsburg, "Social Aspects of Palestinian Jewish Apocalypticism," in Hellholm, *Apocalypticism in the Mediterranean World*, 641–54.

63. He states, "since the definition of 'apocalyptic' has been discussed extensively in recent times [by scholars of apocalyptic literature], every writer or speaker who uses the word is under obligation to make clear what he or she understands by it" (Hagner, "Apocalyptic Motifs," 54).

64. Hagner, "Apocalyptic Motifs," 57.

65. These motifs include dream-visions, angelic mediators and their revelations, its astronomical phenomena, its stress on the unusual, its expression of the coming salvation, and the activity of the Holy Spirit as seen in the birth narrative. Hagner traces these and others also in the baptism of Jesus, the temptation, Jesus's ministry, and the crucifixion narrative. He refers to his definition of apocalyptic perspective as "apocalyptic proper" (Hagner, "Apocalyptic Motifs," 60–62).

1. Approaching Matthew's Apocalyptic Discourse

apocalyptic with future eschatology, he inevitably focuses upon imminent fulfillment of end-time events.

Hagner ends his article by identifying the purpose and function of Matthew's apocalyptic material under four headings: instruction, encouragement, paraenesis, and readiness. With regard to paraenesis as purpose, Hagner suggests that it is one of the main pillars of Matthew's apocalyptic perspective. I suspect that Hagner is correct in recognizing Matthew's apocalyptic discourse as being associated with these four headings. However, like Streeter, he concludes that instruction, encouragement, paraenesis, and readiness are all performed with urgency. He, too, seems to struggle to make sense of notions of the imminent coming end and the strong presence of exhortation.

Hagner makes his perspectives on apocalyptic in Matthew clearer in his second article, in which he deals directly with the topic of imminence and the parousia.[66] There he argues that, given the Gospel of Matthew's apocalyptic eschatological character, its author must have believed that the end-time events and parousia were in fact imminent. For Hagner, Matthew redacts Mark to make it more clear that, like the disciples who ask Jesus, "When will this be and what will be the sign of your coming and the end of the age" (Matt 24:3; cf. 13:39, 40, 49 in reference to final judgment), Matthew makes the two events of the destruction of the temple and parousia inseparable.[67] Hagner claims that the imminence of the former event, as predicted by Jesus, is now transferred onto the latter.[68]

Hagner takes a clue from Mark's dependence on Dan 12. He suggests that Mark's apocalypse, "to a considerable extent functions as a kind of midrash of the Danielic texts." He goes on to make a comparative analysis:

> In view in Daniel 12 is not merely the end of the temple, but a shattering of the nation and the accomplishing of all things, that is, the end of the age (Daniel 12:6–7). If the second temple was to be destroyed, the end of the present world order was also necessarily in the offing. The result of this conviction was that the disciples would have been prone to take the

---

66. Hagner, "Imminence," 77–92.

67. All translations (unless stated otherwise) and Greek texts of the New Testament come from Nestle-Aland, ed., *Novum Testamentum Graece*, 28th rev. ed. (Stuttgart: Deutsche Bibelgesellschaft, 2012).

68. Hagner, "Imminence," 82–86. The redactional insertion of the Greek adverb εὐθέως in 24:29 makes this all the more probable. The addition of this Greek adverb is for Hagner and others an obvious indicator of imminence and a reference to the parousia.

> imminence sayings that referred to Jerusalem and apply them also to the end of the age, and thus to the *parousia* of the Son of Man ... if now the second temple was to be destroyed this must surely signal the tribulation of the end of the age, the birth pains of the Messiah, and accordingly entail the long expected turning of the aeons.[69]

Hagner does not expand further on the suggestion that Matthew's text is a possible midrash on Dan 12, but it is necessary to note that a midrash is hardly just a comparison. Nevertheless, he does suggest that much as Daniel associates "the end of the temple" with "a shattering of the nation and the accomplishing of all things," so, too, do Mark and Matthew understand the destruction of the temple to forebode a similar future. Hagner concludes that the author of the Gospel of Matthew, along with the disciples, surely believed the parousia and the end of the age were to occur in their generation.[70] All of this, for Hagner, is apocalyptic.

Both Stanton and Hagner offer a social perspective in explaining the function of apocalyptic within the Gospel of Matthew. It is obvious that from Streeter to Hagner, scholars have recognized apocalyptic material in the Gospel of Matthew. For the most part, the views of an imminent coming of the end and parousia dominate their focus and definition of apocalyptic. This we see clearly in a monograph by David C. Sim, to which I now turn.

David C. Sim

Employing historical-critical methods, namely, redaction criticism and the social-scientific method, Sim sets out to expound and reconstruct the religious perspective within the Gospel of Matthew that Streeter, Sabourin, and Hagner hinted at and wrestled with, namely, the religious perspective of apocalyptic eschatology. Very much in tune with studies of apocalyptic literature, Sim takes his lead from the influential but controversial works of Koch and Hanson in the 1970s. Sim begins with the discussions of the terminologies surrounding apocalyptic that responded to Koch's earlier call to clarify them. Then Sim turns to Hanson, who provides a convenient way of distinguishing between form, content, and function through the

---

69. Hagner, "Imminence," 79.

70. For Hagner, this would strongly support that Matthew was written before the destruction of the temple or shortly thereafter.

respective terms *apocalypse*, *apocalyptic eschatology*, and *apocalypticism*. The first term denotes a literary genre, the second a religious perspective, and the third a social movement. Sim then utilizes Koch's eight characteristic motifs of apocalyptic and Hanson's term for a religious perspective, apocalyptic eschatology. He uses the former to characterize and identify the latter. Sim agrees with Rowland and Collins that apocalyptic eschatology is a transcendent eschatology that anticipates retribution or judgment beyond the realm of history.[71] The eight characteristics of what warrants an apocalyptic label are dualism, determinism, and six eschatological motifs: eschatological woes, the appearance of a savior figure, the judgment, the fate of the wicked, the fate of the righteous, and an imminent-end expectation.[72] Sim does not limit apocalyptic to notions of eschatology. He uses dualism and determinism as a contextual perspective by which to understand the eschatological motifs. As such, Sim suggests that apocalyptic would refer to more than eschatological judgment. While these are not all present in other apocalypses, Sim argues that some combination of them signifies an apocalyptic eschatological perspective.

Following Hanson and others, Sim also links this perspective to a social setting: to those minority groups who are in situations of great crisis or distress due to oppression and who are experiencing group alienation from society. In fact, for Sim, apocalyptic eschatology is a product of an apocalyptic movement, as the distressed group adopts the religious perspective to create a "symbolic universe" and imagery as seen in apocalypses, such as the time schemas in the Apocalypse of Weeks and the elaborate schemes of imagery and symbolism in Revelation. Sim suggests that symbolic and metaphorical language emerges from this religious perspective. The function of apocalyptic eschatology, according to Sim, serves not only to create this symbolic world; this symbolic world also (1) identifies and legitimates the apocalyptic community, (2) explains the circumstances under the purview of determinism, (3) encourages and instills hope for the future, (4)

---

71. On this, Sim agrees with Rowland and Collins. He agrees with the "more common type," which Collins points out is "reflected in the historical apocalypses and involves the notion of the two ages, including concrete description of the end-times woes, the process of a universal judgement and the bestowal of eternal rewards or punishments" (Sim, *Apocalyptic Eschatology*, 28–29). See also Collins, *Apocalyptic Imagination*, 9.

72. Sim replaces Koch's motif of "glory" for the "fate of the wicked" (Sim, *Apocalyptic Eschatology*, 35).

24   Apocalyptic Sheep and Goats in Matthew and 1 Enoch

envisions vengeance and consolation, and (5) creates group solidarity and social control.

Sim argues that apocalyptic eschatology saturates the entire Gospel of Matthew. For Sim, what makes the application of this religious perspective possible is the argument that a religious perspective and a social movement do not necessarily need to be connected to the literary genre of apocalypse. In other words, they can be found in other genres, such as the gospels. He states,

> The point I wish to make is that the current terminology is no longer serviceable and is in dire need of revision. We must arrive at terms which do not imply that apocalyptic eschatology is the dominant religious perspective of the apocalyptic genre or that apocalypticism is simply the social movement which produced the apocalypses. The historical reality is that apocalypticism is the social phenomenon underlying an apocalyptic-eschatological perspective which can be given expression in the genre apocalypse as well as other literary types.[73]

Sim's general redactional exegetical work on Matthew is thorough, and I will return to some of it later in this study. His specific explanations of apocalyptic material in Matthew are interesting but unconvincing. For Sim, the presence of the eight motifs listed above strongly indicates a religious perspective of apocalyptic eschatology in Matthew. While Matthew is not an apocalypse, Sim argues that it is apocalyptic because it reflects this religious perspective. For that reason, Sim conjectures that Matthew's community is an oppressed community. Essentially, a religious perspective (apocalyptic eschatology) and a social movement of oppression (apocalypticism) are, he says, what connects the Gospel of Matthew with Jewish apocalypses. However, the scholarship on apocalyptic has since shifted, and some views have been advanced and deemed no longer viable.

Sim is correct to suggest that a religious perspective and movement should be considered distinct and separate from the literary genre, apocalypse. For Sim, the religious perspective of apocalyptic eschatology and its embodied alienated group are what created most of the historical apocalypses. To be sure, perspectives of eschatology are present in historical apocalypses, but they do not necessarily make discourses apocalyptic, for eschatology is absent in many other Jewish apocalypses. The conjectured

---

73. Sim, *Apocalyptic Eschatology*, 28.

existence of a religious perspective and, thus, community is only a conjecture, for they simply cannot be found in apocalypses. The list of motifs referred to by Sim is not peculiar to Jewish apocalypses, and they would not be enough to suggest an ideology, let alone a separate social group. Moreover, if the motifs and features are not peculiar to Jewish apocalypses, why would any perspective and movement be called apocalyptic? Sim is also correct that there is a pressing need for a revision of terminology. Yet, he does little to resolve the confusion of terminologies by maintaining the adjective *apocalyptic* to modify his distinctive eschatology and the resulting social group of which he speaks.

According to Sim, this religious perspective of apocalyptic eschatology is responsible for the apocalyptic features of the Gospel of Matthew and its apocalyptic community, which, in the wake of a crisis of the delayed parousia, causes a borderline fanatic reaction regarding an imminent coming end. Seeing eschatological features of Jewish apocalypses in the texts of Matthew does not necessarily make those features in Matthew apocalyptic. To paraphrase Davies, if we find the idea that Jesus is the Messiah in a piece of literature other than the gospels, we would not suggest it to be *gospelic*.

As the scholars above argue, though apocalyptic material and traditions are present within the Gospel of Matthew, these traditions have been interpreted through a particular lens. Since the studies by Hanson, Sacchi, and others on apocalyptic literature, scholars such as Stanton, Hagner, and Sim have used the term *apocalyptic* to describe a community. Apocalyptic also refers to the imminent fulfillment of the eschatological future and is closely related to the crisis of the delay of the parousia.[74] As such, apocalyptic becomes apocalyptic eschatology that associates a marginal or alienated group with ideological and religious convictions of destruction and vengeance against "the wicked" in the very near future. What then

---

74. Richard J. Bauckham has made this clear in his Tyndale Biblical Theology Lecture in 1979 entitled, "The Delay of the Parousia." In those lectures, which he published later, he states that "the problem of eschatological delay was familiar to Jewish apocalyptic from its earliest beginnings. It could even be said to be one of the most important ingredients in the mixture of influences and circumstances which produced the apocalyptic movement." See Richard J. Bauckham, "The Delay of the Parousia," *TynBul* 31 (1980): 4. Some apocalypses do seem to deal with a problem of eschatological delay in its texts, but scholars do not speak of whether in Jewish apocalypses we witness an expression of the problem or an address of the problem.

26   Apocalyptic Sheep and Goats in Matthew and 1 Enoch

do we do with the strong gospel exhortation for moral behavior that both Streeter and Hagner recognize?

To be sure, Weiss and Schweitzer were faced with a similar dilemma on the intersection between an apocalyptic end of the world and ethical and moral exhortations in Jesus's teachings in the Sermon on the Mount. Weiss and Schweitzer reasoned that we should not take seriously the seemingly unreasonable ethical teachings in Jesus's sermon, for the sermon was composed during a time of a heightened expectation of the imminent coming end and would thus be irrelevant. This led Schweitzer to suggest that the Sermon on the Mount is an "interim ethics."[75] Günther Bornkamm points out a problem with Weiss's and Schweitzer's position:

> Or in other and less figurative words: this interpretation would appear to make the apocalyptic end of the world the ground of Jesus' demands, whereas the love of our neighbor and of our enemy, purity, faithfulness and truth are demanded simply because they are the will of God. The inner relationship between Jesus' requirement and his message of the coming of the Kingdom of God is not brought out clearly in the apocalyptic interpretation of the Sermon on the Mount.[76]

Bornkamm makes an excellent point by questioning the idea that the apocalyptic end of the world would be the reason for exhortations of love, purity, faithfulness, and truth. If Weiss and Schweitzer in fact perceived an apocalyptic end of the world, this would be the same idea as that behind Streeter's and Hagner's conclusions. However, Bornkamm takes an equally problematic stance. First, he assumes that apocalyptic equates with notions of the imminent coming end and destruction. Second, this leads him to neglect any serious treatment of Jewish apocalyptic traditions.

The brief survey of Matthean scholars conflating apocalyptic and eschatology may have caused a misrepresentation of apocalyptic and their functions in nonapocalyptic literature. Furthermore, this conflation may have caused many to shy away from Jewish apocalypses or prevented serious literary focus and treatment of apocalyptic material in apocalyptic discourses of Matthew's texts, as already hinted above by Bornkamm. This can also be gleaned from the comments of the German scholar, Gerhard Sauter,

---

75. See the works of Weiss and Schweitzer cited at the beginning of this survey.

76. Gunther Bornkamm, "The History of the Exposition of the Sermon on the Mount," in *Jesus of Nazareth* (New York: Harper & Row, 1960), 223–24.

1. Approaching Matthew's Apocalyptic Discourse   27

who states that some scholars and theologians have perceived apocalyptic as the "quintessence of what is 'eschatologically improper.'"[77] He states further, "Theological eschatology believed that it could best prove its legitimacy by abjuring apocalyptic as firmly and vocally as possible." This was the attitude of New Testament scholars in Germany for most of the twentieth century.[78] While the works of Bornkamm and others occasionally mention apocalyptic features of the Gospel of Matthew, their lack of attention to Jewish apocalyptic literature largely reflects this negative perception of apocalyptic.[79]

1.3.2. Matthew and Apocalyptic Recently

Not all earlier studies on Matthew and apocalyptic focused upon apocalyptic as solely eschatological ideology or as social movement. P. Hadfield and David E. Orton, for instance, depict Matthew as a scribe trained in apocalyptic traditions similar to the authors of the apocalyptic literature.[80]

---

77. Quoted by Klaus Koch, "What is Apocalyptic? An Attempt at a Preliminary Definition," in *Visionaries and Their Apocalypses*, ed. Paul Hanson (Philadelphia: Fortress, 1983), 16–36. Originally published as chapter 3 in his *Ratlos vor der Apokalyptik*, ET: *Rediscovery of Apocalyptic*. Koch quotes Gerhard Sauter, *Zukunft und Verheissung* (Zürich: Zwingli-Verlag, 1965), 95: "'Apokalyptik' wird zum Inbegriff des 'eschatologisch' Unsachgemaessen, weil sie ein Gesamtbild der Katastrophe bekannter Welt auszumalen scheint, das die wiederum hoechst massive Vorstellung eines zeitlich folgenden Weltzustandes zum Hintergrund hat.... Theologische Eschatologie glaubt ihre Legitimität—gerade auch in Rücksicht auf 'weltbildhafte' Konsequenzen—am besten dadurch zu beweisen, dass sie der Apokalyptik entschieden und so laut wie möglich abschwört."

78. Koch, *Rediscovery of Apocalyptic*, 92–93.

79. Gunther Bornkamm, "End-Expectation and Church in Matthew," in *Tradition and Interpretation in Matthew*, Gunther Bornkamm, G. Barth, and H. J. Held (London: SCM, 1963); Wolfgang Trilling, *Das Wahre Israel: Studien zur Theologie des Matthäusevangeliums*, 3rd ed., ETS 7 (Munich: Kösel, 1964); Trilling, *The Gospel according to St. Matthew*, trans. Kevin Smyth (London: Burns & Oates, 1969); Georg Strecker, *Der Weg der Gerechtigkeit: Untersuchung zur Theologie des Matthäus*, 3rd ed., FRLANT 82 (Göttingen: Vandenhoeck & Ruprecht, 1966); Daniel Marguerat, *Le jugemant dans l'evangile de Matthieu*, Le Monde de la Bible (Geneva: Labor et Fides, 1981); Blaine Charette, *The Theme of Recompense in Matthew's Gospel* (Sheffield: JSOT Press, 1992); Ulrich Luz, "The Final Judgment (Matt 25:31–46): An Exercise in 'History of Influence' Exegesis," in *Treasures New and Old: Contributions to Matthean Studies*, ed. David R. Bauer and Mark A. Powell, SBLSymS 1 (Atlanta: Scholars Press, 1996), 271–310.

80. P. Hadfield, "Matthew the Apocalyptic Editor," *London Quarterly & Holborn Review* 184 (1959): 128–32; David E. Orton, *The Understanding Scribe: Matthew and*

28 Apocalyptic Sheep and Goats in Matthew and 1 Enoch

John P. Meier sees Matthew using motifs similar to those in apocalyptic literature to reinterpret and exhort his audience.[81] Rowland points out that scholarship has been dominated by the idea that apocalyptic almost exclusively meant heralding the end of the world.[82] He suggests that this one-sided focus neglects another important aspect of what can be gleaned from Jewish apocalyptic literature: that they unveil secrets.[83]

> First and foremost, apocalypses unveil secrets, some of which relate to the future. They are not, therefore, solely concerned with the end of the world. Their chief task is to reveal truths about God and the universe, and in these attempts, they come close to one understanding of mysticism: the perception of truths which exceed the capacity of human reason and are mediated by means of divine revelation. It is that kind of religious outlook we find in an apocalypse.[84]

Daniel Gurtner concurs with Rowland.[85] Moreover, like Rowland, he places a significant emphasis upon metaphorical and symbolic language within apocalyptic discourses in the Gospel of Matthew. These affirm core aspects of the definition of apocalyptic adopted above: communication of

---

the Apocalyptic Ideal, JSNTSup 25 (Sheffield: Sheffield Academic, 1989). On Matthew's scribal practices, see also Krister Stendahl, The School of St. Matthew and Its Use of the Old Testament (Philadelphia: Fortress, 1968); M. Jack Suggs, Wisdom, Christology, and Law in Matthew (Cambridge: Harvard University Press, 1970), 125–27; Celia M. Deutsch, Lady Wisdom, Jesus, and the Sages: Metaphor and Social Context in Matthew's Gospel (Valley Forge, PA: Trinity Press International, 1996); Lawrence M. Wills, "Scribal Methods in Matthew and Mishnah Abot," in The Gospel of Matthew, vol. 2 of Biblical Interpretation in Early Christian Gospels, LNTS 310 (New York: T&T Clark, 2008), 183–97.

81. John P. Meier suggests that apocalyptic motifs of symbols and revelation serve to exhort. Meier does not define what he means when he uses apocalyptic. While he seems to use apocalyptic confusingly at times to refer to motifs (such as the temple veil and earthquake), on the one hand, and eschatological event, on the other, he concludes that "Matthew uses apocalyptic motifs to reinterpret the traditional Christian message of the death and resurrection of Jesus." See John P. Meier, The Vision of Matthew: Christ, Church and Morality in the First Gospel (New York: Paulist, 1979), 38.

82. Christopher C. Rowland, "Apocalyptic, the Poor, and the Gospel of Matthew," JTS 45 (1994): 504–18.

83. Rowland, Open Heaven.

84. Rowland, "Apocalyptic," 504.

85. Daniel Gurtner, "Interpreting Apocalyptic Symbolism in the Gospel of Matthew," BBR 22 (2012): 525–46.

esoteric knowledge and symbolic language. These are animated in apocalyptic discourses.

Very few studies have investigated the metaphorical language in Matthew's apocalyptic material in the last fifteen years. There have been important works that have dealt with the apocalyptic language of Jesus; however, those works continue the quest for the historical Jesus and trends of New Testament theology of the twentieth century, which mainly approach apocalyptic language as synonymous with eschatological language.[86] Two important books and one essay, respectively by Amy E. Richter, Leslie W. Walck, and Catherine Sider Hamilton, link the books of Enoch to the Gospel of Matthew.[87] I summarize Gurtner, Richter, Walck, and Hamilton's work of the last five years in what follows.

Daniel Gurtner

A recent essay by Daniel Gurtner recognizes the problem of exclusively equating apocalyptic with heralding the end time, as did Rowland, and proposes steps by which to approach apocalyptic material in Matthew without necessarily equating apocalyptic with eschatology. First, Gurtner suggests that we take a different approach from the one taken by Hagner and Sim, who reconstruct Matthew's sociological community and setting from apocalyptic features. Gurtner contends that although Matthew may contain apocalyptic traits, that should not mean that we are to analyze Matthew's sociological setting in the way we analyze an actual Jewish apocalypse. He asks, "since Hanson has argued that apocalypses arise from settings of crisis and community formations, must we conclude that 'apocalyptic traits' found in the narrative of Matthew's gospel suggest the

---

86. For a recent survey of such works, see Alistair I. Wilson, *When Will These Things Happen? A Study of Jesus as Judge in Matthew 21–25* (Waynesboro, GA: Paternoster, 2004). Allison counters the metaphorical readings of Caird and N. T. Wright for a literal reading of eschatological expectations.

87. Leslie W. Walck, *The Son of Man in the Parables of Enoch and in Matthew*, Jewish and Christian Texts in Contexts and Related Studies (New York: T&T Clark, 2011); Amy E. Richter, *Enoch and the Gospel of Matthew*, PTMS (Eugene, OR: Pickwick, 2012); Catherine Sider Hamilton, "Blood and Secrets: The Re-telling of Genesis 1–6 in 1 Enoch 6–11 and Its Echoes in Susanna and the Gospel of Matthew," in *The Synoptic Gospels*, vol. 1 of *'What Does the Scripture Say?' Studies in the Function of Scripture in Early Judaism and Christianity*, ed. Craig A. Evans and H. Daniel Zacharias (New York: T&T Clark, 2012), 90–141.

30   Apocalyptic Sheep and Goats in Matthew and 1 Enoch

origins of Matthew's community?"[88] Gurtner considers such a move to be purely speculative.

Second, Gurtner suggests that we distinguish between eschatology and apocalyptic when interpreting Matthew's eschatological texts. Like Rowland, he recognizes that scholars have understood "apocalyptic ... to mean either eschatological, or symbolic (non-literal), or both."[89] For Gurtner, apocalyptic eschatology is eschatology found in the apocalypses (i.e., the judgment of the dead or a scenario of the end of history), which, as Collins also notes, is not particular to apocalypses.[90]

Third, Gurtner suggests that we must examine the use of apocalyptic symbols. Having observed that apocalyptic elements are interwoven into both narrative and discourse materials of various forms (e.g., pronouncement stories, miracles stories, words of discipleship, controversy sayings, etc.), Gurtner believes that "if apocalyptic symbolism is the point at which to interpret apocalyptic features in Matthew, we must first discern how one identifies and interprets such symbols."[91] Gurtner then sets out to interpret the tearing of the veil in Matt 27:51 as an apocalyptic symbol of the opening of the heavens, revealing Jesus as the Son of God and inaugurating a new age.

To advance the recognition of apocalyptic material prevalent within the Gospel of Matthew, studies of the last five years have explored Matthew more closely by comparing it with other apocalyptic texts. Focusing on 1 Enoch, works by Amy E. Richter, Catherine Sider Hamilton, and Leslie W. Walck have blazed a new trail in this regard. Their insights may deepen our claims about symbols and metaphorical language, and our understanding of apocalyptic discourse, in Matthew.

---

88. Gurtner, "Interpreting Apocalyptic Symbolism," 528–29.

89. Gurtner, "Interpreting Apocalyptic Symbolism," 531. He states, "Scholars like Sabourin and Sim move quickly from apocalyptic to discussing the 'end of the world' in terms of Matthew's *apocalyptic* outlook, when in fact this is more properly an *eschatological* feature that is *sometimes* couched in apocalyptic symbols. Hagner requires that apocalyptic involves 'the near future' of end-time blessings and judgment. This is unnecessarily restricting and problematic in the sense that it conflates two overlapping and related yet distinct concepts: apocalyptic and eschatology."

90. Gurtner, "Interpreting Apocalyptic Symbolism," 532.

91. Gurtner turns to Revelation for "methodological controls" in reading symbolic language (Gurtner, "Interpreting Apocalyptic Symbolism," 532).

1. Approaching Matthew's Apocalyptic Discourse   31

Amy E. Richter

Richter argues in *Enoch and the Gospel of Matthew* that the themes and traditions of the first book of Enoch with regard to the Watcher's transgression (1 En. 1–36) are also evident in the genealogy and infancy narratives of Matt 1:1–2:23,[92] including "the four women in the genealogy, Joseph's suspicions of Mary's pregnancy, the revelatory dreams…, and the magi led by an astral body to worship the child."[93] She makes it clear, however, that she is not claiming direct dependence between Matthew and 1 Enoch, which differentiates her analysis from that of Sim, whose textual analysis is from a purely historical-critical perspective.[94]

Richter concludes that "Matthew shows Jesus to be a divinely appointed figure who completes the work that Enoch is unable to complete according to 1 Enoch." The allusions to the Book of the Watchers in Matthew, says Richter, portray a Jesus who corrects the transgressions of the Watchers, which is foreshadowed by the four women in Matthew's genealogy (Tamar, Rahab, Ruth, and the wife of Uriah, i.e., Bathsheba) who utilize the Watchers' illicit arts and motifs from the Enochic Watchers' narrative to good ends and not evil ones.[95] The unfolding of this portrayal of Jesus

---

92. Richter, *Enoch and the Gospel of Matthew*, 1–3.

93. Richter, *Enoch and the Gospel of Matthew*, 2–3. The "Enochic template" is one of three groupings of Jewish myths about evil in the world composed by John Reeves and others. Though the website Richter cites no longer exists, one may find it at John Reeves, "Sefer 'Uzza Wa-'Aza(z)el: Exploring Early Jewish Mythologies of Evil," https://tinyurl.com/SBL4827a. This template includes: "Humanity already present on earth, women are born among mortals, some angels in heaven see them and desire to possess them sexually and beget children, the angels bind each other with oaths to effect this deed, angels descend from heaven, angels fulfill their desire: engage in sexual activity and teach magical spells, result: bastard race of giants engendered, these hybrids engage in violence and lawlessness against humanity and each other; blood spilled, earth and humanity complain to heaven, loyal archangels relay the complaints to God, God dispatches these archangels to punish the watchers by binding/burial/fire, flood purges earth of giants' corruption, and immortal spirits of dead giants become the origin of demons and continue to plague humankind."

94. Richter, *Enoch and the Gospel of Matthew*, 18–19. She uses an example from Matt 22:13 that David C. Sim examines and attributes to Matthew's use of "the C text of 1 En. 10:4a as his source." See David C. Sim, "Matthew 22:13a and 1 Enoch 10:4a: A Case of Literary Dependence," *JSNT* 47 (1992): 3–19.

95. Each of the four women represents in some form the transgressions by the Watchers in the Enochic typology of the origins of evil (Richter, *Enoch and the Gospel*

becomes more evident through Mary, who conceives via the holy Spirit without sexual activity, and the magi, who use astrological skills and magical arts for good and not evil, as do the Watchers.[96] I find Richter's analysis interesting and largely convincing. Matthew may have been familiar with the first book of Enoch, that is, the Book of the Watchers, and the motifs she mentions are indeed likely apocalyptic allusions within Matthew. Unfortunately, her conclusions remain only hypotheses, as Matthew certainly does not explicitly mention Enoch's name. At best, hers is a highly probable assessment, one that helpfully questions some of the assumptions surrounding the inclusion of the four women in Matthew's genealogy.

Leslie W. Walck

Published in the same year as Richter's work, *The Son of Man in the Parables of Enoch and in Matthew*, by Leslie W. Walck, studies the depictions of the Son of Man in the Gospel of Matthew in light of the Parables of Enoch using literary, redaction, sociological, and narrative criticism. She assumes that the motif of the Son of Man in Dan 7 originates in the Canaanite myth of the Baal cycles, and shows that the Parables of Enoch reinterprets the Danielic vision.[97] Moreover, she notes that the Son of Man figure in the Parables of Enoch is a heavenly and divine figure who does not suffer. Within these parameters, Walck examines the Son of Man depictions peculiar to Matthew, a total of nine sayings: Matt 10:23; 13:37, 41; 16:27, 28; 19:28; 24:30–31; 25:31.[98] The parallels between Matthew and the Parables of Enoch (and Dan 7) based upon the nonsuffering figure of the Son of Man indicate for Walck—and thus she extrapolates for Matthew—the overthrow of those currently in power and a reversal of fortunes. Moreover, the statements about the Son of Man bring consolation and hope to the followers.[99] Walck's work on the Son of Man depictions in Matthew

---

of Matthew, ch. 3). This layout foreshadows Matthew's aims to portray Jesus as a correction for the transgressions of the Watchers, who engage in sexual activities with women and teach forbidden skills and arts.

96. Richter, *Enoch and the Gospel of Matthew*, ch. 4.

97. Walck, *Son of Man*, 52–53. For a recent opposing reading that sees rather two apocalyptic sources for the Son of Man figure in Dan 7, see Daniel Boyarin, "Daniel 7, Intertextuality, and the History of Israel's Cult," *HTR* 105 (2012): 139–62, esp. 147–48.

98. Walck, *Son of Man*, 165–66. Due to redactional implications, Walck adds two more in her analysis: Matt 16:13, 21.

99. Walck, *Son of Man*, 167.

1. Approaching Matthew's Apocalyptic Discourse   33

will be of particular significance to this study in my analysis of the last judgment of Matt 25:31–46. I hope to expand upon her work by focusing on those being judged, an aspect of the accounts that is often neglected. A focus upon the judged will, I hope, throw light on the other Son of Man depictions that are just as important in Matthew, namely, those of the suffering Son of Man. The latter depictions, I will suggest, highlight his human and earthly role in conjunction with the Son of God epithet and righteousness rather than the Son of Man's more familiar and more often studied role of advocate.

Catherine Sider Hamilton

In her illuminating expository essay on Matt 27:24–25, "Blood and Secrets: The Re-telling of Genesis 1–6 in 1 Enoch 6–11 and Its Echoes in Susanna and the Gospel of Matthew," Hamilton calls into question the charge of anti-Judaism that has plagued this passage in the history of interpretation. By tracing the interrelationship between the narratives of Matt 27:24–25, the Daniel addition of the Susanna story (θ 46),[100] and 1 En. 6–11, Hamilton argues that Matt 27:24–25, in which Pilate attempts to relieve himself of guilt for taking the blood of Jesus, is a reflection of the imaginative world created by Scriptures and traditions. She states,

> This scriptural world, this tradition of reflection on scripture—and not simply a historical situation—illuminates the interchange between Pilate and the people in Matt 27:24–25. To explore the world of innocent blood in 1 Enoch and in Susanna is to find the Matthean passion narrative taking its place in an early Jewish interpretive context. It is to find an intricate and intimate relationship between Jewish texts and traditions of interpretation and Matthew's story of Jesus.[101]

Hamilton strings together in a convincing way parallels between Matthew's story of Jesus's trial and the trial of Susanna, who is also condemned

---

100. The Susanna story is not extant in the Masoretic Text (MT) but extant only in the Septuagint (LXX Codex Chisianus) and Theodotion (θ) as part of the book of Daniel. The later Syriac version is believed to be a translation from the Septuagint, while the Coptic and Vulgate stems from Theodotion's Greek text. It is dated by scholars to the second to first centuries BCE. See R. H. Charles, ed. *The Apocrypha and Pseudepigrapha of the Old Testament in English*, vol. 1 (Oxford: Clarendon, 1913).

101. Hamilton, "Blood and Secrets," 92.

to death. While the charges of condemnation are starkly different, what links the two is the cry of innocent blood, which, as Hamilton argues, is a reflection of 1 En. 6–11, which tells of "the blood poured out upon the ground."[102]

Like Richter, Hamilton illuminates the allusions to the Book of the Watchers in the Gospel of Matthew, except rather than the opening genealogy, her focus is on the passion narrative at the other end of the Gospel. Hamilton, like Richter, also suggests that the intertextual allusions function to expand upon themes and motifs evident in the Book of the Watchers. More so than Richter, Hamilton emphasizes the fact that these expansions are Matthew's deliberate interweaving of authoritative texts. For Hamilton, the themes of innocent blood, the cry for justice, and the resulting promises of judgment and restoration are the obvious textual connections between Matthew, Susanna, Genesis, and 1 Enoch.[103]

The presence of apocalyptic themes and motifs abound in the Gospel of Matthew and therefore apocalyptic discourse. Few extant studies elucidate these discourses and the possible ways in which they (re)interpret cultural traditions. Rowland and Gurtner recognize the known value that metaphors play in apocalyptic discourse. Richter, Walck, and Hamilton all look at intertextual influences of the first book of Enoch, namely, the Book of the Watchers and the Parables of Enoch. Hamilton traces the transmission of motifs and themes. All of these harken back to Orton and Philip R. Davies's emphasis upon the literary and social activities of scribal traditions. While some scholars find an informative function in the apocalyptic discourses, Meier, Rowland, and Hamilton make it clear that the discourses' main function is exhortation.[104]

Most recently, in a chapter to a composite of works on apocalypticism and the New Testament and in recognition of Adela Yarbro Collins's important contribution to the field, Kristian Bendoraitis wrote an essay entitled "Apocalypticism, Angels, and Matthew." There, Bendoraitis echoes

---

102. Hamilton, "Blood and Secrets," 124.

103. Hamilton, "Blood and Secrets," 129–41.

104. Cf. Stephenson Humphries-Brooks, "Apocalyptic *Paraenesis* in Matthew 6:19–34," in Marcus and Soards, *Apocalyptic and the New Testament*, 95–112. Brooks dwells upon "an apocalyptic eschatological perspective similar to structures of thought identifiable in both Jewish and Christian literature," which he does not explain (p. 103).

1. Approaching Matthew's Apocalyptic Discourse   35

much of what has already been mentioned thus far in this study.[105] Bendo-raitis rightly points out an important piece of what are often seen in Jewish apocalyptic literature, when he expounds upon angels in the Gospel of Matthew. More importantly, he expounds upon the relationship between angels and the Son of Man as evident in Matthean passages (13:41, 49; 16:27; 24:30; 25:31), all of which will be covered particularly in this study. Overall, his reading of angels in Matthew as buttressing the authority of the Son of Man, being a mediator between the heavens and earth, and indicating God's presence serves as complementary to the work at hand.

1.4. The Scope, Thesis, and Significance

As stated above, our working definition of *apocalyptic* is an adjective that describes the literary communication of esoteric knowledge, which is presented through heavenly revelation and metaphorical language, which may take the form of dreams, visions, or angelic pronouncements. In addition to this working definition, the above recent studies affirm the need for new perspectives and approach to Matthew's apocalyptic material, ones that particularly appreciate its literary and cultural traditions of heavenly communication of esoteric knowledge. A study of metaphorical language will be most beneficial in expounding such communication with an eye toward Jewish apocalyptic literature, namely, 1 Enoch. This study will contribute more fully to this line of reading, refuting the idea that apocalyptic material in Matthew is defined by eschatology. To this end, I will look at a key apocalyptic discourse of Matt 25:31–46 and metaphorical language associated with it. The presence of eschatological imagery, I argue, is only a part of the apocalyptic discourse, and that discourse functions primarily to exhort.[106] In general, apocalyptic discourses involving eschatological imageries are but one example of apocalyptic materials in the Gospel of Matthew.

---

105. See Kristian Bendoraitis, "Apocalypticism, Angels, and Matthew," in *The Jewish Apocalyptic Tradition and the Shaping of New Testament Thought*, ed. Benjamin E. Reynolds and Loren T. Stuckenbruck (Minneapolis: Fortress, 2017), 31–52. I was unaware of this encouraging piece as it was published only after I had submitted a completed draft of my dissertation in the spring of 2017. I am grateful for Vernon K. Robbins and others for pointing this out during the process of publication.

106. I will return to apocalyptic discourse in the context of New Testament studies in the following chapter on methodology.

36 Apocalyptic Sheep and Goats in Matthew and 1 Enoch

Scholars have rightly recognized Matt 25:31–46 as apocalyptic discourse.[107] The topical elements of the last judgment in Matt 25:31–46 are present in some Jewish apocalypses: an enthroned judge, angels, gathered people, two groups separated, the righteous rewarded, and the wicked punished.[108] These elements are also present in the descriptions of a similar image in Matt 13:24–30, 36–43, where weeds are separated from the wheat at the end of the age. At no other place in Matthew do these topical elements all appear explicitly. Both are also peculiar to Matthew.[109] However, these are not all present in Dan 7, let alone Matt 24:29–31 (cf. Mark 13:24–27; Luke 21:25–28). For example, in the latter passage, there is no separation of groups and no judgment scene of the wicked and the righteous.

---

107. J. A. T. Robinson, "The 'Parable' of the Sheep and the Goats," *NTS* 2 (1956): 225–37; O. L. Cope, "Matthew XXV:31–46; 'The Sheep and the Goats' Reinterpreted," *NovT* 11 (1969): 32–44; Meier, *Vision of Matthew*, 177–78; J. M. Court, "Right and Left: The Implications for Matthew 25:31–46," *NTS* 31 (1985): 223–33; John R. Donahue, "The 'Parable' of the Sheep and the Goats: A Challenge to Christian Ethics," *TS* 47 (1986): 3–31; Paul W. Meyer, "Context as a Bearer of Meaning in Matthew," *USQR* 42 (1988): 69–72; M. Hutter, "Matt 25:31–46 in der Deutung Manis," *NovT* 33 (1991): 276–82; Kathleen Weber, "The Image of the Sheep and Goats in Matthew 25:31–46," *CBQ* 59 (1997): 657–78; R. L. Thomas, "Jesus' View of Eternal Punishment," *MSJ* 9 (1998): 147–67; John Paul Heil, "The Double Meaning of the Narrative of Universal Judgment in Matthew 25:31–46," *JSNT* 69 (1998): 3–14; David Cortés-Fuentes, "The Least of These My Brothers: Matthew 25:31–46," *Apuntes* 23 (2003): 100–109; Ulrich Luz, *Matthew 21–28*, Hermeneia (Minneapolis: Fortress, 2005); John Nolland, *The Gospel of Matthew*, NIGTC (Grand Rapids: Eerdmans, 2005); J. S. Suh, "Das Weltgericht und die Matthäische Gemeinde," *NovT* 48 (2006): 217–32: R. T. France, *The Gospel of Matthew*, NICNT (Grand Rapids: Eerdmans, 2007), 217–33; Sigurd Grindheim, "Ignorance Is Bliss: Attitudinal Aspects of the Judgment according to Works in Matthew 25:31–46," *NovT* 50 (2008): 313–31; M. Down, "Exegetical Note on Matthew 25:31–46: The Parable of the Sheep and the Goats," *ExpTim* 123 (2012): 587–89; R. Klein, "Wer sind die 'geringsten Geschwister' in Matt 25?," *Stimmen der Zeit* 237 (2019): 103–5.

108. W. D. Davies and Dale C. Allison, *The Gospel according to Saint Matthew 19–28*, ICC (New York: T&T Clark, 2004), 418–19. Davies and Allison include Dan 7; 1 En. 62–63, 90; Rev 20; 2 Bar. 72–73; Test. Ab. 11–13; and Sib. Or. See also Warren Carter, *Matthew and the Margins: A Socio-political and Religious Reading* (New York: T&T Clark, 2000), 491. Carter adds Joel 3:1–3 and 4 Ezra 7.31–44, as does Stanton, *Gospel for a New People*, 221, 224–25.

109. Yet Matt 13:24–30 may be a version of Mark 4:26–39. Nevertheless, Matt 13:24–30 and its interpretation is largely Matthean.

1. Approaching Matthew's Apocalyptic Discourse   37

The dragnet parable of Matt 13:47–50 is a similar image and also peculiar to Matthew. It lacks the figure of the Son of Man, and the angels seem to separate the bad fishes from good ones on behalf of a judge. A close reading of Matt 3:11–12 shows also another related image. It connects with 13:36–43 in depicting the righteous as wheat. However, the one coming does the gathering, and while he separates the wheat from the chaff, the image emphasizes the burning of the chaff. This text does not have a judgment scene with a judge but rather with a punisher, specifically the grim reaper. What ties these four passages together—25:31–46; 13:24–30 (13:36–43); 13:47–50; and 3:11–12—is the fact that they utilize parables that extend the judgment imagery for further interpretation.[110] Only 3:11–12 is from Q (Luke 3:16–17), indicating a dialogue between Matthew and his sources with regard to Jesus and judgment. John proclaims that the end will happen in the appearance of Jesus. This offers an interesting difference that I hope to capitalize on in this study.

Other similar and prominent passages are 7:21–23; 10:23; 16:27–28; and 19:27–30. Matthew 7:21–23 is from Q and makes no mention of the Son of Man but speaks only of a dialogue between the judge and judged, emphasizing those who fall short. Matthew 10:23 and 16:27–28 lack details. They focus more on the salvific reward of discipleship and have the Son of Man as a judge, although 16:27–28 is more explicit and mentions angels.[111] Matthew 19:27–30 poses the disciples as judges, but like 10:23 and 16:27–28, it addresses the disciples directly and pursues the idea of following Jesus as a way to eternal life. For these passages, the elements of the Son of Man and judgment are more or less alluded to; they address the disciples directly and focus upon the rewards of discipleship. All of the above judgment imageries of Matthew are found within Jesus's five discourses from Matt 3–25 and can be seen in the table on page 38.

---

110. With the exception of Matt 25:31–46, scholars are divided on whether we may consider the shepherd, sheep, and goat metaphors as a parable. I will reserve comment until below in chapter 4.

111. Like Matt 16:27–28, 10:23 seems to speak of an imminent expectation of the parousia. In both, Jesus addresses directly the disciples, and in both, Matthew inserts the Son of Man to his sources. Matthew 10:23 may well be "a mandate to continue the mission task in spite of the persecution." See Eugene E. C. Park, *The Mission Discourse in Matthew's Interpretation* (Tübingen: Mohr Siebeck, 1995), 142. The same force can be witnessed in the idea of taking up one's cross in 16:27–28.

Matthew's Imagery of Judgment	Judge	Angels	Gathered People	Two Groups Separated	Righteous Rewarded	Wicked Punished	Character
24:29–31, Mark	yes/Son of Man	yes	yes	none	none	none	Scripture citation
25:31–46	yes/Son of Man	yes	yes	yes	yes	yes	parable/sheep and goats
13:24–30, 36–43	yes/Son of Man	yes	yes	yes	yes	yes	parable/wheat and weeds
13:47–50	implied/Son of Man	yes	yes	yes	yes	yes	parable/bad and good fishes
3:11–12, Q	yes/Son of God	none	yes	yes	yes	yes	parable/wheat and chaff
7:21–23, Q	yes	none	implied	implied	yes	yes	salvation/do the will of my Father
10:23, Q and Mark	implied/Son of Man	none	none	none	yes	implied	salvation/endure mission
16:27–28, Q and Mark	yes/Son of Man	yes	implied	implied	yes	implied	salvation/take up cross
19:27–30, Q and Mark	yes/Son of Man and disciples	none	implied	none	yes	none	salvation/leave home

1. Approaching Matthew's Apocalyptic Discourse 39

The imagery reflects what may have been visions. Of course, visions characterize apocalyptic discourses and are thought to be actual communications from the divine.[112] Dreams and visions generally are considered to be of two types: symbolic and message visions.[113] Message visions impart a clear message from a deity while symbolic visions need the interpretation of an expert. Both deal with revealed knowledge. The above imagery is of the symbolic type. Jesus interprets this imagery for his disciples that he seems to have received in visions revealed to him by his Father. Thus, if Matthew had to communicate anything definitive in apocalyptic fashion with eschatological judgment, it would involve visions presented in symbolic language.

Judgment imagery peculiar to Matthew may be good indication of how the text of Matthew uniquely uses the imagery. The imagery is found in 13:24–30; (13:36–43); 13:47–52; and 25:31–46. Since the parable of the dragnet (13:47–52) is within the same narrative context of 13:24–30, 36–43, the latter should be read in conjunction with the parable of the weeds in the field and its interpretation (13:24–30, 36–43). John's depiction of Jesus as the Messiah is similar in language to the parable of the weeds in the field, and the contrast to Jesus as the Son of God may be illuminating. Therefore, while Matt 25:31–46 will be the focus, the listed—3:11–12; 13:24–30; (13:36–43); and 13:47–52—will be in the purview of its analysis. These passages all contain the conceptual topos of eschatological judgment and are spread out within the five discourses of Jesus (occurring in the first, third, and fifth).[114] How do the apocalyptic visions and metaphors in these discourses function and interrelate with each other? From the apocalyptic discourse of Matt 25:31–46 and related texts above, what implications are there for the Gospel of Matthew? These will be central questions of this study.

---

112. Hengel, *Judaism and Hellenism*, 1:207. Hengel states that apocalyptic literature derives in part from visions and ecstatic experiences. See Frances Flannery, "Dreams and Visions in Early Jewish and Early Christian Apocalypses and Apocalypticism," in *The Oxford Handbook of Apocalyptic Literature*, ed. John J. Collins (Oxford: Oxford University Press, 2014), 104–22, esp. 106.

113. Flannery, "Dreams and Visions," 107.

114. I refer to imagery as conceptual topos as well. I will return to this in the following chapter on methodology. There, in terms of cognitive linguistics, one may also refer to conceptual frames. In this study, imagery, topos, and conceptual frame are interchangeable. See also appendix A on Aristotle and topos.

The thesis of this monograph is that the apocalyptic discourse involving the topos of eschatological judgment in Matt 25:31–46 functions primarily as the means for the author to speak existentially of the "here and now," that is, as paraenesis for Israel to teach the will of the Father in both word and deed,[115] as did the Son, to the world of gentiles despite expecting—at some unknown time—the end of the age to take place.[116]

If this thesis can be demonstrated, the significance for new approaches to Matthew's apocalyptic material cannot be overstated, especially if it is truly the case that "apocalyptic is the mother of all Christian theology." A study of apocalyptic material as defined above will contribute to literary, cultural, and historical studies of Jewish-Christian relations, specifically relations between Matthew and Judaism. A study on the apocalyptic and eschatological traditions in Matthew contributes to Matthew's soteriology. It will also potentially salvage from the eschatological wreckage what may have been an important Jewish literary and cultural heritage in apocalyptic writing.

In the following chapter, I will describe the method of this study that will serve the above thesis and focus. That description will consist of two parts. First, the analysis of metaphorical language draws from classical and modern theories of metaphor. This will provide a theoretical lens for approaching apocalyptic metaphorical language in a way that contributes to knowledge and thus meaning. Second, sociorhetorical interpretation as a heuristic paradigm for rhetorical analysis will aid in integrating literary, cultural, and historical elements of text as inner textures and intertextures. In order to perceive the function of Matthew's apocalyptic discourses and metaphorical language, we must explain in part some of the cultural and historical elements that are blended within its literary and rhetorical presentation.

---

115. The term *paraenesis* is a transliteration of the Greek noun παραίνεσις whose root meaning comes from the combination of the Greek prefix παρα- and verb αἰνέω, meaning to praise, advise, approve, or recommend (LSJ, s.v. "αἰνέω"). The noun itself means exhortation, advice, counsel, or address (LSJ, s.v. "παραίνεσις"). In the New Testament context, without being limited to ethical issues alone, paraenesis could mean to give positive advice, to suggest a positive action adequate to what is needed under particular circumstances. See Wiard Popkes, "Paraenesis in the New Testament: An Exercise in Conceptuality," in *Early Christian Paraenesis in Context*, ed. James Starr and Troels Engberg-Pedersen (New York: de Gruyter, 2005), 13–46, esp. 16–17.

116. Matthew speaks of the end of the age but never the end of the world.

2

Metaphor and Rhetoric

2.1. Introduction: Apocalyptic Discourse

Studies of various New Testament texts have benefitted greatly from the explorations of apocalyptic literature in the past three decades. Lars Hartman, for example, hints at rhetorical analysis as necessary future work in apocalyptic discourse, when he exhorts readers to attend to communication and its social interplay in apocalyptic texts.[1] It is not surprising that rhetorical studies in general show such interest in the communicative nature of apocalyptic,[2] or that sociorhetorical studies of

---

1. Lars Hartman, "Survey of the Problem of Apocalyptic Genre," in Hellholm, *Apocalypticism in the Mediterranean World*, 329. Hartman states, "Furthermore, one should pay attention to the communication aspects, i.e., consciously connect the literary analysis with the fact that the genre problem is part of the larger one concerning understanding and interpretation of human expressions in social interplay" (Hartman, "Survey of the Problem," 341).

2. For example, Amos Niven Wilder, "The Rhetoric of Ancient and Modern Apocalyptic," *Int* 25 (1971): 436–53. Wilder points to the ecstatic nature of apocalyptic language used in its initial utterance where it speaks to the reality of the chaotic event. He asks, "If we then identify the matrix of apocalyptic language with situations of anomie, what special kinds of rhetoric will we expect to find?" (Wilder, "Rhetoric of Ancient and Modern Apocalyptic," 444). Wilder suggests the language of hope and future. See also Barry Brummett, "Premillennial Apocalyptic as a Rhetorical Genre," *Central States Speech Journal* 35 (1984): 84–93; Brummett, "Using Apocalyptic Discourse to Exploit Audience Commitments through Transfer," *Southern Communication Journal* 54 (1988): 58–73; Brummett, *Contemporary Apocalyptic Rhetoric* (New York: Praeger, 1991); Stephen O'Leary, "A Dramatistic Theory of Apocalyptic Rhetoric," *QJS* 79 (1993): 385–426; O'Leary, *Arguing the Apocalypse: A Theory of Millennial Rhetoric* (New York: Oxford University Press, 1994). For O'Leary, like many others, apocalypse is a literary medium for an apocalyptic ideology that is wholly eschatological. He states, "The particular type of eschatology that is the subject of this book

-41-

42 Apocalyptic Sheep and Goats in Matthew and 1 Enoch

the New Testament in particular have taken an interest in discovering new ways to explicate apocalyptic discourse. To tackle this task, Greg Carey and others have proposed a definition of apocalyptic discourse as follows:

> *Apocalyptic discourse* refers to the constellation of apocalyptic topics as they function in larger early Jewish and Christian literary and social contexts. Thus, apocalyptic discourse should be treated as a flexible set of resources that early Jews and Christian could employ for a variety of persuasive tasks. Whenever early Jews and Christians appealed to such topics as visions and revelations, heavenly journeys, final catastrophes, and the like, they were using apocalyptic discourse.[3]

In an essay from a collection of works on how apocalyptic discourse influences the New Testament, Robbins refines the above definition along the lines of classical rhetorical theory by modifying the first sentence to read: "Apocalyptic discourse refers to the constellation of apocalyptic *topoi* as they function in early Jewish and Christian descriptive, explanatory, and argumentative discourse."[4] That apocalyptic discourse is a "flexible set of

---

is apocalyptic. Eschatology ... is the 'logos' or discourse about the last things.... Apocalypse ... is thus that discourse that reveals or makes manifest a vision of ultimate destiny, rendering immediate to human audiences of the ultimate End of the cosmos in the Last Judgment. Apocalyptic eschatology argues for the imminence of this Judgment, in which good and evil will finally receive their ultimate reward and punishment" (O'Leary, *Arguing the Apocalypse*, 6). As such, apocalyptic metaphor is understood through this lens as well. O'Leary states, "Apocalyptic metaphor cannot be understood apart from apocalyptic logic" (O'Leary, *Arguing the Apocalypse*, 21). What's more, he refrains from observing Jewish apocalyptic literature of the first century or earlier, limiting his studies to millenarian movements of later periods. Thus, his work will not be of much help to this study.

3. Carey, "Introduction," in Carey and Bloomquist, *Vision and Persuasion*, 10. See also the other contributions to this volume.

4. Vernon K. Robbins, "The Intertexture of Apocalyptic Discourse in the Gospel of Mark," in *The Intertexture of Apocalyptic Discourse in the New Testament*, ed. Duane F. Watson, SBLSymS 14 (Atlanta: Society of Biblical Literature, 2002), 11. Robbins highlights the twofold function of topoi: (1) argumentative-enthymematic and (2) amplificatory-descriptive, as recognized by Wilhelm H. Wuellner. In the same volume, L. Gregory Bloomquist presents the definition determined by the editorial board of the Rhetoric of Religious Antiquity section, which reads: "Apocalyptic discourse reconfigures our perception of all regions of time and space, in the world and in the body, in light of the conviction that God will intervene to judge at some time in the future."

2. Metaphor and Rhetoric 43

resources" for the use of Jews and Christians presupposes that the recipients and keepers of these cultural resources are scribes and that apocalyptic discourse as it is conceived is both a tangible and intangible cultural heritage handed down from generations of scribes.

These scholars define apocalyptic discourse in terms of content, that is, in terms of topos. The discourse, they say, consists of a constellation of traditional topoi, which may vary in form, meaning that they may function in descriptive, explanatory, and argumentative discourses to reconfigure the topoi and, thus, the perceptions of the audience. However, from this perspective, nothing really indicates the discourse to be apocalyptic except for the possible use of a topos commonly used in apocalypses.[5] As per the working definition adopted in the previous chapter, an apocalyptic topos identified in a given text would be a communication of esoteric knowledge through heavenly communication and metaphorical language.[6] The topoi utilized in apocalyptic discourse may derive from various traditions. In the texts that we will analyze in this study, we have eschatological judgment as the main apocalyptic topos, where Matthew has Jesus interpret visions of it to exhort Israel to a life of righteousness. The topos in isolation is not apocalyptic. Apocalyptic is the way in which the topos is used to communicate a heavenly sanctioned message, hence an apocalyptic discourse. It is the hopes of this study that at the end of its analysis, it would be made clear what I mean by apocalyptic discourse. Bloomquist suggests that the best way to understand this communication would be through sociorhetorical analysis.[7]

See L. Gregory Bloomquist, "The Intertexture of Lukan Apocalyptic Discourse," in Watson, *The Intertexture of Apocalyptic Discourse*, 45. While this definition may be too limiting in scope, the definition does point toward the reconfiguration of perception, which is an important conceptual aspect of apocalyptic discourse. However, reconfiguring perception is implied in the above definition.

5. As Michael E. Stone argues, it is not enough merely to list motifs to suggest that a discourse be apocalyptic. See Michael E. Stone, "Lists of Revealed Things in the Apocalyptic Literature," in *Magnalia Dei: The Mighty Acts of God; Essays on the Bible and Archaeology in Memory of G. Ernest Wright*, ed. Frank Moore Cross, Werner E. LeMarke, and Patrick D. Miller (Garden City, NY: Doubleday, 1976).

6. Otherwise, it remains a scriptural allusion and nothing more.

7. L. Gregory Bloomquist, "Methodological Criteria for Apocalyptic Rhetoric," in Carey and Bloomquist, *Vision and Persuasion*, 184. Bloomquist states, "I suggest that a potentially fruitful approach to apocalyptic literature may be ... rhetorical analysis, for it is this analysis that is geared to the very communicative aspects to which Hartman

44 Apocalyptic Sheep and Goats in Matthew and 1 Enoch

This chapter on method has two parts. The first part focuses on the ideas of Aristotle and George Lakoff (and cognitive linguists more broadly) concerning *metaphorical language* and the ways in which metaphorical language clarifies reality. Since apocalyptic discourse involves metaphorical and symbolic language, their insights will be helpful in identifying and analyzing the complexities of metaphors in Matthew's apocalyptic discourse. In the second part of the chapter, I employ *sociorhetorical interpretation* as an analytical and heuristic framework to explicate the rhetoric of apocalyptic discourses and metaphorical language in its literary, cultural, and historical context.[8] Together these two foci will help us perceive a possible picture of how apocalyptic metaphors in the judgment imagery of Matthew's apocalyptic discourse function to exhort Matthew's torah-abiding congregation.

2.2. Metaphor Theory

Modern scholars have typically understood metaphor as being chiefly literary (rather than cognitive) and have referred to it mainly in classical works such as those of Aristotle. A recent study in cognitive linguistics on conceptual frames reflects this understanding of metaphorical language:

> Aristotle presents metaphor as a linguistic ornamentation akin to the use of foreign words in a text, not as a way of thinking or a cognitive strategy. It is only relatively recently that metaphor has been reinterpreted as primarily a cognitive process that surfaces in language, rather than a rhetorical strategy that exists only at the level of language itself.[9]

The author goes on to cite the seminal work of George Lakoff and Mark Johnson, *Metaphors We Live By*. However, I suggest that Aristotle saw more in metaphorical language than he is credited as seeing.

---

points. Even more specifically, I suggest that within the category of rhetorical analysis, it will be sociorhetorical analysis that will be the most helpful."

8. Basic to rhetorical theory is the presupposition that speaker, speech, and audience are primary constituents of a situation of communication. Sociorhetorical criticism calls attention to all three. See Vernon K. Robbins, *The Tapestry of Early Christian Discourse: Rhetoric, Society and Ideology* (London: Routledge, 1996), 45.

9. Karen Sullivan, *Frames and Constructions in Metaphoric Language* (Philadelphia: John Benjamins, 2013), 1.

2. Metaphor and Rhetoric

If the conceptual understanding of metaphor is purely modern and not Aristotelian, then ancient metaphors contribute nothing to knowledge and were used only for aesthetic purposes. This may lead us to misconstrue ancient metaphorical language in general, and specifically within apocalyptic discourses. Indeed, G. R. Boys-Stones challenges the modern perception of classical theories of metaphor, saying, "it is worth considering whether this [the limited insights of classical theories] is because the ancients' views were, as a matter of fact, limited; or whether it is more to do with the way in which their position was presented in the later tradition."[10] Boys-Stones suggests it is the latter. According to Boys-Stones, the accounts of metaphorical language (allegory in particular) in antiquity are based primarily on ancient rhetorical handbooks, which present a limited range of texts. He suggests that one would find more about metaphorical language in philosophical texts and reminds us that such metaphorical language was in fact central to philosophical thought, such as that found in the theoretical treatises of Aristotle. This may also be the case in the writings of Cicero and Quintilian.[11]

2.2.1. Aristotle and Classical Metaphor Theory

Aristotle's theory of "invention" depends on the use of oral language (*lexis*),[12] because the understanding of what one says depends upon *how one says it* (*Rhet.* 3.1.2, 1403b16–17),[13] which are two different things, though they are inseparable.[14] They both contribute to the effective communication of

---

10. G. R. Boys-Stones, "Introduction," in *Metaphor, Allegory, and the Classical Tradition*, ed. G. R. Boys-Stones (Oxford: Oxford University Press, 2003), 1–2.

11. See appendix B on Cicero and Quintilian and metaphors.

12. Eckart Schuetrumpf and others have argued that the three parts of rhetoric—argument, ethos, and pathos—in invention were not part of Aristotle's rhetorical theory and that it is anachronistic to say so. See Eckart Schuetrumpf, "Non-logical Means of Persuasion in Aristotle's Rhetoric and Cicero's De oratore," in *Peripatetic Rhetoric after Aristotle*, ed. William W. Fortenbaugh and David C. Mirhady, vol. 6, Rutgers University Studies in Classical Humanities (New Brunswick: Transaction, 1994), 101–2. However, Jakob Wisse and others disagree. See, e.g., James M. May and Jakob Wisse, *Cicero: On the Ideal Orator* (Oxford: Oxford University Press, 2001), 30.

13. See also Amos N. Wilder, *Early Christian Rhetoric: The Language of the Gospel* (Cambridge: Harvard University Press, 1964; repr., 1976).

14. Wilder suggests that what the early Christians said cannot be separated from how they said it (Wilder, *Early Christian Rhetoric*, 2).

46 Apocalyptic Sheep and Goats in Matthew and 1 Enoch

meaning. Plato would suggest that absolute truth needs no persuasion,[15] but this implies that knowledge alone is persuasive. Although Aristotle understands there to be a binary opposition between truth and falsehood, he recognizes the significance of a rhetorical approach of argumentation that employs skills of persuasion in presenting truths. This is particularly helpful when presenting an unfamiliar concept to an audience. For Aristotle, language not only makes this happen but also enhances understanding and even creates new knowledge. This idea he presents in his theory of inventions, that is, through the aims of *logos*, *ethos*, and *pathos*.[16] This holds especially true in the *lexis* of metaphors, as metaphorical language contributes most effectively to the aims of invention, particularly in its sensitivity to social and cultural knowledge.

Definition

To be sure, the Greeks before Plato have used metaphors, similes, and analogies in both prosaic and poetic contexts since Homer in the *Iliad* and *Odyssey*.[17] The Greek terms εἰκών and παραβολή carried the technical meanings of "similarity" and "comparison," respectively, denoting figurative language.[18] In addition to παραβολή, Plato introduced the Greek term

---

15. This conviction is essentially Parmenidian. See, for example, Daniel Boyarin, *Socrates and the Fat Rabbis* (Chicago: University of Chicago Press, 2009), 36–37. Boyarin points out that for Plato, dialectic is not dialogical (in the Bahktinian sense) but rather monological (opposing the aims of rhetoric). Boyarin also points out that Aristotle's epistemology is "in the same traditions as that of Parmenides and Plato, one in which truth and falsehood are absolute binary opposites" (Boyarin, *Socrates*, 45).

16. For a bibliography for each of these, see Duane F. Watson, *The Rhetoric of the New Testament: A Bibliographic Survey* (Blandford Forum: Deo, 2006), 33–37.

17. They were used for ornamentation of speech, didactic purposes, and clarification (especially of the abstract), to name a few. See G. E. R. Lloyd, *The Revolutions of Wisdom: Studies in the Claims and Practice of Ancient Greek Science* (Berkeley: University of California Press, 1989), 172–83. See Doreen Innes, "Metaphor, Simile, and Allegory," in *Metaphor, Allegory and the Classical Tradition*, ed. G. R. Boys-Stones (Oxford: Oxford University Press, 2003), 9–11. See also Marsh H. McCall Jr., *Ancient Rhetorical Theories of Simile and Comparison* (Cambridge: Harvard University Press, 1969).

18. Other meanings are attached as well, that is, "image," "illustration," or "likeness." See McCall, *Ancient Rhetorical Theories*, 1–23. In tracing terms of comparisons, McCall posits that the first rhetorical appearance of a term of simile (εἰκών) is in Aristophanes, particularly in the *Eq.* 864–867 and in the *Ran.* 905–906. Plato seems to have introduced παραβολή ("comparison") and ὁμοίωσις ("likeness" or "resemblance").

2. Metaphor and Rhetoric 47

ὁμοίωσις, meaning "comparison," "likeness," and "resemblance."[19] In the *Critias* and the *Timaeus*, Plato uses the verb μεταφέρω in the technical sense of translation (*Criti.* 113a) and in transferring ideas from fiction to reality (*Tim.* 26c), but he provides no definition of it.[20] The earliest documented use of the actual term μεταφορά in a rhetorical context is found in Isocrates's *Evag.* 8–10 (writing ca. 374 BCE).[21] Isocrates does not define metaphor either, and, what is more, he denies its place in prose, thus taking a contrasting stance to Aristotle (e.g., *Rhet.* 3.2.6, 1404b).[22]

The primary lexical entry for the Greek noun μεταφορά is "transference" or "change," and by extension "transference to a new sense."[23] The noun is derived from the verb form, μεταφέρω, a combination of μετά (among, with, after) and φέρω (to bear, carry, bring), which denotes the carrying of something across, the act of transferring. The latter is a typical effect of the preposition on words of action, as can be seen in μεταβαίνω (to pass over from one place to another), μεταβάλλω (throw into a different position or translate), μεταβιβάζω (carry over, transfer), μεταβοθρεύω (move into another trench), and μετάγω (convey from one place to another). Yet this alone seems to be an incomplete interpretation, for it says little about what is transferred or how it is done. In the *Poetics* and the *Rhetoric*, Aristotle systematizes a theoretical basis for the definition and function of figurative expressions in which he uses the Greek term μεταφορά as a metaphor.[24] Aristotle states in the *Poetics*,

---

19. McCall, *Ancient Rhetorical Theories*, 17–18.

20. See also John T. Kirby, "Aristotle on Metaphor," *American Journal of Philology* 118 (1997): 528–30.

21. As Kirby reiterates, Aristotle did not invent the word μεταφορά, though its uses within classical literature that have survived to our time are not found beyond or before Isocrates (Kirby, "Aristotle on Metaphor," 523).

22. Isocrates uses it in the context of distinguishing between prose and verse. According to Isocrates, *Evag.* 8–9, poets typically use metaphors, along with foreign words and neologisms, for ornamental reasons; they are impermissible for prose writers. The latter seems to be a contentious issue for Aristotle, who suggests that metaphor, along with the common use of words, is most suitable for prose. Interestingly, John T. Kirby points to the strong possibility that Isocrates may have understood the definition of μεταφορά differently than Aristotle (Kirby, "Aristotle on Metaphor," 526).

23. LSJ, s.v. "μεταφορά."

24. Paul Ricoeur, *The Rule of Metaphor* (Toronto: University of Toronto Press, 1975), 25. Ricoeur states, "In order to explain metaphor, Aristotle fashions a metaphor borrowed from the order of movement, that of changing place ... the very word 'metaphor' is thus metaphoric because it is borrowed from another order than that of language."

48   Apocalyptic Sheep and Goats in Matthew and 1 Enoch

A μεταφορά is the application [ἐπιφορά] of a name [ὀνόματος] that belongs to another thing [ἀλλοτρίου]: either from genus [γένους] to species [εἶδος], species to genus, species to species, or by analogy [ἀνάλογον]. By "from genus to species" I mean, e.g., "my ship stands here": mooring is a kind of standing. Species to genus: "ten thousand noble deeds has Odysseus accomplished"; ten thousand is many, and the poet has used it here instead of "many." Species to species: e.g., "drawing off the life with bronze," and "cutting with slender-edged bronze"; here he has used "drawing off" for "cutting" and vice versa, as both are kinds of removing. I call by "analogy" cases where B is to A as D is to C: one will then speak of D instead of B, or B instead of D (*Poet.* 21, 1457b6–19).

First, Aristotle defines μεταφορά as being an application (ἐπιφορά) of a foreign name (ὀνόματος ἀλλοτρίου),[25] or literally, a name (ὄνομα) that belongs

---

25. The Greek noun ἐπιφορά denotes the placing of a thing upon another as indicated by its prefix ἐπι-, further qualifying μεταφορά, as they share the same root. For a discussion of the possible use of the term ἐπιφορά by Aristotle, see Ricoeur, *Rule of Metaphor*, 17–21. See also Kirby, "Aristotle on Metaphor," 532–33. Kirby points out the risk of tautology between μεταφορά and ἐπιφορά, but the latter further clarifies an aspect that is not so clear in the former. In the context of ὄνομα, and without neglecting other possible meanings (See Kirby, "Aristotle on Metaphor," 517–54, esp. 532), ἐπιφορά most likely means "application" (e.g., ὀνομάτων [Plato, *Leg.* 944b; cf. *Crat.* 430d]) as in "transfer upon" (See LSJ, s.v. "ἐπιφορά"). Risking tautology, it is likely that Aristotle uses ἐπιφορά to clarify what may have been ambiguous in the term μεταφορά alone (as in transfer across) and to emphasize the importance of ὄνομα. μεταφορά is not just transference but also the application of a name, transferring attributes of one thing upon another. The adjective ἀλλότριος denotes foreignness. For Aristotle, foreignness is one of μεταφορά's virtues as it elevates one's style (*Rhet.* 2.2.9, 1404b). On virtues of μεταφορά, see Richard Moran, "Artifice and Persuasion: The Work of Metaphor in the Rhetoric," in *Essays on Aristotle's Rhetoric*, ed. Amelie Oksenberg Rorty (Berkeley: University of California Press, 1996), 390. Like foreign terms (γλῶτται) and unusual word forms, Aristotle classifies μεταφορά in the *Poetics* as strange or exotic (ξενικός), which would deviate from the standard or familiar use of language (κύριος) (*Poet.* 22, 1458a21–23). The Greek term κύριος refers to the primary, literal, or proper meaning of a word. All other meanings are tropes. This is not to say that Aristotle makes a distinction between literal and metaphorical. Such distinction comes later. See Innes, "Metaphor," 11. The sense of ἀλλότριος may be best illustrated by the example of analogy (cf. *Poet.* 21, 1457b25–31). Aristotle states, "It is necessary that μεταφορά from analogy correspond always to either of two things of similar genera [τῶν ὁμογενῶν]," not "the same genus" as some would have it (*Rhet.* 3.4.4, 1407a4). Contra George Kennedy's translation, "Metaphor from analogy should always have a correspondence *between the two species* of *the same genus*," in Aristotle, *On Rhetoric: A Theory of Civic*

2. Metaphor and Rhetoric

to another thing.[26] Second, he clarifies μεταφορά by specifying four types (εἴδη μεταφορᾶς, e.g., *Rhet.* 3.2.7, 1405a3).[27] The four kinds of metaphor foreshadow and correspond to (without necessarily influencing) taxonomies of figurative expressions in later rhetorical handbooks.[28] The definition implies a philosophical description of metaphorical language.[29]

Discourse, trans. George A. Kennedy, 2nd ed. (Oxford: Oxford University Press, 2007), 206. The Greek does not suggest necessarily things of "the same genus." Aristotle follows with an example of the wine cup of Dionysus and Ares's shield. The wine cup and shield are certainly not of the same genus, but given the proportion of analogy, they would be things of "similar genera."

26. The ὄνομα (name or noun) literally gives μεταφορά its formative attributes in the *Poetics*. See Pierre Swiggers, "Cognitive Aspects of Aristotle's Theory of Metaphor," *Glotta* 62 (1984): 40–45, esp. 40; Ricoeur, *Rule of Metaphor*, 14; Kirby, "Aristotle on Metaphor," 533. The term ὄνομα is by no means an insignificant aspect of Aristotle's definition. It is an important element within a system of interpretation. See Jacques Derrida, *Margins of Philosophy*, trans. Alan Bass (Chicago: University of Chicago Press, 1982), 232. Aristotle defines it as a "compound meaningful sound, without (expression of) time, and of which no part has a meaning on itself" (*Poet.* 20, 1457a10–12). While ὄνομα seems restricted to nouns, the Greek term may also include adjectives and verbs used nominally. See Derrida, *Margins of Philosophy*, 232–35; Kirby, "Aristotle on Metaphor," 533. When Aristotle speaks of names (ὄνομα), he speaks also of the existence of things (substances/nonsubstances) symbolized by the names (cf. *Int.* 1, 16a14–15). Elsewhere, Aristotle distinguishes between an uncombined ὄνομα ("man," "ox," "runs," "wins") and a combined ὄνομα ("man runs" and "man wins") (*Cat.* 2, 1a16–19; *Int.* 1, 16a19). An uncombined ὄνομα says nothing of existence or reality insofar as it can be said to be true or false (*Cat.* 4, 2a4–10; *Int.* 1, 16a15–19). A combined ὄνομα carries a verb, taking on dimensions of time and reality (*Int.* 3, 16b6–8). The definition of a μεταφορά as an ἐπιφορά implies the verb *to be* by virtue of applying a name to something as a predication, hence, a combined ὄνομα.

27. On the treatment of the four types, see Ingram Bywater, *Aristotle on the Art of Poetry: A Revised Text with Critical Introduction, Translation, and Commentary* (Oxford: Clarendon, 1909). See also Umberto Eco, "Metaphor, Dictionary, and Encyclopedia," *New Literary History* 15 (1984): 255–71; Umberto Eco, Ursula Niklas, and Francis Edeline, "Metaphor," in *Encyclopedic Dictionary of Semiotics*, ed. T. A. Sebeok, 2nd ed. (Berlin: de Gruyter, 1994), 534–49.

28. These include metonymy, antonomasia, metalepsis, synecdoche, catechresis, allegory, hyperbole, and so forth. See Quintilian, *Inst.* 9.1.5. See also George Kennedy, *The Art of Persuasion in Greece* (Princeton: Princeton University Press, 1963), 111–12.

29. What I mean by "rhetorical aspects" are those in which metaphor may be persuasive through ornamentation. Metaphor, as defined, presents a philosophical description as to how it contributes to the aims of the pursuit of truth. Cf. Derrida, *Margins of Philosophy*, 232.

50 Apocalyptic Sheep and Goats in Matthew and 1 Enoch

From the above, we see that the first three types of μεταφορά emphasize secondary nonsubstances and, thus, universals and the abstract; these emphases are common to metonymies, synecdoches, and similes. Nonsubstances point toward relatives, quantities, qualities, and so forth. Standing is a position and, thus, a relative (*Cat.* 7, 6b11), "ten thousand" is a quantity (*Cat.* 6, 4b26–27), and "drawing off" shares the same qualities with "cutting." With respect to qualities, things are called similar and dissimilar (*Cat.* 8, 11a15),[30] such that, in a metaphorical instance, the foreign name symbolizes certain qualities it shares with another. A name in an instance of a μεταφορά transfers its qualities of similarity.[31] In an analogy, Aristotle highlights primaries and particulars and the similarities between them. All four types involve cognition. It follows that what allows for predication between two different things is also where similarities of qualities between universals and particulars are conceptualized and compared (*Cat.* 7, 7b15–8a12). What is more, μεταφοραί for Aristotle are not predominantly matters of ornamentation but are primarily ways to speak about the existence of things, of "things there are," through categories and cognitive activities of comparison.

Metaphor and Cognition

For Aristotle, humans share certain cognitive faculties with animals,[32] notably perception, φαντάσια, and experience. φαντασίαι are persistent traces of perception that Aristotle calls "images" (φαντάσματα, *De an.* 3.3, 428b30–9a6).[33] The accumulation of perceptual information is stored as

---

30. The observation of likeness (ὅμοια) and unlikeness (ἀνόμοια) is in virtue of *qualities* only. Furthermore, things called similar or "like" (ὅμοια) are not just things that are similar in one quality but similar in many or in the most important qualities that when altering those qualities changes occur (*Metaph.* 5.9.5, 1018a15–19).

31. The Rhetorica ad Herennium expresses a similar notion when it states, "*Similitudo* is a manner of speech that carries over an element of likeness to one thing from a dissimilar thing" (Rhet. Her. 4.45.59).

32. Malcolm Heath, "Cognition in Aristotle's Poetics," *Mnemosyne* 62 (2009): 51–75, esp. 53. Aristotle recognized the capabilities of animals to adapt to their environment as well as their intelligence (e.g., *Hist. an.* 9.7, 612b18–31; 9.5, 611a15–30; 9.10, 614b18–30; 9.39, 623a7–26; 9.46, 630b18–21).

33. See also Malcolm Schofield, "Aristotle on the Imagination," in *Essays on Aristotle's* De Anima, ed. Martha C. Nussbaum and Amélie Oksenberg Rorty (Oxford: Oxford University Press, 1992), 249–78.

2. Metaphor and Rhetoric 51

memory (*Mem. rem.* 1, 449b30–451a17). From memory, we acquire experience because "the numerous memories of the same thing eventually produce the effect of a single experience" (*An. post.* 2.19, 100a3–6; *Metaph.* 1.1–6, 980b26–981a13), which results in a judgment.[34] Both animals and humans are able to recollect conceptual images, but, for Aristotle, the former does so involuntarily and passively, while the latter recollections are active, as humans voluntarily call something to mind.

φαντασίαι are conceptual imitations (μίμησις) of things perceived; when drawn, they become portraits and pictures; when written in letters or described with a word, they become names or nouns; when acted out in causal sequences, they form tragedy.[35] Imitations are symbols insofar as they stand for what they imitate. The human voice can best imitate things (*Rhet.* 3.1.8, 1404a21–22). Things spoken are symbols (σύμβολα) of affections of the soul, while things written are the symbols (σύμβολα) of the sound (*Int.* 1, 16a1–5). Substances themselves are also symbols: secondary substances signify (σημαίνω) the qualifications (ποιόν) of primary substances (*Cat.* 5, 3b10–24). In their proper sense, names (ὀνόματα) signify something (*Int.* 1–2, 16a1–34, *Rhet.* 3.10, 1410b11).[36] μεταφορά must be drawn from "the beautiful either in sound or in meaning or in visualization or in some form of sense perception" (*Rhet.* 3.2.13, 1405b). Ideally, then, μεταφορά symbolizes both a thing in its usual context and the qualities it shares with another different thing, prompting the conceptual image(s) and experience(s) attached to it.

---

34. Aristotle cites Polus as saying that "experience produces art, but inexperience chance." According to Aristotle, many notions of experience make a single universal judgment with regard to similar objects. A remedy to a certain disease on Callias is, through experience, the remedy for the same disease on Socrates and many others. The judgment that that is the remedy for that disease comes about through experience, and as a result, the art of curing disease may emerge (*Metaph.* 1.5–6, 981a5–13).

35. The processes and descriptions involved in these examples are far more complex, but for the sake of space, I have simplified them.

36. In this respect, Kirby utilizes the interaction of a triad of semiotic elements as theorized by Charles Sanders Pierce. These elements are "[1] the *object*, the thing being represented; [2] the 'representamen' or *sign*—whatever thing it is that stands for or signifies the object to someone—and [3] the *interpretant*, the all-important vehicle whereby the human brain makes the connection between sign and object—the concept whereby one grasps this connection, so that (for example) a red octagonal traffic sign is accepted as signifying that an automobile must come to a halt at that point" (Kirby, "Aristotle on Metaphor," 535).

52   Apocalyptic Sheep and Goats in Matthew and 1 Enoch

For Aristotle, conceptual images are subjectively interpretive (cf. *De an.* 3, 428a12–15).[37] Though susceptible to logical scrutiny, they do not necessarily equate with the actual sensible object (*Metaph.* 4.5.23, 1010b1–4).[38] This relates closely with thought (διάνοια), as someone thinks that "this is that."[39] The study of thought (διάνοια, see *Poet.* 19, 1456a34–b19) is explicitly assigned to the domain of rhetoric (*Rhet.* 1.1.14 and 1.2.1, 1355b8–11, and 25–27), so that μεταφορά has a place both in the study of cognition (expression of thoughts) and logical argumentation.[40]

Metaphor and Reason

Unlike animals, humans have the ability to "add to, interact with and partially transform" perception, images (φαντασίαι), and experience.[41] In other words, for Aristotle, only humans are able to reason. This allows humans to access the world of universals, to deliberate, and to make inferences (*An.*

---

37. "Further, it is not when we are exercising [our sense] with precision on the object of perception that we say that this *appears* (φαίνεται) *to us* a man, but rather when we do not perceive it distinctly." Schofield makes the point that the appearance of "to us" reveals Aristotle's awareness of the subjectivity of the judgment, and so suggests that Aristotle would not object to the idea that in φαντάσια we consciously or unconsciously interpret the data of our senses (Schofield, "Aristotle on the Imagination," 259).

38. It must be noted that for Aristotle, conceptual images acquired from sense perception are not necessarily true. In the *Metaph.* 4.5.23, 1010b1–4, Aristotle, against Protagoras, suggests that not all appearances (φαινόμενον) are true (ἀληθές) and that sense-perception (αἴσθησις) is not false. However, the image (φαντασία) we get is not the same as the sense-perception. The passage (*Metaph.* 4.5.23, 1010b1–4) constitutes part of his argument against Protagoras's doctrine (see Plato, *Theaet.* 152a–c) that all φαινόμενα, "appearances," are true. See *Metaph.* 4.5.7–9, 1009a38–b9. See also Schofield, "Aristotle on the Imagination," 256–57.

39. See Derrida, *Margins of Philosophy*, 232–33. "Thought," says Derrida, "covers the range of that which is given to language, or of what one is given to think through language, as a cause or an effect or content of language" (Derrida, *Margins of Philosophy*, 232).

40. It is also in the context of argumentative techniques that Aristotle speaks of μεταφορά in the *Poetics* (*Poet.* 21 and 22, 1457a31–1459a16).

41. Heath, "Cognition," 55. For Aristotle, what sets us apart from animals is our capacity to reason. Heath points out that although we share the ability to perceive, create conceptual images (φαντάσματα), and attain experience, reason does not supersede but "interacts with and partially transforms them."

post. 1.31, 87b28–88a7; *Phys.* 1.5, 189a5–8; *De an.* 2.5, 417b21–3).[42] When comparing similarities, the reasoning mind asks why and thus speaks of causality.[43] Simply put, one asks why "this is that." In μεταφορά, we may ask why "this is *said of* that" or why "this is *in* that." For Aristotle, reasoning and asking why gains access to the universals, whereas perception of the senses accesses the particulars.[44]

In μεταφορά, universals interact with particulars through recollected φαντασίαι, which is the memory of imitative images, the perception of existing things, reinforced through experience and symbolized by names. In its interface with universals, the perception of particulars engages in the act of becoming. In other words, φαντάσια combines and recombines with universals in a conceptual place that Aristotle calls τόπος, which may lead one closer to truth or to a more complete imagery of what is perceived through the senses.[45] In this sense, μεταφορά provides the proposition for the middle term: for example, if A is B, *B is C*, then A is C.

---

42. Kirby, "Aristotle on Metaphor," 537. Kirby suggests, "the observation of likeness is a crucial cognitive step in the process of reasoning about the world—and also in the practice of articulating one's perceptions."

43. Reason and the exercise of rationality play a central part in the pursuit of truth or making sense of things. Aristotle states in the *Topics*, "The observation of likeness is useful with a view both to inductive arguments and to hypothetical deductions ... for it is not easy to do this if we do not know the points of likeness" (*Top.* 1.18, 108b7–14). Aristotle points to the usefulness of observing likeness for philosophical argumentations.

44. Heath suggests, "If perception typically prompts humans to exercise their rationality by asking 'why'?, thinking about the 'why' has an effect on perception in turn—at the very least, by influencing how we direct our attention" (Heath, "Cognition," 55). Heath further explains that perception, φαντάσια, and experience constantly interact with reason. It is in this interactive thinking that learning may come about.

45. In the *Physica*, Aristotle compares τόπος with a vessel and describes it as the boundary of a contained body (*Phys.* 4.2, 209b29–34). Aristotle's concept of τόπος is made to correspond with Plato's concept of spaces (χώρα) as he refers to Plato. According to Plato, the process of becoming and perishing of substance occurs within these "spaces" (Plato, *Tim.* 52a–c). In the *Physica*, Aristotle differs from Plato's concept of spaces in that Plato in *Timaeus* suggests place is coextensive with the object/matter occupying the place. For Aristotle, two bodies cannot be coextensive and so place is independent of the object, yet it contains the object. Both form and matter occupy place, where form is the intelligible, definable element in matter/substance. Whereas in Plato (*Tim.* 52a), the imprint of form and its copies are what enters the spaces of becoming, which is witnessed by the senses. See, for example, W. K. C. Guthrie, *The Later Plato and the Academy*, vol. 5 of *A History of Greek Philosophy* (Cambridge:

54   Apocalyptic Sheep and Goats in Matthew and 1 Enoch

The μεταφορά, in a conceptual τόπος, allows possibilities of discovery and novelty.[46] With human reason and logical thought, the comparison of conceptual images reevaluates the κύριος ("proper" name) by way of inference. The transference of a name to be applied to another as a proposition (μεταφορά) may result in change, as different names can be used in new ways for the listener, just as proper names may take on an enlightened or new meaning (cf. *Rhet.* 3.11.6, 1412a26–28). The μεταφορά stands in close affinity with induction (παράδειγμα—rhetorical induction) and thus is connected with similes, parables, and fables.[47] The μεταφορά becomes a potential (δύναμις) for novelty and possible knowledge. Aristotle states, "μεταφορά most [often] brings about learning; for when he calls old age 'stubble,' he creates understanding and knowledge through the genus, since old age and stubble are things that have lost their bloom" (*Rhet.* 3.10, 1410b2). μεταφορά creates clarity, as he realizes "that he learned something different from what he believed, and his mind seems to say,

---

Cambridge University Press, 1996), 262–70. See also Paul Natorp, *Plato's Theory of Ideas: An Introduction to Idealism* (Sankt Augustin: Academia, 2004), esp. chapter 12. See also Francisco J. Gonzalez, "Plato's Dialectic of Forms," in *Plato's Forms: Varieties of Interpretation*, ed. William Welton (Lanham, MD: Lexington Books, 2003), 46–47.

46. The general principle contained within a τόπος analyzes the possibilities of a proposition, that is, what is being predicated. Second, the consideration of combining more than one predicable to finalize a conclusion implies the creativity of knowledge. These two points perhaps lead William Grimaldi to understand τόποι as not just a mere list of mechanical terms but also ways to think about the subject. See William M. Grimaldi, "The Aristotelian Topics," in *Aristotle: The Classical Heritage of Rhetoric*, ed. Keith V. Erickson (Methuchen, NJ: Scarecrow, 1974), 185. Grimaldi states, "This was what was meant by saying that these particular topics are not mere mechanical lists of terms to be tried on a subject, no Procrustean bed to which the subject is fitted; rather we have here a method of analysis originating in the ontological reality of the subject." Richard McKeon suggests topos serves as a "space" for combination and recombination. See Richard McKeon, "Creativity and the Commonplace," in *Rhetoric: Essays in Invention and Discovery*, ed. Mark Backman (Woodbridge: Ox Bow, 1987), 31.

47. In the *Rhetorica*, there are two proofs: enthymemes and paradigms; deductions and inductions, respectively. "To make up an illustration" belongs to the paradigm [παράδειγμα—rhetorical induction] and characterized by two kinds: comparisons [παράβολη] and fables [λόγοι]" (*Rhet.* 2.20.2, 1393a). Quintilian also considers comparisons as belonging to proof (Quintilian, *Inst.* 5.11.5). παράδειγμα is also closely related to personification, which becomes a distinct figurative expression in later rhetorical handbooks.

2. Metaphor and Rhetoric   55

'How true, and I was wrong'" (*Rhet.* 3.11, 1412a6).[48] This places the use of μεταφορά well within the purview of creating knowledge and pursuing truth and reality.

2.2.2. Modern Metaphor Theory

For Aristotle, metaphorical language (metonymy, synecdoche, simile, and analogy) is a way to speak of ontological existence and realities. By applying a name from another thing or context to be used in a new context, metaphorical language aims to understand, while at the same time it proposes realities about something known, an unnamed thing, or an abstract thought through comparison. Thus, the application of a name (metaphor) as a conceptual proposition, involving recollected imagery and imitation, allows metaphorical language to access reasoning for or against what may be true or false.

In their seminal work on metaphorical language, George Lakoff and Mark Johnson devise and also argue for a conceptual understanding of metaphor.[49] For them, metaphorical language functions on principles of predication or categories.[50] Metaphorical language is the means of understanding realities through the interactive relationship between cognitive thought (memory, established experiences, and realities within the mind) and bodily experiences (e.g., sight, touch, emotions, smell, habit, behavior, etc.). These are categorized and structurally created by the mind in what cognitive linguistics call conceptual frames and mental spaces.[51]

---

48. Innes, "Metaphor," 14. Innes posits, "The audience perceives a likeness between a and b which stirs a sudden new understanding (or recognition) of a relationship between species and genus."

49. George Lakoff and Mark Johnson, *Metaphors We Live By* (Chicago: University of Chicago Press, 2003).

50. George Lakoff and Mark Johnson, *Philosophy in The Flesh: The Embodied Mind and Its Challenge to Western Thought* (New York: Basic Books, 1999); George Lakoff, *Women, Fire, and Dangerous Things: What Categories Reveal about the Mind* (Chicago: University of Chicago Press, 1987).

51. Charles J. Fillmore, "Frame Semantics," in *Linguistics in the Morning Calm*, ed. the Linguistic Society of Korea (Seoul: Hanshin, 1982), 111–37; Fillmore, "Frames and the Semantics of Understanding," *Quaderni di Semantica* 6 (1985): 222–53. For a recent study on frames, see Karen Sullivan, *Frames and Constructions in Metaphorical Language* (Philadelphia: John Benjamins, 2013). George Lakoff calls this the Idealized Cognitive Model (ICM). The smaller and more specific frames of experiential

The philosophical backbone of cognitive linguistics is *embodied realism*, which is similar to an Aristotelian perception of truth in the sense that the material world exists (realism) and that there is no gap between the mind and body (embodied mind).[52] They differ significantly in that, although the material world exists, for cognitive linguists, absolute truth (absolutism) cannot be accessed. Cognitive linguists adopt a relativist view, meaning that they believe that "concepts do change over time, vary across cultures, have multiple inconsistent structures, and reflect social conditions." They do not subscribe to extreme relativism in the sense that "it [cognitive linguistics] has an account of how real, stable knowledge, both in science and the everyday world, is possible."[53]

Cognitive linguists are realists, but absolute truth is *unattainable*, because there is no gap between the mind and body (embodied).[54] There exist in the human perception empirical realities.[55] This view is closer to Aristotle than it is to Plato. In fact, it is the opposite of Platonic epistemology. The embodied realism of cognitive linguistics claims that "the same

---

reality are called mental spaces. See Zoltan Kovecses, *Language, Mind, and Culture: A Practical Introduction* (Oxford: Oxford University Press, 2006), 251. On the idea of "mental spaces," see Gilles Fauconnier, *Mental Spaces* (Cambridge: Cambridge University Press, 1994), originally published in 1985 by MIT Press. The theory of mental spaces is further developed by Gilles Fauconnier and Mark Turner, *The Way We Think: Conceptual Blending and the Mind's Hidden Complexities* (New York: Basic Books, 2002).

52. Lakoff and Johnson, *Philosophy in the Flesh*, chapter 7. With regard to culture and language, I lean heavily upon Kovecses, *Language, Mind, and Culture*. With regard to figurative language in cognitive linguistic terms, I refer to Barbara Dancygier and Eve Sweetser, *Figurative Language* (Cambridge: Cambridge University Press, 2014).

53. Lakoff and Johnson, *Philosophy in the Flesh*, 96.

54. Although Aristotle was a realist, he believed that absolute truth is *attainable* in the material world. Plato also was a realist but believed that absolute truth is *unattainable* because of a gap between the mind and body (metaphysical).

55. The embodied realist approach of the cognitive linguists' metaphorical program is not total relativism. It does not claim that there is no correct knowledge or knowledge of the real world. Lakoff recognizes that embodied realism is still a form of realism. Though it retains a notion of objectivity, it follows the philosophical contention that there cannot be a privileged correct description such as the one taken up by metaphysical realism or objectivism that there is only a God's eye view of reality. Lakoff agrees with Hillary Putnam's argument for an "internal realism," in Hillary Putnam, *Mind, Language, and Reality: Philosophical Papers*, vol. 2 (Cambridge: Cambridge University Press, 1975). See the discussion in Lakoff, *Women, Fire, and Dangerous Things*, esp. 260–68.

cognitive operations that human beings use for making sense of empirical realities are also used for making sense of language."[56] Those cognitive operations take place in a metaphorical structure, as in "A is B" (in its simplest form), in which experience plays an indispensable role. Thus, Lakoff and Johnson state, "metaphor is a matter for empirical study, not for *a priori* definition."[57] This difference sees cognitive linguistics taking a sharper turn toward cultural sensitivities of metaphorical language than Aristotle does. This is seen especially in the way cognitive linguistics understands categorization of realities.

Categorization and Metaphorical Language

The process of categorization and its products (frames) is indispensable in making sense of the world and producing meaning. Metaphorical thought and language are dependent upon categorization in its ability to produce knowledge and understanding. Cognitive linguists rightly point out that Aristotle categorizes things that exist in accordance with essential features or sets of necessary and sufficient conditions that form rigid boundaries. Such essentials act as rules that determine whether something is or is not in a category. Although metaphors can change those boundaries, categories are nevertheless rigid. Thus, things in the same category share the same features and are of equal status. Classical categorization operates on objective truth, an issue regulated by principles and contained in conceptual topoi.[58] As such, propositions are judged true or false through philosophical disputation or rhetorical argumentation. Aristotle accounts for human subjectivity through rhetorical argumentation, but it is for the direct pursuit of objective truth. On the other hand, categorization for cognitive linguistics operates largely in response to empirical reality, issues of which are regulated by the nature of the thinking and communicating organisms.[59]

---

56. Zoltan Kovecses, *Where Metaphors Come From: Reconsidering Context in Metaphor* (Oxford: Oxford University Press, 2015), 75.

57. Lakoff and Johnson, *Philosophy in the Flesh*, 124.

58. See appendix A.

59. Lakoff and Johnson, *Women, Fire, and Dangerous Things*, 266. Lakoff and Johnson explain that this does not mean just the individual but "the nature and experience of the species and of communities." He states, " 'Experience' is thus not taken in the narrow sense of the things that have 'happened to happen' to a single individual. Experience is instead construed in the broad sense: the totality of human experience and everything that plays a role in it—the nature of our bodies, our genetically inherited capacities,

58   Apocalyptic Sheep and Goats in Matthew and 1 Enoch

Conceptual theory of metaphor has dominated metaphorical studies of the past decade since emerging some four decades ago. However, it is not within the scope of this study to cover the intricacy into which the study has developed with regard to the links of linguistics and neuroscience. In order to understand how metaphors can be used, I aim only to highlight what underlines metaphorical language and culture and how that aids how metaphors work ideally.

Based on studies of Ludwig Wittgenstein, John L. Austin, and Eleanor Rosch, George Lakoff understands categories in terms of prototypes.[60] Wittgenstein and Austin find that categories cannot be defined only by their essential features. Using the conceptual category "game," Wittgenstein shows that there is no single essential feature that characterizes all instances of the category of game. Instead, there are only family resemblances among various members (games) within a category.[61] This leads to the insight that the boundaries of categories are not always fixed but are often fuzzy and expandable. What creates categories are the relations between the members. Its members are based on family resemblances to each other.

Austin extends this conceptual understanding of category to the senses of words. He shows further how family resemblances can be realized. Austin utilizes the various senses of the word *healthy* as an example:[62]

---

our modes of physical functioning in the world, our social organization, etc. In short, it takes as essential much of what is seen as irrelevant in the objectivist account."

60. Lakoff, *Women, Fire, and Dangerous Things*; John R. Taylor, *Linguistic Categorization* (Oxford: Clarendon, 1995), originally published in 1989; Ludwig Wittgenstein, *Philosophical Investigation* (New York: Macmillan, 1953); John L. Austin, *Philosophical Papers* (Oxford: Oxford University Press, 1961). Austin extends Wittgenstein's "family members" and "exemplars" to the study of words. See Eleanor Rosch, "Principles of Categorization," in *Cognition and Categorization*, ed. Eleanor Rosch and B. B. Lloyd (Hillsdale, NJ: Lawrence Erlbaum, 1978), 27–48; Eleanor Rosch and Carolyne Mervis, "Family Resemblances: Studies in the Internal Structure of Categories," *Cognitive Psychology* 7 (1975): 573–605.

61. Zoltan Kovecses explains this: "Family member A has properties x and y, family member B has properties y and z, and family member C has properties x and z. There is no single property that they all share, but they resemble one another and are members of the same family by virtue of sharing a property with only some family members but not others" (Kovecses, *Language, Mind, and Culture*, 23). See also Lakoff, *Women, Fire, and Dangerous Things*, 17.

62. This example and others like it are cited by Lakoff, *Women, Fire, and Dangerous Things*, 18–21.

2. Metaphor and Rhetoric   59

> The adjective "healthy": when I talk of a healthy body, and again of a healthy complexion, of healthy exercise: the word is not just being used equivocally ... there is what we may call a *primary nuclear sense* of "healthy": the sense in which "healthy" is used of a healthy body: I call this *nuclear* because it is "contained as a part" in the other two senses which may be set out as "productive of healthy bodies" and "resulting from a healthy body".... Now are we content to say that the exercise, the complexion, and the body are all called "healthy" because they are similar?[63]

Here body becomes the nuclear or central representation of the sense of the word *healthy* under which complexion and exercise become peripheral or noncentral. In other words, body, complexion, and exercise (which are different things) form a category of health (a state of being) whose members are related through metonymic relations to the nuclear representation, healthy body; healthy body can stand for the cause (healthy exercise) and for the results (healthy complexion) of being healthy. Metonymy in this particular case is just one mechanism among others that acts as the principle of family relationship between the members of the category.[64]

The works of Rosch and her associates are largely responsible for making this understanding of categorization into an empirical issue, resulting in "the theory of prototypes."[65] Rosch's experiments show that prototypical or central and noncentral members of a category are culturally dependent.[66] She proves that categories are conceptually created not only a priori but largely by human understanding and experience.[67] The

---

63. Austin, *Philosophical Papers*, 71.

64. Lakoff, *Women, Fire, and Dangerous Things*, 19.

65. Lakoff, *Women, Fire, and Dangerous Things*, 39.

66. See also Kovecses, *Language, Mind and Culture*, 24–25, 46. For a fuller discussion, see Lakoff, *Women, Fire, and Dangerous Things*, 39–57.

67. See also Lakoff, *Women, Fire, and Dangerous Things*, 69. Studies along this line of inquiry are currently ongoing. However, studies conducted by scholars in more recent times show that categories might not be stable abstract mental representations, that is, chair, bird, boat, and so forth. They can also be created to fulfill a goal or an aim. Lawrence Barsalou gives examples of categories such as "food to eat on a diet," or "things to take on a camping trip," or "clothing to take on a vacation," and so forth. All of these categories are created for a purpose (to lose weight, to do things on a camping trip, etc.). Brasilia shows that, for each of these, people consider differently what types of items best represent each category. See Lawrence Barsalou, "Structure, Flexibility, and Linguistic Vagary in Concepts: Manifestations of a Compositional

60   Apocalyptic Sheep and Goats in Matthew and 1 Enoch

cognitive linguist Zoltan Kovecses, in his studies of language, culture, and mind, substantiates the above findings, concurring that

> categorization in general and levels of categorization for particular people is just as much a matter of culture as it is a matter of cognition. The cultural contexts in which the categorization takes place play a crucial role in why people categorize particular objects and events at particular levels of abstraction.[68]

Lakoff combines family resemblance and prototype semantics. For Lakoff, while the borders of the category expand (due to shared properties and family resemblance) to include other things normally excluded in Aristotle's category (due to governing principles and logic), those things are structured in a graded fashion, from a central representative to peripherals of the category.[69] Lakoff and Johnson applied the above insights along with the theory of prototype to linguistics (noun, verb, modifier, phrase, clause, sentence, etc.), most notably in his work on expressions and structure of conceptual metaphor theory.

Conceptual Metaphor

For Lakoff and Johnson, "*The essence of metaphor is understanding and experiencing one kind of thing in terms of another*."[70] Metaphor means metaphorical concept. This does not mean that metaphor reduces an abstract thought or meaning to literary thought or meaning. It means that abstract thought remains figurative and is expressed by figurative means.[71] In conceptual metaphorical structure (A is B), conceptual frames (A, B) are idealized and correlated. The frame A is an abstract reality, while frame B is some concrete reality of experience.[72] These frames are themselves

---

System of Perceptual Symbols," in *Theories of Memory*, ed. A. C. Collins, S. E. Gathercole, and M. A. Conway (London: Lawrence Erlbaum Associates, 1993), 29–101.

68. Kovecses, *Language, Mind and Culture*, 48.

69. See Kovecses, *Language, Mind, and Culture*, 26; Lakoff, *Women, Fire, and Dangerous Things*, 16–17.

70. Lakoff and Johnson, *Metaphors We Live By*, 5, emphasis original; see 6 for the following point.

71. Kovecses, *Language, Mind, and Culture*, 183, 194.

72. Lakoff states in his 2003 afterword to their seminal work that metaphor "is typically based on cross-domain correlations in our experience, which give rise to the

2. Metaphor and Rhetoric   61

partially structured. For example, in the metaphorical concept ARGUMENT IS WAR, argument, abstractly known with its structural elements, is structured in terms of war. Lakoff and Johnson call the ARGUMENT frame the *target* domain and the WAR frame the *source* domain. However, the structure and elements of WAR do not cover every structural element that is known of ARGUMENT. Thus you have ARGUMENT IS JOURNEY, AN ARGUMENT IS A CONTAINER, and AN ARGUMENT IS A BUILDING.[73] As the name of the domain suggests, these are *sources* from which to understand the *target* frame, ARGUMENT. For example, a journey, as it is structured conceptually through our experiences, can be used to speak of argument in terms of goal, direction, or progress: "We have *set out* to prove that bats are birds."[74] The process of using one to understand or speak of the other is called mapping a source domain onto the target domain. It requires coherence between domains or frames in which elements of the structure correlate.[75]

The above are the more universal metaphors from which other metaphors can emerge. The most universal metaphors are called primary metaphors. To use ARGUMENT IS JOURNEY as an example: we know that JOURNEY (1) defines a path and that path (2) is a surface. It then follows that ARGUMENT DEFINES A PATH (e.g., "He *strayed* from the line of argument") and THE PATH OF AN ARGUMENT IS A SURFACE (e.g., "We have already covered those points.").[76] These logical connections between elements of experiential frames are called metaphorical entailments. Furthermore,

---

perceived similarities between the two domains within the metaphor" (Lakoff and Johnson, *Metaphors We Live By*, 245).

73. Lakoff and Johnson, *Metaphors We Live By*, 89.

74. In this example, "set out" uses elements of the concept of JOURNEY as we understand to speak metaphorically of intentions or goals of the argument, bats are birds. Also in terms of BUILDING, we have, "We've got the *framework* for a *solid* argument." Here, elements of the conceptual structure of BUILDING are used metaphorically to speak of certain elements with the conceptual structure of ARGUMENT. See Lakoff and Johnson, *Metaphors We Live By*, 90.

75. While this section aims only to point out the basics of metaphorical language, metaphorical language is not simply a comparison of one or two frames of reality. Metaphorical language often contains a blend of various frames of realities that are integrated, from which a salient meaning emerges. Fauconnier and Turner call these various frames mental spaces, and the process of blending is referred to as "running the blend." What emerges is a unique meaning. At least four components are involved: Input Space 1, Input Space 2, Generic Space, and Blend. On the blends of various mental spaces of input, see Fauconnier and Turner, *Way We Think*.

76. Lakoff and Johnson, *Metaphors We Live By*, 90–91.

62   Apocalyptic Sheep and Goats in Matthew and 1 Enoch

sometimes two source domains have the same metaphorical entailments and overlap.[77]

Thus, frames are conceptual ways to organize *our* knowledge of things via human experience in order to think and speak about them.[78] This may be analogous to the Aristotelian topos, which is also a conceptual way to organize knowledge albeit via laws and principles of objective reality in order to think and speak about them. The prototypical model of categorization skews more toward culturally accepted realities. For instance, the category JOURNEY in its structural elements is structured in terms of prototypes of experience. This means that the reality as it is understood varies from culture to culture, for every culture has its own preferences or salient features that are used to understand the category JOURNEY.[79] The preference for concept and salient features of reality appears in speech or literature, and in our case metaphorical language. It is to these prototypical entities of a category for any given culture that all other categories, frames, or elements relate.

The more similarities or family resemblances there are to the prototype, the closer that entity is to the center of the category. The fewer there are, the more peripheral an entity is within that category and the more incomprehensible a connection becomes. These more peripheral entities would have been deemed false under classical categorization and, theoretically, would not appear in language. Cognitive linguists argue that they can and do. Thus, categories can overlap and are creatively extended by adding new members.[80] This means that metaphors also have the ability to contain multiple meanings as they create multiple connections between entities. It would also mean that some meanings are goal or ideologically oriented.[81] For Lakoff, prototype categorization allows the

---

77. ARGUMENT IS A JOURNEY and AN ARGUMENT IS A CONTAINER share a similar entailment: As we make an argument, more of a surface is created. For example, as more of a surface is created, the argument covers more ground (JOURNEY); as more of a surface is created, the argument gets more content (CONTAINER). See Lakoff and Johnson, *Metaphors We Live By*, 94.

78. Lakoff, *Women, Fire, and Dangerous Things*, 68–76; Fillmore, "Frame Semantics," 111–37.

79. Kovecses, *Language, Mind, and Culture*, 167. Kovecses states that metaphors vary for at least two reasons: difference of experiences and difference of cognitive preferences.

80. Kovecses, *Language, Mind, and Culture*, 23.

81. Kovecses, *Language, Mind, and Culture*, 152. Kovecses suggests that metaphorical frames are chosen on the basis of one's goals or ideology. He suggests that

2. Metaphor and Rhetoric 63

aboriginal language of Australia in the Dyirbal tradition to categorize together women, fire, and dangerous things, correlating them in countless metaphorical expressions.[82] This understanding of metaphors and the way we think allow, if not motivate, the interpreter to sympathize and be less dismissive when confronted with the polyvalency that underlines religious communication and language.

2.2.3 Apocalyptic Metaphorical Language

Metaphors are ways to make sense of the world, to render it intelligible through bodily experiences, that is, through cultural and social realities. In the Gospel of Matthew, visions of judgment include Jesus as the Son of Man judging the righteous and condemning the wicked in a future setting of the end time. In the judgment imagery of the last judgment in the Gospel of Matthew, metaphors depict the judge as a shepherd, the righteous as sheep, and the condemned as goats in Matt 25:31–46. In Matt 3:11–12, the same characters are depicted as a reaper, the righteous as wheat, and the condemned as chaff. In another judgment image in Matt 13:24–30, we have a sower, the righteous as wheat, and the wicked as weeds. The above discussion on metaphor theory may explain how these metaphors came to be or how these metaphors contain more than one meaning. It may also explain how it is that we can blend multiple layers of meaning to produce a new meaning. Consistent with our working definition of apocalyptic, one may then define apocalyptic metaphorical language as figurative expressions of Jewish reality conceptually conceived that aid in the revelation of esoteric knowledge. Such reality may, for example, describe or reveal for the relationship between the heavens and the earth or the supernatural and humanity, a relational that would otherwise be unintelligible in literal expressions. For the most part, metaphors create new perception and understanding of old concepts without any real substantial change in the essence of those concepts. For instance, as we will see below, the messianic Son of God image is evoked by the metaphors of a baptizer (3:11), a sower (13:24), a shepherd (25:32) and a king (25:34). Righteous Israel and humanity are depicted as wheat (3:12; 13:25) and sheep (25:32), while the wicked are depicted as chaff (3:12), weeds (13:26), and goats (25:32). This

---

this is because of the different consequences that different frames (of source or target) have.

82. Lakoff, *Women, Fire, and Dangerous Things*, 92–96.

64 Apocalyptic Sheep and Goats in Matthew and 1 Enoch

study is mostly concerned with ways in which these metaphors add to the different presentation of the judgment topos and the means by which they assist the revelation of esoteric knowledge, that is, the dynamics of the apocalyptic discourses.

In antiquity and late antiquity within Jewish circles, metaphors were the stock-in-trade of scribes, sages, and priests. Apart from their simple use, metaphors were present in midrash especially in the context of *meshalim*, parables, and allegories. The same can be said of apocalyptic discourses. As we will see in the following chapters, the allegorical interpretation of biblical accounts within the Animal Apocalypse can be seen as a case in point.

In distinguishing between the *mashal*, parable, and allegory, David Stern suggests that "the mashal is a literary-rhetorical form, a genre of narrative that employs certain poetic and rhetorical techniques to persuade its audience of the truth of a specific message relating to an ad hoc situation."[83] Allegory, on the other hand, is "a mode of literary discourse," and the *meshalim* are not. The parable is "an illustrative parallel" that includes "narratives that serve as illustrations."[84] These literary features will be touched upon in this study, and all contain metaphors that attempt "to persuade its audience of the truth of a specific message."

The persuasive value of metaphorical language has long been used in the ancient practice of biblical interpretation and rabbinic midrash. It cannot be denied that the author(s) of the Gospel of Matthew is such a scribe and interpreter of scriptural texts. Matthew utilizes midrash in his interpretive activities, activities that are often far ranging and intertextual. Daniel Boyarin has argued convincingly that midrash is an intertextual reading of the Torah and that the *mashal* has intertextual qualities.[85] For Boyarin, the *mashal*, often translated as parable, can be a figure, simile, or paradigm that serves to give "handles to the Torah." The structural elements with which to fill in the gaps and make connections are the *mashal*. Although Matthew has been considered a scribe of the rabbinic pedigree,[86]

---

83. David Stern, *Parables in Midrash: Narrative and Exegesis in Rabbinic Literature* (Cambridge: Harvard University Press, 1991), 12.

84. Stern, *Parables in Midrash*, 10. See also McCall, Ancient Rhetorical Theories, 27.

85. Daniel Boyarin, *Intertextuality and the Reading of Midrash* (Bloomington: Indiana University Press, 1990), chapter 5.

86. For example, Michael D. Goulder, *Midrash and Lection in Matthew* (London: SPCK, 1974). In an important article published in 1928, Ernst von Dobschütz made

2. Metaphor and Rhetoric 65

the text points more specifically to a Jewish scribe well versed in apocalyptic traditions,[87] albeit this distinction does not necessarily suggest
much difference.

In apocalyptic literature, scholars recognize the pervasiveness and
polyvalent qualities of metaphorical language. Such language evokes
imaginative participation, and it cannot be reduced to descriptive and
factual references.[88] For this reason, its exposition must be seen from a
literary perspective.[89] In response to theological inconsistency within

---

the claim that Matthew might have been a converted rabbi. For the English translation,
see Ernst von Dobschütz, "Matthew as Rabbi and Catechist," in *The Interpretation of
Matthew*, ed. Graham Stanton (Philadelphia: Fortress, 1983), 19–29. For more recent
studies of Matthew and scribal activities, see Lawrence M. Wills, "Scribal Methods in
Matthew and Mishnah Abot," *CBQ* 63 (2001): 258–64; Craig A. Evans, "Targumizing
Tendencies in Matthean Redaction," in *When Judaism and Christianity Began: Essays
in Memory of Anthony J. Saldarini*, ed. Alan J. Avery-Peck, Daniel Harrington, and
Jacob Neusner, JSJSup 85 (Leiden: Brill, 2004), 1:93–116.

87. David E. Orton, *The Understanding Scribe: Matthew and the Apocalyptic Ideal*
(New York: T&T Clark, 1989), 116. Following E. Janssen, who argues for scribal characters of apocalyptic literature, Orton adds one characteristic. Janssen lists that (1)
the central figures reflect distinctively scribal interest, (2) the issues that occupy the
authors are typically scribal, and (3) the methods employed by the authors (midrashic
exposition on a scriptural base) are also scribal. Orton adds that the scribal nature
of the literature also carries with it the visionary or revelatory qualities of the scribal
figures whom the literature reveres.

88. In his monograph *Apocalyptic Vision of the Book of Daniel*, Collins devotes a
chapter to the language of Dan 7–12, where he makes the point that symbolic language
is polyvalent and disagrees with Norman Perrin, who sees the symbols of apocalypses
as examples of "steno-symbols," which maintain a one-to-one relationship with their
referents. See John J. Collins, *The Apocalyptic Vision of the Book of Daniel*, HSM 16
(Missoula, MT: Scholars Press, 1977). See also John J. Collins, "The Symbolism of
Transcendence in Jewish Apocalyptic," *BR* 19 (1974): 5–22.

89. Elisabeth Schüssler Fiorenza, "The Phenomenon of Early Christian Apocalyptic: Some Reflections on Method," in Hellholm, *Apocalypticism in the Mediterranean World*, 295–316. Schüssler Fiorenza states, "The metaphoric and symbolic
character of apocalyptic language resists any attempt at logical reduction and closed
one-dimensional interpretation. Its aim is not explanation and information but the
expression of visionary wholeness. It elicits understandings, emotions, and reactions
that cannot fully be conceptualized and expressed in propositional language. Since
apocalyptic language appeals to the imagination it has to be analyzed from a literary
perspective." Schüssler Fiorenza's point is that the study of symbolic language takes
precedence because the literary context is the means of understanding the essence of
apocalyptic texts (304–5).

apocalypses or Jewish thinking in images, Krister Stendahl states, "Over against stringent logic stands Jewish thinking in images, where the contradictory facts and conceptions can be put together in a kind of significant mosaic."[90] George Nickelsburg and James VanderKam see this as dipping a brush "into a variety of colors available on his [the author's] palette without a concern that they might clash with one another."[91]

The layers of meaning within apocalyptic metaphors also harken back to historical traditions. Some metaphors are themselves historical symbols. Paul Ricoeur's foreword to André LaCocque's commentary on the book of Daniel recognizes the nature of the use of past myths in the language of apocalypses.[92] He highlights not only the symbols utilized in apocalypses but also the literal meaning that comes along with it. For Ricoeur, symbols used in apocalypses unpack historical references of the past to project them upon the current situation. He calls this "analogical assimilation" or "the process of symbolization," which, like Collins and von Rad, involves an interpretive process that sees the symbols as containing several layers of meaning. In this sense, metaphorical and symbolic language functions typologically.[93] However, one must be careful not to suggest a complete transference of meaning in metaphors from one historical context to another. Rather, one should assume that the metaphors may also have accrued other meanings over the course of time and through transference, that is, by being (re)used in a different context.

---

90. The quotation is taken from George W. E. Nickelsburg and James C. VanderKam, *1 Enoch 2: A Commentary on the Book of 1 Enoch 37–82* (Minneapolis: Fortress, 2012), 7. See Krister Stendahl, "The Called and the Chosen," in *The Root of the Vine: Essays in Biblical Theology*, ed. Anton Fridrichsen (New York: Philosophical, 1953), 67.

91. Nickelsburg and Vanderkam, *1 Enoch 2*, 7.

92. Paul Ricoeur, foreword to *The Book of Daniel*, by André LaCocque (Atlanta: John Knox, 1979).

93. Paul Ricoeur, foreword, xxii. Ricoeur states, "The author constitutes the past as the model for his own time and prophecy *post eventum* is transformed according to a schematic rule into new prophecy." The transference of the past underlines for Ricoeur the very operation of apocalyptic discourse. His referring to past myths as a model typifies the present situation. For example, he states, "The statue which the three young men of chapter three [of Daniel] refuse to worship is just as much the golden calf as it is any other idol. In chapter two, the statue in the king's dream, whose different levels allegorically represent four empires, virtually signifies every empire and all hubris by any political-religious power because the statue brings them together in a single reign covering four empires."

2. Metaphor and Rhetoric 67

For Ricoeur, this ideal-type perspective by the author employs a possible model from past myths in response to a challenge in the present, with the hopes of transforming the perspective of the latter.[94] Interestingly, Ricoeur distinguishes between the informed reader of the symbols (i.e., the author, esoteric audience) and those who are ignorant (i.e., the broader public). In Matthew, for example, we may see this distinction between the disciples and the crowd. The polyvalence of the symbols, which he insists upon, activates for the uninformed audience the act of discourse within apocalypses as they respond to existential situations of the present. Ricoeur's attention toward the transference of traditions of the past for the purposes of transformation in the present speaks to the interpretive intentions of the author and the hermeneutical character of metaphors and symbolism across time. The insight that the metaphors play to different types of audiences seems to highlight the prototypical nature of the "process of symbolization."

Apocalyptic metaphorical language within judgment imageries of Matthew's apocalyptic discourses is certainly polyvalent, as are metaphors in apocalyptic discourses in general. As such, they contribute to new perceptions of realities and the interpretation of Scriptures that reflect new experiences and situations. The analytical approach of sociorhetorical interpretation will help trace the communicative and interpretive values of apocalyptic discourse and metaphors, which involves looking at the texts in their literary, cultural, and historical contexts.

2.3. Sociorhetorical Interpretation

2.3.1. Rhetorical Criticism and the New Testament

Following Aristotle's own theory of rhetoric, scholars define rhetoric as "the deployment of available means of persuasion on the part of an author or speaker wishing to exercise influence on the response of one or more readers or hearers to their situation."[95] The description forms the basic foundation

---

94. Ricoeur, foreword, xxiii. He states, "This movement of analogical assimilation, this process of symbolization, which the author spontaneously practices, may be taken into account—and systematized by the exegete—he thereby forms what I have called the ideal-type of apocalyptic, that is, one possible model of response to a certain type of challenge."

95. The above quotation comes from David A. deSilva, "Rhetorical Criticism," *OEBI* 2:273–83. For a survey of the history of rhetoric, see George Kennedy, "Historical

68   Apocalyptic Sheep and Goats in Matthew and 1 Enoch

for modern rhetorical criticism in biblical studies.[96] In the second half of the twentieth century, the seminal works of Hans D. Betz and George A. Kennedy revived the ancient art of rhetoric for New Testament studies.[97] James Muilenburg is credited for this revival in his infamous address at the 1968 conference of the Society of Biblical Literature, in which he challenged biblical scholars to go beyond form critical application of Scripture and toward a keen observation of rhetorical formulations.[98]

Survey of Rhetoric," in *Handbook of Classical Rhetoric in the Hellenistic Period 330 B.C.– A.D. 400*, ed. Stanley Porter (Leiden: Brill, 1997), 3–42. For a survey of scholarship of rhetoric up to the 1980s, see Winifred Horner, *The Present State of Scholarship in Historical and Contemporary Rhetoric* (Columbia: University of Missouri Press, 1990). On the scope in the New Testament, see Watson, *Rhetoric of the New Testament*.

96. Hans Dieter Betz, in his work on Pauline Epistles, and George A. Kennedy, in the New Testament, including the Gospels. These seminal works began the foundation of applying the ancient art of persuasion to the interpretation of New Testament texts. It was made possible through at least two main premises. First, Aristotle understood his systematization of the art of rhetoric as a universal approach in antiquity. See George A. Kennedy, *New Testament Interpretation through Rhetorical Criticism* (Chapel Hill: North Carolina University, 1984), 10. Second, it is undeniably understood that Jews of the first century were exposed to rhetorical practices and treatises of Greco-Roman traditions either directly or indirectly. See, for example, C. Clifton Black, "Rhetorical Criticism," in *Hearing the New Testament: Strategies for Interpretation*, ed. Joel B. Green (Grand Rapids: Eerdmans, 1995), 256–77, esp. 257–58. Black cites also Donald L. Clark, *Rhetoric in Greco-Roman Education* (New York: Columbia University Press, 1957). See also George A. Kennedy, *Classical Rhetoric and Its Christian and Secular Tradition from Ancient to Modern Times* (Chapel Hill: University of North Carolina Press, 1980); Burton L. Mack, *Rhetoric and the New Testament* (Minneapolis: Fortress, 1990), 9.

97. Betz deals especially with the studies of Paul, while Kennedy, a classicist, applies classical rhetorical parameters to the criticism of New Testament texts in general. See Hans Dieter Betz, "Literary Composition and Function of Paul's Letter to the Galatians," *NTS* 21 (1975): 353–79; Betz, *Galatians: A Commentary on Paul's Letter to the Churches in Galatia*, Hermeneia (Philadelphia: Fortress, 1979); Kennedy, *New Testament Interpretation*. For a brief history of biblical scholarship on the New Testament and rhetoric before Betz, see Mack, *Rhetoric and the New Testament*, esp. 10–11.

98. James Muilenburg, "Form Criticism and Beyond," in *Beyond Form Criticism: Essays in Old Testament Literary Criticism*, ed. P. House, SBTS (Winona Lake, IN: Eisenbrauns, 1992), 49–69. As shown in the works of his students, Muilenburg's application of rhetorical theory focuses on stylistic and aesthetic features of texts in order to unveil the "fabric of the writer's thought" (Muilenburg, "Form Criticism," 56). Prominent among his students is Phyllis Trible, *Rhetorical Criticism: Context, Method, and the Book of Jonah*, Guides to Biblical Scholarship (Minneapolis: Fortress, 1994).

2. Metaphor and Rhetoric   69

For Jewish texts of the first century, the above description remains a starting point to approach rhetoric as an object of study.[99] As a benefit to rhetorical analysis in New Testament texts, in 1984 Kennedy laid out a five-step method that investigates a given unit,[100] ranging from a

---

99. There exists an obvious tension between guilds of rhetorical studies in the New Testament. For example, Ben Witherington III categorizes scholarly works by disassociating the classical art of persuasion as practiced by Hans D. Betz and George A. Kennedy from scholars such as Vernon K. Robbins and, by implication, the new rhetoric of Perelman and Olbrichts-Tyteca, who elevate the importance of audience in rhetorical communication. See Ben Witherington III, *New Testament Rhetoric: An Introductory Guide to the Art of Persuasion in and of the New Testament* (Eugene, OR: Wipf & Stock, 2009), 6. See also Black, "Rhetorical Criticism," 256–77. Black discerns five scholarly patterns of the classical approach. First is the employment of Kennedy's method. Second is the study of the *chreiai*. Third is utilizing classical rhetoric to solve "longstanding questions of NT exegesis" and, fourth, to reformulate "tradition-historical forms of interpretation." Finally, it is using "ancient rhetorical precepts and practices … as a springboard for revising the concept of rhetoric and rhetorical analysis" (Black, "Rhetorical Criticism," 262). This distinction seems to be based upon two types of rhetorical analysis: a historical rhetorical criticism that limits analysis to classical rhetorical tools (e.g., Margaret Mitchell, *Paul and the Rhetoric of Reconciliation: An Exegetical Investigation of the Language and Composition of 1 Corinthians* [Louisville: Westminster John Knox, 1993], esp. 6) and a more modern rhetorical criticism that employs modern means to expound ancient rhetoric. Such a distinction may stem from a confusion since Betz's seminal work, "whether rhetoric is the tool used for analysis or the object of study" (Anders Eriksson, "Enthymemes in Pauline Argumentation: Reading between the Lines in 1 Corinthians," in Rhetorical Argumentation in Biblical Texts, ed. Anders Eriksson, Thomas H. Olbricht, and Walter Übelacker [Harrisburg, PA: Trinity Press International, 2002], 246). I am indebted to Vernon K. Robbins for directing me toward this discussion as documented by Robert H. von Thaden Jr., "A Cognitive Turn: Conceptual Blending within a Sociorhetorical Framework," in *Foundations for Sociorhetorical Exploration: A Rhetoric of Religious Antiquity Reader*, ed. Vernon K. Robbins, Robert H. von Thaden Jr., and Bart B. Bruehler (Atlanta: SBL Press, 2016), 314–16. Von Thaden suggests that the multitexture approach that Robbins takes in sociorhetorical analysis offers New Testament exegesis a "both/and" opportunity. He states, "The historical investigation of ancient rhetorical forms and praxis always has a place within SRI on at least the level of intertexture, that is, the NT's relationship to other texts that aim to persuade." He further notes that Mitchell's work cited above can be seen as an intertextual investigation.

100. Kennedy, *New Testament Interpretation*, 33–38. These are (1) identifying an *inclusio/rhetorical unit*, (2) defining the *rhetorical situation*, (3) considering the rhetorical problem or stasis and the species of rhetoric, (4) analyzing the *invention, arrangement, and style* of the discourse, and (5) *reviewing* the whole analysis for its

70   Apocalyptic Sheep and Goats in Matthew and 1 Enoch

short expression to an entire piece of writing.[101] This model as a tool for rhetorical analysis continues to impact New Testament studies.[102] However, Kennedy's model lacks what today we would call cultural sensitivity, for he restricts his source of ancient rhetoric to Hellenistic and Roman handbooks.[103] Despite this, Kennedy recognizes a universal character in Aristotle's ideas on rhetoric that allows for cross-cultural applications, opening analysis to cultural traditions.[104] As Karl Möller has noted, "Aris-

---

effectiveness. Or six if one considers a rhetorical problem a separate point of analysis from the rhetorical situation. With regard to the fifth step, "effectiveness," Duane F. Watson explains it in terms of the constituents of the other steps. He states, "5. Evaluate the rhetorical effectiveness of the rhetorical unit in utilizing invention, arrangement, and style in addressing the needs of the rhetorical situation" (Duane F. Watson, "The Influence of George Kennedy on Rhetorical Criticism of the New Testament," in *Words Well Spoken: George Kennedy's Rhetoric of the New Testament*, ed. C. Clifton Black and Duane F. Watson [Waco, TX: Baylor University Press, 2008], 43.) For a summary of these, see also Wilhelm Wuellner, "Where Is Rhetorical Criticism Taking Us?," *CBQ* 49 (1987): 448–63, esp. 455–58. C. Clifton Black lists six, naming the rhetorical problem (Black, "Rhetorical Criticism," 261–62).

101. See, for example, Duane F. Watson, "Influence of George Kennedy," 43.

102. See Black and Watson, *Words Well Spoken*.

103. Indeed, Kennedy takes on a well-informed analysis, which is understandably a reflection of his expertise. In spite of this drawback, Kennedy is well aware of the fact that Aristotle's system of rhetoric intends to be a universal paradigm. He states, "Though rhetoric is colored by the traditions and conventions of the society in which it is applied, it is also a universal phenomenon which is conditioned by basic workings of the human mind and heart and by the nature of all human society. Aristotle's objective in writing his Rhetoric was not to describe Greek rhetoric, but to describe this universal facet of human communication.... What we mean by classical rhetorical theory is this structured system which describes the universal phenomenon of rhetoric in Greek terms.... Though the Jews of the pre-Christian era seem never to have conceptualized rhetoric to any significant degree, the importance of speech among them is everywhere evident in the Old Testament, and undoubtedly they learned its techniques by imitation. In understanding how their rhetoric worked we have little choice but to employ the concepts and terms of the Greeks" (Kennedy, *New Testament Interpretation*, 10). Kennedy may have overjustified his point to state that Jews never conceptualized rhetoric to any significant degree. To his defense, he would mean to suggest at least not in the way that it was laid out systematically by classical theorists of the pre-Christian era.

104. Kennedy makes this especially apparent in his later study. See George A. Kennedy, *Comparative Rhetoric: An Historical and Cross-Cultural Introduction* (Oxford: Oxford University Press, 1998). Here he applies classical rhetorical theory to illuminate rhetorical activities of other cultures, as well as animals. However, as I will

2. Metaphor and Rhetoric 71

totle and his successors ... did not *invent* rhetorical discourse.... Aristotle and others merely investigated rhetorical utterances and then developed a concept of rhetoric that was based partly on their observations and partly on philosophical ideas and concepts."[105] At best, classical rhetoric brings us closer to how persuasion may have been conceptualized in other cultures in classical times. Sociorhetorical analytics capitalize upon this universal aspect of classical rhetorical theory.

2.3.2. Sociorhetorical Criticism

Robbins finds classical rhetoric to be foundational in thinking of rhetoric in the context of the first century. Unlike Kennedy, he accounts for the multiple traditions and cultural elements of the rhetoric of early Christian texts, which he calls sociorhetorical interpretation.[106]

In order to allow the inclusion of other cultural traditions in rhetorical analysis, Robbins departs from the three classical species of rhetoric.[107] Instead, Robbins lists six conventional forms in which early Christian discourses of rhetoric were expressed: wisdom, prophetic, apocalyptic, precreation, priestly, and miracle argumentation.[108] He calls these "rhetorolects" and states, "During the first century, early Christians filled these modes of discourse with action, speech, and thought attributed to God, Jesus Christ, Holy Spirit, and the followers of Jesus to negotiate social,

---

show in the section on metaphor theory, Aristotle's categorization is itself limited and confined to Greek logic and reasoning.

105. Karl Möller, *A Prophet in Debate: The Rhetoric of Persuasion in the Book of Amos*, JSOTSup 372 (Sheffield: Sheffield Academic, 2003), 43.

106. Robbins lays out his interpretive program in the following two works: Vernon K. Robbins, *Exploring the Texture of Texts: A Guide to Socio-rhetorical Interpretation* (Valley Forge, PA: Trinity Press International, 1996), and Robbins, *Tapestry of Early Christian Discourse*. Duane F. Watson, a student of Kennedy's, sanctions this shift by stating that "the work of Robbins will be the greatest catalyst for the future influence of Kennedy on New Testament rhetorical analysis" (Watson, "Influence of George Kennedy," 56).

107. See, for example, Vernon K. Robbins, *The Invention of Christian Discourse* (Blandford Forum: Deo, 2009), 1:1–3. According to Robbins, judicial, deliberative, and epideictic forms of speech did not view New Testament texts in a positive light, for the law court, political assembly, and civil ceremony cause strife to and do not account for the social and cultural lives of early Christians of the first century.

108. Robbins, *Invention of Christian Discourse*, 14–16.

72   Apocalyptic Sheep and Goats in Matthew and 1 Enoch

cultural, and ideological relationships in the contexts in which they lived."[109] Through frames of various cultural traditions, which include frames of apocalyptic traditions, Robbins provides space for conceptualizing persuasion in the texts and contexts of early Christians with strong Jewish roots.

To be sure, each cultural convention listed above is broad and not easily defined. All are still debatable in terms of definition, some more than others. Each is itself a blend of traditions. There is also the possibility that, for example, not all apocalypses share the same traditions. Certainly, as Robbins argues, these various conventions blend with one another within Christian writings.[110] The difficulty is finding out which cultural conventions and traditions are blended within any given literary work. Jesus as a Messiah emerges from a blend of prophetic and kingly traditions, at the least, but from which cultural convention? The theological meaning and implications of Jesus's death would certainly need creativity to describe them. Some of the early attempts in understanding Jesus are hinted at in the Pauline Letters, and, perhaps, an articulation seems more fully expressed in the gospels. Early Jesus followers were not all in agreement, as various blends of thought about Jesus and his teachings existed within different circles, for example, Paul, Peter, Apollos (1 Cor 3), James, or even John of Patmos. It would be unwise to paint all of these with one broad brush; rather, each distinct text should be dealt with separately within the broader Jewish world of people and literature.

Robbins suggests five ways of exploring the rhetoric within the social and cultural dynamics of early Christian texts. These are by looking at its (1) inner texture, (2) intertexture, (3) social and cultural texture, (4) ideological texture, and (5) sacred texture.[111] My study sees Matt 25:31–46 as an apocalyptic discourse and a cultural text. As such, Robbins's categorization may provide a heuristic model to flesh out possible communication of

---

109. Robbins, *Invention of Christian Discourse*, 13–16. *Rhetorolect* is an elision of *rhetorical dialect*.

110. On Robbins's views of blending, see Robbins, "Social Location and Conceptual Blending in Early Christian Story," ch. 3 in *Invention of Christian Discourse*; Robbins, "Conceptual Blending and Early Christian Imagination," in *Explaining Christian Origins and Early Judaism: Contributions from Cognitive and Social Science*, ed. Petri Luomanen, Ilkka Pyysiainen, and Risto Uro, BibInt 89 (Leiden: Brill, 2007), 161–95. Robbins adopts the vocabulary of cognitive linguistics. See Fauconnier and Turner, *Way We Think*.

111. Robbins, *Exploring the Texture of Texts*; Robbins, *Tapestry of Early Christian Discourse*.

2. Metaphor and Rhetoric 73

apocalyptic discourse within the last judgment. I will use a combination of inner texture, scribal, and cultural intertextures as my heuristic framework.

Inner Texture

The first category of inner-texture analysis pays attention to literary features of the text. It observes and identifies the argumentative features and aesthetics of language and expressions.[112] Robbins lists six textures to look for: repetitive, progressive, narrational, opening-middle-closing, argumentative, and sensory-aesthetic texture.[113] These are covered less explicitly by Kennedy's modes of analysis and are important for initial analysis prior to interpretation. I will give attention to these when it is most suitable to expound the literary and textual elements of the imagery and metaphors that this study treats.

Intertextures

As Robbins defines it, "Intertexture … is the interaction of the language in the text with 'outside' material and physical 'objects,' historical events, texts, customs, values, roles, institutions, and systems."[114] Intertexture means more than just an allusion. It examines how possible allusions and echoes interact within the text in a way that makes it persuasive to the audience. Intertexture is the broader category under which Robbins places the more specific categories of oral-scribal, social, cultural, and historical intertextures.[115] To be sure, the term and concept of intertexture is not unique to Robbins. It is a similar concept to what Daniel Boyarin sees in midrash, what Julia Kristeva sees in literature in general, and what Mikhail Bakhtin sees in language. In fact, Robbins's concept is borrowed from the

---

112. Robbins, *Tapestry of Early Christian Discourse*, 28–29. It takes into consideration the initial rhetorical and interactive communication between the author and audience.

113. For a description, see Robbins, *Exploring the Texture of Texts*, 8–36.

114. Robbins, *Exploring the Texture of Texts*, 40, 58. "Intertexture is a text's representation of, reference to, and use of phenomena in the 'world' outside the text being interpreted."

115. Robbins, *Exploring the Texture of Texts*, 40–70; Robbins, *Tapestry of Early Christian Discourse*, 121–43.

74   Apocalyptic Sheep and Goats in Matthew and 1 Enoch

intellectual discussions in Europe of poststructuralists in the second half of the twentieth century.[116]

Kristeva, a Bulgarian linguist, is a prominent partner in these discussions and is credited with coining the term *intertextuality*.[117] In one of her essays, Kristeva speaks of texts as productivity, in that text redistributes the language it uses—a process in which text becomes a "permutation of texts," or what she calls intertextuality.[118] She defines intertextuality as being "the space" of a given text where "several utterances, taken from other texts, intersect and neutralize one another."[119] She states, "any text is constructed as a mosaic of quotations; any text is the absorption and transformation of another."[120] Her insights are inspired by the work of Russian literary theorist Mikhail Bakhtin, who saw at work within the novel heteroglossia or multiple languages in dialogue, including the utterances of the author, the addressee, and the context, which together he describes as *dialogism*.[121] This is neither a dialogue in the narrative sense of conversation nor in the Platonic sense of dialectical debate. He states, "[Rather] it is a dialogue between points of view, each with its own concrete language that cannot be translated into the other."[122] These languages are diverse in voices and utterances, which are artistically linked and interrelated in the novel.[123]

---

116. Robbins, *Tapestry of Early Christian Discourse*, 30.

117. See Julia Kristeva, *Desire in Language: A Semiotic Approach to Language and Art*, trans. Thomas Gora, Alice Jardine, and Leon S. Roudiez, ed. Leon S. Roudiez (New York: Columbia University Press, 1980). See especially her second essay, "The Bounded Text," in the above book.

118. Kristeva, "Bounded Text," in *Desire in Language*.

119. Kristeva, *Desire in Language*, 36.

120. Julia Kristeva, "Word, Dialogue and the Novel," in *The Kristeva Reader*, ed. T. Moi (Oxford: Blackwell, 1986), 37.

121. Defined as "the characteristic epistemological mode of a world dominated by heteroglossia. Everything means, is understood, as a part of a greater whole—there is a constant interaction between meanings, all of which have the potential of conditioning others. Which will affect the other, how it will do so and in what degree is what is actually settled at the moment of utterance. This dialogic imperative, mandated by the pre-existence of the language world relative to any of its current inhabitants, insures that there can be no actual monologue … unitariness is relative to the overpowering force of heteroglossia, and thus dialogism." See M. M. Bakhtin, "Glossary," in *The Dialogic Imagination: Four Essays*, ed. Michael Holist, trans. Caryl Emerson and Michael Holist (Austin: University of Texas Press, 1981), 426.

122. Bakhtin, *Dialogic Imagination*, 76.

123. Bakhtin, *Dialogic Imagination*, 262–63.

2. Metaphor and Rhetoric

For Kristeva, intertextuality is not simply quotations, allusions, or a form of source criticism.[124] It involves the influences of prior texts or the prehistory of the text by the way they engage in a dialogical interaction.[125] She sees text as a system of signs, understood to have both horizontal (synchronic) and vertical (diachronic) dimensions that interact with one another. As such, it would be futile to understand intertexts or influences in a positivistic way, as the utterance of the pretexts often lose their original meaning. That would weaken a referential designation of meaning. In other words, what one text says about a certain term or theme another text would not necessarily mean in the same way.

Intertextuality has useful implications in biblical studies, particularly in its social and cultural aspects. Precautions must be in place, however, for an infinite number of intertexts would make intertextuality unworkable. Critics note that "Kristeva blurs any difference between textuality and intertextuality."[126] For this reason, scholars labor to determine exactly how intertextuality manifests itself in ancient texts in more quantitative and concrete ways. What would demarcate an intertext? What determines the degree of influence such demarcation implies?

The ways of identifying how texts, traditions, culture, or history influence other texts is a difficult endeavor when dealing with texts in antiquity, and in fact there is no scholarly consensus about it.[127] Richard B. Hays has

---

124. Julia Kristeva, "Intimate Revolt," in *The Portable Kristeva*, ed. Kelly Oliver, 2nd ed. (New York: Columbia University Press, 2002), 446. "Intertextuality 'encourages one to read the literary text as an intersection of other texts. It has often been understood in a formalist or structuralist perspective, as an appeal to citations or a variant of the old criticism of sources. For me, it has always been about introducing history into structuralism.… At the same time, by showing how much the inside of the text is indebted to its outside, interpretation reveals the inauthenticity of the writing subject: the writer is a subject in process, a carnival, a polyphony without possible reconciliation, a permanent revolt.'"

125. *Text* here does not refer to literary text. It connotes multiple utterances, which, for Kristeva, is the product of the human subject that includes the surrounding social, cultural, historical, and ideological context of both the present and the past.

126. As summarized by Moises Mayordomo, "Matthew 1–2 and the Problem of Intertextuality," in *Infancy Gospels: Stories and Identities*, ed. Claire Clivaz et al. (Tübingen: Mohr Siebeck, 2011), 259.

127. Moises Mayordomo compares the categories of Gérard Genette, Manfred Pfister, Richard B. Hays, Regula Hohl Trillini, and Sixta Quassdorf. See Mayordomo, "Matthew 1–2," 261–63. Many see quotations as a marker of intertext. See, for example, Heinrich F. Plett, "Intertextualities," in *Research in Text Theory (Untersuchungen zur*

76 Apocalyptic Sheep and Goats in Matthew and 1 Enoch

been influential in positing ways that intertextuality (though Hays's favorite term is *echoes* or intertexts) may take form in New Testament texts and in Pauline letters in particular.[128] With his particular interest in historical questions, his approach to intertextuality is an author-centered perspective.[129] For Hays, the author becomes a voice of an interpretive community interacting with other texts in contributing to the production of the text. In this light, the implied author becomes not the subject but the object of texts.[130] In Robbins's category of intertexture, he utilizes, simplifies, and improves upon Hays's list of echoes or intertexts. In fact, Robbins divides Hays's list in two, differentiating between oral-scribal and cultural categories of intertextures.[131] For Robbins, references and echoes are cultural rather than oral-scribal. In addition, he supplements Hays's categories with two more: social and historical intertextures.

Under oral and scribal intertextures, the rhetorical analysis examines instances that include "recitation, recontextualization, and reconfiguration of other texts, both oral and scribal, in the foregrounded text."[132] For

---

Texttheorie), ed. Janos S. Petofi (New York: de Gruyter, 1991), 3–29. Some take clues from formulas (e.g., "It is written.... [Matt 4:4; Luke 19:46; Mark 14:27; John 6:45]). For others, text typologies. Others see echoes as primary to programs of determining intertexts. See Richard B. Hays, *Echoes of Scripture in the Letters of Paul* (New Haven: Yale University Press, 1989). The determination of echoes consists of analyzing rules: availability, volume, recurrence, thematic coherence, historical plausibility, and history of interpretation. For an application on the gospels, see Nathan Lane, "An Echo of Mercy: A Rereading of the Parable of the Good Samaritan," in *Exegetical* Studies, vol. 2 of *Early Christian Literature and Intertextuality*, ed. Craig A. Evans and H. Daniel Zacharias (New York: T&T Clark, 2009), 74–84. Still others see the contemporary and historical exchanges as important, for to them the future reception of a text factors in to some extent the determination and reinforcement of intertexts. See William W. Hallo, ed., *Canonical Compositions from the Biblical World*, vol. 1 of *The Context of Scriptures* (Leiden: Brill, 2003), xxvi.

128. Hays, *Echoes of Scripture*. See important reviews of Hays's work in Craig A. Evans and James A. Sanders, eds., *Paul and the Scriptures of Israel* (Sheffield: JSOT Press, 1993).

129. On the position of intertextuality from the author's perspective, see Mayordomo, "Matthew 1–2," 260.

130. Mayordomo, "Matthew 1–2," 260.

131. Robbins, *Tapestry of Early Christian Discourse*, 102.

132. Robbins, *Tapestry of Early Christian Discourse*, 97. In his earlier text (*Exploring the Texture of Texts*, 51–53), Robbins includes also narrative amplification and thematic elaboration.

2. Metaphor and Rhetoric

cultural, social, and historical intertextures, the interpreter examines references and echoes in the text ranging from those that are explicit to those that are implicit.[133] References pertain to words and phrases that refer to personages or traditions. Echoes denote words and phrases that evoke or potentially evoke cultural, social, and historical traditions. Of the six cultural conventions mentioned by Robbins, apocalyptic and wisdom conventions are especially assessed as cultural intertextures. Historical intertextures consist of historical events or happenings outside of the text that may have occasioned or influenced the text. Social and historical intertextures will be gleaned from the text itself and be assessed from the results of scribal and cultural intertextures.

2.3.3. Apocalyptic Metaphorical Language as Intertexture

Robbins takes intertextuality further through cognitive linguistics. In this recent interest in cognitive linguistics, Robbins means to establish more concretely the intertextual links of influence between texts.[134] Through cognitive linguistic models, influences are conceptualized as frames, analogous to Aristotelian topoi. For example, the image of the Messiah could be a byproduct of the traditions of the Davidic Messiah blended with a frame of wisdom traditions to produce metaphorical expressions that perceive the messianic figure in new ways.

The descriptions of intertextures—for example, recitation, reconfiguration, recontextualization, reference, and evocation—are essentially the

---

133. Robbins, *Tapestry of Early Christian Discourse*, 108–15.

134. Robbins states that he moves biblical interpretation forward by focusing on analysis of conventional forms of discourse, referring to the six rhetorolects. He states, "At its foundations human cognition is metaphorical. Humans continually use reasoning in one domain to sort through cognitive items in another domain. This means throughout the millennia humans have continually used forms, which cognitive scientists now call 'frames,' in one conceptual domain to understand and interpret forms in another domain. This view of semantic frames underlies the argument in this volume about early Christian rhetorolects. The argument is that the six early Christian rhetorolects investigated and interpreted [in the volume cited below] ... are cultural-religious frames that introduce multiple networks of thinking, reasoning, and acting that were alive and dynamic in early Christian thought, language, and practice." Thus, Robbins makes a turn from a focus on form and genre criticism to "frames and prototype criticism" (Robbins, *Tapestry of Early Christian Discourse*; Robbins, *Exploring the Texture of Texts*, 99–100).

(re)utilization of texts (utterances) from another context to express or help express a thought (meaning) in a new context. Robbins extends the concept of intertextuality from Kristeva and Hays into the argumentative logic of New Testament texts, where the above examples are external and cultural utterances and influences that contribute to the persuasiveness of a given communication. They are used either consciously or unconsciously and help produce the thought (meaning) in a text for the purposes of persuading the audience or communicating a message that may be credible. This is also essentially the process of metaphorical thinking and language in apocalyptic discourses. Thus, metaphorical language can conceptually contribute its own utterance(s) and influences from other texts (traditions) within the text.

As noted above, Matthew's judgment imagery identified in the previous chapter (3:11–12; 13:24–30, 36–43; 25:31–46) utilizes apocalyptic metaphorical language. The metaphors within apocalyptic discourse not only harken back to and anticipate materials within the narrative, they also evoke cultural memories and traditions. This will be seen especially in the metaphor of sheep utilized in 25:31–46. Thus, they contribute not only to the analysis of inner textures but also of intertextures in Matthew's apocalyptic discourses.

2.4. Plan of Study

The sociorhetorical and metaphorical analysis will show how each of the texts (3:11–12; 13:24–30, 36–43; 25:31–46) is apocalyptic discourse dealing with the revelation of esoteric knowledge through heavenly communication and metaphorical language that include the topos of eschatological judgment. It will show how apocalyptic metaphorical language therein aids in revealing the function and identity of Jesus as the Son of God (3:1–4:17) and the Son of Man (13:24–30, 36–43), and how this works toward exhorting Israel to a life in line with its election and the torah. It will show how Matt 25:31–46 provides a third eschatological imagery in a midrashic fashion that explicitly shows Jesus as both the Son of God and the Son of Man to reinforce and exhort Israel to a life of righteousness via teachings of the torah. This means that together the topoi related to judgment in the above three passages are themselves in dialogue with each other in the narrative, made possible through the different metaphorical language and presentation. Ultimately, the topoi exhort righteous living in accordance with the torah in the here and now. This may be substantiated by the Book

2. Metaphor and Rhetoric　　　　　　　　　79

of Dreams (1 En. 83–90) as a significant intertext to the metaphor of sheep in Matt 25:31–46 and the apocalyptic discourses identified in this study.

I utilize a combination of literary, cultural, and historical-critical tools of hermeneutics when applicable, and narrative, cultural, and redactional readings of the texts to analyze inner textures and intertextures. The literary and narrative readings may delineate the rhetorical units and structures and point out the metaphors as inner textures that expound upon the possible meanings of the metaphors and respective discourses. The cultural and redactional readings will illuminate possible cultural traditions and historical intertextures that contribute to the multiple voices at play within the apocalyptic discourses and metaphorical language.

In a historical reading, for example, John's baptism is a tradition from Matthew's Mark and Q sources (two-source hypothesis). Analyzing both literary and conceptual interaction between Matthew and its sources illuminates historical intertextures that contribute to the layers of meaning within the text. As I will argue below, this interaction between Matthew and its sources in Matt 3:11–17 conceptually carries on toward Matt 13:24–30, 36–43 and 25:31–46, highlighting the rhetoric of these discourses within the narrative.

In a cultural reading, for instance, the central significance of the torah must not be overlooked in Jewish thought. The way in which the relationship between Israel and torah is perceived and described in wisdom traditions are closely attached to the sheep metaphor in the Book of Dreams (1 En. 83–90). If Matthew had the Book of Dreams as one of its possible sources, which I argue it does, these blends of cultural traditions make for prototypical designations in Matthew's thought world, which then function as cultural intertextures within Matt 25:31–46. Such perception would also linger conceptually behind similar metaphors of righteous Israel and humanity (i.e., wheat), for metaphorical language, as Kovecses states, "is just as much a matter of culture as it is a matter of cognition."[135]

In chapter 3, I will begin first with an analysis of the Book of Dreams (1 En. 83–90; Animal Apocalypse: 1 En. 85–90) as a possible cultural precedent and significant intertexture to the metaphor of sheep of Matt 25:31–46. I will then provide, in chapter 4, an inner-textural analysis of the visions and metaphorical language of the Gospel of Matthew (Matt

---

135. Kovecses, *Language, Mind and Culture*, 48. See quotation above, p. 60. I take this to mean that how one thinks is culturally induced.

3:11–17; 13:24–30, 36–43; and 25:31–46) to show the progression and development of the topos of judgment within its five discourses and its apocalyptic character. I will then proceed to show the intended persuasive force of the apocalyptic discourse in Matt 25:31–46 by combining the analysis of apocalyptic intertexture and inner-texture analyses with an interpretation of conceptual blending in chapter 5 and present possible implications. Finally, I will end this study with a conclusion of its findings.

3
Animal Apocalypse: A Metaphorical Reading

3.1. Introduction

Within the Book of Dreams, Israel is depicted as sheep in an allegory that tells the narrative of humanity from creation to the day of judgment, where sheep and other animals all are turned into white cattle. Scholars have labeled this allegory as the Animal Apocalypse. Aside from the Hebrew terms, the Greek translations of sheep within the Hebrew Bible are corroborated within the surviving Greek versions of the Animal Apocalypse, all with the exception of ἀμνός.[1] Fragments of the Aramaic version of the Animal Apocalypse exist as well. In Aramaic, we find the terms אמר, דבר, and ען. The Aramaic דבר (the Greek, κρίος) can be viewed as the equivalent of the Hebrew כר, as both can mean "pasture" and "ram." The Aramaic terms אמר and ען are the usual expressions for sheep in the allegory.

The sheep metaphor in apocalyptic discourse is apt be taken for granted, perhaps due to its seeming simplicity and obvious meaning. However, studies of metaphorical language and the polyvalence of scriptural texts teach us that we must not accept even a demonstrative without question. The interpretation of the Animal Apocalypse would be crucial for understanding the various layers of meaning in the sheep metaphor, and potentially suggests the inadequacy of equating sheep with a simple metaphor that represents just Israel. In this chapter, I hope to highlight the expressive nature of the sheep metaphor within the Book of Dreams. I argue that the sheep metaphor takes on layers of cultural meaning in apocalyptic context involving judgment, which is evoked by the Gospel of Matthew in scenes of

---

1. For references to the relevant terms for sheep in the Animal Apocalypse, see Patrick A. Tiller, *A Commentary on the Animal Apocalypse of 1 Enoch*, EJL 4 (Atlanta: Scholars Press, 1993), 275.

82 Apocalyptic Sheep and Goats in Matthew and 1 Enoch

end-time judgment. In other words, we may find a significant culture intertexture to the sheep metaphor of Matt 25:31–46 in the Animal Apocalypse.

3.2. Animal Apocalypse

The influence of the Animal Apocalypse in later Jewish literature is not altogether clear. The writings of 1 Enoch may have been authoritative Scriptures within some Jewish circles of first-century Palestine and beyond. Certainly, some traditions therein are traceable especially in later Christian writings of the first century. Most recently, Amy Genevive Dibley has written an illuminating dissertation that argues for the Book of Dreams as "the precedent for Paul's program of gentile reclamation qua gentiles."[2] From a slightly different vein from Dibley's reading of the Book of Dreams, I argue rather a case for the Book of Dreams as a precedent to Matthew's program of salvation for Israel in light of their obligations to humanity. This is indicative of the developments evident in the Animal Apocalypse about the interpretation of the contractual blueprint of salvation via the torah: that Israel's election is an obligation to humanity and creation.

In a recent commentary on the Animal Apocalypse, Daniel C. Olson lists the "three most fundamental issues" for scholars as being:

(1) The scope and focus of the allegory. Is the salvation of the nation of Israel the central concern, or is the real subject of the Animal Apocalypse humanity in general?

(2) The relationship between human history and divine salvation. Does the Animal Apocalypse champion one or more traditions within Israel's history as the main avenue for the working out of God's salvific plans, or does the allegory abandon traditional articulations of *Heilsgeschichte*? What roles, if any, do the Abrahamic or Mosaic covenants, or the Davidic throne, or the prophets, or the temple play in the story of salvation?

(3) The basis for moral responsibility. Are humans (a) free moral agents, (b) creatures who act according to predetermined fate, or (c) some kind of third option? And what implication does this question have for a right standing with God in the allegory?[3]

---

2. Amy Genevive Dibley, "Abraham's Uncircumcised Children: The Enochic Precedent for Paul's Paradoxical Claim in Galatians 3:29" (PhD diss., Graduate Theological Union and University of California at Berkeley, 2013).

3. Daniel C. Olson, *A New Reading of the Animal Apocalypse of 1 Enoch: All Nations Shall be Blessed*, SVTP 24 (Leiden: Brill, 2013), 4.

3. Animal Apocalypse: A Metaphorical Reading   83

As Olsen sees it, the first topic covers the salient features of the Animal Apocalypse: salvation and universal perspective. The second speaks to "the working out of God's plans," and the third deals with questions of determinism and human choice. This study touches upon aspects of each of these to some degree with regard to the metaphor of the sheep. Yet the general thesis is that the allegory is about the righteousness of humanity and knowledge, with these seen as inseparable concepts.

3.2.1. The Figure of Enoch

Enoch is the pseudonymous figure responsible for the Animal Apocalypse. The predeluge patriarch, Enoch, is considered to be one of Israel's notorious biblical figures. For the most part, the apocalyptic literature that bears its name helped to create this notoriety. The book of Genesis informs the modern reader that Enoch is a seventh-generation descendent of the archetypal figure, Adam, and is three generations behind yet another figure of biblical fame, Noah (Gen 5–6).[4] It is safe to say that scribes and sages concerned with apocalyptic literature view these three men as an important set of Israelite heroes as regards the Mediterranean and Mesopotamian world at large. Enoch stands out as the set's all-star. He lives up to one meaning of his name as a seeker of knowledge. The name Enoch in Hebrew relates to the verb meaning "to dedicate."[5] The author of Jubilees correlates the name with wisdom, describing Enoch as "the first among the children of men, born of the earth, who had learned writing, science, and wisdom, and he described in a book the signs of heaven according to the order of their months, that the children of men might know the periods of the year according to the order of all their particular months" (Jub. 4.17). At the end of the passage, Jubilees refers to Enoch's knowledge of the cosmos, a trait also mentioned in the Book of the Watchers and the Astronomical Books. The attribute recurs in Hellenistic Jewish history, as Enoch is recorded to have been the inventor of astronomy.[6]

---

4. For a late twentieth-century discussion about the debate surrounding the editors of P and J on the generations from Adam to Noah and Enoch, see James C. VanderKam, *Enoch and the Growth of an Apocalyptic Tradition* (Washington, DC: Catholic Biblical Association of America, 1984), 8–19.

5. VanderKam, *Enoch and the Growth*, 29. See also BDB, 335.

6. Jozef T. Milik, *The Books of Enoch: Aramaic Fragments of Qumran Cave 4* (Oxford: Clarendon, 1976), 8–9; VanderKam, *Enoch and the Growth*, 84–87. Milik

84 Apocalyptic Sheep and Goats in Matthew and 1 Enoch

Indeed, in Genesis, Enoch is taken by God (*Elohim*, Gen 5:24 RSV), a translation that comes about from the rendering of *Elohim* as God.[7] In apocalyptic literature, Enoch is escorted by the angels, a translation that could be an interpretation of Genesis by scribes. In the Book of the Watchers and the Astronomical Books, he journeys the heavens and records the movements of the cosmos. He is a heavenly scribe (1 En. 82.1), a feature that Enoch shares with other figures in cultures of antiquity.[8] He is also a scribe of righteousness (1 En. 12.4) and a mediator between the angels and God (e.g., 1 En. 13). All of this notoriety would have placed him in competition with ancient Egyptian and Hellenistic astrologers, wise men, and heroes.

Just as a picture says a lot about the painter, this biblical figure speaks volumes about the thinking of the contemporary scribes and sages. Enoch becomes an archetype from which the cultural convictions of ancient Jews were presented upon the world stage. At the same time, the figure of Enoch and his legends provide a renewed and necessary perspective from which to make sense of events in their context.

3.2.2. The Texts of Enoch

Of the literature classified as the genre apocalypse, the writings attributed to Enoch are among the earliest texts. Aside from later writings credited to Enoch (2 Enoch), the chosen book of 1 Enoch contains at least five

---

cites an allusion made by a Hellenistic Jewish historian by the name of Eupolemos (ca. second century BCE), whose writing is no longer extant but recorded only in quotations by Eusebius of Caesarea (*Praep. ev.* 9.17.2–9), who in turn may have drawn from the writings of Alexander Polyhistor, a Greek compiler of the first century BCE. VanderKam, who labels the source of the quotations as Pseudo-Eupolemos, concludes from these allusions that "Pseudo-Eupolemos was clearly acquainted with more than just the technical astronomical teachings of the book; he also knew the editorial framework into which the scientific material had been placed: Enoch learned his astronomy (and geography) from an angel, taught it to Methuselah, and Methuselah conveyed it to posterity."

7. See VanderKam, *Enoch and the Growth*, 31. VanderKam renders *Elohim* in Gen 5:24 as angels rather than God. For VanderKam, this would be a characteristic of a Priestly (P) text as opposed to a Yahwist (J) text, which designates God as YHWH. As such, the priestly scribes interpreted the Genesis text as meaning angels in the apocalypses involving Enoch.

8. VanderKam, *Enoch and the Growth*, 104.

3. Animal Apocalypse: A Metaphorical Reading

independent works: The Book of the Watchers (1 En. 1–36), the Parables (1 En. 37–71), Astronomical Books (1 En. 72–82), the Book of Dreams (1 En. 83–90), and the Epistle of Enoch (1 En. 91–107).[9] The Book of Dreams contains the Animal Apocalypse (1 En. 85–90), and the Epistle of Enoch contains the Apocalypse of Weeks (1 En. 93.1–10; 91.11–17). From the Epistle, some scholars also identify the Exhortation (91.1–10) and the Birth of Noah (106–107).[10] Despite the orderly sequence of chapters, these are not chronological.

The texts of Enoch most likely were originally written in Aramaic and later translated into Greek. From the Greek texts, we have the Ethiopic (Geʿez—ancient Ethiopic) translations, the only language in which the entire corpus of 1 Enoch survives.[11] Exactly when these translations were done is not known.[12] However, the Aramaic fragments discovered at Qumran (4Q) provide more precise dating of these texts.[13] Using paleographic analysis of the scrolls, it has been determined that the early Enochic texts span approximately four centuries, from the third century BCE to the first century CE. The first of these writings are the Book of the Watchers and Astronomical Books, which probably stem from the beginning of the

---

9. R. H. Charles, *The Book of Enoch or 1 Enoch* (Oxford: Clarendon, 1912), xxx–xlvi.

10. For example, Loren T. Stuckenbruck, "The Early Traditions Related to 1 Enoch from the Dead Sea Scrolls: An Overview and Assessment," in *The Early Enoch Literature*, ed. Gabriele Boccaccini and John J. Collins (Leiden: Brill, 2007), 41.

11. For overviews of the Ethiopic manuscripts, see Michael A. Knibb, *The Ethiopic Book of Enoch: A New Edition in the Light of the Aramaic Dead Sea Fragments*, 2 vols. (Oxford: Clarendon, 1978), 2:1–6, 21–37; George W. E. Nickelsburg, *1 Enoch 1*, Hermeneia (Minneapolis: Fortress, 2001), 15–17. For the Greek texts generally, see Matthew Black, *Apocalypsis Henochi Graece: Fragmenta pseudepigraphorum quae supersunt graeca una cum historicorum et auctorum judaeorum hellenistarum fragmentis collegit et ordinarit Albert-Marie Denis*, PVTG 3 (Leiden: Brill, 1970). For an overview of extant Greek texts, see also Stuckenbruck's, "Early Traditions Related to 1 Enoch," cited above.

12. Milik suggests that a good starting point in possibly dating the Greek translations is through comparisons of the language with classical texts and papyri from the Hellenistic and Roman periods (Milik, *Books of Enoch*, 70). On the comparison of translations, see also Michael A. Knibb, "The Book of Enoch or Books of Enoch? The Textual Evidence for 1 Enoch," in Boccaccini and Collins, *The Early Enoch Literature*, 21–40.

13. See Milik, *Books of Enoch*. See also the following discussions by Knibb, *Ethiopic Book of Enoch*; VanderKam, *Enoch and the Growth*.

third century, with the Astronomical Books being the first of the two. Most likely, the Epistles of Enoch and the dream visions of the Book of Dreams were created at least in part from the knowledge these had provided, and possibly along with the final portion of the book of Daniel. Judging from external and internal evidence, the composition of the Epistles of Enoch, the Book of Dreams, and Daniel may have been composed in their final forms during the second half of the second century BCE. The Parables are considered to be the last of these texts, dating from about the first half of the first century CE.[14]

The influence of these texts on the formulation of Jewish thought and early Christian texts has become the subject of many studies over the past two decades. A particular area of interest to scholars has been the canonization of the text and, therefore, issues of authority. Was the Enochic corpus authoritative to Jews of antiquity? The discovery of Enochic texts at Qumran and scholarly analyses of the Book of Jubilees attest to the widespread and authoritative use of these texts among early Jewish communities. Annette Yoshiko Reed agrees with James VanderKam when she states, "Our evidence suggests that the boundaries of scriptural authority remained fluid in the second century BCE, and that a variety of texts continued to vie for elevated status, functioning as Scripture for some Jews but not for others."[15] The latter point is important because a canon would certainly presuppose some unified and centralized body that did not seem to have existed in the second century or at the time of Jesus. However, for the purposes of this study, suffice it to say that in the first century BCE/CE, the Enochic corpus was authoritative enough to be influential among various Jewish circles, including possibly those circles responsible for the Gospel of Matthew.

---

14. Besides the fact that no fragments of the Parables are among the Enoch collections from Qumran, James H. Charlesworth recently argues for a date of composition from the time of Herod the Great (40–4 BCE) to the early decades of the first century CE. See James H. Charlesworth, "The Date and Provenience of the *Parables of Enoch*," in *Parables of Enoch: A Paradigm Shift*, ed. Darrell L. Bock and James H. Charlesworth (London: Bloomsbury, 2013), 40.

15. Annette Yoshiko Reed, "'Revealed Literature' in the Second Century BCE: Jubilees, 1 Enoch, Qumran, and the Prehistory of the Biblical Canon," in Boccaccini, *Enoch and Qumran Origins*, 97. See also James C. VanderKam, *From Revelation to Canon: Studies in the Hebrew Bible and Second Temple Literature*, JSJSup 62 (Leiden: Brill, 2000).

3.2.3. Book of Dreams

As discussed at length in chapter 1 above, scholars distinguish between two general types of Jewish apocalypses: historical and otherworldly journeys.[16] The Book of the Watchers (1 En. 1–36) and the Astronomical Books (1 En. 72–82) are the earliest apocalypses classified under otherworldly journeys, while the book of Daniel, the Animal Apocalypse (1 En. 85–90), and the Apocalypse of Weeks (1 En. 91, 93) are the earliest historical apocalypses.[17] The former have particular interest in cosmology, while the latter factor in the development of history.

The fragments of the Book of Dreams in Aramaic come to us from Qumran, where we find a quarter of the original text preserved.[18] The oldest of the fragments from 4QEn[f] date to the third quarter of the second century BCE (150–125 BCE). Greek fragments are scattered and survive from a manuscript of a Byzantine chronicle in Greek (1 En. 89.42–9) and the Oxyrhynchus Papyrus (1 En. 85.10–86; 87.1–3).[19] The first two chapters (83–84) do not exist in either Aramaic or Greek. Like most of the other books of 1 Enoch, the Book of Dreams survives in its entirety only in Ethiopic.[20]

3.2.4. Dating and Unity

J. T. Milik's attribution of the manuscript 4QEn[f] to the early Hasmonean period, as mentioned above, provides a *terminus ante quem* for the Animal Apocalypse (1 En. 86.1–3).[21] Given the *vaticinium ex eventu* character of the Animal Apocalypse, scholars suggest a more specific dating during the Maccabean revolt, which is described in 1 En. 90.6–19, and which scholars have determined must have happened sometime between 165 and 160

---

16. Collins, "Introduction," 1–20; Collins, *The Apocalyptic Imagination: An Introduction to Jewish Apocalyptic Literature*, 2nd ed. (Grand Rapids: Eerdmans, 1998), 6.

17. For a list of apocalypses under "historical" and "otherworldly journeys," see Collins, *Apocalyptic Imagination*, 7.

18. Milik, *Books of Enoch*, 41, 244. The fragments come from four manuscripts: 4QEn[c], 4QEn[d], 4QEn[e], and 4QEn[f].

19. See Black, *Apocalypsis Henochi Graece*. See also Knibb, *Ethiopic Book of Enoch*, 2:15–21.

20. Milik, *Books of Enoch*, 45–46, 74.

21. Tiller, *Commentary*, 61. Tiller notes that 100 BCE may be the *terminus ad quem*.

BCE, since Judas Maccabeus died around 160 BCE.[22] Perhaps, the eschatological condemnation of the fallen angels, shepherds, and blind sheep (1 En. 90.20–27) makes the revolt against persecution a highly probable scenario for the time frame of the Animal Apocalypse.[23] It is hard not to read the judgment (1 En. 90.20–27) into 1 En. 90.6–19, linking the judgment to the rise (and perhaps the fall) of Judas referenced in the latter. It is also possible that the final composition was completed later, after Judas's death in 160 BCE, which means we may also perceive the fall of Judas in 1 En. 90.6–9.

Indeed, 1 En. 90.6–19 seems to indicate the ideal place for a specific dating.[24] Yet scholars are divided in making sense of the redactional activi-

---

22. Milik, *Books of Enoch*, 44; VanderKam, *Enoch and the Growth*, 161–63; Matthew Black, *Book of Enoch or 1 Enoch: A New English Edition with Commentary and Textual Notes*, SVTP 7 (Leiden: Brill, 1985), 21; Nickelsburg, *1 Enoch 1*, 396.

23. Anathea E. Porter-Young, *Apocalypse against Empire: Theologies of Resistance in Early Judaism* (Grand Rapids: Eerdmans, 2011), 350–52. Porter-Young, for example, states, "The apocalypse envisions imminent divine intervention and judgment precisely because the sheep are being attacked and devoured (e.g., 90.11)" (350).

24. 1 En. 90.6–19: "[6]And look, lambs were born of those white sheep, and they began to open their eyes and to see and to cry out to the sheep. [7]But they did not listen to them nor attend to their words, but they were extremely deaf, and their eyes were extremely and excessively blinded. [8]And I saw in the vision that the ravens flew upon those lambs and seized one of those lambs and dashed the sheep in pieces and devoured them. [9]And I saw until horns came out on those lambs, and the ravens were casting down their horns. {And I saw until a great horn sprouted on one of those sheep. [10]And it looked on them, and their eyes were opened, and it cried out to the sheep, and the rams saw it, and they all ran to it.}[11]And besides this, all those eagles and vultures and ravens and kites were still tearing the sheep in pieces and flying upon them and devouring them. And the sheep were silent, but the rams lamented and cried out. {[12]And those ravens were struggling and fighting with it and wished to do away with its horn, but they did not prevail against it. [13]And I saw until the shepherds and the eagles and those vultures and the kites came, and they cried to the ravens to smash the horn of that ram, and they struggled and made war with it, and it was struggling with them and cried out that its help might come. [14]And I looked until that man came who wrote the names of the shepherds and brought (them) before the Lord of the sheep and he helped it and showed it everything; his help came down to that ram. [15]And I saw until the Lord of the sheep came upon them in wrath, and all that saw him fled and all fell into darkness before him. [16]And all the eagles and vultures and ravens and kites gathered and brought with them all the wild <beasts>, and they all came together and helped one another smash the horn of that ram.} [17]And I looked at that man who wrote the book at the word of the Lord, until he opened the book of

3. Animal Apocalypse: A Metaphorical Reading   89

ties that seem to be evident in the doubling of the passages.[25] Even more puzzling is how 90.19 fits with the rest of the unit, 1 En. 90.6–18. I concur with Tiller that the reference to Judas Maccabeus in 1 En. 90.16–18 is original to the vision. I also agree with Tiller that the giving of the sword in 1 En. 90.19 could likewise allude to a historical event. However, I do not agree that the mention of a sword here is meant to record only the giving of the sword to Judas, as it is evident in 2 Macc 15:15–16.[26] As it were, the

---

the destruction that those last twelve shepherds worked, and he showed before the Lord of the sheep that they had destroyed more than those before them. [18]And I saw until the Lord of the sheep came to them and took in his hand the staff of his wrath and struck the earth, and the earth was split, and all the beasts and all the birds of heaven fell (away) from among those sheep and sank in the earth, and it covered over them. [19]And I saw until a large sword was given to those sheep, and the sheep went out against all the wild beasts to kill them, and all the beasts and the birds of heaven fled before them."

25. For the scholarly discussion of the redactional debate, see Tiller, *Commentary*, 63–79. See also Nickelsburg, *1 Enoch 1*, 396–98. Nickelsburg sees the texts as heavily redacted and that there are two levels of tradition. He places these side by side in the attempt to show tension and duplication, which creates disjunctions to the final form of the text. For Nickelsburg, the later tradition updates the earlier tradition, which suggests at least two datings of the material in 90.6–19. He states, "[I] suggest that a vision composed either in the last decade of the third century BCE, or after the death of Onias III (169 BCE) … was updated late in that decade before the death of Judas Maccabeus." Jonathan A. Goldstein makes a similar redactional proposal, except he sees three stages of redaction. See Jonathan A. Goldstein, *1 Maccabees: A New Translation*, AB 41 (Garden City, NY: Doubleday, 1976), 41–42. The first stage tells of plural horned lambs or rams, who may be pietists who could not resist the assault of the animals but receive heavenly aid. The second stage tells of a singular horned ram "who will win repeated victories for the Jews." The finals stage tells of all Jews winning a victory over Nicanor in 90.19. Tiller argues in a different fashion. Instead of suggesting that the reference to Judas Maccabeus (90.16–18) is the later interpolation, as proposed by Goldstein and Nickelsburg, it is for Tiller the earlier form of the vision, "because it is coherent and vs 17 is necessary to the form of the An. Apoc." (Tiller, *Commentary*, 72). I agree with Tiller on this point. He concludes that the redactions he proposes were written before Judas's death in 160 BCE, perhaps some time in the fall of 163 BCE. Thus, he sees the sword in 90.19 as futuristic and symbolic.

26. In 2 Macc 15:15–16, Jeremiah offers to Judas "a holy sword, a gift from God, with which you will strike down your adversaries." This speaks of Judas alone. Our passage in 1 En. 90.19 tells of the sword given to "those sheep." Second Maccabees 15:15–16 suggests only that the accomplishments of "those sheep" in 1 En. 90.19 are a direct result of Judas's actions. Tiller sees 2 Macc 15:15–16 as the prooftext that 90.19 is referring to Judas (Tiller, *Commentary*, 72–73).

90 Apocalyptic Sheep and Goats in Matthew and 1 Enoch

"large sword" in 1 En. 90.19 is given to "those sheep" to kill "all the wild beasts … [after which] all the beasts and the birds of heaven fled before them."[27] First Enoch 90.19 does not refer to a particular person as 2 Macc 15:15–16 does. The imagery of issuing a large sword to "those sheep" and not "a ram" seems symbolic rather than being merely a reference to the text of 2 Maccabees. There is also the possibility that the death of Judas Maccabeus may be indicated in 1 En. 90.16: "And all the eagles and vultures and ravens and kites gathered and brought with them all the wild beasts and they all come together and helped one another *to smash the horn of that ram.*"[28] From this passage, it seems that the horn is smashed and, apparently, the ram falls, especially when no further mention is made of it. If these assumptions are correct, the issuance of a large sword to "those sheep" symbolizes succession and the establishment of Jewish religious freedom and self-governance under the leadership of the Maccabees. This would mean that the composition of the Animal Apocalypse could have been written sometime after Judas's death, perhaps under Jonathan's leadership and priesthood (160–143BCE), or Simon's rule (143–135 BCE), or John Hyrcanus (135–104 BCE).[29] It seems most likely to be sometime between the aftermath of Judas's death and Simon's rule, which is between 160 and 135 BCE. The symbolic value of the sword becomes more evident when we learn that it is returned by the sheep (plural) to that house in

---

27. All translations of 1 Enoch, unless otherwise stated, are taken from George W. E. Nickelsburg and James C. VanderKam, *1 Enoch: The Hermeneia Translation* (Minneapolis: Fortress, 2012), 134–35.

28. The mystery that surrounds the animal metaphors in this passage precludes an exact historical event. I do not think the allegorist intends to do so but only to depict symbolically with a broad stroke, which means that the allegorist is looking back in reflection. Concerning this passage (1 En. 90.16), Tiller states, "No historical referent of this collection of Israel's enemies is possible. According to Charles, "the eagles, ravens, vultures, and kites represent all the hostile heathen nations in their last Gog and Magog struggle against Israel" (Tiller, *Commentary*, 363).

29. This falls before 100 BCE, which Tiller takes to be the *terminus ad quem* for the Animal Apocalypse (Tiller, *Commentary*, 61 n. 3). August Dillman, *Das Buch Henoch übersetzt und erklärt* (Leipzig: Vogel, 1853), makes the suggestion that the great horned ram could be John Hyrcanus (taken from Tiller, *Commentary*, 365). Tiller notes that for Dillman, the sword represents the period of Israel's "forcible subjugation of the Gentiles" and their rule over them. Tiller argues that "there is no attempt by Israel in this verse to subjugate the gentiles. The beasts and birds are being killed and fleeing; they are not becoming subject to Israel." However, it seems that Dillman may be referring to subjugation more in terms of futuristic hope as we see in 1 En. 90.28.

3. Animal Apocalypse: A Metaphorical Reading   91

1 En. 90.34. The return of the large sword follows the subjugation of the beasts and birds. I will revisit this below and explain in greater detail how this subjugation could be envisioned. The point I wish to make here is that the period between the giving of the large sword and its return reflects Israel's religious freedom, self-governance, and even empowerment. It is only then that ideas of a divine sovereignty come to mind, capturing the hopes described in the futuristic imagery in 1 En. 90.28–36. Thus, the issuing of the sword expresses both historical and futuristic values. I will come back to this in the latter part of this chapter and consider a possible social and historical scenario.

Daniel Assefa points out that the Animal Apocalypse makes no mention of any political revolt. He suggests that it transcends any particular crisis, is too imaginative and complex to have been composed in a great crisis, and is not militant in nature.[30] As such, Assefa places the Animal Apocalypse before the Maccabean uprising. It may be obvious that Assefa finds it difficult to reconcile the setting of a crisis with the fabric of the Animal Apocalypse, which seems to oppose violence and is open to inclusiveness. Anathea E. Porter-Young rightly rejects such dating. However, her disagreement with Assefa's above-mentioned points already sees the text of the Animal Apocalypse through an anti-imperial lens. The fact that she reads only the judgment of 1 En. 90.20–27 into 1 En. 90.6–19 delimits the temporal scope. She does agree with Assefa's first and third point above, and she totally dismisses his second point, suggesting instead that "the work's complexities necessitate neither an earlier nor a less stressful date." Moreover, she states, "a crisis that threatened everything that mattered could kick a determined writer into high gear."[31] She might be overstating her claims for a twenty-first-century gung-ho writer or computer warrior. I do not suggest that writers in the antiquities did not possess both the resources and the intellect needed to write while a crisis is unfolding outside their door––especially a crisis affecting loved ones, but I do point out that the emotional strength needed at the time of such a crisis certainly would deplete the spirit, time, and energy needed for such a complex piece of creativity. On this point, I agree on a "less stressful date" but would date it after the height of the rebellion.

---

30. Daniel Assefa, *L'Apocalypse des animaux (1Hen 85–90): une propaganda militaire?* (Leiden: Brill, 2007), 208, 254, 321.

31. Portier-Young, *Apocalypse Against Empire*, 351.

A number of scholars derive the integrity of the unity of the Book of Dreams from the shared themes of the first (1 En. 83–84) and second vision (1 En. 85–90).[32] I concur with these readings. I agree wholly with Carol Newsom, who states in an unpublished essay on 1 En. 83–90 that the first vision acts as a hermeneutical key for a proper interpretation of the subsequent beast vision.[33] Throughout the years, the Book of Dreams may have been edited to fit current situations. I choose to read it and the Animal Apocalypse in their final forms, which to a large extent may have been as they were on the above date.

3.3. The Animal Apocalypse as Allegory

The final form of the Book of Dreams consists of two dream visions, with the Animal Apocalypse (1 En. 85–90) making up the second and larger part (1 En. 83–90).[34] In the first part (1 En. 83–84), the first dream vision reveals to Enoch what will become of the cosmos. As he recounts the revelation, he sees the sky falling upon the earth and all sinking into the great and deep abyss of destruction. It disturbs Enoch greatly, mobilizing him to petition on behalf of all that is righteous on earth, for a remnant (cf. 1 En. 83.8)—in other words, a generation that will succeed him. The sovereignty of the Lord comes to the fore as Enoch prays, "O Lord of all the creation of heaven, King of kings and God of the whole world.... For you have created (all), and all things you rule" (1 En. 84.2–3).

The second part of the Book of Dreams is the Animal Apocalypse, which clearly is an allegory. Its metaphorical language draws from bestial language found in the narrative books of Gen 1 to 2 Kgs 25, possibly Ezra-Nehemiah,

---

32. For example, James VanderKam suggests that because "there is no indication in the text which would suggest that the apocalypse was written by someone other than the author of the entire BD, establishing a date for the AA should reveal the date for the complete booklet" (VanderKam, *Enoch and the Growth*, 161). At the end of his analysis of the Animal Apocalypse, Nickelsburg admits to "a certain unity" despite his redactional approach to the Book of Dreams (Nickelsburg, *1 Enoch 1*, 408).

33. Carol A. Newsom, "Enoch 83–90. The Historical Resume as Biblical Exegesis," unpublished seminar paper, Harvard University, 1975.

34. First Enoch 83.1 closely parallels the wording of 1 En. 85.1 (Nickelsburg, *1 Enoch 1*, 370). The first-person speech in 1 En. 85.1 links it also to the first-person account in 1 En. 83.1. As Tiller points out, "The An. Apoc. is a third person narrative of an account of a dream, enclosed within a first person narrative" (Tiller, *Commentary*, 225).

3. Animal Apocalypse: A Metaphorical Reading 93

and this causes some to label the work as *Rewritten Bible*.[35] It also accounts for contemporary events from oral traditions or the books of the Maccabees. In his commentary on the Animal Apocalypse, Patrick Tiller portrays the allegory and its language as being symbolic and classifies this symbolism on three levels. He states:

> There are at least three levels of symbolism in the An. Apoc. Accordingly I will use three different words: allegory, sign, and symbol. By allegory, I mean the literary convention by which a narrative about one set of things can refer to another set of things that is entirely external to the narrative itself. By sign, I mean the individual characters, events, and things of the narrative each of which points to an external referent. I use the more general term symbol of any of the more evocative representations that seem to be more culturally loaded, rather than simple ad hoc signs whose representations work only within the allegory.[36]

The way in which Tiller defines and uses the terms *sign* and *symbol* intimates that allegorical language is largely steno-language; he admits: "it does seem to lean in that direction."[37] Rather than understanding sign and symbol as simply referring to external things, I approach the figurative language as metaphorical, in other words, as language that uses the comparative parts of the metaphor to create metaphorical expressions. For example, instead of simply seeing sheep as a symbol that represents Israel, I understand sheep as a metaphorical blend of what is culturally known of both sheep and Israel, which may involve following the torah, an understanding of

---

35. The term *Rewritten Bible* was first coined by Geza Vermes in his *Scripture and Tradition in Judaism: Haggadic Studies* (Leiden: Brill, 1983), first published in 1961. The Animal Apocalypse and the Apocalypse of Weeks may well fall generally under this classification. See concluding remarks by Andreas Bedenbender, "The Place of the Torah in the Early Enoch Literature," in Boccaccini and Collins, *The Early Enoch Literature*, 78–80. For a convenient table of the biblical histories, see Nickelsburg, *1 Enoch 1*, 358–59.

36. Tiller, *Commentary*, 24.

37. Tiller, *Commentary*, 26. John J. Collins suggests that the use of "steno-symbols" to examine apocalypses "shows little appreciation for the allusive and evocative power of apocalyptic symbolism" (Collins, *The Apocalyptic Imagination*, 16). On "steno-language," see Norman Perrin, "Eschatology and Hermeneutics: Reflections on Method in the Interpretation of the New Testament," *JBL* 93 (1974): 3–14. For a critique on the application of "steno-language" to apocalyptic metaphors, see Collins, "Symbolism of Transcendence," 5–22.

94   Apocalyptic Sheep and Goats in Matthew and 1 Enoch

election, possibly a people with a purpose, and so forth. Together, this then creates the expressions within the allegory. Thus, we are not only imagining all the possible representations of sheep that may be applicable to the culture and propping these up alongside Israel. We are also imagining how those possibilities are used to express the relationships between sheep and Israel. Newsom seems close to this interpretation when she states, "Caught in the mesh of transparent allegory are genuine symbols whose surplus of meaning imparts added significance to the allegorical ciphers and makes the narrative a witness to certain esoteric traditions of the Enoch circle."[38] The task of this study is not to find the possible sources for the animal metaphor but to understand the expressive nature of the metaphors and elucidate the possible layers that create those expressions. Given the obvious problems of language, such attempts must be made with caution.[39]

As mysterious, vivid, and tantalizing as the vision might seem, there lies beneath the visuals a more predictive outcome that becomes realized at some point as biblical accounts unfold, thereby activating the allegory. In coming to such a realization, we find the story becoming less mysterious. The conceptual neurons of the mind fire up their connections, as the stories of Adam, Eve, Cain, and Abel, for example, put flesh on the metaphorical language. Generally speaking, the narrative of the Bible creates one conceptual frame, and the narrative of the allegory forms another, and they combine for a blended perception of a resulting narrative. The ensu-

---

38. Newsom, "Enoch 83–90," 30.

39. There is an obvious caveat in an analysis of the text. The issue of language is problematic to some degree. The Ethiopic language is twice removed from its original language. This means that some of the rhetorical features of the text in its original form may be lost in translation or interpretation. Scholars caution against relying too heavily upon the Ethiopic wording due to the significant differences with the Aramaic (VanderKam, *Enoch and the Growth*, 83). There are published works that rely heavily on the languages of the surviving texts of the Animal Apocalypse with textual notes, which will prove to be helpful. Tiller places the Ethiopic, Greek, and Aramaic versions alongside each other in his commentary. With a keen eye on rhetorical features of the text, Nickelsburg is able to work out meaning between the languages. Where the Aramaic still exists, he substitutes it for the Ethiopic portion of a given passage. Working closely with Tiller's commentary, Olson expands upon the theological aspects of the Animal Apocalypse, which discussion provides insights that may be missing in Nickelsburg's textual observation. While the analysis of inner texture aims primarily for a narrative reading of texts, it will work between these three studies primarily for points of agreement and departure.

3. Animal Apocalypse: A Metaphorical Reading   95

ing story becomes neither the Bible's nor the allegorist's, but metaphorical to the extent that the reader creates his or her own version. Clearly, I am presenting only one possibility of the allegorist's narrative in this study. As such, it is more fruitful if we treat the allegory first as a literary text and only secondarily look at its layers of cultural and, possibly, historical meaning. I will discuss the cultural and possible historical layers more fully in the latter part of this chapter. This sequencing is not meant to reflect any particular order of importance, but the examination of the relationships between words, phrases, and structural patterns may reveal the argumentative and aesthetic patterns produced by the text.[40] After all, it is the surface text that the reader encounters first.

3.4. A Reading

A rhetorical and narrative reading of key sections of the Animal Apocalypse highlights the structure and central metaphors of the allegory. Animal metaphors are significant in pointing out three key sections of the allegory. These occur at the beginning with the emergence of the cattle; then there is the shifting point of metaphors from cattle to sheep; and finally, there is the eschaton when both sheep and predators turn into cattle. These areas coincide with the structure of the Animal Apocalypse if we divide it into three unequal sections.[41] The first is comprised of the emergence of humanity in history, the interference of angels, and condemnation (1 En. 85.3–89.8). The second deals with the regeneration of humanity, the election of Israel, the interference of angels, and condemnation (1 En. 89.9–90.27). The third ends the apocalypse with the restoration of the temple, gathering of the nations and Israel alike, the transformation of the animals, and closes with blessings (90.28–38). This division of the text is of course not set in stone. Other markers of division do not really fit this three-part structure. For instance, the judgment in 1 En. 90.20–27 could be only a partial judgment. Does that condemnation go together with the blessing of 1 En. 90.33 and 1 En. 90.38 to constitute one judgment for all humanity? If that be the case, then we would have only a two-part structure. Nevertheless, since the

---

40. Robbins, Tapestry of Early Christian Discourse, 46.

41. For a three-part structure of the Animal Apocalypse, see Tiller, *Commentary*, 15–20, 383. Tiller argues that the appearance of a patriarchal white bull in each case is the dividing indicator. So also Nickelsburg, *1 Enoch 1*, 354–55, but with different division markers. I follow Nickelsburg more closely.

96   Apocalyptic Sheep and Goats in Matthew and 1 Enoch

focus of this study is on the actual animal metaphors, highlighting them is easier if we adhere to a three-part setup.

3.4.1. The Emergence of Cattle: 1 Enoch 85.3–10

> [3]Before I took your mother Edna (as my wife), I saw in a vision on my bed, and behold, and look, a bull came forth from the earth, and that bull was white. And after it a young heifer came forth. And with her two bull calves came forth; one of them was black, and one was red. [4]And that black calf struck the red one and pursued it over the earth. And from then on I could not see that red calf. [5]But that black calf grew up, and a young heifer came to it. And I saw that many cattle that came forth from it, that were like it and were following after it. [6]And that female calf, that first one, went forth from the presence of that first bull; she searched for that red calf, but did not find it, and she lamented bitterly over it and searched for it. [7]And I looked until that first bull came to her and quieted her; and from that time on she did not cry out. [8]After this she bore another white bull, and after it she bore many black bulls and cows. [9]And I saw in my sleep that white bull, that it grew likewise and became a large white bull, and from it came forth many white cattle, and they were like it. [10]And they began to bear many white cattle, which were like them, and each one followed the other.

The Beginnings

The above passage is the first significant unit of the second vision (1 En. 85–90). Enoch constantly invites the reader to share his vision with him: I saw; and behold; I looked; I could not see (85.3, 5, 7, 9).[42] The repeated prompts call the reader to attention, while at the same time stimulating curiosity. The reader finds him- or herself as it were at Enoch's feet, next to his son Methuselah (85.1–2).

Four types of cattle mysteriously appear out of nowhere: white, black, and red cattle, along with a young heifer. Only the white bull emerges from the earth. However, at the end, two seem to be in view: one white and one black. The color black typically is associated with negativity: with plague

---

42. Here we witness the vision-report formula "I saw" that occurs throughout the Animal Apocalypse (1 En. 86.1, 2, 3; 87.1 etc.; 88.1 etc.). It is also common in Dan 7, 8. See Paul A. Porter, *Metaphors and Monsters: A Literary-Critical Study of Daniel 7 and 8*, ConBOT 20 (Lund: Gleerup, 1983), esp. chapter 4.

3. Animal Apocalypse: A Metaphorical Reading   97

and famine (e.g., Exod 10:15; Lam 5:10), death (e.g., Job 30:30), and even blindness (e.g., Mic 3:6). The intimidating black calf seems to live up to its color as it gores the red calf. The colors and the violent action already imply death for the red calf as the reader is told that Enoch sees it no more (85.4). Even more daunting, as Enoch continues to watch, is that many more of the black bull's kind come forth and follow it. Suddenly, the focus shifts toward the first heifer, perhaps the mother of the red calf as she seeks her calf, stressed by its absence. Convinced that it has been killed, the heifer laments. Fortunately, when Enoch looks again, the first bull, being the white bull that it is, consoles her in her sorrow.

While the existence of Adam to Seth in the form of cattle emerge from the earth as accounted for in Genesis, much of the other details of their accounts and beyond are left out. Yet allegory is not so much about what it leaves out as what it captures with the language it uses and of what emerges through the allegorical filter. For instance, if the author(s) of the Animal Apocalypse knew about Gen 1 and 3, then Adam and Eve cannot be conceptualized without the creation story and original sin. That it is in fact left out explicitly does not necessarily mean the author(s) thinks nothing of it or that the text does not presuppose it.[43] Often there are subtle clues, some of which I will point out in this chapter. Three immediate features of the text's reality surface from an initial comparison of the biblical account and the metaphors.

First and rather obviously, the vision paints an image of these cattle as the progenitors of all the cattle in existence in the present and future. The black bull (Cain) and the second heifer bore many black bulls like it, while the white bull (Adam) and the first young heifer (Eve) bore a white bull (Seth) and many other black bulls and heifers. From that white bull (Seth), many like it came forth. Thus, both white and black bulls, as well as heifers, come into being and multiply. Simply put, Adam and Eve populate the earth.

---

43. Nickelsburg, *1 Enoch 1*, 370. Nickelsburg suggests that since Adam "comes forth" from the earth, it reflects only the accounts of Gen 2 and not Gen 1. He notes that the Ethiopian verb for "come forth" suggests patrilineage, since it is being used to describe the birth of Eve, the births of Cain and Abel, and the disembarkation of Noah and his sons at the beginning of a new creation. But this is not so obvious. The verb for "come forth" can also emphasize the relationship between humanity and creation. I will come back to this point throughout this study. Nickelsburg further highlights that Gen 3 is also omitted.

98   Apocalyptic Sheep and Goats in Matthew and 1 Enoch

What can easily be missed is the fact that that first bull (Adam) "came forth from the earth" (1 En. 85.3). This is significant especially when the last white bull at the end of the allegory in 1 En. 90.37 is said to have been born, indicating that it, too, comes forth from the earth. I am not suggesting a second Adam typology.[44] Rather, I am proposing that this detail constitutes in part the rhetoric of the Animal Apocalypse that highlights a mediating feature in the animal metaphors, namely, that the animal metaphors emphasize an inseparable link that mankind has with the earth and creation and thus the creator, further substantiating the connection of this section with Gen 1 and 3.

The relationship between humanity and creation is one that interpreters of scriptural texts often overlook.[45] However, this relationship is very much evident in Jewish culture, particularly within its wisdom traditions. This is made especially clear in 1 En. 84.1–3 as Enoch praises YHWH for his creative deeds of and dominion over both heaven and earth. The text of the Book of the Watchers expresses anxiety in this regard when it narrates the descent of the angels who are seeing "much blood being shed upon the earth, and all the oppression being wrought upon the earth." To which they say to one another, "The earth, (from) her empty (foundation), has brought the cry of their voice unto the gates of heaven" (1 En. 9.1–2). Earth is important and cannot be imagined without mankind. This relationship underscores the use of animals as metaphor. I will argue later in this chapter that an eye to the relationship between humanity and creation

------

44. On a second Adam typology, see Milik, *Books of Enoch*, 45; Black, *Book of Enoch*, 20–21, 279–80; Florentino Garcia Martinez, "Qumran and Apocalyptic: Studies on the Aramaic Texts from Qumran," STDJ 9 (Leiden: Brill, 1992), 75; Andre Lacocque, "Allusions to Creation in Daniel 7," in *The Book of Daniel: Composition and Reception*, ed. J. J. Collins and P. W. Flint, VTSup 83 (Leiden: Brill, 2001), 1:114–31. Olson notes that the proposition of the last bull being a "second Adam" was first suggested by Johs. Pedersen in his work back in 1926. See Olson, *New Reading*, 27 n. 33.

45. The neglect of earth and creation in the interpretation of texts is due to the androcentric hermeneutics of Western thought and hermeneutics. However, this unity is often expressed if not implied in religious cultures, which is usually expressed in metaphors. It is also used in the expression of power. This is seen in a recent essay by Tina Dykesteen Nilsen and Anna Rebecca Solevag, "Expanding Ecological Hermeneutics: The Case for Ecolonialism," *JBL* 135 (2016): 665–83, esp. 676–80. I hope to show in this chapter that the Animal Apocalypse is not immune to this use of metaphorical language. See also Norman C. Habel and Peter Trudinger, *Exploring Ecological Hermeneutics*, SBLSymS 46 (Atlanta: Society of Biblical Literature, 2008).

3. Animal Apocalypse: A Metaphorical Reading   99

may prove to be beneficial in our analysis of the Animal Apocalypse, particularly in its close association with the heavens and God.

Second, it is undeniable that color is symbolic. The red calf represents the murdered Abel. The color black attributes a negative image to Cain and his offspring. The color white seems to symbolize the elect or purity,[46] but in the context of the Animal Apocalypse as a whole, it suggests another possibility. The relationship between the brother calves (Cain and Abel) underscores the proposition that righteousness, which encompasses the knowledge of God, is represented by the color white.[47] If the color black signifies an unwanted trait that strikes or gores other cattle to death,[48] then the red denotes the results, as in the color of blood (cf. 89.9).[49] If, as I suggest, white can be considered a symbol of righteousness, then the vision thematizes the color black and equates it with conflict of a violent nature that results in murder. Such actions are contrary to the knowledge of God and considered unrighteous. Indeed, the sin of fraternal hostility is an important motif in the Animal Apocalypse.[50] That the actions of the black cattle cause the first heifer to lament affirms and adds to the repertoire of attributes for the color black, that is, that unrighteous acts cause grief and lamentation. Throughout the allegory, as in many cases in the

---

46. Just as white generally symbolizes the inclusion of someone within the race, Tiller suggests that black signifies being excluded from the race. For Tiller, color generally symbolizes lineage or the elect (Tiller, *Commentary*, 226). Nickelsburg suggests white symbolizes purity (Nickelsburg, *1 Enoch 1*, 371). These suggestions, in my opinion, are possible, but given the allegory as a whole, they may be problematic, for none of the sheep other than Jacob and the ones before the last judgment are explicitly labeled as white. Jacob stands in a transitional point when cattle shift to sheep. So also do the ones at the last judgment when sheep turn back into cattle.

47. Unlike Nickelsburg and Tiller, Olson is less settled. He suggests that white can indicate either righteousness or divine favor (Olson, *New Reading*, 76). If white symbolizes the elect, then the sheep between Jacob and those sheep before the last judgment are not, which is unlikely. I agree with the first option Olson provides, that white symbolizes righteousness. Nevertheless, he does not expound on what he means by it. What many neglect to explain is the fact that the heifer is colorless, which may hint further regarding the meanings of the color.

48. Here, I refer to color as a trait to maintain a language befitting the context of animal genetics. I will become more specific as the analysis develops.

49. Nickelsburg, *1 Enoch 1*, 371; Tiller, *Commentary*, 226.

50. Olson, *New Reading*, 90–91. While this may be referring to the hostility of Jews persecuting other Jews, it may also refer to the hostility of one human persecuting another. Both are possible in the Animal Apocalypse.

100   Apocalyptic Sheep and Goats in Matthew and 1 Enoch

Hebrew Bible, lamenting is a result of violence and death (1 En. 85.6; 87.1; 89.15–16, 20, 53, 57, 69; 90.3, 11).

If these colors are associated with a set of human characteristics that centers on humankind's response to the knowledge of God, then the color white stands in contrast to the unwanted traits associated with black cattle. The white bull's ability to console the lamenting heifer is a case in point. It reflects the way in which the Lord of the sheep (1 En. 89.16) and the angelic scribe (1 En. 90.13) answer the cries of the sheep by comforting them. Thus, the identity of Adam in the allegory is defined in part by the encounter of the red (Abel) with the black cattle (Cain), placing Adam in a positive light. This detail is missing in Genesis, but the color symbolism of the allegory suggests it.[51]

I would like to suggest allusions to creation at Gen 1–3 in the use of the white and black symbolism. Nickelsburg points out that in the Animal Apocalypse, Cain's murder of Abel is the first explicit instance of human evil (Gen 4:4). However, Gen 4:7, which speaks of Cain's inability to make the correct choice, may suggest that that evil should be read back into the creation story of Gen 1 and into the garden story of Gen 3. In other words, the color black both reflects Cain's evil act (Gen 4:7) that defies the image in which humanity was created in Gen 1 and enacts the darker side of the knowledge that Eve was lured into accepting (Gen 3:6). It would explain why the account in the garden is excluded, because what the author intends to highlight is already sufficiently well represented in Cain's evil deed. Paradigmatically, it represents an evil that disobeys God and embodies violence.

Interestingly, the color of heifers is not mentioned. Essentially, the second heifer and Eve are colorless. If indeed we do place cattle, and thus humans, along a continuum of wanted and unwanted traits with white and black representing the opposite poles, then femininity seems to be neutral, standing in the middle of this continuum. Like the red calf, females seem to be victimized in the struggle between white and black.

---

51. In part, it plays a role in popularizing the motif of the glory of Adam as seen in other Jewish literature. It can also harmonize well with the eschatological imagery of all white cattle in the eschaton (1 En. 90.38). See Sir 49:16; Philo, *Creation* 136–150; CD III, 18–20; 1QH XVII, 15–16; and 1QS IV, 23. See also Olson, *New Reading*, 146. However, I do not see the figure in the eschaton as a new Adam, for Adam is not the only white bull in the Animal Apocalypse.

3. Animal Apocalypse: A Metaphorical Reading   101

Some scholars have noticed the emphasis on Eve's grief over Abel. Peculiar is the superfluous searching for Abel by Eve in 1 En. 85.6, which is a detail added by the allegory to the biblical account, perhaps drawing on a haggadic tradition.[52] However, Eve could be contemplating revenge to some extent as part of her lamenting. When the first heifer searches a second time after she laments, it causes one to wonder whether she is searching for something other than the red calf. The ambiguity in the text allows for such interpretation. It could be that her lamenting (after her first search) presupposes that the red calf may already have perished and that she is now searching for the black calf, which is responsible for the death. George W. Nickelsburg suggests that perhaps there is a mistranslation of the verb בעא, which could mean both "search" and "make petition" in the sense of crying out. He points out that the root of the Ethiopic verb for "cry out" in 85.7 (*sarha*) is found elsewhere in the context of vengeance (1 En. 8.4; 89.19).[53] That the first heifer pleads for the blood of Abel and cries out in vengeance would fit well within the context of violence. If this is the case, then the white bull's intervention suggests a possible attempt to turn her away from unrighteousness, quieting her to silence, perhaps through some revelation. In Apoc. Mos. 3.3–4, Adam receives a revelation that they will bear another son, Seth, which eases their grief over Abel. This attributes additional positive qualities to Adam and the color white. We will find the same three colors represented in the renewed earth after the flood.

Third, in the context of progeny, the logic that white cattle beget white cattle (just as good fruit produces good fruit and bad fruit bad) is employed.[54] The second offspring, which the first black bull (Cain) brings forth, begets many black bulls. The vision says nothing of them producing white bulls. How then do white bulls create black bulls?[55] It appears that black bulls beget only black, not white ones. This remains consistent

---

52. Tiller, *Commentary*, 229. Tiller suggests that the myth of Demeter's search for Kore or the search of Isis for Osiris may have been incorporated here. Nickelsburg sees this as drawing on a haggadic tradition (Nickelsburg, *1 Enoch 1*, 372).

53. Nickelsburg, *1 Enoch 1*, 372.

54. Tiller, *Commentary*, 226.

55. This is explained away by some by suggesting that white symbolizes the elect and black means the nonelect. See Newsom, "Enoch 83–90," 39 n. 25. Also Olson, *New Reading*, 76. The explanation would suggest that all the sheep between Jacob, who is a white sheep, and those white sheep (1 En. 90.6) before the last judgment are not elect. It may be premature to adopt a theological perspective on the metaphors at this point of the narrative.

102   Apocalyptic Sheep and Goats in Matthew and 1 Enoch

throughout the Animal Apocalypse. It may be the case that the white bull generates offspring of black bovines by some innate or external reason. This suggests that both color cattle, seen as humankind, have an inclination toward unrighteousness and violence or that some external force causes cattle as humanity to gravitate toward that darker side of the continuum of righteousness. Given the case of Cain discussed above in Gen 4:7, this possibility cannot be ruled out.

The evil or unrighteousness to which humanity inclines itself becomes the biblical legacy of Adam and Eve (e.g., 2 Bar. 17.2–18.2; 23.4). In the Animal Apocalypse, it would also explain why a white bull (Adam) and the first heifer (Eve) bore black cattle. It would follow then that the color of cattle or humanity is a reflection of human choice—a choice heavily influenced, though not determined, by an innate evil or external force. In the following chapters of the Animal Apocalypse, this external force takes on an extended form of fallen angels who add to the knowledge of humans, much like the force that wooed Eve with the prospect of knowledge. This calls into question the argument of determinism in apocalyptic contexts. The allegory simply designates the color according to how the characters turn out in the biblical accounts.[56] Although heifers or the female side of humanity are able to make choices, they are susceptible to persuasion or deceit, as it were (e.g., see LAE 9–11). The heifers in the above passage are only reported as being with the respective colored cattle. This vulnerability and position of victimization would have them colorless and situated in the middle of the continuum of righteousness and unrighteousness, being tugged to either side, as was the case in which the white bull silenced the first heifer.

Coupled with an innate propensity for evil, the new knowledge that the fallen angels introduce in the next chapter (1 En. 86) leads humankind and creation to further chaos. This ultimately results in judgment of the angels (1 En. 89) and humanity via the flood (1 En. 89.1–8). Together, these constitute a structural unit, just as the narrative following the flood

---

56. While the prospect of determinism looms in the use of Enoch being the visionary of history and current events in the Animal Apocalypse, it seems more likely that Enoch is being used for its authoritative status, which has been established in the Book of the Watchers and the Astronomical Books, in which his knowledge surpasses any person that ever lived. His knowledge is received from God and the heavenly beings, which does not necessarily mean determinism but authoritative prediction. The biblical accounts would affirm his predictions, adding to his authority.

3. Animal Apocalypse: A Metaphorical Reading 103

potentially constitutes another, for it, too, leads toward judgment upon the angels and humanity.

Increase of Violence

Chapters 86–88 and the destruction caused by the offspring of these stars are allusions to the Book of the Watchers. This section tells of what seems to be an invasion of the earth by stars (1 En. 86.1–4).[57] The stars themselves become cattle and begin to mingle sexually with the cattle of the earth, creating larger and different forms of animal beings. These relations between cattle add other unwanted traits along the continuum of righteousness with the creation of animals such as elephants, camels, and donkeys. Thus, to return to the notion of a continuum, we now have white cattle at one end, and on the other end, we find black cattle and giant animals. This creates a social imbalance. They not only gore one another, as was the case in 1 En. 85.4, now they also devour one another and bite with their teeth while the earth cries out (1 En. 86.5; 87.1). This causes fear among "the children of the earth" as they tremble and flee (1 En. 86.6). The conflict between cattle in 1 En. 85 has now escalated, which seems to be the result of the blending. This struggle becomes the reason for the judgment that follows.

Condemnation

Four other heavenly beings appear, one of whom takes Enoch by the hand and leads him back to heaven (1 En. 87.2–4). From there he witnesses the gathering of the fallen stars by these newly appeared heavenly beings. They bind the stars, hand and foot (if one can imagine such a thing), and cast them into a deep and dark Abyss within the earth (1 En. 88.1–3). Not only does the invasion of stars bring into existence giant animals, it also triggers divine judgment upon the fallen stars, including the wrath of the flood, all of which is understood here in the Animal Apocalypse as secrets revealed (1 En. 87.4; 89.1).[58]

---

57. I will return to this below.

58. In this section, allusions are made to the Book of the Watchers and the accounts of the flood in Genesis.

104 Apocalyptic Sheep and Goats in Matthew and 1 Enoch

3.4.2. The Emergence of Sheep: 1 En. 89.9–12

[9]That white bull who had become a man came out of that vessel, and the three bulls with him. And one of those three bulls was white like that bull, and one of them was red like blood, and one of them was black. And that white bull departed from them. [10]And they began to beget wild beasts and birds, so that there arose from them every kind of species: lions, leopards, wolves, dogs, hyenas, wild boars, foxes, conies, pigs, falcons, vultures, kites, eagles, and ravens. But among them a white bull was born. [11]And they began to bite one another, but that white bull that was born among them begat a wild ass and a white bull with it, and the wild asses increased. [12]But that bull that was born from it begat a black wild boar and a white ram of the flock. And that (wild boar) begat many boars, and that ram begat twelve sheep.

Beginnings

The above passage (1 En. 89.9–12) is a significant turning point of the Animal Apocalypse. It has one main agenda: to narrate the lineage from Noah to Jacob. It is significant for our purpose because this narrative marks the shift from cattle to sheep, which dominates the narrative until the last several verses of the Animal Apocalypse. The above passage lacks the visual prompts of the previously cited passage, but it is, nonetheless, conceptually stimulating. Indeed, a reader familiar with the biblical accounts of Genesis is keen to compare it with the allegorical narrative.

Much like 85.3–10, the section begins with the appearance of a white bull. The white bull, to which one of the stars reveals the secret of the flood (1 En. 89.1), comes out of the vessel as a man to a new beginning—a cleansed earth (1 En. 89.9). The transformation from white bull to man points to his angelic status and that he belongs rather to the old world. It is his offspring that are credited with populating the renewed world. Nevertheless, with him come three cattle, the same number that emerged from the earth in 1 En. 85.3.[59] One bull is white, one is red like blood, and one is black.

The white bull does not emerge from the purified earth. Rather it and the other three bulls come out of "that vessel," indicating a continuation of

---

59. Tiller (*Commentary*, 258) and George W. E. Nickelsburg and James C. VanderKam (1 Enoch: The Hermeneia Translation [Minneapolis: Fortress, 2012], 123) translate these three cows as bulls or male cattle.

3. Animal Apocalypse: A Metaphorical Reading   105

the previous generations of humanity. This image of setting foot upon the earth from "that vessel" suggests that the earth itself has been renewed but the cattle and their moral predispositions before the flood remain; both the evil and the righteousness of the old world carry over into the new. The negative traits of the color black and the different varieties of animals caused by the intermingling of the stars and cattle blend with the progenitors of the renewed earth. If the colors of the cattle are placed on a continuum of wanted and unwanted traits, as posited above, both in the beginning (1 En. 85) and in the renewal of the earth, we find both ends of that continuum well represented. The only difference between the two beginnings (85.3–10; 89.9–12) is that now we have an added unwanted trait of "different animals" born by the unnatural invasion of the stars that resulted in sexual intercourse with the cattle.[60] We have black cattle and other animals on one side of the continuum, and white cattle on the other. The red calf along with heifers remain situated in the middle of this continuum as victims caught between the struggles of the violent and the righteous.

Once again, in 1 En. 89.9–12, these colored cattle become the ancestors of the earth. However, the cattle metaphor quickly disappears from the allegory. Instead of bulls begetting bulls, as was the case in 1 En. 85, much of what was caused by the intermingling of the fallen stars (1 En. 86–88) remains as predispositions in subsequent generations. In other words, the colored cattle now beget wild beasts and birds, which in turn beget all kinds of species: lions, leopards, wolves, dogs, hyenas, wild boars, foxes, conies, pigs, falcons, vultures, kites, eagles, and ravens (1 En. 89.10). This stands in contrast to the elephants, camels, and asses created before the flood (1 En. 86.4; 87.4). The black cattle are completely replaced. The conflict of kin noted in 1 En. 85 continues and progressively becomes more violent as the new species of various animals not only bite with their teeth (cf. 1 En. 86.5) but also bite one another (1 En. 87.1; 89.11).

In this new scenario, we have only two white bulls (Noah and Shem) that come out of that vessel and two more white bulls (Abraham and Isaac)

---

60. VanderKam, *Enoch and the Growth*, 119–22. In his comments on 1 En. 1–5, VanderKam points to the laws of natural order as examples for laws of morality. He discusses the possibility of a paraenetical use of natural order. See also Lars Hartman, *Asking for a Meaning: A Study of 1 Enoch 1–5*, ConBNT 12 (Lund: Gleerup, 1979). In other words, the intermingling of the stars with the cattle is seen as a negative addition to humanity and the natural order.

106   Apocalyptic Sheep and Goats in Matthew and 1 Enoch

that emerge from the species of animals. Other than the fact that they begat one another, not much else is heard about those white bulls, except that the last white bull (Isaac) produces a new kind of animal (1 En. 89.12), a white ram (Jacob), which in turn brings forth twelve sheep (Jacob's sons). After the appearance of the white ram, cattle disappear altogether from the revelation. Thus, just as the various species of animals substitute for giant animals, from here on, the sheep take the place of cattle. What's more, subsequently in the allegory, the black and white coloring of the cattle, which symbolizes the different poles of the continuum of wanted and unwanted traits, is replaced with a new set of qualities. On one side of the continuum, there are sheep with open eyes following the path and gathering in the house, while on the other side of the continuum are wild animals and blind sheep straying from the path and abandoning the house. That the white ram (Jacob) remains white symbolically reflects the transition from cattle to sheep, a motif that does not reappear in the vision when the dream begins to predict the beginning of the judgment in 1 En. 90.20–27. There, sheep change back to cattle (1 En. 90.6, 32).[61] The symbolic value of particular details in the narrative that seem to form an *inclusio* is not uncommon in the Animal Apocalypse. As discussed above, this is also seen in the symbol of the "large sword" (1 En. 90.19 and 90.34). Nevertheless, in a very significant way, the sheep resemble the cattle that emerge in 85.3–10. The question becomes how. I will return to this important question later and remain with the story of the sheep for now.

The sheep are initially led by the Lord of the sheep (1 En. 89.16, 22, 24, 28) and another sheep from among them that acts as a guide, showing the flock the path and instructing them (1 En. 89.32). The obedience of the sheep in following this path is reflected in the vision in terms of sight or the lack thereof (1 En. 89.32, 33, 39–40, 44) and in terms of staying on the path or straying from it (1 En. 89.35, 51, 53). The choice made results in gathering in the house of the Lord of the sheep (1 En. 89.36) or abandoning it altogether. The Lord of the sheep then raises rams to lead the sheep (1 En. 89.42, 45, 48, 49), and these rams are also subjected to the same conditions (1 En. 89.44). However, blindness and straying from the path increase to the point that the sheep abandon the house of the Lord (1 En. 85.53–54). Consequently, the Lord of the sheep gives them over to

---

61. Nickelsburg sees 1 En. 90.6–19 as the section that "recounts events in what the author expects to be the last years of human history before the eschaton" (Nickelsburg, *1 Enoch 1*, 396). Thus, it is a section that describes a transitional stage.

3. Animal Apocalypse: A Metaphorical Reading 107

the wild animals (1 En. 89.54–58). Within the above structural frame, the encounters of the righteous and the unrighteous escalate into increasing violence and blindness until finally angelic beings (1 En. 86), in the guise of shepherds, intervene, which leads also to judgment.

Increased Violence and Blindness

What the author of the Animal Apocalypse narrates next is quite interesting: the Lord of the sheep (God) hands over the leadership and pasturing of the sheep to seventy shepherds who are divine beings acting as foreign kings (1 En. 89.59).[62] Along with the shepherds, the Lord of the sheep separately recruits another shepherd to keep watch over the seventy shepherds' actions and to report back any excessive violence they might enact upon the sheep (1 En. 89.61–64). The fact that these are shepherds and not animals suggests that they are angels. Therefore, just as angels intrude upon the earth in 1 En. 86 on their own, here they are directly appointed by God to intervene on earth as rulers of the nations. They seem to be operating according to a different set of instructions than those given to the sheep that ascended to the Lord of the sheep at "the summit of that rock" (1 En. 89.32). Like the fallen angels in 1 En. 86, the shepherds disobey the Lord as they cause great destruction. They incite the wild beasts and animals to violence. As a result, they kill, destroy, and hand over many more sheep to be devoured by wild beasts than they are commanded to do by the Lord of the sheep (1 En. 89.65–68, 74–75; 90.3–4, 17). All the while, the appointed angelic scribe responsible for record-keeping reports their deeds (89.70–71, 76; 90.17) to the Lord of the sheep. In addition to being handed over and killed, many more sheep are also blinded (89.74; 90.7). This increase of disobedience by both shepherds and sheep, together with the increase of aggression by the animals, leads to yet another intervention by the Lord of the sheep.

Condemnation

As in the first section above, this section ends with divine intervention. Instead of a flood, this time the Lord's staff stomps upon the earth, creating an earthquake that causes those who were tyrannizing the sheep to

---

62. Nickelsburg, *1 Enoch 1*, 390.

108   Apocalyptic Sheep and Goats in Matthew and 1 Enoch

fall into the fissures. A throne is erected on the land by the Lord of the sheep. From it, he reviews the records that have been kept and metes out judgment on all the culpable, beginning with the fallen stars. Yet unlike with the flood, here not all are judged; only those who have sinned are adjudicated. The fallen angels who have been tied up since the flood and the seventy shepherds "who took and killed more than … commanded" (1 En. 90.22) are condemned. Moreover, the blinded sheep are also judged. All are found to be sinners and thrown into a fiery abyss (1 En. 90.23–27). Astonishingly, both the sheep that kept to the path as well as the wild animals are not judged! Are not wild animals sinners? How did they survive judgment? What follows is even more astonishing.

3.4.3. The (Re)emergence of Cattle: 1 En. 90.37–38

[37]And I saw how a white bull was born, and its horns were large. And all the wild beasts and all the birds of heaven were afraid of it and made petition to it continually. [38]And I saw until all their species were changed, and they all became white cattle. And the first one became <leader> among them (and that <leader> was a large animal), and there were large black horns on its head. And the Lord of the sheep rejoiced over it and over all the cattle.

This last segment of the Animal Apocalypse presents yet another new beginning. It becomes the climax of a unit that begins with 1 En. 90.28.[63] After the condemnation described above, the Lord of the sheep establishes a new house where all the sheep that survived the judgment gather (90.28–29, 32) as all the wild animals and birds fall down to worship the sheep and obey their instructions. All the animals' eyes are opened (90.35), and then a white bull, as described in the above passage, emerges once again. He has large black horns. Apparently fear of the white bull causes all the other animals, including the sheep, to transform not just into cattle, but specifically into white cattle. The continuum of unwanted and wanted traits disappears, and there remain only positive traits. This beginning is very unlike the previous two. There are no more colors; all are white. There is no variety among the animals; now all are cattle. The state of being seems to harken back to creation, when there were no black cattle. All seem to be righteous and know God. There is no end of the cosmos or of creation, in

---

63. Nickelsburg designates 1 En. 90.28–38 as a vision of "a new beginning" (Nickelsburg, *1 Enoch 1*, 402).

3. Animal Apocalypse: A Metaphorical Reading

fact no end of anything. There seems only to be a continuation of life on earth but now in an ideal state. Evil appears to have been eradicated completely. That the white bull is *born* suggests that this white bull is not from the heavens but from the earth, as was the original white bull. Whether this is a return to a second Adam, as Tiller suggests, is not clear. Adam was not the only white bovine born on earth. What is clear is that the essence of all that is righteous in white cattle is all that remains.

3.4.4. Conceptual Metaphors

From this preliminary reading of the Animal Apocalypse, we are able to list several salient metaphors in the narrative.

Generic Space: Entity is Nature	Input Space 1: Scriptural Account	Input Space 2: Natural World	Blend: Animal Apocalypse
Agent 1	God	Lord of the Sheep	GOD IS LORD OF THE SHEEP
Agent 2	Jacob and Israel	Sheep	ISRAEL IS SHEEP
Agent 3	Gentiles	Predator	GENTILES ARE PREDATORS
Agent 4	Righteous Humanity	White Cattle	RIGHTEOUS HUMANITY ARE WHITE CATTLE
Agent 5	Unrighteous Humanity	Black Cattle	UNRIGHTEOUS HUMANITY ARE BLACK CATTLE
Agent 6	Violent Humanity	Giant Animals	VIOLENT HUMANITY ARE GIANT ANIMALS
Agent 7	Woman	Heifers	WOMAN IS HEIFER
Agent 8	Angels	Shepherds/Stars	ANGELS ARE SHEPHERDS/STARS

The allegory utilizes three general metaphors for humans (sheep, cattle, and other animals[64]) that merge figures in Scripture with those in the natural world, for example, ISRAEL IS SHEEP. How do all the metaphors interrelate? Conceptual frames of creatures transfer onto humans. It

---

64. Here I am referring to the various creatures that are not sheep or cattle as animals.

appears that creaturely characteristics are transferred to express the divine elements of humans. From Gen 1 and 3, it appears that this divine element consists of knowledge. In this sense, humanity is inseparable from both creation and God. This is the imagery that the Animal Apocalypse asks us to believe, the imagery that I will explore further below. From the above reading, the violence observed in black cattle, giant animals, and predators is equated to the unrighteousness that results from the type of knowledge that humanity chooses to accept. The prototypical metaphor pertaining to Israel involves sheep, which is attested to in Scripture (e.g., Ps 100:3) and is obviously important for the Animal Apocalypse. Its creaturely characteristics are closely related to the knowledge of God, who is metaphorically referred to as the Lord of the sheep. Humans and stars are displaced by angelic beings. Since angels are in the realm of the heavens, they are much closer to the cosmos and God but inseparable from humanity. Thus, angels and animals have a common denominator in humanity. In the Animal Apocalypse, the earth and its creatures—humans, angels, and the cosmos—are all creations of God. Only angels and humanity are subject to his judgment because of the knowledge they are able to attain.

The structure (beginning, increase in violence, and judgment) seems to indicate that the animal metaphors evolve from one form to another and then back to what they were. After the flood, sheep replace righteous humanity (white cattle). Unrighteous humanity metamorphoses into violent humanity, which is then replaced after the flood by predators.[65] In the end, all return to being righteous humans. What is the rhetoric behind the structure of this narrative? What does it all say about the sheep? I would like to begin this discussion by considering the relationship between the sheep and their Lord.

3.5. Sheep and the Lord of the Sheep

The way in which the allegorist uses Scripture is telling. Such intertextual activity reflects Scriptures *recited*, *recontextualized*, and *reconfigured*.[66] The

---

65. I am distinguishing violence from unrighteousness here in terms of knowledge. The term *violence* refers to actions obtained from the knowledge received from the fallen angels. Unrighteousness refers to actions of black cattle that choose to ignore the righteous knowledge of God obtained at creation.

66. Robbins, *Tapestry of Early Christian Discourse*, 97. Recitation can be defined as "the presentation of speech or narrative or both, either from oral or writ-

3. Animal Apocalypse: A Metaphorical Reading 111

Animal Apocalypse largely recites and reconfigures, as all of the scriptural accounts to which it refers are compressed and allegorized. It also recontextualizes biblical accounts with themes in mind. This is not to suggest that biblical accounts are the only intertexts present. The use of Scripture underscores the metaphor GOD IS THE LORD OF THE SHEEP, in which the sheep follow and the Lord leads. It also emphasizes that leading the sheep is necessary.

As mentioned, Jacob is the first snow-white sheep. From Jacob, twelve more sheep emerge (89.13). The one sheep (Joseph) that was sold by the eleven sheep (Joseph's brothers) later becomes a ram who pastures the other eleven sheep that later multiply among wolves in Egypt. Nickelsburg, following Tiller, suggests that the use of sheep and predators is perhaps to reflect issues of purity and impurity or cleanliness and uncleanliness. Tiller states that the modifier, "snow-white," indicates purity, yet this is attributed to particular individuals only (e.g., Jacob, 1 En. 89.12) and not to the others (e.g., Moses, 1 En. 89.16) nor to the collective (e.g., the twelve sheep, 1 En. 89.13–14). Moreover, Leviticus to Judges seems to be of little interest to the Animal Apocalypse.[67] It is likely that the color white is a metaphorical characteristic of cattle and it is being used here for Jacob to signify the transition from cattle to sheep. It creates a trail of positive figures, tracing the biblical accounts from Gen 2 to 2 Kings.[68]

---

ten tradition, in words identical to or different from those the person has received" (Robbins, *Tapestry of Early Christian Discourse*, 103). Recitations occur in six possible forms within a given text: as *chreia*, with omissions, with different words, and then with narrative words and sayings from biblical text, paraphrase, and summary (Robbins, *Tapestry of Early Christian Discourse*, 103–7). Recontextualization differs from recitation in that it recites "without mentioning that the words 'stand written' anywhere else." It utilizes words from another text in a new context without suggesting the words it uses are from elsewhere (Robbins, *Tapestry of Early Christian Discourse*, 107). Robbin uses an example from 1 Pet 2:3: "Like newborn babes, long for the pure spiritual milk, that by it you may grow up to salvation; for you have *tasted the kindness of the Lord*." The italicized words are from Ps 34:8, which are now used in a different context. Reconfiguration refers to "the restructuring of an antecedent tradition."

67. Tiller, *Commentary*, 299. Martha Himmelfarb states, "The Animal Apocalypse … says nothing at all that could be construed as relevant to purity laws and hardly mentions priests." See Martha Himmelfarb, *Between Temple and Torah* (Tübingen: Mohr Siebeck, 2013), 89.

68. And possibly Ezra-Nehemiah (Nickelsburg, *1 Enoch 1*, 358–59).

112   Apocalyptic Sheep and Goats in Matthew and 1 Enoch

There are several terms used for sheep throughout the Hebrew Bible. Some are used more than others. These include the collective term צאן (e.g., Gen 4:2), which technically means flock of small ruminants, sheep or goats. The Hebrew terms כשב (e.g., Gen 30:32–33; Lev 22:19), כבש (e.g., Exod 12:5; Lev 9:3), and כר (e.g., Deut 32:14; 1 Sam 15:9) are often used to denote sheep and lambs. The Septuagint translations are not consistent. The Greek πρόβατον often renders צאן, but it is also equated with the three above-mentioned Hebrew terms for sheep and lambs. Other LXX translations include ἀρήν and ἀμνός. The Hebrew term איל, though at times כר is also used, is rendered in English as "ram" since it may refer to a male lamb or pasture.[69] The LXX translates the Hebrew as κριός. Aside from the Hebrew terms, their Greek translations are corroborated within the surviving Greek versions of the Animal Apocalypse, all with the exception of ἀμνός.[70] As noted at the outset, in Aramaic fragments of the Animal Apocalypse we find the terms דבר, אמר, and ען: Aramaic דבר (Greek κριός) is the equivalent of Hebrew כר, as both can mean "pasture" and "ram," while Aramaic אמר and ען are the usual expressions for sheep in the allegory.

The Hebrew Bible provides us with the basic information to conceptualize sheep in their natural context, that is, a conceptual framework. From Jacob's dealings with Laban, we understand that a shepherd does not necessarily mean the actual owner of the sheep, though the shepherd may be related to the owner, often one of the owner's children, as exemplified in the cases of Rachel, the daughter of Laban (Gen 29), and David, the son of Jesse (1 Sam 17). Both were shepherds of their fathers' sheep. The duties of the shepherd include pasturing the sheep, feeding and watering them, and protecting the flock from wild animals, such as lions and bears (cf. Ezek 34:11–31). In addition to owners and shepherds, we also have sheep breeders (Amos 1:1; 2 Kgs 3:4) that may have raised sheep as a commodity, as they were of great value in those days. They were a source of both food and clothing (cf. Job 31:20; Prov 27:26). Color was of great cultural importance when attaching value to sheep. White sheep were preferable, while spotted and speckled or black sheep were undesirable (e.g., Gen 30:32–42). Sheep provided a form of sacrifice for one's well-being, freewill, or burnt and sin offerings (e.g., Lev 1:10; 4:32–35; 22:27). In addition to sacrificial offerings, lambs were also used to mend broken relationships,

---

69. BDB, 499.

70. For references to the relevant terms for sheep in the Animal Apocalypse, see Tiller, *Commentary*, 275.

3. Animal Apocalypse: A Metaphorical Reading 113

maintain existing relationships (cf. 2 Kgs 3:4), and to create new ones, as was the case with Abraham and Abimelech (Gen 21:27–34). Thus it seems that the animal sheep is an important means for Israel to uphold its relationship with both neighbors and God.

With the above, we have laid out a conceptual framework for sheep from Scripture. Thus, it is not surprising that sheep are readily used as a metaphor, for the animal figures in every aspect of life: from consummation, bargaining, cultic practices, to cultural behaviors. It is also not surprising that Israel's relationship with God is expressed through the sheep metaphor on more than one level of abstraction. Numerous examples from the Hebrew Bible illustrate the use of the sheep as a metaphor for Israel in times of judgment (e.g., 2 Sam 24:17; Ps 44; Jer 51:40), distress (e.g., Ezek 34), and hope (Ps 78:52; Mic 5:8). What's more, animals share much with humans.[71] The Animal Apocalypse selectively utilizes some of these characteristics of sheep to blend its own conceptual frames to express its metaphorical depictions of Israel and create its narrative.

3.5.1. Leading Israel: Jacob to Moses

First Enoch 89.14 is where the Animal Apocalypse begins to speak extensively of sheep.

> And the *ram* led forth the eleven sheep to dwell with it and to pasture with it among the wolves. And they multiplied and became many flocks of sheep.[72]

In this section of the Animal Apocalypse, biblical stories are retold and compressed immensely to highlight the fact that God himself leads Israel in the beginning. In comparison with the Aramaic text at Qumran, scholars point out that the Ethiopic text of the passage above contains an error

---

71. Porter considers animal and human souls to be of the same kind (Gen 1:20–21; cf. 2:7). They observe the Sabbath (Exod 20:10; Deut 5:14), were shipmates with Noah in the ark, and were party along with Noah to God's covenant (Gen 9:9–10). He also points out that Lev 20 places equal blame on man and animal in cases of unnatural union between the two (20:15–16) (Porter, *Metaphors and Monsters*, 47–48).

72. See also Nickelsburg, *1 Enoch 1*, 365; Tiller, *Commentary*, 270. For the Ethiopic and Aramaic text, see Tiller, *Commentary*, 168–69. See also Florentino Garcia Martinez and Eibert J. C. Tigchelaar, *The Dead Sea Scrolls: Study Edition* (Grand Rapids: Eerdmans, 1997), 1:423, 427.

114   Apocalyptic Sheep and Goats in Matthew and 1 Enoch

that may stem from a Greek copy of the Animal Apocalypse. The Ethiopic text uses *Lord* instead of *ram*, which is what we find in the Aramaic (4QEn^d ar and 4QEn^e ar). Scholars surmise that either the Greek term χύριος (Lord) may have been mistaken for χρίος (ram) by the Ethiopic translator or that a scribal misspelling by the Greek text caused the Ethiopic interpreter to translate it as Lord.[73] The Greek χρίος would fall in line with the Aramaic דכר (ram) from the two extant texts found in Qumran. Both types of errors are possible and may have easily been overlooked since references are made shortly thereafter to "their Lord" in 89.15, which denotes the "Lord of the sheep," who descends to earth, as it were, for the first time in 89.16. The idea that the original was written in Aramaic adds weight to the choice of utilizing the term *ram* instead of *Lord*.[74] In that case, as seen in the above passage, the ram points to Joseph as one of the twelve sheep.

Along with 89.13, the above passage compresses a large amount of material that tells of the selling of Joseph into slavery and culminates in the arrival of Jacob and his entire household in Egypt (Gen 37:12–46:4). The only explicit reference to these events in the Animal Apocalypse is in two sentences that relate that Joseph led the family to Egypt, which, according to Joseph in Genesis, is technically all God's doing. Joseph states,

> And now do not be distressed, or angry with yourselves, because you sold me here; for God sent me before you to preserve life.... God sent me before you to preserve for you *a remnant on earth*, and to keep alive for you many survivors. So it was not you who sent me here, but God (Gen 45:5–8).[75]

It seems likely that the Ethiopic text erred deliberately. In other words, the translation "Lord" instead of "ram" may not be a mistake but rather a new version of the old.[76] The translator of this text not only translates but

---

73. The Greek translation does not exist for this particular section. The Ethiopic term used, *wa'egzi'*, means Lord. For the Ethiopic text and translation, see Tiller, *Commentary*.

74. See translations by James H. Charlesworth (*OTP*, 1:65).

75. Translations of the Revised Standard Version will be used unless my own translations of the Hebrew text differ substantially.

76. Knibb, "Book of Enoch or Books of Enoch?," 22. Knibb questions whether the differences between the Ethiopic and Aramaic texts are completely due to "the activity of an editor" or whether some if not most of the differences "represent a new edition." Knibb points toward the evolution of the subsequent Greek and Ethiopic translations that contain different literary and historical contexts from the original.

3. Animal Apocalypse: A Metaphorical Reading

also interprets in accord with scriptural accounts. This is clear when we compare Ethiopic translations with the Greek and Aramaic versions (e.g., 89.44–45).[77] Nonetheless, the Animal Apocalypse derives from the Bible story the fact that the Lord of the sheep leads the sheep, or literally, the Lord leads Israel.

The emphasis upon the Lord leading the sheep is at the expense of compressing the large amount of material found in Scriptures. That the Lord himself leads is made more realistic when it is said that the Lord of the sheep "descended from a lofty chamber at the voice of the sheep" (1 En. 89.16). For example,

> And the Lord of the sheep went with them, leading them, and all his sheep followed him. And his face was dazzling and glorious and fearful to look at. (1 En. 89.22)

The above passage alludes to Exod 13:17–22:

> When Pharaoh let the people go, God did not lead them by way of the land of the Philistines.... So God led the people by the roundabout way of the wilderness toward the Red Sea.... The Lord went in front of them in a pillar of cloud by day, to lead them along the way, and in a pillar of fire by night, to give them light, so that they traveled by day and by night.

The psalms of Israel often recall this imagery (e.g., Ps 77:20; 78:52). Yet in the Animal Apocalypse, the spectacular and elaborate details of the exodus are excluded. The theophany of the Lord in the pillar of cloud and fire are not described in the way seen in Enoch's account with the Great Glory (1 En. 14.8–25), which starts with Enoch seeing a cloud. Notable is that everything here in this section (1 En. 89.22–23) is toned down to something less than spectacular, which makes the task of leading more pronounced and the experience of the Lord of the sheep more real. Yet the Israelites see the face of the Lord as dazzling and fearful (1 En. 89.22, 30). Many more examples of scriptural stories and narratives are being compressed in order to highlight the Lord leading Israel.

The image of the Lord leading Israel to a place where they may once again multiply under the Lord's protection is an important feature as well,

---

77. In 89.44–45, what is described in the Aramaic and the Greek as "the ram" losing its "way," the Ethiopic clearly interprets from Scripture in 1 Sam 15 when it translates "the sheep that left its glory," while also translating out of its metaphorical context.

for this requires Israel to follow specific directives from God. The passage 1 En. 89.28 states:

> But the sheep departed from that water and went out to a desert, where there was no water or grass, and they began to open their eyes and see. And I saw <until> the Lord of the sheep was pasturing them and giving them water and grass, and that sheep was going and leading them.

This passage marks an important part of what the author of the Animal Apocalypse retains from the biblical narratives as Israel is led through the wilderness of Shur to Sinai (Exod 15:22–19:25). From 1 En. 98.28–36, the narrative takes a short but significant break to define how the Lord of the sheep leads Israel. It is at this point of the Animal Apocalypse that the themes of sight and blindness come to the fore, adding to the characteristics of the sheep metaphor. It strongly implies a purpose for the Lord of the sheep, for leading in the Animal Apocalypse enables others to attain sight by showing the right path and guiding them along. In retrospect, knowing the path and acknowledging the one leading is metaphorically expressed in terms of sight or "open eyes."

In contrast to some other images of God as shepherd that we find in other biblical accounts, in the Animal Apocalypse God does not lead as a shepherd but rather as the owner or "the Lord of the sheep." In the Animal Apocalypse, God is not a shepherd per se; in other words, he does not perform shepherd-like duties. In fact, the term shepherd is seen in a negative light. Culturally, the Lord of the sheep and the shepherd are two quite different roles. The shepherd is employed by the owner. At this point of the allegory, God as an owner plays a direct role in leading. Indeed, at times, the leading roles are given to another sheep from among the flock. As we will see, prophets, judges, and kings become the head sheep and rams that participate in leading Israel. These sheep are not to be thought of as shepherds either, but rather, to use another metaphorical expression, as leaders of the pack with whom God communicates directly. The owner leading says much about the perceived relationship with God. That the owner leads and pastures the sheep himself illuminates the lasting intimacy for the sheep that may be taken for granted if God is seen as a temporary employer, like a shepherd.

The Animal Apocalypse also highlights the fact that the sheep failed to follow. The following alludes to Exod 32 when Moses goes up the mountain again.

3. Animal Apocalypse: A Metaphorical Reading   117

And again that sheep that led them went up to the summit of that rock, and the sheep began to be blinded and to stray from the path that it had shown them, but the sheep [Moses] did not know about these things. (1 En. 89.32)

In Gen 32, Moses leaves Israel to Aaron (Exod 32:1–6; 21–25) as he goes up the mountain again. The Lord informs Moses, who up until now did not know that Israel has "acted corruptly" (Exod 32:7, שחת) in a wicked sense.[78] The Septuagint translates this as having "acted unlawfully" (Exod 32:7 LXX, ἀνομέω). In the following verse (Exod 32:8), the Lord explains to Moses:

סרו מהר מן־הדרך אשר צויתם עשו להם עגל מסכה וישתחוו־לו ויזבחו־לו ויאמרו
אלה אלהיך ישראל אשר העלוך מארץ מצרים

They have been quick to turn aside from the way that I commanded them; they have made for themselves an image of a calf, and have worshiped it and sacrificed to it, and said, "These are your gods, O Israel, who brought you up out of the land of Egypt!"

The last quotation stems from previous verses, which describe Aaron collecting gold from Israel and forming it into a mold or image (Exod 32:4, מסכה), about which the people say, "These are our gods, O Israel, who brought you up out of the land of Egypt!" In later verses, when Moses comes down from Mount Sinai, he asks Aaron, "What did this people do to you that you have brought so great a sin upon them?" (Exod 32:21). Aaron responds, "Do not let the anger of my Lord burn hot, for you yourself know the people have 'an inherent evil'" (Exod 32:22, ברע). The Septuagint translates this inherent evil as violence (Gen 32:22 LXX, τὸ ὄρμημα). Thus, in this recounting of the incident in Exodus, the metaphorical expressions of blindness and straying away from the path are defined specifically in terms of not knowing God and violence respectively. One cannot help but recall the symbolism of the color black attributed to Cain in 1 En. 85.3–10. As such, leading becomes all the more important, for an inherent evil will cause Israel to be unrighteous and violent. As already noted, leading enables others to see, and this also guards them against these unwanted traits.

---

78. *HALOT*, s.v. "שחת."

3.5.2. Leading Israel: Judges to Kings

When Israel crosses the Jordan after Moses dies, leaders among the sheep become a crucial theme. Although leaders may help in fostering sight, they themselves are also susceptible to the folly of being blind. The accounts of the judges are severely condensed in terms of sight and how the Lord of the sheep begins to raise up rams. The biblical accounts of Samuel and Saul are condensed to the point of only highlighting their turns at leading.

> [41]And sometimes their eyes were opened, and sometimes they were blinded, until another sheep arose and led them and brought them all back, and their eyes were opened. [42]And the dogs began to devour the sheep, and the wild boars and the foxes were devouring them, until the Lord of the sheep raised up a ram from among the sheep, which led them. (1 En. 89.41–42)

Likewise, the Animal Apocalypse is supported in this focus by the accounts of David and Solomon:

> [44]And the sheep whose eyes were open saw the ram among the sheep until it forsook its path and began to walk where there was no path. [45]And the Lord of the sheep sent this sheep to another sheep to appoint it to be ram, to rule the sheep instead of the ram that had forsaken its way. [46]And it went to it and spoke with it secretly, alone, and appointed it to be ram and ruler and leader of the sheep. And during all these things, the dogs were oppressing the sheep. (1 En. 89.44–46)

As David dies, Solomon takes over:

> And that ram begat many sheep, and it fell asleep. And a little sheep became ram instead of it, and it became ruler and leader of those sheep. (1 En. 89.48b)

It becomes evident that leading not only entails keeping the sheep on the right path but also protecting the sheep from being slaughtered or eaten by predators. This suggests that the very existence of the sheep has some purposeful significance (1 En. 89.42, 43, 46, 49, 55–58).

3. Animal Apocalypse: A Metaphorical Reading 119

3.5.3. Leading Israel: Rulers of Nations to the Future White Bull

It is only when blindness increases, and the house of the Lord is abandoned, that the Lord abdicates his post of direct leadership of Israel.

> [54]After that I saw when they abandoned the house of the Lord and his tower, they went astray in everything, and their eyes were blinded. And I saw that the Lord of the sheep worked much slaughter on them in their pastures, <because> those sheep invited that slaughter and betrayed his place. [55]And he abandoned them into the hands of the lions and the leopards and the wolves and the hyenas and into the hands of the foxes and to all the beasts; and those wild beasts began to tear those sheep in pieces. (1 En. 89.54–55)

At this point, the Lord appoints seventy shepherds to lead Israel:

> And he summoned seventy shepherds, and he left those sheep to them, that they might pasture them. And he said to the shepherds and their subordinates, "Every one of you from now on shall pasture the sheep, and everything that I command you, do." (1 En. 89.59)

The above passage marks a new *modus operandi* in which the Lord assumes an indirect role in leading the sheep. It is generally understood that the shepherd, being a human figure, is a metaphor for angels who become gentile rulers. The introduction of a shepherd tends to relieve the owner of some of the duties of leadership, particularly that of pasturing. The Lord of the sheep gives the responsibility of pasturing the sheep to the shepherds with the condition that they follow his commands. These responsibilities of the shepherds continue until the last judgment. First Enoch 89.60–61 states,

> [60]'I am handing them over to you duly numbered, and I will tell you which of them are to be destroyed. Destroy them.' And he handed those sheep over to them. [61]And another one he summoned and said to him, "Observe and see everything that the shepherds do against these sheep, for they will destroy more of them than I have commanded them."

A subtext here suggests that the appointment of overseer becomes in part a punishment, as it were, for the sheep. It also reflects the sovereignty of God over the earth to do as he pleases (cf. Jer 27:5–7). However, the appointment of another to supervise the shepherds' duties suggests a concern not

120 Apocalyptic Sheep and Goats in Matthew and 1 Enoch

only that the shepherds will not follow God's commands, which, indeed, they ultimately do not (e.g., 1 En. 89.65, 69, 74; 90.17, 23, 25), but also the possibility that the sheep will disappear altogether (cf. 1 En. 90.4) as a result of the shepherds not obeying orders. Whereas the Israelite rulers fought off the predators, these appointed rulers hand the sheep over to them (1 En. 89.65, 68, 74; cf. 90.1–4).

The future scenarios (90.6–38) present interesting images on the theme of leadership. For instance, lambs begin to open their eyes and a ram (Judas Maccabeus) takes the lead in fighting off the predators again (1 En. 90.6–19), just as it was in the days when the Lord of the sheep was directly in charge. At the very end of this situation, the sheep lead the predators: "And all the animals upon the earth and all the birds of heaven were falling down and worshiping those sheep and making petition to them and obeying them in every word" (1 En. 90.30–33). Only then does a white bull emerge as a leader: "And I saw until all their species were changed, and they all became white cattle. And the first one became <leader> among them (and that <leader> was a large animal), and there were large black horns on its head" (1 En. 90.37–38).[79]

3.5.4. Conceptual Metaphors

Below is a metaphorical projection of how four of the metaphors listed in chart 1 above relate, with the addition of the metaphor, ISRAELITE LEADER IS RAM/SHEEP.

Generic Space:	Input Space 1: Biblical Account	Input Space 2: Owning Sheep	Blend: Animal Apocalypse
Owner of Property			
Agent 1: Owner	God	Lord of the Sheep	GOD IS THE LORD OF THE SHEEP
	*elects Israel	*owns the sheep	*elects sheep
		*instructs the shepherd regarding the sheep	*commands the shepherd regarding the sheep
	*leads/instructs Israel	*guides the sheep to a pasture	*leads/instructs sheep

---

79. Nickelsburg, *1 Enoch 1*, 402.

3. Animal Apocalypse: A Metaphorical Reading — 121

Agent 2: Property	Israel and Judah	Sheep	ISRAEL IS SHEEP
	*Genesis to 2 Kings; Ezra-Nehemiah?		
	*obey God's commands	*follow the path	*Israel follows path
	*worship idols, transgress, etc.	*go astray	*Israel goes astray
	*prophets, judges, kings lead Israel and Judah	*dominant sheep/ ram of the flock	*prophets, judges, kings of Israel pasture the sheep
Agent 3: Intermediary 1	Inner Leaders (prophets, judges, kings)	Ram or Sheep	ISRAELITE LEADER IS RAM/SHEEP
	*obey God's commands	*follows instructions	*follows commands from the Lord of the sheep
	*lead Israel	*goes before the sheep	*leads the flock
Agent 4: Intermediary 2	Gentile Rulers	Shepherd	ANGELS/GENTILE RULERS ARE SHEPHERDS
	*summoned by God	*follows instructions from the Lord of the sheep	*summoned by the Lord of the sheep
	*punish/persecute Israel	*hands over for slaughter	*slaughter/persecute the sheep
	*keep Israel	*pastures the sheep	*keep the sheep
Agent 5: External Threat	Gentile	Predator	GENTILE IS PREDATOR
	*oppresses, persecutes	*eats and slaughters the sheep	*persecutes the sheep

In summary, biblical accounts are prevalent in apocalyptic literature. In the Animal Apocalypse, Scripture substantiates God directly leading Israel from the time of Jacob all the way to the last kings of the Israelite monarchy. At the same time, it highlights the significance of leading Israel in such a way that it can maintain the path. Equally significant is that Israel must follow. The need to emphasize this is not the result of a lack of leaders, but because without a leader, an innate evil will cause Israel to go blind and astray with the result that predators will slaughter the sheep. Thus, leading is a necessity. The metaphors in the above chart are linked together through God's relationship as owner of Israel as property. This relationship is taken from the history of Israel itself, as depicted in Genesis to 2 Kings and Ezra-Nehemiah, from oral traditions, and from the present time of the Animal Apocalypse. From the chart, it is clear that obedience to God's commands and instructions dominates the second half of the allegory, whether it concerns the sheep or the shepherd that is to follow them. Such commands and instructions are cultural and can be understood only when viewed that way.

3.6. Torah: Path of the Sheep

In this second part in the study of the Animal Apocalypse, I examine the predominant cultural features of the animal metaphors.[80] I will show that the sheep metaphor embodies a divine purpose for the salvation of humanity and hence represents creation in the Animal Apocalypse. Scholars rightly point out the lack of explicit reference to the torah, or the covenant, in the Animal Apocalypse even though the allegory in 1 En. 28–40 describes the events in Exod 15–40. This lack of mention causes Nickelsburg to suggest that the torah is insignificant to the author(s) of the Animal Apocalypse.[81] Andreas Bedenbender, on the other hand, has posited that the writer(s) may have been unaware of or might have rejected the covenant at Sinai outright.[82] In making a comparison to the book of Daniel, Gabriele Boccaccini postulates that this absence of the Mosaic torah becomes one of the important characteristics that differentiated Enochic Judaism from Zadokite Judaism.[83] For him, its omission

---

80. Robbins, *Tapestry of Early Christian Discourse*, 110. In examining cultural intertextures within texts, Robbins refers to *references* and *echoes*. References are described by Robbins as "the occurrence of a word, phrase or clause that refers to a personage or tradition known to people in a culture." Echoes are evident "when a word or phrase evokes, or potentially evokes, a cultural tradition." These are certainly debatable terms if not interchangeable. However, I will simply refer to such occurrences as allusions.

81. Nickelsburg, *1 Enoch 1*, 50.

82. Bedenbender, "Place of the Torah," 65, 74–75.

83. Gabriele Boccaccini, *Beyond the Essene Hypothesis: The Parting of the Ways*

3. Animal Apocalypse: A Metaphorical Reading   123

by Enochian scribes, as it were, points to a decisive ideological difference between the two groups.[84]

It is outside the scope of this study to argue against such compartmentalization. Suffice it to say that I subscribe to the idea that such characterizations may be oversimplifications of something that was quite possibly more fluid and complex.[85] Indeed, 1 Enoch lacks explicit paral-

---

between Qumran and Enochic Judaism (Grand Rapids: Eerdmans, 1998); see also Boccaccini, *Roots of Rabbinic Judaism: An Intellectual History, from Ezekiel to Daniel* (Grand Rapids: Eerdmans, 2002). Boccaccini states, "In spite of any similarities, however, a fundamental difference makes Daniel representative of a different party. While sharing the same apocalyptic worldview as Dream Visions, Daniel opposes the Enochic doctrine of evil and strenuously defends the tenets of Zadokite Judaism: the Mosaic torah and the legitimacy of the second temple" (Boccaccini, *Beyond the Essene Hypothesis*, 83). Zadokite Judaism is "a society that unceasingly and persistently defined the boundaries of cosmic and societal structure; rules and regulations were enforced to restrict or control interaction and avoid trespassing" (Boccaccini, *Roots of Rabbinic Judaism*, 73). It is a society of a priestly order that sets the boundaries of cosmic and societal structure. Such society has the priest at the top of a hierarchical structure: high priests of the Zadokite line, priests of the Aaronite line, Levites, male Jews, female Jews, gentiles, clean and unclean animals. The world is God's orderly and perfect creation. For Boccaccini, "There is no room in the Zadokite worldview for extreme measures that would lead to the end of times and a new creation" (Boccaccini, *Roots of Rabbinic Judaism*, 76). What stands in opposition to this worldview and ideology was Enochic Judaism, which sees the fallen angels as the ultimate cause for the spread of evil and impurity on earth. From the Book of the Watchers, Boccaccini states that "despite God's reaction and the subsequent Flood, the divine order of creation was not restored. The cosmos did not return to what it was" (Boccaccini, *Roots of Rabbinic Judaism*, 90–91). According to Boccaccini, the Enochians see humans as powerless against evil, and only God's intervention can save it. Bedenbender supports Boccaccini's hypothesis entirely (Bedenbender, "Place of the Torah," 67–74).

84. Boccaccini actually lays out three groups of distinctive Judaisms. The third group is Sapiential Judaism, which is associated with the authors responsible for wisdom writings, that is, Proverbs, Job, Jonah, and Qoheleth. Others in the past have also hypothesized about the attribution of Second Temple ideology and tradition and their writings to ancient Jewish groups. For a brief overview, see James C. VanderKam, "Mapping Second Temple Judaism," in Boccaccini and Collins, *The Early Enoch Literature*, 1–20.

85. Matthias Henze, "Enoch's Dream Visions and the Visions of Daniel Reexamined," in Boccaccini, *Enoch and Qumran Origins*, 17–22. In positing the fluid nature of the relationship between Enochic and Danielic texts, Henze states, "The nature of the material suggests that we should not think of apocalyptic groups of the second century BCE in terms of continuous and independent strands of traditions that are ultimately

124 Apocalyptic Sheep and Goats in Matthew and 1 Enoch

lels to specific laws and commandments. However, does the absence of explicit reference suggest a unique ideology, or does it mean the ignorance or rejection of the covenant at Sinai or the torah? In her review of Boccaccini's *Essene Hypothesis*, Hindy Najman concedes, "Indeed, the claim that Enochians 'ignored' the torah of Enoch's 'rival Moses' is supported only by an argument from silence: 1 Enoch's omission of the Mosaic covenant and the gift of torah. It is unclear what such omissions prove, especially since Boccaccini does not explain which traditions and laws were then thought to compromise Mosaic torah."[86] I echo this sentiment and suggest that conclusions should not be drawn from the absence of particular elements of a biblical story when we are dealing with an allegorical presentation of that story—especially when the biblical version is deliberately compressed. It is more reasonable to extend the benefit of the doubt to the allegorist's creative use of Scripture. I would like to begin with what is actually explicit.

One wonders why the Animal Apocalypse allots more space to the recounting of Israel's time in the desert than most other biblical accounts. It rivals the Noachian stories of the flood. Together with the narratives from Egypt, the Animal Apocalypse spends more time recounting events involving Moses than any other biblical figure. The section that devotes the greatest amount of attention to Moses can be found in 1 En. 89.28–36. As mentioned above, the narrative pauses significantly to define how the Lord of the sheep leads Israel in 1 En. 89.28–36, which is the section that corresponds with Exod 15–40.

In 1 En. 89.28–36, Moses's two-fold ascension of the mountain and the explicit blindness of Israel to the commands given to Moses, as well as allusions to Genesis and Exodus, are especially telling. While the Animal Apocalypse generally follows the biblical account, it does more than simply reference the Bible story in this section. In what follows, I intend to show that the goal of the allegorist in this particular section was not so much to relate sequences of biblical accounts as it was to highlight the torah, that is, the instructions and commandments stipulated within the Pentateuch. If this can be accepted as a reasonable

---

opposed to one another. After all, apocalyptic literature is characterized by a high degree of fluctuation and translatability, with later apocalypses constantly recycling language, imagery, and entire literary genres found in earlier material."

86. Hindy Najman, review of *Beyond the Essene Hypothesis*, by G. Boccaccini, *Association for Jewish Studies Review* 26 (2002): 352–54.

3. Animal Apocalypse: A Metaphorical Reading 125

possibility, then our understanding of the sheep metaphor and related expressions in the Animal Apocalypse exemplify adherence to the torah. This may explain the metaphorical expressions of open eyes and being blinded. It may also clarify phrases such as following or straying from the path that are used throughout the allegory. Later, we will define this, and its understanding will relate with other animal metaphors that turn up in the Animal Apocalypse.

We begin with the 1 En. 89.28–36 passage:[87]

> [28a]But the sheep departed from that water and went out to a desert, where there was no water or grass, and they began to open their eyes and see. [b]And I saw <until> the Lord of the sheep was pasturing them and giving them water and grass,
> [c]and that sheep was going and leading them. [29a]That sheep went up to the summit of a high rock, [b]and the Lord of the sheep sent it to them. [30a]And after that, I saw the Lord of the sheep who stood before them, [b]and his appearance was majestic and fearful and mighty, and all those sheep saw him and were afraid before him. [31a]And all of them were afraid and trembling because of him, [b]and they were crying out after that sheep with the other sheep that was in their midst, "We cannot stand before our Lord or look at him." [32a]And, again, that sheep that led them went up to the summit of the rock, the one towering high, [b]and the sheep began to be blinded and to stray from the path that it had shown them, [c]but the sheep did not know about these things. [33]And the Lord of the sheep was filled with great wrath against them, and that sheep discovered it and went down from the summit of that rock and came to the sheep and found most of them blinded and straying. [34]And when they saw it, they were afraid and trembled before it, and wished to return to their folds. [35]And that sheep took other sheep with it and went against those sheep that had strayed and began to slaughter them, and the sheep were afraid of it. And that sheep returned all the straying flock to their folds. [36]And I saw in this vision, until that sheep became a man and built a house for the Lord of the sheep and made all the sheep stand in that house.[88]

---

87. Here I have grouped the passage for convenience of reference, as I get into the exegesis later below.

88. Other than slight changes to the translation of the Aramaic, this translation is taken largely from Nickelsburg, *1 Enoch 1*, 366. Here I have organized the passage in the way I wish them to be read. I will show why in the analysis that follows.

126 Apocalyptic Sheep and Goats in Matthew and 1 Enoch

Scholars differ in how they allocate the above passage to a structural unit. Tiller unifies this passage in a unit that extends to 89.36, while Nickelsburg ends it at 89.35.[89] Recently, Olson extended the unit to 89.40.[90]

Nickelsburg correctly sees this section (89.28–35) as depicting Israel's journey to Sinai and its ensuing events but does not see how it connects to 89.36. Indeed, 89.36 switches topic, for it begins to speak of "the house" as a metaphor for the tabernacle or a dwelling place.[91] It wanders even further away in 89.37–40 as it narrates the detour, the death of Moses, and eventually the crossing of the Jordan. However, I would like to show below that 89.36 actually connects thematically to 89.28, which would render Tiller's analysis more fitting. As Tiller points out, 89.28–36 summarizes the Sinai narrative in Exod 15–40. He links 89.36 with 89.28–35 by suggesting that the house in 89.36 replaces the sheepfolds in 89.28–35. I agree with him on that point, but he does not share his opinion on why this detail from the biblical accounts is important enough to be included in the Animal Apocalypse.

Despite the fact that the Aramaic is too fragmented to allow definitive conclusions, we can still ascertain the emphasis of certain significant features in the text.[92] Verses 28a–b open with metaphorical themes of sight and pasturing, utilizing metaphors of open eyes (89.28b, ועיניהון התפתחו)

---

89. Nickelsburg, 1 Enoch 1, 379–81; Tiller, Commentary, 291–97.

90. Olson, New Reading, 173–77. "[37]And I saw until that sheep that had met that sheep that had led them fell asleep. And I saw until all the large sheep perished, and little ones arose in their place, and they came to a pasture and approached a river of water. [38]And that sheep that had led them, that had become a man, was separated from them and fell asleep, and all the sheep searched for him and cried bitterly because of him. [39]And I saw until they ceased crying for that sheep and crossed that stream of water, and two sheep arose that led them instead of those that had fallen asleep; and they led them. [40]And I saw the sheep until they were entering a good place and a pleasant and glorious land. And I saw those sheep until they were satisfied, and that house was in their midst in the pleasant land." Translation taken from Nickelsburg, 1 Enoch 1, 366.

91. Nickelsburg, 1 Enoch 1, 379, 381. Tiller sees it as the tabernacle or the entire desert camp (Tiller, Commentary, 297). For Tiller, the metaphor is significant, as the house continues to be used to refer to the city of Jerusalem (Tiller, Commentary, 312–13). Olson and I agree with Tiller (Olson, New Reading, 59).

92. First Enoch 89.28–35 is extant in the Aramaic in three fragments found in Qumran: Frag. 5 col. III (4Q205 2 III), Frag. 2 col. II (4Q206 5 III; 4Q204 4), and Frag. 4 (4Q205 2 II). However, a little over 50 percent of the text is reconstructed from the Ethiopic. See Milik, Books of Enoch, 41.

3. Animal Apocalypse: A Metaphorical Reading 127

and feeding with water and grass.[93] Nickelsburg believes that this passage alludes to Exod 15:22–26. He states,

> God had opened the eyes of the sheep (i.e., given them revelation) already at Marah (89.28), where according to Exod 15:25–26 God had made a statute and ordinance with Israel and promised not to punish them if they "listened to his commandments and observed his statutes."[94]

Nickelsburg's assumptions might be too restrictive. He implies that the Animal Apocalypse follows the biblical order and that 1 En. 89.28a–b mentions only the commandments in Marah. What follows in 1 En. 89.29–35, according to Nickelsburg, focuses only on the theophany of God and Israel's fearful reaction to God's anger at Israel's apostasy. The commandments and instructions at Sinai are then ignored. However, the passage in Exod 15:25–26 may only account for the need for water and grass, but Israel was also in need of water in Rephidim (Exod 17:1) where they fought Amalek. Moreover, the saying concerning open eyes in 89.28a–b does not seem to apply to Exod 15:25–26, since the people are complaining there about the lack of water as they also do in Rephidim. Indeed, Moses in Exod 15:25–26 advises Israel to follow the commandments and keep the statutes, for God has promised to heal them on this condition. But acts of healing are not evident in the allegory. Significant is the fact that the same conditional statement is said to Israel as they reach Mount Sinai, except the promise is on terms of election: to be a priestly kingdom and a holy nation. This notion of election is an important theme in the Animal Apocalypse as Enoch cries out for a remnant.[95] Thus, it seems more likely that by the description of open eyes and pasturing, 1 En. 89.28a–b encapsulates events including Mount Sinai in the form of a summary that highlights the fact that the Israelites are gathered and will open their eyes to all of the commandments and instructions God will reveal to them as sheep. This is to

---

93. On the scholarly discussion of the "open eyes," see James C. VanderKam, "Open and Closed Eyes in the Animal Apocalypse (1 Enoch 85–90)," in *The Idea of Biblical Interpretation: Essays in Honor of James L. Kugel*, ed. Hindy Najman and Judith H. Newman (Leiden: Brill, 2004), 279–92.

94. Nickelsburg, *1 Enoch 1*, 379; Nickelsburg, "Enochic Wisdom and Its Relationship to the Mosaic Torah," in Boccaccini and Collins, *The Early Enoch Literature*, 83.

95. I hope to show below that the Animal Apocalypse gives a sapiential twist to this notion of election in Deuteronomy.

128   Apocalyptic Sheep and Goats in Matthew and 1 Enoch

say, it introduces and foreshadows what is to follow in 89.28c–35d, which includes the giving of the torah.[96]

After 89.28a–b above, 89.28c–29a makes reference to Moses leading the sheep and going up to the summit of the rock, the one towering high (89.29a, סלק לראש כף חד ראם). An interesting phrase is found in 89.29b, "and the Lord of the sheep sent *it* to them." This phrase did not survive in the Aramaic. Daniel Olson notes that the various Ethiopic versions offer three possible meanings of the pronoun *it* or *him*: Moses, law, or tablets.[97] All of them seem good possibilities. Whether *it* refers to one or other of these, the context of the phrase would indicate that all of these would metaphorically point toward God's commands and instructions in the torah. Verse 30 stresses the motif of sight as the sheep see the Lord (89.30b, "and his appearance was strong and great and fearful," וחזיה תקיף ורב ודחיל). Verse 31a ends with the sheep trembling and afraid (89.31a, וכולהון הווא דחלין ורעדין). This fear equates to their reverence and acknowledgment of the Lord of the sheep as expressed in their statement, "We are not able to stand before [the owner]" (89.31b, [לא יכלין אנחנא למקם למקבל [מריא). The fear of YHWH reflects wisdom (Sir 1:27a). It may also equate with the love for YHWH (Sir 2:16). Such fear is associated with the observance of the law (cf. Deut 28:58).

This is repeated in 89.32–34 but reflects a negative imagery. Like 89.28c, 89.32 references Moses leading Israel and, like 89.29a, refers to *again* going up to *that* summit of the rock (89.32a, תנינא וסלק לראש כפא דן). Both 89.29a and 89.32a emphasize a particular "summit of the rock" with the demonstrative (89.32a, דן) and an appositional description (89.29a, חד ראם). The following 89.32b–33b, like 89.30, stresses the motif of sight.

---

96. VanderKam believes "that one should search for the source of the opened eyes/seeing imagery, not in the chapters of Exodus preceding the Sinai pericope [i.e., Exod 15] but within it." He further states, "This would be consistent with 1 En. 89.28 which locates the Israelites in a desert after crossing the sea, with v. 29 mentioning Moses's ascent of the mountain" (VanderKam, "Open and Closed Eyes," 287). VanderKam argues that the source of the "open eyes" comes from the etymology of the name of Israel given to Jacob, "the one who sees God," which is transferred upon Israel as a people in the event at Sinai. I find this proposition more plausible, though I argue here not so much regarding the origin of the expression but about a thematic reason for its use.

97. Olson, *New Reading*, 174. Olson notes that the Ethiopic versions have either a masculine singular object, a feminine singular object, or a masculine plural. According to Olson, these could correspond to either Moses, the law, or the tablets, respectively.

3. Animal Apocalypse: A Metaphorical Reading 129

However, it describes the failure of knowing the Lord, as they are blinded and have strayed from the path (cf. 89.32b–c, "and the sheep began to go blind … and the sheep did not know," וענא שריוא לאתס[מיה...ל[הון ואמרא לא ידעבהון). In 89.32b, "the path it had shown them" harkens back to the commandments and instructions referred to in 89.29b. After the Lord informs Moses, they come down from the rock, and Moses discovers that the sheep were in fact blinded (cf. 89.33b, ואתה על ענא ואשכח כול שגאהון מתסמין, "and he came upon the sheep and found a great number blinded"). In 89.34, the Lord becomes quite angry, and, like 89.31, the sight of the Lord causes the sheep to tremble, except this is now out of true fear, as they are desperate to return to the fold.[98]

Verses 35–36 end with how the scene began in 89.28a–b, an *inclusio* that suggests Israel was gathered for a special purpose. In 89.28a–b, the Lord gathers Israel and takes them from danger to a pasture where he feeds them. In 89.35–36, Moses gathers Israel back to the fold after they strayed, and this immediately precedes the gathering in the desert camp (89.36).[99] The following structure reflects the above analysis:

I. Sheep "open their eyes" (ועיניהון התפתחו). The Lord of the sheep pastures (89.28a–b).
    A. That sheep leads and goes up to the summit of a high rock (29a, סלק לראש כף חד ראם) (89.28c–29a).
        B. 89.29b–30 *The Lord sends the torah.* The sheep see the Lord who appears majestic, fearful, and mighty (89.30b, וחזיה תקיף ורב ודחיל).
            C. 89.31 Sheep see the Lord and were afraid and trembling (89.31a, וכולהון הווא דחלין ורעדין), saying, "We cannot

---

98. That they were in fear and trembling standing before the Lord is material absent in the Aramaic, which is reconstructed as follows: ובמחזאהו שריוא למדחל מן ק] ודמוהי] (89.34a). See Tiller, *Commentary*, 177. For the contents of the fragment, see v. 6 Frag. 4, 4Q205 2 II in Martinez and Tigchelaar, *Dead Sea Scrolls*, 419.

99. Tiller suggests since the tabernacle would correspond with the temple as "tower" in 1 En. 90.54, where the "tower" is distinguished from "the house," which refers to Jerusalem, then the house in our passage (89.36) must be referring to the desert camp (Tiller, *Commentary*, 42). Nickelsburg suggests that "the house" could refer to the tabernacle, as its construction is recorded in Exod 35–40. But he also allows for the possibility that the metaphor refers also to the entire Israelite camp, since it is built around the tabernacle (Nickelsburg, *1 Enoch 1*, 381). So also Himmelfarb, *Between Temple and Torah*, 87.

130 Apocalyptic Sheep and Goats in Matthew and 1 Enoch

stand before our Lord or look at him" (89.31b, לא יכלין
[אנחנא למקמ לקובל [מריא).

A'. That sheep that leads goes up to that summit of the rock (89.32a,
תנינא וסלק לראש כפא דן).

B'. The sheep began to be blinded and to stray from *the path that
it had shown them*. The Lord is filled with great wrath, and
that sheep witnesses them blinded and straying (89.33b, ואתה
על ענא ואשכח כול שגאהון מתסמין) (89.32bc–33).

C'. Sheep see the Lord and were afraid and trembled, wishing
to return to their folds. That sheep slaughters those straying, and the sheep were afraid of it (89.34–35d).

I'. That sheep returns sheep to the fold. That sheep becomes a man,
builds a house for the Lord of sheep, and made all the sheep stand in
that house (89.35e–36).

We may have an antithetical parallel here in 89.28c–34 that is bracketed by
the gathering of Israel by God and Moses to be fed within its pasture and
fold (89.28ab, 35e–36).[100] What is being narrated, and therefore retained
from Exod 15–40 is Israel being gathered and fed. The narrative centers
upon the instructions and commands that presumably came from *that*
"summit of the rock." While the theophany is a salient feature of the section, it is viewed in light of the instructions and laws that the Lord sends
with Moses (89.29b), reflecting sapiential traditions regarding the fear of
the Lord.[101] The theophany is not separate from the revelation of God's
laws and instructions but rather is their affirmation.[102] As such, it emphasizes Israel's reactions.

It is well known that seeing is a metaphor for knowing. Israel's reaction
consists of knowing the Lord (89.30) and being blind or lacking knowledge
of the Lord (89.33). Knowledge of the Lord is central, and recognizing the

---

100. Literary and rhetorical constructions like these are also presented elsewhere,
for example, in 1 En. 90.6–19. See Nickelsburg, *1 Enoch 1*, 396–98.

101. See Roland E. Murphy, "Religious Dimensions of Israelite Wisdom," in
Ancient Israelite Wisdom: Essays in Honour of Frank Moore Cross, ed. Patrick Miller,
Paul D. Hanson, and S. Dean McBride (Philadelphia: Fortress, 1987), 452–53; Henri
Blocher, "The Fear of the Lord as the Principle of Wisdom," *TynBul* 28 (1977): 3–28.

102. Nickelsburg sees the theophany as the focus of the section 89.29–35 and
separates 89.28 as the revelation of God's laws and instructions (Nickelsburg, *1 Enoch
1*, 50, 379–80).

3. Animal Apocalypse: A Metaphorical Reading   131

theophany affirms the recognition of that knowledge (cf. Exod 19:9). If the above structural proposal stands, then Israel's open eyes (cf. 89.28b, ועיניהון התפתחו) do not necessarily describe an actual event that precedes the ascension of Moses.[103] Rather, it foreshadows and describes thematically what the allegory highlights in 89.28c–36 from the exodus event within chapters 15–40.[104] It emphasizes the acknowledgment of the torah, the knowledge of God's commandments and instructions as revealed to Moses and Israel at Mount Sinai. Metaphorically, the torah becomes the path and cannot be understood apart from knowing the Lord. Thus, open eyes and following the path are inseparable.

The Aramaic expression of sheep *opening* their eyes in 1 En. 89.28b above comes from the root פתח, "to see,"[105] and its references to the torah, Israel, and God may allude to wisdom traditions of identifying the wise.[106] We need not go any further than Exod 23:8 for such a reference, where we find the Hebrew equivalent in the adjective פקח. There, we read:

ושחד לא תקח כי השחד יעור פקחים ויסלף דברי צדיקים

You shall not take a bribe, because the bribe blinds the open-eyed ones, and perverts the words of the righteous.

The adjective refers here in the plural to the "open-eyed ones," which is rare in the Hebrew Bible. It occurs in only one other place, Exod 4:11. Its verbal form פקח, "to open," is more common. In Exod 4:11, Moses is hesitant to lead because of his professed difficulty with speaking. Yet, in typical wisdom fashion,[107] the Lord answers with rhetorical questions:

---

103. Contra Tiller, *Commentary*, 292.

104. The Ethiopic translation or perhaps interpretation utilizes the subjunctive of the verb "to begin" (89.28b, *wa'axazu*) with the auxiliary verb "to open." The Aramaic simply states, "their eyes were opened." The sense of foreshadowing of what follows may be implied in the subjunctive. For the Ethiopic and Aramaic versions side by side, see Tiller, *Commentary*, 174. See also Thomas O. Lambdin, *Introduction to Classical Ethiopic*, HSS 24 (Missoula, MT: Scholars Press, 1978), 150.

105. The Aramaic verb פתח, meaning "to open," is the same and common in the Hebrew (e.g., Gen 8:6; 29:31; 30:22; 41:56; Exod 2:6; 21:33; 28:9; Num 16:32; 19:15; Deut 15:8, 11; 20:11; etc.).

106. *Pace* Nickelsburg ("Enochic Wisdom," 83), who restricts the phrase of opened eyes to Exod 15:25–26.

107. See Stone, "Lists of Revealed Things," 414–52.

"Who gives speech to mortals? Who makes them mute or deaf, the seeing [פקח] or the blind [עור]? Is it not I, the Lord?"

The above passage in Exodus is reproduced in Deut 16:19,[108] which reads:

לא־תטה משפט לא תכיר פנים ולא־תקח שחד כי השחד יעור עיני חכמים ויסלף דברי צדיקם

You must not distort justice; you must not show partiality; and you must not accept bribes, because the bribe blinds *the eyes of the wise* and subverts the words of the righteous.

In proverbial form, these texts speak of administering justice and righteousness within the community through prohibitions. Similarly, Ben Sira warns, "Favors and gifts blind the eyes of the wise; like a muzzle on the mouth they stop reproofs" (Sir 20:28). The proverb from Deuteronomy and Exodus cautions against bribery. Apparently, both the wise and the open-eyed are susceptible to the deceit of bribery that alters their decisions. More important for this study, the open-eyed (פתח//פקח) are identified with the wise (חכמים) by the Deuteronomist and are synonymous with the righteous (צדיקם) in both texts. All of this is linked through the giving of the torah at Mount Sinai in the Animal Apocalypse, and from there on, the torah dictates the standard by which the sheep are measured.

It may be possible that the Animal Apocalypse looks favorably upon a particular group of sheep. In 1 En. 90.6–19, where it contains details of the actual historical setting of the Animal Apocalypse, a group of sheep referred to as lambs are said to begin opening their eyes and crying out to the "white sheep," who were "extremely and excessively blinded."[109]

---

108. Reinhard Müller, "The Blinded Eyes of the Wise: Sapiential Tradition and Mosaic Commandment in Deut 16:19–20," in *Wisdom and Torah: The Reception of 'Torah' in the Wisdom Literature of the Second Temple Period*, ed. Bernd U. Schipper and D. Andrew Teeter (Leiden: Brill, 2013), 14.

109. Quotation from Nickelsburg, *1 Enoch 1*, 388. The verses survive only in Ethiopic, and the translation distinguishes between an adult and young sheep, which may not have been made in the original Aramaic. As Tiller explains, the Aramaic term for lamb is also used to refer to an adult sheep elsewhere in the Animal Apocalypse. However, he does suggest that if there was a distinction, it is meant to indicate that the group represented by lambs are new (Tiller, *Commentary*, 351). Following

3. Animal Apocalypse: A Metaphorical Reading 133

Those sheep with their eyes open may refer to a particular group that is speaking out against the injustices and unrighteousness of some of the priests. At this point, those lambs are seen favorably by the author(s) of the Animal Apocalypse as righteous, but nothing substantially indicates that the author(s) of the Animal Apocalypse identifies with them. Moreover, those lambs who open their eyes take on a leading role, just as Judas Maccabeus is referred to as a ram. Other than this, their identity is vague, and their recognition by the Animal Apocalypse is one of legitimation for their struggles.[110]

The act of leading involves pasturing. Pasturing is a metaphor for feeding, which also involves gathering, as expressed in the above verses (89.28a–b, 35e–36). Being fed is a metaphor for imparting knowledge. Gathering Israel allows her to attain knowledge. The motif of gathering forms the *inclusio* of the above parallelism. Shortly after, a reference to Samuel in 1 En. 89.41 illuminates this further. There, the Ethiopic version states,

> And sometimes their eyes were opened, and sometimes they were darkened, until another sheep arose. And it led them and *caused them all to return*, and *their eyes were opened*.[111]

The first part of this verse refers to the judges, although it is difficult to pinpoint which ones. Given its brevity, it seems to anticipate the second part. There, it speaks of Samuel from 1 Sam 7:3–6.[112] In that biblical passage, Samuel, who acts as judge, gathers all Israel at Mizpah (1 Sam 7:5) and demands that they put away the Baals and the Astartes (1 Sam 7:4) and offers prayers of repentance and petition. These actions parallel the mediating actions of Moses. The correspondence between Samuel and Moses has long been recognized by scholars. Moses was to "teach the statutes and instructions and make known to them the way they are to go and

---

the proposition that white refers to the elect, Tiller suggests that the white sheep carries a collective connotation to mean Israel. But as noted above, white represents righteousness. I believe that white here does not carry the same metaphorical value it does with "white cattle," and thus I agree with Tiller to the extent that "white sheep" carries a collective connotation to mean Israel without necessarily referring to election. The color here simply refers to the fact that all sheep are white in their natural color, which Tiller himself notes in passing.

110. Henze, "Enoch's Dream Visions," 21.

111. Tiller, *Commentary*, 302.

112. Tiller, *Commentary*, 302.

134   Apocalyptic Sheep and Goats in Matthew and 1 Enoch

the things they are to do" (Exod 18:20). Samuel's duties (1 Sam 8–11) fall along these same lines (cf. Deut 18:15–19).[113] Thus the act of gathering to enable eyes to open metaphorically refers to the acquisition of knowledge divinely revealed at Mount Sinai. The purpose is to be able to see and follow the path (the torah) that the Lord of the sheep has set forth. The risk is that they will go off "on many paths" (1 En. 89.51).

It is for this reason that the motif of the fold comes to the fore (1 En. 89.35). The building of "the house" and "tower" becomes the extension of the metaphor of the sheepfold into which Israel is gathered (1 En. 89.36). As we find later, Israel eventually loses sight of the path and is blinded. As a result, the sheep desert the fold. This abandonment leaves them vulnerable to violence and away from the protection of their owner: "After that I saw when they abandoned the house of the Lord and his tower, they went astray in everything, and their eyes were blinded" (1 En. 89.54). Interestingly, the Second Temple is viewed negatively in the Animal Apocalypse (1 En. 89.73).[114] The sheepfolds are then dispersed as "the sheep were scattered over the field" (1 En. 89.75). The fold is not to be seen again until the last days (1 En. 90.29, 35–36):

> [29]And I saw until the Lord of the sheep brought a new house, larger and higher than that first one, and he erected it on the site of the first one that had been rolled up. And all its pillars were new, and its beams were new, and its ornaments were new and larger than (those of) the first one, the old one that he had removed. *And all the sheep were within it....* [35]And the eyes of all were opened, and they saw good things; and there was none among them that did not see. [36]*And I saw how that house was large and broad and very full.*

Thus, gathering within the sheepfold not only provides protection but also a place in which the eyes of the sheep are opened. From 1 En. 89.28–36, the expression of open eyes throughout the Animal Apocalypse evokes the events at Mount Sinai.

---

113. See Antony F. Campbell, *1 Samuel*, FOTL 7 (Grand Rapids: Eerdmans, 2003), 88. It is also at 1 Sam 7 that the transition to the monarchy begins, just as it is depicted here in the Animal Apocalypse (1 En. 89.41).

114. The negative portrayal of the Second Temple may be a critique of the temple cult but not necessarily the rejection of the torah by authors of Enochian literature. The use of Scriptures is prevalent throughout the ancient world of Jewish circles. The capacity of these Scriptures varies.

3. Animal Apocalypse: A Metaphorical Reading   135

It is obvious that cultural elements of wisdom traditions work throughout the discourse of the Animal Apocalypse. While prophetic traditions of the law and the covenant are certainly also brought to mind, they are cloaked in wisdom fabric. In wisdom literature, the metaphors for the torah are associated with the eye. Proverbs 7:2 states, "Keep my commandments and live, keep my teachings as the apple of your eye." The Psalms metaphorically speak of the Lord's commandments as light to the eyes (Ps 19:8; cf. Prov 6:23). The passage that we visited above in 1 En. 89.28–36 encapsulates the words of Ben Sira: πᾶσα σοφία φόβος κυρίου καὶ ἐν πάσῃ σοφίᾳ ποίησις νόμου, "All wisdom is fear of the Lord, and in all wisdom there is doing of the law" (Sir 19:20).[115] Therefore, the sheep metaphor is associated with those considered wise, measured by their fidelity to the torah. In metaphorical terms, those with open eyes see and follow the path. I will elaborate this motif further when we turn to other heavenly communications.

3.7. Apocalyptic Communication

As defined earlier, apocalypse as a genre is a literary communication of esoteric knowledge, which describes celestial revelations through symbols. This knowledge is acquired only through heavenly revelation and not by means of human observation and reason. In the Animal Apocalypse, heavenly knowledge of the future is revealed in a dream to Enoch and involves judgment insofar as it can also be considered revealed knowledge. The use of dreams as a way for the divine realm to communicate with humans is attested in both the Hebrew Bible and the literature of the ancient Near East. It is also a common phenomenon in the mantic art of divination.[116] In the Animal Apocalypse, the dream is juxtaposed with an apocalypse. The apocalyptic communication of esoteric knowledge occurs

---

115. Skehan and Di Lella argue that this is "the fundamental thesis of the book." See Patrick W. Skehan and Alexander A. Di Lella, *The Wisdom of Ben Sira*, AB 39 (New York: Doubleday, 1987), 75–76.

116. For a study on dreams in the ancient Near East, see A. L. Oppenheim, *The Interpretation of Dreams in the Ancient Near East, with a Translation of an Assyrian Dream-Book* (Philadelphia: American Philosophical Society, 1956). For the influence of such practice upon the Enochic texts, see VanderKam, *Enoch and the Growth*. For a recent discussion of dream/visions in the context of apocalypses, see Flannery, "Dreams and Visions," 104–20. Flannery refers to a "dream logic" or "vision logic" that liberates the dreamer or visionary from constraints of the physiological, spatial, and temporal of the real world.

136   Apocalyptic Sheep and Goats in Matthew and 1 Enoch

when Enoch is taken up to the heavens by three angels (1 En. 87.3) and brought back down by these same three before "the judgment" of the flood (1 En. 90.31). As events unfold in the Animal Apocalypse between these passages, the three angels disclose to Enoch in metaphorical terms what will come about in the future. It is this that he is relating to his son (cf. 1 En. 85.1–2). In what follows, I focus only on how these cultural and literary phenomena may have contributed to constructing the conceptual framework of the sheep metaphor. I argue that the sheep metaphor also embodies the apocalyptic communication between God, angelic beings, and Enoch in such a way that Israel becomes a remnant elected for the salvation of humanity.

Tiller states in his commentary,

> The *An. Apoc.* removes the screen to show history as it really is, a great playing field.... By means of the allegory, the author has been able to level this playing field so that he can imaginatively present the whole hierarchy of God, angels and demons, and humans as acting on the same playing field ... and the angels are seen as being as much a part of the life of Israel as a shepherd is a part of the life of a sheep.[117]

My contention is that this is not just a linguistic trick to stimulate the imagination but a sort of realism expressed in metaphorical language that characterizes heaven and earth, as a holistic system of reality for the Animal Apocalypse heaven is reachable. Heaven and earth are on the same continuum of reality, separated, it seems, by a veil of limited understanding and knowledge. There is no difficulty in crossing from one realm to another. The fallen angels came as they wished (1 En. 86). In 1 En. 89.16, Enoch sees that the "Lord of the sheep descended from a lofty chamber at the voice of the sheep." Using a modern metaphor, the Lord came to the lobby after a phone call to his room. Enoch himself is taken by angels from earth to heaven (1 En. 87.3) and back again (1 En. 90.31). That angels as shepherds become rulers of nations makes this connection visual. In fact, this bond is also audible. In 1 En. 87.1, the earth cries out due to violence caused by the fallen angels, giant animals, and black cattle. In 1 En. 90.3, 11, and 13, the sheep and that ram cry out because of the shepherds and predators. The cries prompt the heavenly intervention of angels (as men) and God (as the Lord of the sheep) who save Israel (the sheep) from the

---

117. Tiller, *Commentary*, 27–28.

3. Animal Apocalypse: A Metaphorical Reading 137

violent ones (predators). Although the Lord of the sheep may not always answer, he does so for a reason (1 En. 90.58). For the scribes of the Animal Apocalypse, heaven is but a call away (also 1 En. 89.16; 90.52).

Direct communication with the heavenly realm is significant in the Animal Apocalypse, and the primary function of direct communication with heaven is to impart knowledge. From its reception at Sinai, the torah is also alluded to in the Animal Apocalypse as revealed knowledge. This revelatory aspect of torah is expressed by Ps 119:18, "Open [ἀποκαλύπτω, LXX] my eyes, so that I may behold wondrous things out of your law." It defines in part the sheep metaphor by the way in which the torah becomes the path that the sheep are to follow, thereby defining the relationship between the sheep and the Lord of the sheep. The revelatory discourse of the torah as narrated in the Animal Apocalypse ties itself in a timeless way to the identity of Israel. However, it cannot be fully appreciated without looking at the overarching discourse that involves angelic and heavenly communication. The revelatory event at Sinai must be seen as a part of a broader discourse of humans acquiring knowledge from the heavens. The way in which the Sinai event plays out in this broader discourse reveals more about what the sheep metaphor stands for in the Animal Apocalypse.

3.7.1. Sheep and Remnant

It is important to understand that Enoch receives visions in the first dream communicating that "the earth has been destroyed" (1 En. 83.3–5) and that humans will be obliterated (cf. 1 En. 84.5). Acting upon advice given to him by his grandfather Mahalalel (1 En. 83.8), he makes a plea to the "Lord of all the creation of heaven" (1 En. 84.2). It appears that the blame for God's wrath in Enoch's dream rests upon both angels and humans (1 En. 84.4). The following are the words of Enoch's petition (1 En. 84.5–6):

> And now, O God and Lord and great King, I make supplication and request that you fulfill my prayer, to leave me *a remnant* on the earth, and not obliterate *all human flesh*, and devastate the earth, that there be eternal destruction. And now, my Lord, remove from the earth the flesh that has aroused your wrath, but *the righteous* and *true flesh* raise up *a seed-bearing plant* forever. And hide not your face from the prayer of your servant, O Lord.[118]

---

118. Translation from Nickelsburg, *1 Enoch 1*, 346, emphasis added.

138   Apocalyptic Sheep and Goats in Matthew and 1 Enoch

The prayer here may in fact be the one of which Enoch makes mention in 1 En. 83.10.[119] Enoch's plea is clearly for the salvation of both humanity and the earth. His petition is made on the basis of God's greatness, sovereignty, power, and eternity (cf. 83.11; 84.1). Significant is Enoch's reference to creation as a whole: that is, God's creation of the heavens and the earth.

The first part of Enoch's prayer asks to save a "righteous and true flesh." This true flesh stands in contrast to the flesh that tainted the earth with blood in the second dream. In the second dream, as we learn, the earth is not destroyed but only cleansed, and Noah, a white bull, is saved by angelic intervention (cf. 1 En. 10.1–2). The destruction of the earth and the wrath of God that Enoch envisioned in his first dream appear to be postponed or resolved. The second dream shows three angels taking Enoch to heaven (1 En. 87.3), and another tells Noah about the mystery of the flood (1 En. 89.1), which is that a righteous remnant will be saved, symbolizing true flesh not being destroyed. Indeed, it seems that the visions of the second dream serve as a response to Enoch's plea in the first. It is important to note that there is a gap of time between the occurrence of the first dream and the second. The first dream happened when Enoch was a child. The second occurred when he has a son of his own. If indeed the second dream is a response to the first, the survival of Noah as a righteous remnant is the result of Enoch's petition. In the context of the Book of Dreams, Jacob (as well as some other Israelites) would also be considered a righteous remnant as the result of Enoch's plea, and Jacob's status as such would be understood as an extension of that symbolism from Noah in representing "true flesh."[120] This is especially marked when we consider that both Abraham and Isaac, like Noah, are symbolized as white cattle.[121] Thus, Israel depicted as sheep is meant to portray a righteous remnant on earth.

----

119. Nickelsburg, *1 Enoch 1*, 351.

120. The phrase "true flesh" comes from Nickelsburg's translation of Enoch's petition in 1 En. 84.6. Nickelsburg translates "the righteous and true flesh." Charlesworth translates, "the flesh of righteousness and uprightness" (*OTP*, 1:62). Jacob certainly would fit the description as "true flesh" in terms of a "righteous" remnant. Because of Abraham, Isaac, and Jacob, it transfers onto its descendants as a privileged status, though many fall short in fulfilling such status of a righteous remnant. I will explain this more below.

121. Nickelsburg, *1 Enoch 1*, 347. Nickelsburg sees the centrality of the remnant and the flood in Enoch's petition of 1 En. 84.5. He states, "Central are the flood and the concern about a remnant that would survive its universal destruction." However, I

3. Animal Apocalypse: A Metaphorical Reading   139

Therefore, the second vision communicates to Enoch what will come to pass. Not only does Noah, a descendant of his, survive the destruction that causes him to lament, but also Abraham and Isaac emerge from the midst of predators. Then God plants a "seed-bearing plant" in Jacob and Israel, maintaining a righteous remnant throughout. Moreover, Enoch's vision of the future shows heavenly beings communicating with the righteous in ways that fulfill his petition. One salient feature of this communication is the revealing to Enoch of the knowledge of future judgment and heavenly intervention.[122] This is significant because the judgment of the wicked runs hand in hand with a saved remnant, as the former ensures the existence of

---

take Enoch's concern for the survival of a righteous remnant further to extend it upon Jacob and Israel, since Abraham and Isaac are also white cattle.

122. For example, having seen the beginnings of wickedness and the increase of violence on earth through the fallen angels (1 En. 86.1–87.1), heavenly beings reveal to Enoch the judgment that will ensue in 1 En. 87–88. In 1 En. 87, Enoch is again astonished with what unfolds next, as he says again, "And I lifted my eyes again to heaven, and I saw…, and behold" (cf. 86.4: "I looked … I saw and behold"). Imagine his astonishment at seeing seven angels descending from heaven. Three grab Enoch by the hand and take him up (cf. Gen 5:24) to what seems to be a heavenly temple, in order for him to witness the fate of the giant animals and stars alike on earth. Equally important is 1 En. 89.1, in which one of the four angels tells Noah about the mystery of the flood. This angelic communication of esoteric knowledge allows Noah to build for himself and his family an ark that allows him to survive the calamity. First Enoch 90.2–19 depicts events of the recent past and what the Animal Apocalypse expects to take place in the near future (Nickelsburg, *1 Enoch 1*, 396). In the immediate past, the sheep and Enoch cry out for the destruction that befalls the sheep (1 En. 90.3) and brings them to near extinction (1 En. 90.4, "and the sheep became few"). In more contemporary events and possibly the near future, Enoch sees that the rams, who seem to assume some form of leadership role, lament and cry out (1 En. 90.11). One ram, who also makes war, also cries out (1 En. 90.13). This one is most likely Judas Maccabeus, whom the angelic scribe aids by revealing everything (1 En. 90.14). At this time, the last of the seventy shepherds that the Lord appointed was reigning over Israel. The Lord of the sheep then intervenes with wrath and later strikes the earth with his staff, which causes all the predators to sink into the earth. Moreover, the sheep are given a large sword, with which they triumph over the beasts and birds of the heaven. Again, the heavenly intervention in this section helps the sheep to survive the onslaught of violence upon them. In 1 En. 90.20–27, Enoch watches as the Lord of the sheep takes his seat upon a throne on the earth, "in the pleasant land" to be exact (1 En. 90.20). The angelic scribe opens the books before him, and judgment commences. The stars, the seventy shepherds, and the blinded sheep are all found to be sinners and are thrown into the fire. The rest of the sheep, who presumably had their eyes opened, and other animals remain. Again, like Noah, a righteous remnant is saved.

140 Apocalyptic Sheep and Goats in Matthew and 1 Enoch

the latter. The communication between God, angels, and Enoch functions to inform and save a "righteous and true flesh" on earth from being destroyed (1 En. 84.6). In such a way, apocalyptic communications are interwoven into biblical accounts through the metaphorical language of the allegory. But how does the status of a remnant thus defined differ from the notion of election?

3.7.2. Sheep and Election

The second part of Enoch's petition quoted above hints at a purpose for the righteous and true flesh; that is, to be a "seed-bearing plant" (cf. 1 En. 84.6). As the vision in the second dream begins to relate a future time, the divine purpose for Israel as sheep becomes more evident. First, in 1 En. 90.28–38, we find that predatory animals were not condemned in the judgment of 1 En. 90.20–27. One would expect the predators to be considered sinners as well, since they, too, were responsible for destroying the sheep along with the angelic beings and blind sheep (cf. 1 En. 90.24–26). That is not the case. We appear to have both a righteous remnant in the open-eyed sheep and the predatory animals. This is a different imagery from the one we get from the judgment of the flood, where all are condemned.

Judgment was passed on both the angels as shepherds and the apostate Israelites for disobeying the instructions and commandments that God gave them. We are told in the Book of the Watchers that the fallen angels went against the will of God by mingling sexually with and revealing forbidden knowledge to humans (cf. 1 En. 86). We learn that the seventy shepherds were appointed to pasture the sheep and not kill more than commanded (1 En. 89.59–60). Moreover, some sheep choose to be blinded after being appointed a path to follow. Thus, the condemnation is based upon failure of the angels and Israel to adhere to the instructions and commandments that God gave them.

Second, we find that survival continues after the condemnation in 1 En. 90.29–38. Enoch sees an extraordinary image of the sheep interacting with the animals of the earth in 1 En. 90.30, 33:

> [30]And I saw all the sheep that remained. And all the animals that were upon the earth and all the birds of heaven were falling and bowing down to those sheep and beseeching them and obeying them in *every word*[123]

---

123. The Ethiopic (*kwellu qal*) literally means "every word." However, an Aramaic equivalent that is no longer extant may mean "thing" (מלה), which is why Nickelsburg

3. Animal Apocalypse: A Metaphorical Reading   141

... [33][all] *assembled in that house*. And *the owner of the sheep rejoiced* with great joy because *they had all become good* and they had returned to his house.[124]

That all the animals "gathered in that house" is reminiscent of why sheep are brought together in the fold—to be fed and watered. The torah, as was disclosed at Mount Sinai, deemed Israel to have been appointed or elected for a divine task. That the animals are "obeying them in every word" suggests that Israel's identity as sheep involves both following the path and instructing the other animals along the same path to be "all good" or violent.[125] Therefore, it seems that the depiction of Israel as sheep signifies being elected by way of the revelation at Sinai to make themselves and humanity as a whole a "righteous and true flesh," that is, a remnant of the idea that God created humanity to be.

In conjunction with the judgment scene, the future scenario speaks pragmatically of ideal roles that angels and Israel are to play on earth. They are to bring about righteousness in their own respective roles as they were instructed to do. This explains why the animals are not judged. The aim of the Animal Apocalypse, and thus of the Lord of the sheep, is to have the elect (the sheep) teach humanity (the animals) the knowledge of God (to follow the path of the torah) so that humanity and creation may return to having God rejoice (white cattle in a renewed earth). Israel's election in this sense underlines the fundamental difference that exists between sheep and animals in the Animal Apocalypse. Here, I pause briefly in the discussion of the pragmatic nature of the future scenario to make some conceptual clarifications.

3.7.3. Historiography

The Animal Apocalypse is classified as a historical apocalypse. Historical apocalypses are "characterized by visions with an interest in the devel-

---

renders the text as "obeying them in every*thing*." Nickelsburg, *1 Enoch 1*, 403. See textual note 30b. Yet "everything" has no substantial context in the Animal Apocalypse. Commandments and instructions are the reasons for gathering in the house and means to be good or righteous. Thus, the Ethiopic rendering of "word" may be correct. See comments in Tiller, *Commentary*, 377.

124. Translation from Tiller, *Commentary*, 373–74, emphasis added.

125. Charlesworth, *OTP*, 1:71. Charlesworth renders the Ethiopic as "gentle."

142   Apocalyptic Sheep and Goats in Matthew and 1 Enoch

opment of history."[126] One of the features scholars use in defining this subcategory is "a new worldview," one of "determinism." This constitutes history as a measurement of time from beginning to end, with time as a separate entity. However, while the Animal Apocalypse does seem to lay out history in a linear fashion, it does so not in terms of an abstract understanding of time but in terms of the relationship between God and humanity.[127] In other words, it outlines history in terms of events and not necessarily as having time dimensions. I have shown that the theme of leading seems to be one way in which the allegory is narrated. It is done in the form of collective memory that does not call for the calculation of time. The recollection of biblical accounts in this fashion can be likened to a calendar; it is set, unchangeable, interpretive, and it conveys a collective memory that can transmit a single incontestable message.[128] This does not necessarily imply determinism, for the events are human actions and heavenly reactions (and so forth) already recorded and subject for interpretation.[129] In this sense, the Animal Apocalypse may not fall under historical apocalypse in the way that that category has been defined. As Richard A. Horsley says:

---

126. Collins, *Apocalyptic Imagination*, 6.

127. In speaking of "Calendar, Chronology, and History," Sacha Stern states, "The calendar should not be perceived, necessarily, as a time-measuring scheme. Its primary purpose … is to facilitate the co-ordination of events and activities, and to measure the duration of activities and processes. It is only perceived as a time-measuring scheme if one has a preconception of time as a self-standing dimension that is susceptible of being measured, and that needs, for whatever reason, to be measured; but even then time-measuring as such remains a marginal function of the calendar. In the context of early rabbinic culture, there is little doubt that the main, if not sole, purpose of the calendar is to co-ordinate and measure the duration of activities, events, and processes: for instance, to determine the date of festivals, establish the length of contracts and agreements, etc. The calendar is fully purposeful without any underlying notion of the time-dimension." See Sacha Stern, *Time and Process in Ancient Judaism* (Oxford: Littman Library of Jewish Civilization, 2003), 60.

128. Nissan Rubin, *Time and Life Cycle in Talmud and Midrash: Socio-anthropological Perspectives* (Boston: Academic Studies, 2008), 30. Rubin here speaks of calendrical events. I am only making a comparison.

129. Rubin, *Time and Life Cycle*, 31. "It is not history, as a historian reconstructs it, that shapes the worldview of the Jewish culture of the Sages, but the collective memory of a society, constructed of a combination of past memories of individuals and groups, that transforms and combines these memories into a continuum with significant meaning."

3. Animal Apocalypse: A Metaphorical Reading   143

Since neither "Enoch's" ten-week survey, his Animal Vision, nor "Moses" testamentary survey exhibits the features that supposedly constitute the scholarly subcategory of "historical apocalypse," it is unclear why they should be discussed in such terms. It makes more sense to focus on each text and its principal message as it addresses its historical context, while also looking for how it creatively adapts key forms and materials from the Judean cultural repertoire, and for features that it has in common with similar texts.[130]

There is a rhetorical reason for my brief pause here. I wish to look at the Animal Apocalypse in the context of the Jewish idea of historiography, as such an approach may serve to illuminate further the metaphor of sheep as an elected remnant. In the heavenly communications to Enoch, the events of both the past and future point toward the present, such that the past explains the present, and the future projects an ideal existence on earth with God. Thus, it seems that setting side by side past events with hopeful ones in the future creates a focus on the present. This is indicative of Jewish thought in general rather than being peculiarly apocalyptic.

Scholars have argued that in antiquity the Israelites' understanding of the concepts of history and time was fairly unique compared to their Greek and Roman counterparts. For example, Abraham J. Heschel states, "It was the glory of Greece to have discovered the idea of cosmos, the world of space; it was the achievement of Israel to have experienced history, the world of time.... Biblical history is the triumph of time over space."[131] The Greeks, and later Romans, viewed temporality as a cyclical movement that derives from a naturalistic ideology inherited from Greek philosophy.[132] This dichotomy suggests, on the one hand, that the very nature of cycles deprives history of any ultimate meaning. On the other

---

130. Richard A. Horsley, *Revolt of the Scribes: Resistance and Apocalyptic Origins* (Minneapolis: Fortress, 2010), 65.

131. Abraham J. Heschel, *God in Search of Man: A Philosophy of Judaism* (Philadelphia: Jewish Publication Society, 1955), 206.

132. The cyclical movement of time can be seen among the writings of the Greeks, which was later passed on to the Romans, as asserted by Seneca: "all things are connected in a sort of circle; they flee and they are pursued. Night is close at the heels of day, day at the heels of night; summer ends in autumn, winter rushes after autumn, and winter softens into spring; all nature in this way passes, only to return" (*Ep.* 24.26; trans. R. M. Gummere, LCL). Such understanding has nature revealing the divine. Taken from a quotation in C. A. Patrides, *The Grand Design of God: The Literary Form of the Christian View of History* (London: Routledge, 1972), 2–3.

144   Apocalyptic Sheep and Goats in Matthew and 1 Enoch

hand, the Israelites projected history along a linear path, a consequence of a theological conception of YHWH, which makes every point of time within this projected history meaningful.[133] It culminates in a goal. Both approaches have been dismissed and rejected as being flawed or over-simplified.[134] In actuality, both linearity and cyclicality can be attested in Jewish sources, and neither one is a clear cultural divider. Such is the case in the Animal Apocalypse. While a projection from Adam to contemporary times seems to trace a clear linear history from white cattle to sheep, the future age of the new beginning returns to white cattle. In other words, there does not seem to be a linear progression toward the end of a particular development (an apocalyptic end) as implied. There is only a need for order, for a restoration of what must be, in the guise of white cattle. Nevertheless, what remains fairly clear is how the concept of historical time, whether understood as linear or cyclical, correlates closely with Israel's relationship with God, which consistently places an emphasis upon the present.

Henry Dumery, an influential mid-twentieth-century philosopher of religion, sees no separation between thought and lived experience or, in some circles, faith and reason. For him, actions characterize human existence. He believes that history becomes the means of expressing and revealing God,[135] such that God spoke primarily through events in history, in the actions of those responding to the divine will, which in turn becomes divine revelation.[136] The perception of history as events of responsive actions to the will of God makes the concept of history a "social and religious category," which takes shape in fulfilling the covenantal relationship between God and man, making every action

---

133. See Millar Burrows, "Ancient Israel," in *The Idea of History in the Ancient Near East*, ed. Robert C. Dentan (New Haven: Yale University Press, 1955), 127–28; Heschel, *God in Search*, 200–208; Henry Dumery, *Phenomenology and Religion: Structures of the Christian Institution* (Berkeley: University of California Press, 1958); Patrides, *Grand Design of God*, 6.

134. For example, Bertil Albrektson, History and the Gods: An Essay on the Idea of Historical Events as Divine Manifestations in the Ancient Near East and in Israel (Lund: Gleerup, 1967); James Barr, *Biblical Words for Time*, 2nd ed. (London: SCM, 1969), 143–50; A. Momigliano, *Essays in Ancient and Modern Historiography* (Oxford: Blackwell, 1977), 179–204; Y. H. Yerushalmi, *Zakhor: Jewish History and Jewish Memory* (Seattle: University of Washington Press, 1982), 107–9 nn. 4 and 7.

135. Dumery, *Phenomenology and Religion*, 6.

136. Heschel, *God in Search*, 200.

3. Animal Apocalypse: A Metaphorical Reading 145

meaningful.[137] History encourages transformation, which must be born out of a free will to act. The relationship between Israel and YHWH becomes one of both privilege and obligation. For this reason, Dumery posits, "Judaism is a deliberate humanism, a humanism that attests that the world has not been given to man as a natural entity but as a cultural entity … [whereby] Man appears as the great maker of sense and meaning, and the universe, so humanized, becomes the most radical, vast, and fruitful of institutions."[138]

In recent years, Sacha Stern has argued this point convincingly from an anthropological perspective. She observes that a word for abstract time is absent in extant Jewish literary sources.[139] Stern's basic thesis is that the concept of time in ancient Judaism as a whole did not exist.[140] The idea of time as an entity separated from reality is a modern construct. Rather, ancient Jewish timing, calendar, and chronology were predicated on the concept of events and processes. Stern argues that "reality was conceived in empirical terms, as consisting of a multitude of discrete and concrete phenomena—activities, motions, changes, and events—occurring simultaneously or in sequence, i.e., processes."[141] From data gathered by anthropologists,[142] Stern suggests that time is not an entity independent of reality but an intrinsic part of environmental change and human activity. On this point, Nissan Rubin makes a similar observation, suggesting that

---

137. Dumery, *Phenomenology and Religion*, 16–17. Dumery states, "Every step, every event has meaning: they become stages in the long journey from the Covenant to the final reconciliation between man and nature."

138. Dumery, *Phenomenology and Religion*, 9.

139. Stern, *Time and Process*. As did Simon J. DeVries, though with a much broader scope of materials. See Simon J. DeVries, *Time and History in the Old Testament: Yesterday, Today and Tomorrow* (Grand Rapids: Eerdmans, 1975).

140. See also DeVries, *Time and History*, 39. DeVries sets out to study words and concepts within the Bible that resemble the idea of time. He begins by observing that the Hebrews had no word for abstract time and that there was no way of speaking about the abstract past, present, and future. He points out that linguistically the Hebrew language seem to have been more two-dimensional than three-dimensional with respect to time, as the majority of Hebrew words for the past and future were essentially the same.

141. Stern, *Time and Process*, 3.

142. Stern draws mainly from anthropological studies of E. Evans-Pritchard, *The Nuer* (Oxford: Clarendon, 1940), and A. Gell, *The Anthropology of Time: Cultural Constructions of Temporal Maps and Images* (Oxford: Berg, 1992).

146   Apocalyptic Sheep and Goats in Matthew and 1 Enoch

God's essence is made visible through historical deeds such as prayers, rituals, and celebrations.[143]

In the Animal Apocalypse, as mentioned above, the spatial separation between heaven and earth is nonexistent, and as such, heavenly beings enter into history, into the realm of life and death, where God's presence and human action interact and correlate.[144] The term *history* then refers to the sequence of events as recorded in Scriptures, not to a mechanism of measuring some entity that we call time. For example, the vertical correlation between Israel's actions and God's presence is seen in the Animal Apocalypse as tracing biblical events. After the flood, the allegory acknowledges that Abraham, Isaac, and Jacob's actions receive favorable attention for their righteousness, as they are depicted as white cattle and, in Jacob's case, as a ram of the flock. Presumably this is the reason why the Lord of the sheep descends from a lofty chamber once the sheep "cried to their Lord." Conversely, when the sheep abandon their Lord by abandoning "that house" and become blinded, it is said that the Lord of the sheep abandons them, though not completely. In the sections of the Animal Apocalypse that we understand to be speaking of the recent past, an angelic scribe descends to give aid to the ram that cries out and presumably opens his eyes as well (cf. 1 En. 90.6, 13–14). Immediately thereafter, the Lord comes upon the predators with wrath (1 En. 90.15). Such is also the case in the future scenarios where the animals gather in "that house." At that time, it is said that the Lord greatly rejoices. Thus, time in the Animal Apocalypse is evident in the spatial relations between Israel and God through the events that occurred. Running parallel to this projection is the horizontal relationship between the sheep and the animals or the violent. It, too, is expressed with events known. Through the actions of the past to the present, it is certainly one of increasing violence. In the future, however, it is one of peace and gentleness. I will return to this below, but this focus upon the reflection of Israel's deeds and its relationship with God and humanity ultimately leads toward the present. Though future scenarios are hopeful, they look to the present for their realization.[145] For Enoch to descend and a white bull to be born depends upon the gathering of all into "that house."

---

143. Rubin, *Time and Life Cycle*, 29–30.

144. For example, the fallen angels "fell from heaven, and it arose and was eating and pasturing among those cattle" (1 En. 86.1). When Enoch was taken to the heavens by an angel, it was said that he was raised from "the generations of the earth" (1 En. 87.3).

145. Rubin, *Time and Life Cycle*, 30. See also Jacob Neusner, *Between Time and Eternity: The Essentials of Judaism* (Encino, CA: Dickenson, 1975), 110.

3. Animal Apocalypse: A Metaphorical Reading   147

Heschel highlights the uniqueness of present time and the uniqueness of the day in ancient Jewish culture. The moment in which an
event occurred was just as important as the event itself, as a talmudic
sage exclaimed: "If not for that day…!"[146] The uniqueness of the present
moment, which stands alone and sovereign among the countless and subsequent events in history, underscores the significance of the particular
and the concrete rather than the ideal and the abstract.[147] Heschel makes
a significant observation about events and time for Israelites when he
notes that their view presupposes a hierarchy of moments, as God does
not speak equally at all times.[148] This also points to the importance of the
present, because it is in the concreteness of existential life that Israel experiences the present active relationship with God.

Simon J. DeVries introduces a similar argument but in a different way.
He suggests that the past and future are expressed relatively, that is, from
the point of view of the present, and not exclusively as time moving linearly from the past, through the present, to the future.[149] DeVries suggests,

> We can say, then, that Israel's concern for the future was related to its
> momentary existential responsibility in a way analogous to its concern
> for the past. Israel's historiography was not simply antiquarian. The past
> was important because it informed the present. "That day" was the illu-
> minating image of "this day," helping the nation see how it should act
> now. So too the "that day" of the future, which we so often find deriving
> its model from an ideal in the past that no longer is, but which one hopes
> may be recovered through responsible action in the here and now. Thus,
> in an ultimate meaning, both historiography and eschatology are forms
> of *paraenesis*, holding the covenant people to an ever-present choice
> between "life and good, death and evil" (Deut 30:15).[150]

---

146. Heschel, *God in Search*, 203; b. Pesah. 68b.

147. Heschel, *God in Search*, 202, 204. "In the realm of space a process which happened once can happen all the time, but we have not the power to understand that in
the realm of time certain events do not happen again and again. Now, revelation is an
event that does not happen all the time but at a particular time, at a unique moment
of time."

148. Heschel gives the example of how, at a certain moment, the spirit of prophecy departed from Israel (Heschel, *God in Search*, 205).

149. DeVries, *Time and History*, 40–42. He concludes that *et* is not the primary
Hebrew "time-word." A synonymous term, *yom* is the most frequently occurring biblical expression for a unit of time.

150. DeVries, *Time and History*, 282.

148   Apocalyptic Sheep and Goats in Matthew and 1 Enoch

The focus upon the present factors significantly into perspectives of being able to shape history as God awaits their actions.[151] Sandra Beth Berg concurs. Having observed a symmetrical series of thesis and antithesis, situations and their reversals within the organization of the narrated events of the book of Esther, Berg shows that the author(s) understood that humans share in determining their fate. She concludes that the future of the Jewish community resides not only with God (who controls history and shapes events) but with both God and humanity.[152] Thus, if Israel controls her own fate, her actions in the present become all the more important.

The interplay between past, present, and future is blurred in biblical Hebrew. In contrast, in Attic Greek and in Latin,[153] one is able to distinguish clearly between the three. Infixes and endings offer clues to the tenses of verbs. An augment or sigma added to the verb stem basically denotes past and future tense in Greek. Certain Latin prefixes and suffixes are applied to the verb root to denote time as well. However, in Hebrew, tense markings are not as clear. Much is dependent upon context. Augments are added in the beginning of verbs to differentiate imperfects from perfects, but nothing clearly suggests a verb is in the present tense unless one reads the context of the passage in which it occurs. In other words, forms of the past and future verb can both be used in the present. This is related to the fact that in biblical Hebrew, the temporal forms of verbs express both tenses and modalities of action, or aspects.[154] To speak of actions in the present is to speak in terms of actions either in the past or in the future.

The layout of biblical events in the Animal Apocalypse from Adam to Judas Maccabeus calls into sharp focus where Israel stands in the historical present, the "here and now," *hic et nunc*. The end of the reign of seventy shepherds brings them not only to the end of persecution but also to a

---

151. DeVries, *Time and History*, 281.

152. Sandra Beth Berg, "After the Exile: God and History in the Books of Chronicles and Esther," in *The Divine Helmsman: Studies on God's Control of Human Events, Presented to Lou H. Silberman*, ed. James L. Crenshaw and Samuel Sandmel (New York: Ktav, 1980), 118.

153. Herbert W. Smyth, *Greek Grammar* (Harvard: Harvard University Press, 1984); Andrew Keller and Stephanie Russell, *Learn to Read Latin* (New Haven: Yale University Press, 2004).

154. Paul Joüon and Takamitsu Muraoka, *A Grammar of Biblical Hebrew*, 2nd ed. (Rome: Gregorian and Biblical Press, 2011), 327.

3. Animal Apocalypse: A Metaphorical Reading 149

beginning of a new experience.[155] For the allegorist, God brings Israel to a particular point in the present. The question becomes, What now? As argued earlier concerning the dating of the text, the issuance of the large sword in 1 En. 90.19 and its return in 1 En. 90.31 channels the historical present, and, more pointedly, it speaks to Israel's election as a remnant with a divine purpose in the here and now. In other words, the allegorist may be calling to gather the nations, including both Jews and gentiles, which speaks more to the state of success achieved through the Maccabean revolt. In this sense, the days of judgment (1 En. 90.20–27) and the gathering of the nations (1 En. 90.28–36) are speech acts in nature. Similar is the general outlook of Wisdom, which dictates the way in which the sheep are to act now; the sheep of the Lord must maintain fidelity and are appointed to face the daunting mission of a universal purpose that results in a righteous humanity (and thus saves humankind) by teaching to the sheep the path of the Lord of the sheep. Israel's status as a remnant and as elected becomes both privilege and obligation. What then is the use of future judgment in the Animal Apocalypse?

3.7.4. Last Judgment?

Judgment as revealed knowledge is significant in the Animal Apocalypse. However, the Animal Apocalypse makes no mention of a last judgment in

---

155. Much discussion of the seventy shepherds among scholars has appeared in print of late. Certainly, the numbering organizes the period of foreign rulers over Israel and is a technique taken over from Jer 25. In its reuse in other texts such as Daniel and the Animal Apocalypse, one wonders whether the authors of these writings are using such organization as interpretation of the future or amplifying the present. The above statement to which this footnote applies comes about from a reading of the Animal Apocalypse that could be using this periodization as a way to highlight the importance of the present. The idea of an independent nation of Judah may have been high in the minds of the Maccabees as they continued to fight, even after regaining their temple and the right to worship as they chose. See Lester L. Grabbe, *An Introduction to Second Temple Judaism: History and Religion of the Jews in the Time of Nehemiah, the Maccabees, Hillel and Jesus* (New York: T&T Clark, 2010), 16; see also Shaye J. D. Cohen, *From the Maccabees to the Mishnah* (Philadelphia: Westminster, 1987), 30–31. Such independence has not been actualized for many centuries. Could the realization of power be an inspiration of such proportion among the Maccabees that they interpret the current situation as God acting in the present for a reason? Maybe, maybe not. Of course, not all were on board with such an idea.

150   Apocalyptic Sheep and Goats in Matthew and 1 Enoch

the eschatological sense.[156] The "great day of judgment" that Enoch envisioned in his first dream (1 En. 84.4), when the earth is destroyed (1 En. 83.5; 84.5) and human flesh obliterated (1 En. 84.5), is realized in the flood in the Animal Apocalypse. As mentioned above, that judgment seems modified since a remnant of true flesh is saved. The condemnation of the angels and blinded sheep in 1 En. 90.20–27 is thought to be the second and last judgment. I propose that this is not the last judgment (1 En. 90.20–27) per se. Rather, it is a divine sentencing that saves the sheep with opened eyes as a righteous remnant from the oppression of predators, the shepherds, and blinded sheep, while condemning the disobedient and apostates to eternal destruction.

There is another judgment narrated in the Animal Apocalypse, which is mentioned in 1 En. 90.31:

> After that, those three who were clothed in white and who had taken hold of me by my hand, who had previously brought me up (with the hand of that ram also taking hold of me), set me down among those sheep before *the judgment* took place.

Here Enoch narrates an encounter with the three angels that first took him to heaven before the flood. The three angels bring him down to earth, together with Elijah "before the judgment took place."[157] Because the judgment of the shepherds and blind sheep has already taken place in 1 En. 90.20–27, some scholars consider this temporal statement to be a mistake or a scribal gloss to link Elijah and Enoch to the tradition of their joint participation in the judgment.[158] However, they may have overlooked the possibility that divine judgment doesn't always mean condemnation. There is both wrath and rejoicing, just as there is condemnation and reward.

---

156. For example, Matthew Black sees 1 En. 90.20–42 as constituting the last judgment, referring to 1 En. 90.20–27, which leads to the following details from 90.28–42: the new Jerusalem, the new Eden, and the second Adam (Black, *Book of Enoch*, 20).

157. Nickelsburg, *1 Enoch 1*, 405. Nickelsburg may be correct in understanding the descending of Elijah and Enoch as agents of judgment, perhaps attesting to later traditions of such imagery.

158. Tiller states, "The text is unclear and probably completely corrupt. Although the judgment has already taken place in vv. 20–27, this seems to expect another judgment; but there is no other judgment" (Tiller, *Commentary*, 379). See also Nickelsburg, *1 Enoch 1*, 405.

3. Animal Apocalypse: A Metaphorical Reading   151

In 1 En. 90.33b, the Lord rejoices over "all the wild beasts and all the birds of heaven [who] were gathered in that house." Before this imagery, Enoch descends. After this imagery, the sword is sealed up in that house in the presence of the Lord (1 En. 90.34). The gathering of the beasts and animals in the house is the result of the animals obeying "every word" of "those sheep" (1 En. 90.30). There seems to be another judgment made. In 1 En. 90.38c, where Enoch ends the recounting of his dream, he sees the following from the Lord of the sheep, "And the Lord of the sheep rejoiced over it and over all the cattle."

The above two judgments differ from all previous judgments in that they are positive and speak to the election status of the sheep and the righteous state of humanity. The sheep have fulfilled their appointed role in leading humanity to righteousness. Three details further elaborate the character of these two judgments.

First, in 1 En. 90.33b, "those sheep" were "white and their wool was thick and pure" (1 En. 90.32), and in 1 En. 90.37a, the white bull has large horns. These images indicate figures of authority. Second, the beasts and animals worship and make petition to "those sheep" with white, thick, and pure wool. We have the same imagery with the white bull, as "all the wild beasts and all the birds of the heaven were afraid of it and made petition to it continually" (1 En. 90.37b). The act of petition cries out for a judgment, whether that judgment involves cleansing (1 En. 87.1), salvific acts of deliverance (1 En. 89.16), wrath (1 En. 90.11, 13), or retribution (1 En. 89.69, 76; 90.3). Having had their eyes opened, the animals petition for acceptance. Third, Enoch awakens immediately after and "blessed the Lord of righteousness and gave him glory" (1 En. 90.39–40). Thus, the future scenario speaks of three judgments, one for the salvation of the sheep as a remnant, the other two for the vindication of the sheep as the elect and the salvation of humanity and creation. All of these divine judgments are done on earth.

Indeed, a righteous remnant is saved and the elect is vindicated. The gathering and transformation of the animals (1 En. 90.30, 38a) ultimately leads God to rejoice (1 En. 90.33b, 38c)—a joy that is a reflection of a saved humanity, which harkens back to Enoch's lament.[159] The connection of

---

159. Leann S. Flesher, "Rapid Change of Mood: Oracles of Salvation, Certainty of a Hearing, or Rhetorical Play," in *My Words Are Lovely: Studies in the Rhetoric of the Psalms*, ed. Robert L. Foster and David M. Howard (New York: T&T Clark, 2008), 34. In expounding upon the roles of lamentation in the Psalms, Leann S. Flesher reasons

152   Apocalyptic Sheep and Goats in Matthew and 1 Enoch

this positive judgment upon a return to righteous humanity or true flesh with Enoch's lament would explain why Enoch is brought down to earth "before the judgment took place": so that he may witness the fulfillment of his petition as well as the righteousness and glory of God.

However, we cannot say for sure that the positive judgment was also the last. Immediately after the transformation (1 En. 90.38a), the first one among them who becomes a leader is said to have large black horns (1 En. 90.38b). The image of large black horns suggests a figure of authority and possibly an instrument of continuous judgment on earth since humanity's existence continues and certainly the human inclination toward evil remains. Altogether, the future imageries above may be the makings of the concept of the kingdom of God on earth that is so prevalent in the Gospel of Matthew.[160] Nevertheless, while judgment is significant, eschatology, insofar as it refers to the end of days or the end of humanity or the end of the earth, is not of any importance in the Animal Apocalypse. Moreover, hope for the future is as much vindication as it is a matter of removing Israel from a state of suffering. This is to say that future judgment consists not only of being saved as a remnant from unrighteous humanity but also as the elect saving humanity from unrighteousness.

3.7.5. Revealed Knowledge

The judgments of the angels, blind sheep, open-eyed sheep, and animals above bring to mind the motif of revealed knowledge in the form of the instructions and commandments by which they were judged. This implies that there is knowledge that only the angels and the Lord know. This distinction of heavenly knowledge is made evident by the way it disrupts the order of humans and earth, as it is unnatural to the earthly realm (e.g., 1 En. 86). It explains why Noah (1 En. 89.1) and Moses (1 En. 89.38) become men,[161] who immediately drop out of the allegory after that designation.

---

that "these prayers are an endeavor to move the heart of God not the psalmist." Enoch's lament, culturally, would have the same sense.

160. Milik seems to make this connection between the advent of eschatology and the kingdom of God in the Animal Apocalypse (Milik, *Book of Enoch*, 42).

161. The transformation of Noah into a man does not occur in the Aramaic fragment 4QEne4i. See Milik, *Books of Enoch*, 205. Whether it was missed by the copyist or added later, the detail is related to the manner in which knowledge was received by Noah, as first proposed by R. H. Charles. See Charles, *Apocrypha and Pseudepigrapha*,

3. Animal Apocalypse: A Metaphorical Reading   153

An angel reveals a mystery to Noah, and he then builds the ark.[162] God reveals the torah to Moses, and he builds the tabernacle. The knowledge allows them to build while elevating them to angelic status. The heavenly communication brings these men extremely close to God and heavenly beings.[163] This also explains why Enoch and Elijah are taken into heaven (1 En. 89.52).

The torah, as a special type of knowledge that is revealed to Israel, stands separately from the knowledge that the angels possess. If what differentiates sheep from animals is this revealed knowledge, then ultimately what also differentiates sheep from animals is knowing the path of the Lord of the sheep. This makes for righteousness, or as Enoch puts it, it

---

2:251–53. Dillman follows Charles, suggesting that the transformation is because it is difficult to imagine a man holding a hammer. See August Dillman, *Das Buch Henoch übersetzt und erklärt* (Leipzig: Vogel, 1853), 257. Porter takes a slightly different stance by suggesting that building skills are angelic wisdom. He refers to the angelic building of the ark in 1 En. 67.2 (Porter, *Metaphors and Monsters*, 53). Devorah Dimant, in her essay "Jerusalem and the Temple in the Animal Apocalypse (1 Enoch 85–90) in Light of Qumran Sectarian Thought"9 [Hebrew], *Shenaton* 5–6 (1981–1982): 183 n. 2, which is cited by Patrick Tiller, seems to concur with Porter's proposition by also suggesting that the transformation symbolized the divine wisdom granted to Moses for building the tabernacle. In my opinion, Porter and Dimant represent a significant improvement on Charles and Dillman. Patrick Tiller dismisses Dillman's claims and suggests that Moses's transformation may be referring to Exod 34:29–35 where Moses's face shines when he is face to face with God. In his commentary, Tiller also argues against Dimant on this basis, yet Dimant's suggestion of a divine wisdom and Tiller's suggestion of a divine personal encounter may not be incompatible. Nickelsburg seems to hint at this when he says, "Does this author find it impossible to imagine a bull or sheep with a hammer in his paw, or is it suggested that Noah and Moses attained an angel-like status? Clearly, Tiller, Porter, and Dimant are all speaking of an angel-like status in relation to heavenly wisdom. It seems to be a difference of exact reference. On this, I think Tiller is correct, but it doesn't preclude the suggestion that Noah and Moses became men or angels because of the knowledge revealed to them.

162. Nickelsburg sees that the acts of building an ark and tabernacle follow the expression of "becoming a man" in each case (Nickelsburg, *1 Enoch 1*, 375).

163. The metamorphosis of Moses from a sheep to a man in order to establish the tabernacle is thought to have been either a temporary angelic status or an inconsistency on the author's part (Tiller, *Commentary*, 299). Klaus Koch suggests that "the human form characterizes an extraordinary nearness to the divine." See Klaus Koch, "The Astral Laws as the Basis of Time, Universal History, and the Eschatological Turn in the Astronomical Book and the Animal Apocalypse in 1 Enoch," in Boccaccini and Collins, *The Early Enoch Literature*, 132.

makes everything good and makes the Lord rejoice. We can go further and suggest that this knowledge allows for the transformation of all animals, including sheep, into white cattle. This would mean that the knowledge of the torah must be related to the symbolism of the color white, which stands in contrast to black. It then seems that the color symbolism is based on righteousness or the lack thereof. If this is true, then the righteousness and wisdom obtained from the torah correlate to the righteousness attributed to white cattle as opposed to the black cattle.

In summary, Israel's status as an "elected remnant" is directly linked to the salvation of humankind. The theme of a remnant is pervasive among the prophets (e.g., Amos 3:12; Zeph 3:11–13; Mic 2:12). The mighty and proud are destroyed, while a remnant of Israel will be gathered from the places they have scattered. Remnant is often understood solely through the lens of Israel's history from Abraham on and consists of its salvation or the discourse of being saved. However, the Animal Apocalypse combines these traditions of the remnant with Israel's status as being elected to define her role as an instrument of salvation, that is, of saving humanity from unrighteousness and thus creation from impurity. To note that Israel is appointed to face such a mission does not mean to say that it is separate from humanity, but rather that the Israelites are the representation of humanity in the exchange of knowledge between God, angels, and creation. Israel's role of *saving* humanity can be seen elsewhere in the book of Isaiah, but it is granted via a prophetic oracle (e.g., Isa 42:1; 43:10; 45:4) and is narrated in terms of Israel's own history. Here, it is sanctioned through apocalyptic communication between God, angels, and Enoch and narrated in terms of the history of humanity. It is an example of merging nonwisdom traditions of remnant and election with a wisdom outlook for righteous humanity and creation through apocalyptic means.[164] For the Animal Apocalypse, the identity of the sheep as a remnant and an appointed elect is not a matter of ethnocentric myth but rather a matter of YHWH-centered discourse that aims to inspire the sheep to continue to be sheep for the sake of humanity and creation. Thus, future judgment, like the torah as revealed knowledge, is not the ends but the means by which the Animal Apocalypse relates to Israel the necessity of continuing

---

164. Wisdom is seen as having a universal appeal. See Gerhard von Rad, *Wisdom in Israel*, trans. James D. Martin (London: SCM, 1972), 4; James L. Kugel, "Wisdom and the Anthological Temper," *Proof* 17 (1997): 9–32, esp. 9.

3. Animal Apocalypse: A Metaphorical Reading

to obey God's commandments and instructions in spite of things being the way they are.

3.8. Wisdom

I would like to return to the aforementioned merging of traditions of the elect and this universalistic outlook of Wisdom. Essentially, it involves the relationship between traditions of the torah and Wisdom insofar as they define the knowledge that underlies each of the conceptual systems. This relationship touches upon issues of particularism and universalism. So far, we have discussed the torah and apocalyptic dimensions of the sheep in the Animal Apocalypse. I will now consider the possible wisdom dimensions of the sheep metaphor in the Animal Apocalypse. This may help further clarify the relationship between the sheep, cattle, and predators touched upon in previous discussions. I argue that wisdom traditions aid the Animal Apocalypse in creating the sheep metaphor and embodying the righteousness of white cattle.

The merging of these two concepts creates a sort of tension and seems to be a paradox in the Animal Apocalypse. It seems untenable to suggest that Israel as an elected remnant must maintain both its fidelity to the torah and serve as a universal role for humanity. How is it that the very foundation of election is based on a mission for the salvation of humanity? Moreover, how is it that one imagines such a purpose as a basis for inspiration, especially when that humanity continuously attempts its own demise? We can make some sense of this seeming paradox if we perceive election not in terms of particularism or exclusivism. If we understand that God does not choose one ethnic group over another, then it would make sense that, as exemplified in the Animal Apocalypse, God selects parts of a whole. In other words, a specific part is chosen out of the whole for a particular divine purpose. This understanding is attributable largely to wisdom traditions. In what follows, I refer to the book of Sirach.

3.8.1. Sheep and Animals

The relationship between the sheep and animals is in some ways parallel to the relationship between the torah and Wisdom. The book of Sirach is written by the Jewish scribe Yeshua ben Eleazar ben Sira (Sir 50:27; hereafter Ben Sira). To understand the close relationship between Israel's election and the universalistic perspective as proposed above for the Animal Apocalypse,

156   Apocalyptic Sheep and Goats in Matthew and 1 Enoch

one must understand the relationship between the founding knowledge behind these two systems of thought: the relationship between the torah and Wisdom.[165] This relationship has been much discussed among scholars. Here, I point out only Ben Sira's perspective on election with respect to this relationship and in comparison to the Animal Apocalypse.

First, one must understand that torah is a special type of knowledge revealed to Israel. Ben Sira seems to make the distinction between the special wisdom of the torah and wisdom in general. In the first chapter, where creation is the central theme, Ben Sira asks about "the root of wisdom" (ῥίζα σοφίας); to whom has it been revealed, and who knows it (Sir 1:6)? Shortly after, he delineates two types of wisdom. In Sir 1:9–10, he states,

κύριος αὐτὸς ἔκτισεν αὐτὴν καὶ εἶδεν καὶ ἐξηρίθμησεν αὐτὴν καὶ ἐξέχεεν αὐτὴν ἐπὶ πάντα τὰ ἔργα αὐτοῦ (Sir 1:9)
The Lord himself created her and he saw and took her measure and poured her out upon all his works;

μετὰ πάσης σαρκὸς κατὰ τὴν δόσιν αὐτοῦ καὶ ἐχορήγησεν αὐτὴν τοῖς ἀγαπῶσιν αὐτόν. (Sir 1:10a–b)
among all living flesh according to his gift and he lavished her to those who love him.

The root of wisdom (ῥίζα σοφίας), as Ben Sira states later in the chapter, is defined as fearing the Lord (1:20). The above passage indicates how the Lord pours out Wisdom, personified here with the feminine pronoun (αὐτήν). First, Wisdom is poured out on all his works (1:9, πάντα τὰ ἔργα αὐτοῦ), among all living flesh (πάσης σαρκός) according to his gift (1:10a, τὴν δόσιν αὐτοῦ). Second, he lavishes (1:10b, ἐχορήγησεν) Wisdom on those who love him. In Sir 1:26, Ben Sira then defines more precisely what he means by the phrase "those who love him":

ἐπιθυμήσας σοφίαν διατήρησον ἐντολάς καὶ κύριος χορηγήσει σοι αὐτήν. (Sir 1:26)

---

165. For a recent bibliography on the subject, see Benjamin G. Wright III, "Torah and Sapiential Pedagogy in the Book of Ben Sira," in *Wisdom and Torah: The Reception of 'Torah' in the Wisdom Literature of the Second Temple Period*, ed. Bernd U. Schipper and D. Andrew Teeter, JSJSup 163 (Leiden: Brill, 2013), 157–58. Here Wright lists three footnotes of helpful bibliography (nn. 3–5).

3. Animal Apocalypse: A Metaphorical Reading 157

> If you desire wisdom, keep the commandments, and the Lord will lavish her upon you.

By utilizing the same verb to lavish, provide, or supply (χορηγέω) as in 1:10b above, Ben Sira correlates those who love the Lord with those who keep his commandments. Clearly, the conditional sense we have here in supplying wisdom to those who love him and keep the commandments is distinguished from the wisdom gifted to all living flesh in 1:10a.[166] Rather than being opposing groups, the former is a subset of the latter.[167] Apparently, the one who loves the Lord and keeps the commandments receives an unequal share of wisdom.

The commandments mentioned here seem to mean the torah. Another oft-quoted passage in Sir 24:23 seems to do the same: "All this [wisdom] is the book of the covenant of the Most High God, the torah that Moses commanded us as an inheritance for the congregations of Jacob." In the past, scholars have largely interpreted the relationship between the torah and Wisdom in two ways based on the above passages. First, the torah falls under Wisdom in a way that universalizes torah.[168] Second, Wisdom falls under torah in a way that nationalizes Wisdom.[169] In a recent study on the topic of election in the book of Sirach, Greg Schmidt Goering finds these interpretations "unsatisfactory in that they define one idea—Wisdom or Torah—in terms of the other. One category subsumes the other, with the result that the subsumed category wanes in importance." He makes a

---

166. I owe this analysis in part to Greg Schmidt Goering, *Wisdom's Root Revealed: Ben Sira and the Election of Israel*, JSJSup 139 (Leiden: Brill, 2009), 22–23.

167. Goering, *Wisdom's Root Revealed*, 24.

168. For example, Gerhard von Rad contends, "It is not that wisdom is overshadowed by the superior power of the Torah, but, vice versa, that we see Sirach endeavouring to legitimatize and to interpret the Torah from the realm of understanding characteristic of wisdom" (von Rad, *Wisdom in Israel*, 245). See also John J. Collins, *Jewish Wisdom in the Hellenistic Age*, OTL (Louisville: Westminster John Knox, 1997), 55; Joseph Blenkinsopp, *Wisdom and Law in the Old Testament* (New York: Oxford University Press, 1995), 162–63.

169. For example, E. P. Sanders believes that for Ben Sira, "Wisdom which is universally sought is in fact truly represented by and particularized in the Torah given by God through Moses." See E. P. Sanders, *Paul and Palestinian Judaism* (Philadelphia: Fortress, 1977), 331. So also Menahem Kister, "Wisdom Literature and Its Relation to Other Genres: From Ben Sira to Mysteries," in *Sapiential Perspectives: Wisdom Literature in Light of the Dead Sea Scrolls*, ed. John J. Collins, Gregory E. Sterling, and Ruth A. Clements, STDJ 51 (Leiden: Brill, 2004), 13–47.

158   Apocalyptic Sheep and Goats in Matthew and 1 Enoch

strong case that the relationship between Wisdom and torah is in fact congruent in the book of Sirach. He argues that there are two kinds of wisdom for Ben Sira: general wisdom and special wisdom. General wisdom is that knowledge given to all human beings through creation, while special wisdom is that which is given to a chosen people through the torah.[170] For Ben Sira, both are creations of God.

Interestingly, he ponders the very paradox we pointed out above:

> If Wisdom represents the teachings of the ancient Near Eastern sages, which were considered universally applicable to all human beings, and if Torah denotes the particular teachings of Israel's God, which were intended for Jews alone, in what sense could Ben Sira possibly relate these two seemingly disparate entities? To state the problem abstractly, how does the sage correlate the universal and the particular?[171]

Goering argues that Ben Sira explains this relation by borrowing the concept of election found in nonwisdom biblical traditions and linking it with his creation theology.[172] In other words, unlike these biblical traditions, Ben Sira roots election in the original acts of creation and the sovereignty of God to choose as he wills.[173]

Furthermore, for Goering, Ben Sira's perception of the election of Israel is not based upon a doctrine of opposites that suggests the elected stand in opposition to the nonelect.[174] Such an interpretation seems to

---

170. Goering, *Wisdom's Roots Revealed*, 8, 9.

171. Goering, *Wisdom's Roots Revealed*, 4. See also his n. 10. He goes on to define what he means by universal and particular. For the former, he means something that applies to humanity, and, for the latter, he means something that applies to a subset of humanity. He notes that he takes this definition from the works of Ellen Birnbaum, who studies Philo and defines universalism as "the position that anyone can participate in these relationships" and particularism as "the position that only Jews can participate in these relationships." See Ellen Birnbaum, *The Place of Judaism in Philo's Thought: Israel, Jews, and Proselytes*, BJS 290 (Atlanta: Scholars Press, 1996), 1–14. The relationships referred to here are between God and Israel. In defining universalism and particularism, I will take these understandings of the concepts as well.

172. Goering, *Wisdom's Roots Revealed*, 61.

173. Goering here makes the distinction between rooting election in the history of Israel (e.g., Exod 19:3b–8; Deut 7:6–8; 9:4–9; Isa 14:1–2; 43:8–13) and rooting it in creation theology (Goering, *Wisdom's Roots Revealed*, 63).

174. Randall A. Argall defines the "doctrine of opposites" as the notion that "every element in creation obeys God and carries out its purpose for which it was

3. Animal Apocalypse: A Metaphorical Reading   159

hover over traditional understanding of passages such as Sir 42:24a: "All of them are in pairs, this corresponding to that."[175] Goering points out that pairs in this passage can also mean "side by side with," "parallel to," or "corresponding to" and argues that the election of Israel in relation to humanity is analogous to the distinction between the roles of the sun and moon, which are not opposites but rather correlations.[176] He states, "By analogy, then, Ben Sira suggests that Yhwh has similarly set apart certain people from all others for a special divine purpose even though all persons derive from the same basic substance, the dust of the earth."[177]

In lieu of a doctrine of opposites, which presumes a dyadic or binary classification of the elect and the nonelect, Goering borrows the schematics posited by Joel Kaminsky and argues that Israel's election in the Hebrew Bible is not strictly understood on binary terms (e.g., inclusive and exclusive or particular and universal).[178] For Kaminsky, "The Israelite idea of election presupposes three categories": the elect, the antielect, and

---

designed, either good or bad." He interprets a "built-in polarity" and a "duality of creation" within Sir 42–43. See Randall A. Argall, *1 Enoch and Sirach: A Comparative Literary and Conceptual Analysis of the Themes of Revelation, Creation and Judgment*, EJL 8 (Atlanta: Scholars Press, 1995), 135, 145.

175. Goering does not deny that such a doctrine exists in Ben Sira. In fact, the dyads of evil/good and wise/fool are prevalent in the Hebrew Bible (Prov 11:27; 13:21; 14:19; 17:13, 20; Qoh 7:14). Goering sees these as serving a minor role in Ben Sira's theology of creation. The duality evident in Ben Sira, according to Goering, attempts to wrestle with the problem of theodicy, of why evil exists if a unitary world is good. What is central and primary is God's sovereignty to choose as he wills (Goering, *Wisdom's Roots Revealed*, 34–35).

176. Goering, *Wisdom's Roots Revealed*, 33–34. Sir 42:24a: "All of them are *in pairs*, this corresponding to that." This translation is gleaned from the Greek and Syriac textual witnesses. This reconstruction utilizes the Hebrew לעמת with the preposition to render "in pairs." Goering argues that it can also mean "side by side with," "parallel to," or "corresponding to" (e.g., Exod 25:27; 28:27; 1 Kgs 7:20; Qoh 7:14; Ezek 40:18; 42:7). He also makes a strong case that Ben Sira does not see the sun and the moon as opposites. Thus Goering reconstructs 42:24a as "All of them are *different*, the one from the other."

177. Greg Schmidt Goering, "Divine Sovereignty and the Election of Israel," in *The Call of Abraham: Essays on the Election of Israel in Honor of Jon D. Levenson*, ed. Gary A. Anderson and Joel S. Kaminsky (Notre Dame: University of Notre Dame Press, 2013), 159.

178. Joel Kaminsky, "Did Election Imply the Mistreatment of Non-Israelite?," *HTR* 96 (2003): 398.

160   Apocalyptic Sheep and Goats in Matthew and 1 Enoch

the nonelect.[179] The antielect for Kaminsky includes those who are viewed as enemies, evil, or dangerous. These would include the Amalekites, the Canaanites, and the Midianites.[180] As for the nonelect, Kaminsky classifies this group from the Hebrew Bible as those who are "neither members of the people of Israel, God's elect, nor are they counted among those who are utterly beyond the pale of divine and human mercy in the Israelite imagination, the anti-elect."[181] These individuals, groups, or nations Kaminsky regards positively and as moral models to ancient Israel. For Goering, the gentiles were considered the unelect, separate from those who are antielect or cursed.

Much of Goering's analysis of Ben Sira is an affirmation of our reading of the Animal Apocalypse thus far. Yet, while I am less inclined to adopt his three-category schema of human classification as an all-encompassing system, I admit that it may be helpful as a convenience. What is more significant is the fact that we can go beyond binary or dualistic classifications of humans in the Animal Apocalypse. By extension, Goering argues, we should forgo perceiving election in terms of dual categorization of particularistic versus universalistic views. Ben Sira merges the election tradition of the nonwisdom literature that roots it to the history of Israel with its universal outlook toward creation as a unitary whole, by suggesting that the torah is specially given to Israel as a part of humankind. In wisdom traditions, particularism and universalism are not mutually exclusive categories. The former is understood in terms of the latter, specifically that the special wisdom imparted to Israel is for the benefit of humanity. However, this does not answer why Israel came to be elected.

Ben Sira's metaphor of inheritance may be significant here. He relates inheritance to portion, as in Sir 17:17, "For every nation he appointed a ruler but Israel is Yhwh's own portion," which is based upon ideas in Deuteronomy, namely, 32:8 (cf. Deut 4:19; 10:13–21).[182] In Sir 24:6–7, the creator instructs Wisdom to "obtain your inheritance" in Israel, which

---

179. Kaminsky, "Did Election Imply the Mistreatment of Non-Israelite?," 398. See also Kaminsky, *Yet I Loved Jacob: Reclaiming the Biblical Concept of Election* (Nashville: Abingdon, 2007), 109.

180. Kaminsky, *Yet I Loved Jacob*, 112. Kaminsky reads those texts that show anti-Canaanite (e.g., Gen 9:20–27), anti-Amalekite (e.g., Exod 17:8–16; Deut 25:17–19; 1 Sam 15), anti-Midianite (e.g., Num 31) polemics, though the Midianites are less obvious.

181. Kaminsky, *Yet I Loved Jacob*, 121.

182. Goering, *Wisdom's Roots Revealed*, 99.

Goering suggests parallels the command to "pitch your tent" in Jacob (Sir 24:8). When this instruction is fulfilled, Wisdom states later in 24:12, "the portion of YHWH is my inheritance." Thus, through the notions of inheritance and portion, Ben Sira correlates Wisdom and torah. He argues that this underscores Sir 24:23, "All this is the book of the covenant of the Most High God, the torah that Moses enjoined upon us as an inheritance for the congregations of Jacob." Here the election of Israel is described as God's inheritance. In the Animal Apocalypse, this would be because of the righteousness of Abraham, Isaac, and Jacob. The inheritance of God is enacted through the wisdom of torah; likewise wisdom is imparted to the sheep for a divine purpose in the Animal Apocalypse. Thus, the sheep metaphor embodies the wisdom of God.

If torah falls under a larger categorization of divine instructions and commandments for a divine purpose, then based on these criteria, angels would also be classified as the elect. Those who defy the instructions and commandments of the Lord are the antielect, which, in the Animal Apocalypse includes the fallen angels, the disobedient shepherds, and the blind sheep. The rest of the animals are the nonelect. This categorization, however, fits only after the flood in Jacob and Israel. It nevertheless highlights further the sheep's divine purpose—to lead creation to purification and humanity back to righteousness, that is, to knowing the Lord.

3.8.2. Sheep and White Cattle

How then do we explain humanity of white, black, and other types of cattle before the flood? The classification of election in terms of purpose does not apply. Humanity is symbolically identified in terms of righteousness and is classified along a continuum, abbreviated as three types of human beings: those who know the Lord, those who decide otherwise, and those who stand in the middle of the continuum. Those who stand in the middle are vulnerable to either side. The unrighteousness of the black and giant animals causes the earth to be impure through the blood that their acts of violence spill upon the earth.

As stated above, Enoch's cry is for a righteous remnant, and thus the Animal Apocalypse links the sheep to Noah, Abraham, and Isaac. Noah and Abraham are connected to each other through acts of righteousness (cf. Sir 44:17–19; Jub. 6.18). Through the metaphor of the open eyes discussed above, acts of righteousness mean acts of recognizing God or having knowledge of God. It is this role of the sheep to teach and enact

162   Apocalyptic Sheep and Goats in Matthew and 1 Enoch

righteousness that links them to white cattle before the flood and, in this way, to creation.

In Gen 3, humans first acquire knowledge. After Eve converses with the snake, the eyes of humanity open: "[then] the woman saw that the tree was good for eating, and that it was pleasing to the eyes, and that the tree was desirable to make one wise" (3:6). Then, having eaten the fruit, "the eyes of the two were opened, and they knew..." (3:7). It is at this point that one may argue that righteous knowledge, or the lack thereof, is born. If this can be read into the first part of the Animal Apocalypse— which it can and must be—then the righteous knowledge attained and revealed by the sheep who have their eyes open is, in essence, the same righteous knowledge that cattle obtain that are designated as being white. The giant animals are certainly a hybrid metaphorically express-ing the fact that humanity attains an unnatural knowledge revealed to them by the fallen angels. This kind of knowledge allows humankind to create further violence upon the earth. It is the unnatural knowledge that remains after the flood that explains why animals were born from those white cattle that emerged from that vessel. They choose to use that knowledge for further unrighteousness and be farther estranged from the Lord of creation. The blind sheep choose to neglect God's instruc-tions. Taken altogether, it is ample reason to find the mission of the sheep daunting.

The fact that the white bull has large horns (1 En. 90.37) suggests a figure of authority. He is not an angel. He seems to be a new elect born among humankind as an animal. He becomes a leader who will maintain unbiased leadership on earth, continue the enforcement of righteousness, and sustain the joy of the Lord, who interestingly remains the Lord of the sheep (1 En. 90.38). The white bull, along with the rest of the white cattle, becomes the "remnant and true flesh" that Enoch petitioned for in the beginning. While some may see Messianic features in this figure, it is closer to Daniel's figure of one like the son of man, as it has humanity wholly in its purview. Thus ends the Animal Apocalypse.

3.9. A Possible Social and Historical Scenario?

I close this chapter by outlining a possible social and historical setting for the Animal Apocalypse. Its authors, as well as its contemporary writers, such as those of the book of Daniel, found themselves in a situation where they felt compelled to interpret the events and crises of the Maccabean era.

3. Animal Apocalypse: A Metaphorical Reading   163

These arose from the internal power struggles for aristocracy and the policies of the Greco-Syrian king, Antiochus IV Epiphanes. While the struggles were sociopolitical in nature, some may have been philosophically intellectual, which I suspect is the case with the Animal Apocalypse. I do not deny the political facets of the Animal Apocalypse. In fact, the image of the sword (90.19, 34) is an example that undoubtedly arises out of this very atmosphere. Nor do I attempt to dichotomize politics and Jewish intellect, for these are not mutually exclusive attributes of apocalyptic discourse. I mean only to highlight that a social intellectual layer to the metaphor of sheep is more involved when one has to rationalize further how the sheep's universal purpose coincides with their continuous fidelity to the torah. Such rationalization involves intellectual creativity, which is political in and of itself and possibly even resistant. I argue that the sheep metaphor in the Animal Apocalypse is socially and politically engaging, and also intellectually stimulating such that it is resistant to competing knowledge and culture.

The Animal Apocalypse clearly favors the efforts of the Maccabean revolt, for we see Judas Maccabeus portrayed positively as a ram with horns (1 En. 90.16). This is peculiar since this same imagery denotes the notables of Israel's history that include a company of prophets, judges, and kings. It also seems to look unfavorably on the temple cult (cf. 1 En. 89.73).[183] If we can take the historical setting to be sometime after the death of Judas Maccabeus, that is, after 160 BCE, then the political situation under Jonathan and Simon Maccabeus could explain what seems to be scribal support for a pressing desire to gather the nations to Jerusalem with a "large sword." The desire was not as intense in the time of Mattathias Maccabeus as it was during the successive reigns of his sons, Judas, Jonathan, Simon, and John Hyrcanus. The shift from fighting for religious freedom to political independence surely caused tensions with other officials and many in Israel, perhaps also in the diaspora. In commenting on the Maccabean era, Shaye Cohen articulates this attitude in antiquity as follows:

> The basic political stance of the Jews of both the land of Israel and the diaspora was not rebellion but accommodation. The Jews must support the state until God sees fit to redeem them. That was the counsel of Jeremiah in the sixth century BCE, of Josephus in the first CE, and of the

---

183. Nickelsburg, *1 Enoch 1*, 405.

164 Apocalyptic Sheep and Goats in Matthew and 1 Enoch

rabbis of the second through the twentieth centuries CE. This advice was accepted by the masses of the Jews throughout antiquity. [184]

I would perhaps add Jesus to this list as well, given his reply to Jewish officials about Caesar's coin. Josephus, however, may be suspect in his pride for the Hasmonean dynasty.[185] Nevertheless, this general attitude in antiquity makes the favorable status under which Judas is placed in the Animal Apocalypse even more peculiar.

Scholars make a convincing case that "the house" spoken of in 1 En. 90.28–29 would not be the temple but rather Jerusalem.[186] The temple is referred to as the "tower," as in 1 En. 89.54 where both the house and the tower are clearly distinguished. In 1 En. 90.28–29, the rebuilding of the pillars, beams, and ornaments of "that house" express both the realization and hope of a new and godly state of Israel under the Hasmoneans. What this may suggest is that everything up to this point in the text is partly historical, even the judgment of 1 En. 90.20–27. In that judgment, the denunciation of the seventy shepherds marks the end of absolute rule of gentiles over Israel. The condemnation of the blind sheep would mark, among other things, the shift to a new priesthood, which may be the key to dating the Animal Apocalypse, probably to Jonathan's era or slightly after. What then lies only in the future in the Animal Apocalypse is the gathering of all the animals into that house, the coming of Enoch, and the messianic figure of the white bull, each followed by a verdict of God rejoicing. Thus, these figures come for judgment and, in the Animal Apocalypse, for vindication. All of this seems utopic. According to the Animal Apocalypse, if the gathering of the animals in the house is successful, then the sword can be sealed and God will rejoice, for all have come to know the Lord. Thus, the zeal of the Maccabees for all to follow the law (e.g., 1 Macc 3:5–6) colors the historical present of the Animal Apocalypse. For Judas to be seen favorably in an apocalypse by Enoch, it would make more sense for it to have been written under the watch of the high priest Jonathan or after.[187] Priests do not appear in the Apocalypse

---

184. Cohen, *From the Maccabees to the Mishnah*, 34.

185. Goldstein, *1 Maccabees*, 56.

186. Tiller, *Commentary*, 376; Horsley, *Revolt*, 68.

187. Philip R. Davies suggests, "The social background of 'apocalyptic' writing thus furnished is more fully described and precisely documented by the activity of politically 'established' and culturally cosmopolitan scribes than of visionary 'counter-

3. Animal Apocalypse: A Metaphorical Reading 165

of Weeks or in Daniel but are not viewed negatively in the Book of the Watchers.[188]

In terms of the broader context of the Animal Apocalypse and its metaphors, there is a side to the divine purpose discussed in a previous section that can be articulated in terms of politics. This is a godly politics in which sheep and white cattle refer to humanity under a unified reign and rule of God's torah. The animals, on the other hand, seem ignorant of that reality in the Animal Apocalypse. I am not suggesting that the characters in the Animal Apocalypse resist foreign rule, since the gentile rulers were appointed and instructed by God to rule. However, the entities in the Animal Apocalypse resist foreign rule insofar as they rule in an ungodly fashion that leads to violence and unrighteousness. The restoration of sheep and all white cattle expresses not only a rejection of unjust rule of the past but also a longing for God's rule, a rule that will be centered in Jerusalem. This seems to be the closest thing to Matthew's concept of a kingdom of God on earth.

Yet the question remains: Why is the figure of Enoch used to narrate such propaganda? The use of Enoch could be a response to Hellenization and the legitimation of Jewish existence. As mentioned previously, Enoch was an astrologer after the model of the Sumerian king Enmeduranki.[189] He is known later in history as the possible inventor of astronomy. Jubilees describes his talent that exceeds "the children of men" in writing, science, and wisdom (Jub. 4.17). The evidence for this is the earliest of the Enochic writings, the Astronomical Books, which scholars date back to the earlier second century or even to the third century BCE. It places Enoch, and thus the Jewish people, alongside heroes of great civilizations. According to VanderKam, the Astronomical Books quite possibly are rooted in Mesopotamian soil and were composed against the backdrop of "Babylonian astronomy in which scientific and superstitious interests were combined."[190] Interestingly enough, there is no mention of angels sinning or any escha-

---

establishment' conventicles." See Phillip R. Davies, On the Origins of Judaism, Bible World (Oakville, CT: Equinox, 2008), 110.

188. Some have argued that the Book of the Watchers also has the sense of rejecting priests. However, Martha Himmelfarb argues convincingly that the criticism of the priests therein is not directed at all priests (Himmelfarb, *Between Temple and Torah*, 86). For Himmelfarb, the Book of the Watchers is interested in priests but only worried about defilement.

189. VanderKam, *Enoch and the Growth*, 91–92.

190. VanderKam, *Enoch and the Growth*, 98–102.

166   Apocalyptic Sheep and Goats in Matthew and 1 Enoch

tological references (72.1 with the exception of "the new creation") in the
Astronomical Books.[191]

The Animal Apocalypse presents Enoch through mantic means—in
dreams and visions. In a most creative way, it intertwines this figure of
supreme knowledge with genealogical traditions from biblical accounts,
wisdom, and prophetic traditions. Enoch's knowledge of Israel's God far
exceeds any knowledge of the gods of the gentiles. What the Animal Apocalypse does is make the connection between this highly distinguished man
and the torah, as well as the history of Israel and creation. Thus, intellectually, the sheep metaphor embodies the cultural conviction that rejects the
superiority of gentile knowledge and wisdom.

3.10 Animal Apocalypse as Scripture

The significance of the torah to this known historical apocalyptic text
("historical apocalypse"), in conjunction with treatments of the theme of
the elect in wisdom traditions, attests to the ever-changing situations of
knowledge and experience that requires new forms of literary presentation
of cultural memories. This is crucial in a culture centered in a particular
canon or rather a set of authoritative Scriptures from which identity and a
way of life is justified, preserved, formed, and reformed.

The torah, Israel, and humanity has always been a point of contention
in Jewish circles as seen in biblical Scriptures. Joachim Schaper attempts to
elucidate the rise of the torah in the midst of the return of the exile during
the Achaemenid period (first Persian Empire ca. 550–330).[192] He argues
from texts of Isa 56:1–8 and Ezra 10:2–3 that there existed two traditions
of exclusivity and inclusivity with regard to foreigners and the torah, or a
corpus of authoritative instructions. For Schaper, the torah or a form of it
existed during the Persian period. He points out that Isa 56:1–8 refers to
the torah implicitly and Ezra 10:2–3 explicitly as "teachings" (תורה). The

---

191. VanderKam suggests that 1 En. 80–81 are later additions (VanderKam,
Enoch and the Growth, 106–9). For VanderKam, the Astronomical Books are only an
apocalypse with the addition of chapters 80–81. The original form of them was not an
apocalypse, according to Collins's definition of the genre.

192. Joachim Schaper, "Torah and Identity in the Persian Period," in *Judah and
the Judeans in the Achaemenid Period: Negotiating Identity in an International Context*, ed. Oded Lipschits, Gary N. Knoppers, and Manfred Oeming (Winona Lake, IN:
Eisenbrauns, 2011), 27–38.

3. Animal Apocalypse: A Metaphorical Reading 167

Trito-Isaiah text above makes allusions to Deut 23:2–9, which is known as the Law of the Assembly. In fact, as Schaper points out, along with the text of Ezek 44:6–9, scholars argue that these texts are two interpretations of the laws of Deut 23:2–9 and that the issue is proselytism.[193]

The text Ezek 44:6–9, like Ezra 10:2–3, uses the reference to "torah" (perhaps Deuteronomy) to strictly exclude gentiles, while the lack of reference in Trito-Isaiah is closely related to its more inclusive sentiments for gentiles. In fact, the text of Isa 56:1–8 suggests the gentiles are able to attach themselves to the God of Israel. Isaiah 42:4 (Deutro-Isaiah), which was also written during the Persian period,[194] attaches the gentiles to the torah: ולתורתו איים ייחילו "and for his Torah, the coast regions shall await." The Septuagint (LXX) translation of Isa 42:4, dating to around the third to second century BCE, is quite interesting. Apparently, the translator was not too fond of the inclusiveness of the Masoretic Text (MT). The text translates: καὶ ἐπὶ τῷ ὀνόματι αὐτοῦ ἔθνη ἐλπιοῦσιν, "and upon *his name* the nations will hope." This LXX translation is alluded to in Matt 12:21, καὶ τῷ ὀνόματι αὐτοῦ ἔθνη ἐλπιοῦσιν, "and in his name the gentiles will hope." The translation of the LXX may have led some to believe it was a corrective measure to the MT and that it reflects the idea that the torah belongs only to Israel (cf. Deut 4:5–8). I like to read this in a more expanded form, namely, that the LXX and thus Matthew perhaps mean to suggest that the knowledge of the true God and life for humanity and creation comes from the torah via the elect. In this interpretation, the hope for gentiles lies with the elect in expounding upon this knowledge. The LXX translation refers to Israel (Isa 42:1 LXX, Ιακωβ ὁ παῖς), and the Gospel of Matthew refers to Jesus (Matt 12:18, ὁ ἀγαπητός μου; cf. Matt 3:17, ὁ υἱός μου ὁ ἀγαπητός). The former is seen in the Animal Apocalypse through the metaphor of the sheep. It seems that by the time of the Gospel of Matthew, Jesus and his disciples would aim to bring Israel up to par. Nevertheless, an important issue surrounding the torah is the relationship between Israel and the gentiles, which, as seen in the Animal Apocalypse, is reflected in the literary contexts of apocalyptic discourse.

To be sure, the basic structure of the torah is not just a law code but largely a narrative in Mosaic tradition. It is essentially a story of the origins of Israel. The Animal Apocalypse incorporates this story in a rhetorical

---

193. Schaper, "Torah and Identity," 30.

194. Joseph Blenkinsopp, *Isaiah 40–55*, AB 19A (New York: Doubleday, 2002), 92.

168   Apocalyptic Sheep and Goats in Matthew and 1 Enoch

narrative that largely justifies the importance of its existence. The laws can hardly be understood outside the context of the narrative. James Sanders describes the story in Mosaic tradition as including three pivotal points: the exodus from Egypt, the wandering in the desert, and the entrance into the land. For Sanders, besides arguing for the Hexateuch, 1 Sam 12:8 is writ large of the story of the torah. The story of the *ethnos* of Israel begins from Abraham and climaxes with the conquest or entrance in the land. This entire story of the torah, according to Sanders, is condensed into one verse in 1 Sam 12:8: "When Jacob went into Egypt and the Egyptians oppressed them, then your ancestors cried to the Lord and the Lord sent Moses and Aaron, who brought forth your ancestors out of Egypt and caused them to dwell in this place." This same story is compressed into five verses in Deut 26:5–9. Sanders points out these stories as both being in the context of the harvest festival. In other words, these stories were recitals, and they were constantly being recited. In arguing for the Hexateuch, the book of Joshua, where the land was conquered, ends with a conference at Shechem, which was a symbolic settlement that refers back to where Abraham's settlement in Canaan began. Furthermore, Sanders suggests that the "Exodus-Wanderings-Conquest" experiences (Mosaic tradition), at some point, extended to include the "David-Jerusalem" event (Davidic tradition).[195] The passages, writ large to this respect, are Ps 78 and Exod 15, which were a combination of J and E traditions.[196] These passages extend the story of the torah in Mosaic tradition unto the story as including the Davidic tradition.[197] Sanders says, "Other than the latter half of the Book of Isaiah, Psalm 78 and Exodus 15 are the only short-compass recitations of the full Moses-cum-David traditions."[198] Israel recited these traditions at cultic and cultural festivals to constantly remind themselves of their origins and identity, as evident in 1 Sam 12:8 (Mosaic traditions) and Ps 78 (+ Davidic traditions). All of which came from the story of the torah. In

---

195. James A. Sanders, *Torah and Canon* (Eugene, OR: Cascade, 2005), 23–24.

196. Sanders dates Ps 78 to between the fall of Samaria in 722 BCE and the fall of Jerusalem in 587 BCE (Sanders, *Torah and Canon*, 24).

197. For example, Exod 5:17 adds, "on your own mountain, the place, O Lord, which you made for your abode, the sanctuary, O Lord, which your hands have established."

198. Sanders, *Torah and Canon*, 24. Sanders states, "Despite the observation that the Bible contains only a few short compass recitations of the full Moses-cum-David traditions, scholars know that the basic structure of the materials in the complex which runs from Genesis through the Books of Kings in the Hebrew Bible is in fact a magnificent amalgam of the great patriarchal, Mosaic, and Davidic traditions."

3. Animal Apocalypse: A Metaphorical Reading 169

apocalyptic literature and discourse, namely, the Animal Apocalypse and sections of the Gospel of Matthew, the torah story is expanded or modified to include life in the realm of the angels and the supernatural. This is, on the one hand, purposed as a sort of evolution and adaptation to new knowledge and experience and, on the other, to maintain the justification of identity in the midst of competing ethnic cultures.

In terms of ethnicity, these torah narratives include all six features listed by A. D. Smith and J. Hutchinson.[199] Yet boundaries of ethnicity are never rigid, especially in the Jewish diaspora. As Geoff Emberling correctly recognizes, boundaries are best understood as perceptions of difference that are not absolute or physical.[200] In fact, they are fluid and permeable. Fredrik Barth sees identity as the perception of both the self and the other.[201] Thus, the torah becomes a lens of differentiation and motives for actions between Israel and gentiles. Sander states,

> At any rate, it is abundantly clear … that all these traditions had as their principal characteristic a story about how the origins of ancient Israel, or Israel and Judah, came about under the aegis and sovereignty of their God, Yahweh. It is the story that is always at the center of the memory in cultic recitations, whether it is recalled or recited in the compass of one festival service or spread out over a longer calendar period embracing the annual festivals, each of which celebrated some aspect of the story…. No matter where Jews might be, the full recitation cycle [torah story of Mosaic and Davidic traditions] functions as the vehicle for the corporate memory of each Jew—of who they are and what they stand for.[202]

---

199. A. D. Smith and J. Hutchinson, *Ethnicity* (Oxford: Oxford University Press, 1996), 6–7. Smith and Hutchinson lists six cultural features of an ethnic group: (1) a common proper name to identify the group, (2) a myth of common ancestry, (3) a shared history or shared memories of a common past, including heroes, events, and their commemoration, (4) a common culture, embracing such things as customs, language, and religion, (5) a link with a homeland, and (6) a sense of communal solidarity.

200. Geoff Emberling, "Ethnicity in Complex Societies: Archaeological Perspectives," *Journal of Archaeological Research* 5 (1997): 295–344, esp. 301–304. Emberling states that ethnicity is best viewed as a "process of identification and differentiation, rather than … an inherent attribute of individuals or groups" (Emberling, "Ethnicity," 306).

201. Fredrik Barth, "Introduction," in *Ethnic Groups and Boundaries: The Social Organization of Culture Difference*, ed. Fredrik Barth (Boston: Little, Brown, 1969), 13–15. Barth includes an examination of boundaries or significant features that differentiate groups.

202. Sanders, *Torah and Canon*, 27–30.

170   Apocalyptic Sheep and Goats in Matthew and 1 Enoch

How important these stories are to the identity of Israel cannot be overstated. They have become the essence for Israel's survival in the diaspora, centering all aspects of their being. In many respects, the text themselves *are* Israel's identity. However, it is significant to point out, especially in the diaspora, that different Jewish communities may not necessarily share the same canon (authority) of texts. In other words, as pointed out with the different interpretations of the torah and the different traditions that have emerged, canonical texts vary among Jewish communities in the diaspora. The torah is the reference point or source of origin that is reinterpreted and constantly reused, made possible through the process of canonization.

Moshe Halbertal, in his *People of the Book*, explains how Israel is known as the "text-centered people." When texts are canonized within the community, functions are assigned that can be likened to a piece of writing that has been published. They take on an authoritative status within the group. The canonizing of text in Jewish communities assigns authority to texts that define behavior (of all stratums of society—political, religious, social, etc.) and social status within the community. Halbertal explains that canonical texts function in three ways: normative, formative, and exemplary. The normative canon is obeyed (Scriptures and legal codes), but rather than in a strict sense, it is "taught, read, transmitted, and interpreted."[203] Formative canon provides a society with a shared vocabulary, and an exemplary canon provides paradigmatic examples, a model for imitation.

Jewish communities centered on canonical texts. This centeredness on canonical texts is especially significant in periods when the institution of the temple is in nonexistence. Halbertal dates the earliest evidence of canonizing texts in the Hellenistic period around 150 BCE.[204] He points out that almost all of the biblical books except Esther were found among the Dead Sea Scrolls and that Josephus mentions the existence of twenty books of the Bible. All of the books of 1 Enoch, except for the Similitudes, were also found at Qumran.

Although each community may have had different canonical texts, it is important to note that the Jewish communities in the diaspora find their central identity within the torah story, that is, identity within legal codes in controlling social behaviors (both inside the group and outside), which

---

203. Moshe Halbertal, *People of the Book: Canon, Meaning, and Authority* (Cambridge: Harvard University Press, 1997), 3, 12.
204. Halbertal, *People of the Book*, 17.

were embedded within the narratives about their origins. Habertal points out that "Jewish culture evolves through the interpretations of the canon, and authority is attached to knowledge of the Torah."[205] I argue that the Book of Dreams is one of the canonized interpretations of the torah for the author of the Gospel of Matthew, if not Matthew's Jewish community. This is to say that it provides a shared and intertextual vocabulary for cultural memories such as the sheep metaphor in Matt 25:31–46. The Book of Dreams may have also been taught, read, transmitted, and contextualized, which, as I argue, may be evident in the emphasis the Gospel of Matthew places upon the teachings of the torah in its apocalyptic discourses in conjunction with eschatological judgment and sheep.

---

205. Halbertal, *People of the Book*, 7.

4
The Inner Textures of Matthew 25:31–46

4.1. Introduction

The overall purpose of this chapter is to present a new interpretation of Matt 25:31–47 through dialogue with David C. Sim's approach to the apocalyptic characteristics of the Gospel of Matthew.[1] While Matt 25:31–46 is one of the most discussed passages of the Christian Testament going back to the third century,[2] there is great debate about its apocalyptic characteristics. In my view, J. A. T. Robinson points toward an analytical direction that is more suitable to its linguistic complexities.[3] Noticing past failures of analytical methods with special mention of form-criticism, Robinson makes "linguistic tests" in an attempt "to analyze out the work of the evangelist himself and to peel away different layers in the tradition, as and if they become apparent."[4] The present study builds on Robinson's attempt with a heuristic framework conditioned "to peel away different layers in the tradition" and language with the aid of sociorhetorical interpretation.

In more recent time, David C. Sim takes what is perhaps the single most influential stance regarding the argument that the Gospel of Matthew expected an imminent fulfillment of all the eschatological events it

---

1. David C. Sim, *Apocalyptic Eschatology in Matthew*, SNTSMS 88 (Cambridge: Cambridge University Press, 1996).

2. Sherman W. Gray, *The Least of My Brothers: Matthew 25:31–46; A History of Interpretation*, SBLDS 114 (Atlanta: Scholars Press, 1989); Graham N. Stanton, "Once More: Matthew 25:31–46," chapter 9 in his *A Gospel for a New People: Studies in Matthew* (Louisville: Westminster John Knox, 1992), 207–31; Luz, "The Final Judgment," 271–310.

3. J. A. T. Robinson, "The 'Parable' of the Sheep and the Goats, *NTS* 2 (1956): 225–37.

4. Robinson, "The 'Parable' of the Sheep," 226.

174   Apocalyptic Sheep and Goats in Matthew and 1 Enoch

describes.[5] For Sim, the very existence of apocalyptic in Matthew functions for this purpose. The eschatological events are eschatological woes, the arrival of a savior figure, and a final judgment that describes the fate of the wicked and the righteous. These are features of apocalyptic eschatology, which is an ideology containing primary and conceptual elements of dualism and determinism that was adopted by Matthew and his groups of Christians.[6]

The main text of Sim's study is Matt 24, which he rightly describes as eschatological. Sim argues that we can be confident that a document embraces apocalyptic eschatology if most of the features he lists can be shown to be present. Indeed, the Gospel of Matthew shows discourses that are apocalyptic in character, but it is for the most part the aim of the present study to show that apocalyptic characteristics are not only as Sim and others see them.

In contrast to Sim, our focus is on Matt 25:31–46, which has often been viewed primarily as wedded to its literary and narrative context.[7] We will examine the inner textures of Matt 25:31–46, both in its immediate literary context and the broader narrative context of Jesus's five discourses. This means we will examine the inner textures of the metaphorical language and also explore the cultural intertextures by peeling away possible cultural traditions that are attached to and evoked by the language of Matt 25:31–46.[8] In this way we hope to grasp a better understanding of the apocalyptic discourse it portrays. Let us first chart our text's contours.

What the present study offers is a more existential connection between the discourse of Matthew and that which is apocalyptic in char-

---

5. Sim, *Apocalyptic Eschatology*, 174.

6. Sim, *Apocalyptic Eschatology*, 35–52. He lists a total of eight features. The primary conceptual elements that provide the framework are dualism and determinism. The other six are eschatological woes, the arrival of the savior figure, the judgment, the fate of the wicked, the fate of the righteous, and the imminence of the end.

7. Robinson, "The 'Parable' of the Sheep," 226. See also Cope, "Matthew XXV:31–46," 33.

8. Donahue, "The 'Parable' of the Sheep," 3–31. Donahue believes the passage should be called "an apocalyptic parable" (9–10). Bultmann calls it an "apocalyptic prediction." See Rudolf Bultmann, *History of the Synoptic Tradition* (New York: Harper & Row, 1963), 123. Some have attempted to go beyond cultural parameters by placing our text in parallel with the Book of the Dead from religious literature of Egypt. See V. Hermann, "Anmerkungen zum Verständnis einiger Paralleltexte zu Matt 25:31ff. aus der altägyptischen Religion," *BibNot* 59 (1991): 17–22.

4. The Inner Textures of Matthew 25:31–46

acter. It hopes to expound Matthew's apocalyptic discourse as a literary phenomenon that is culturally and traditionally rich and thereby goes beyond simply being a product of eschatological ideology. This way of rereading Matthew's apocalyptic discourse may provide a meaningful and enriched reading that, I believe, coincides with a reading of Matthew's Gospel that removes the tension some interpreters see between some of its major themes, for example, judgment and love. Judgment in Matthew, as is well known, has created anti-Semitic interpretations. As I hope to show, judgment in Matthew's apocalyptic discourse is intended more as a deterrent to hate—whether of the neighbor or the enemy—and a stimulant for paraenesis. We will see in the following chapter that the reading this study offers rejects anti-Semitic notions that have emerged around eschatological renderings of the past and instead fosters love for humanity as a whole.

4.2. The Text of Matthew 25:31–46

Scholars often perceive Matt 25:31–46 as a dialogue with a three-part structure: introduction, dialogue, and conclusion.[9] The dialogue is further divided into two sections and is seen to contain similar formulations: 25:34–40 and 25:41–45. Likewise, Luz sees them as two judgment dialogues. Davies and Allison in their commentary suggest these two as twin conversations. While these observations are helpful, they overlook cultural-specific formulations. Allison more recently suggests our passage to be an antithetical parallelism created from the reformulation of sayings.[10] This would be partly true. The reformulation of scriptural texts is a common scribal feature of Jewish and rabbinic traditions familiar to Matthew. Considering this, an attempt will be made with regard to a working structure of our passage that falls more in line with its cultural context. I will argue generally throughout this study that the composition of this passage involves the reformulation, reinterpretation, and contextual application of Scripture. This would also mean to suggest general characteristics of Jewish apocalyptic discourse in the first century.

---

9. For example, Davies and Allison, Matthew 19–28, 417; Luz, Matthew 21–28, 264; Luz, "Final Judgment," 271–310.

10. Dale C. Allison, Studies in Matthew: Interpretation Past and Present (Grand Rapids: Baker Academic, 2005), 210. I will argue below the reformulation of Scripture.

176   Apocalyptic Sheep and Goats in Matthew and 1 Enoch

Matthew 25:31–46 certainly contains eschatological features insofar as it refers to end-time events. The passage is deemed the final judgment, and the climax to the eschatological discourse that runs from Matt 24:1, or indeed to all of Matthew's five discourses of Jesus.[11] The first two verses (25:31–32b) center on judgment as it identifies the agent of judgment in the Son of Man, while at the same time highlighting its authoritative nature as they speak of "his throne of glory." Moreover, they illuminate the very act of judgment by uttering the act of separation. These verses project the dominance of this theme throughout the rest of the pericope:

^{31}"Ὅταν δὲ ἔλθῃ ὁ υἱὸς τοῦ ἀνθρώπου ἐν τῇ δόξῃ αὐτοῦ καὶ πάντες οἱ ἄγγελοι μετ᾽ αὐτοῦ, τότε καθίσει ἐπὶ θρόνου δόξης αὐτοῦ· ^{32}καὶ συναχθήσονται ἔμπροσθεν αὐτοῦ πάντα τὰ ἔθνη, ^{32b}καὶ ἀφορίσει αὐτοὺς ἀπ᾽ ἀλλήλων.
^{31}When the Son of Man comes in his glory with all of his angels, then he will sit upon his throne of glory. ^{32}And all the nations will be gathered before him, ^{32b}and he will separate them from one another.

Matthew 25:31–32b has been seen often as a vision.[12] When compared with what seems to be a citation from Dan 7 in Matt 24:30–31,[13] the above can be described more specifically as a scriptural recitation of eschatological imagery of past apocalyptic discourses.[14] Referencing past apocalyptic

---

11. Margaret Pamment, "Singleness and Matthew's Attitude to the Torah," *JSNT* 17 (1983): 73–86. Nolland states, "Probably the level of Matthean intervention here is unusually high since Matthew uses this final piece to provide a climax for and to draw together not just the Eschatological Discourse but the whole set of five linked discourses" (*The Gospel of Matthew*, 1023–24). So also Stanton, *Gospel for a New People*, 210; Cortés-Fuentes, "The Least of These," 100–109.

12. Curtis Mitch and Edward Sri refer to Matt 25:31–46 as a vision (*The Gospel of Matthew*, Catholic Commentary on Sacred Scripture [Grand Rapids: Baker Academics, 2010], 325). So also Stanton, *Gospel for a New People*, 163. Davies and Allison call it a "word picture of the Last Judgment" (*Matthew 19–28*, 418). Warren Carter and R. T. France refer to it as a "judgment scene." See Carter, *Matthew and the Margin*, 491; France, *The Gospel of Matthew*, 960. France sees it as being closer to the majestic visions of divine judgment in Revelation than to parables in the Synoptic Gospels. Given the fact that Matthew portrays the scene as temporally uncertain, I will refer to it as imagery, falling somewhere between a word picture and a scene, both of which can be considered a presentation of a vivid image of the mind as opposed to a more certain declaration of a prophetic vision.

13. For example, France, *Gospel of Matthew*, 923, 957–60.

14. Discourses, when taken out of their original context, lose their affects. Like-

4. The Inner Textures of Matthew 25:31–46

discourses and visions are good indicators of apocalyptic discourse in New Testament texts. It resembles what is cited in Matt 24:30–31, which states,

³⁰καὶ τότε φανήσεται τὸ σημεῖον τοῦ υἱοῦ τοῦ ἀνθρώπου ἐν οὐρανῷ, καὶ τότε κόψονται πᾶσαι αἱ φυλαὶ τῆς γῆς καὶ ὄψονται τὸν υἱὸν τοῦ ἀνθρώπου ἐρχόμενον ἐπὶ τῶν νεφελῶν τοῦ οὐρανοῦ μετὰ δυνάμεως καὶ δόξης πολλῆς· ³¹καὶ ἀποστελεῖ τοὺς ἀγγέλους αὐτοῦ μετὰ σάλπιγγος μεγάλης, καὶ ἐπισυνάξουσιν τοὺς ἐκλεκτοὺς αὐτοῦ ἐκ τῶν τεσσάρων ἀνέμων ἀπ' ἄκρων οὐρανῶν ἕως [τῶν] ἄκρων αὐτῶν.

³⁰And then the sign of the Son of Man will appear in the heaven, and at that time all the tribes of the earth will mourn, and they will see the Son of Man coming upon the clouds of the heaven with power and great glory. ³¹And he will send his angels with a loud trumpet call, and they will gather his elect from the four winds, from one end of heaven to the other.

The Son of Man resumes the seat of glory and gathers (ἐπισυνάγω) those who have been judged. In the context of judgment, gathering coincides with mourning (κόπτω). As it were, those deemed wicked would mourn and those blessed are considered his elect (τοὺς ἐκλεκτοὺς αὐτοῦ). What is not present in Matt 24:30–31, as it is in 25:31–46, is a parable, which would further indicate that the imagery in Matt 25:31–32b is scriptural in origin. The vision in Matt 25:31–32b goes right into a parable (25:32c–33), which is introduced by the comparative particle ὥσπερ:[15]

³²ᶜὥσπερ ὁ ποιμὴν ἀφορίζει τὰ πρόβατα ἀπὸ τῶν ἐρίφων, ³³καὶ στήσει τὰ μὲν πρόβατα ἐκ δεξιῶν αὐτοῦ, τὰ δὲ ἐρίφια ἐξ εὐωνύμων.

³²ᶜJust as the shepherd separates the sheep from the goats, ³³and he will make the sheep stand on his right, and the goats on the left.

Scriptures that are followed by parables are a good indication of midrash, a method of interpretation in Jewish traditions.[16] The parable of Matt 25:32c–33 would act like a midrash that explains in more detail about

---

wise, apocalyptic discourses, when taken out of their original literary context, lose their rhetorical affects. What is often left, when segments are reused, is judgment imagery.

15. This is a typical feature of Matthew's parables. See Matt 6:2, 7; 12:40; 13:40; 18:17; 20:28; 24:27, 37; 25:14.

16. Davies and Allison also see 25:31–46 as an exposition of 24:29–31 (*Matthew 19–28*, 420).

178   Apocalyptic Sheep and Goats in Matthew and 1 Enoch

those being gathered and the fact that gathering is done for the purpose of separating.

In Matthew, this same eschatological vision is repeated more than twice, albeit with variations. We have a similar and related imagery within Jesus's third discourse in Matt 13:24–30, 36–43. Matthew 13:41–43 states,

> [41]ἀποστελεῖ ὁ υἱὸς τοῦ ἀνθρώπου τοὺς ἀγγέλους αὐτοῦ, καὶ συλλέξουσιν ἐκ τῆς βασιλείας αὐτοῦ πάντα τὰ σκάνδαλα καὶ τοὺς ποιοῦντας τὴν ἀνομίαν [42]καὶ βαλοῦσιν αὐτοὺς εἰς τὴν κάμινον τοῦ πυρός· ἐκεῖ ἔσται ὁ κλαυθμὸς καὶ ὁ βρυγμὸς τῶν ὀδόντων. [43]τότε οἱ δίκαιοι ἐκλάμψουσιν ὡς ὁ ἥλιος ἐν τῇ βασιλείᾳ τοῦ πατρὸς αὐτῶν. ὁ ἔχων ὦτα ἀκουέτω.
> [41]The Son of Man will send out his angels, and they will gather out of his kingdom everything that causes stumbling and all who do lawlessness. [42]They will throw them into the blazing furnace, where there will be weeping and gnashing of teeth. [43]Then the righteous will shine like the sun in the kingdom of their Father.

In the above passage from the parable of the sower of good seeds, judgment also involves gathering (συλλέγω). Unlike 24:30–31 and similar to 25:31–33, gathering is done for the act of separating, which is described in figurative language.[17] As gathering becomes the task of the Son of Man, the figurative language of separating livestock and weeding out in 25:32c–33 and 13:41–43 respectively explains the scriptural imagery in more details. An obvious detail in both 25:31–46 and 13:24–30, 36–43 is the fact that the Son of Man, in his act of judging, will separate those he gathers into two groups. Thus the parables in 25:32c–33 and 13:24–30, 36–43 not only contain features that are midrashic in nature, but they also explain *how* the Son of Man will carry out his judgment.

Unlike the parable of the sower of good seeds, one may suggest that the parable of the sheep and goats (25:32c–33) serves only to highlight the act of separation done by the shepherd. However, that the parable of the shepherd is followed by the metaphor of the king means that the parable and what follows are meant to be understood together. The shepherd and king metaphors (i.e., 25:32, 34) are often seen in correlation, as they are familiar expressions of David and messianic figures in Jewish tradition and literature.[18] As I will argue further below, the correlation of the Son of

---

17. The Greek verb συλλέγω may also be taken to mean "to collect," as in the collection of weeds at harvest while leaving the wheat to shine under the sun.

18. David's domestic role as shepherd is transferred over to his kingship. Walter

4. The Inner Textures of Matthew 25:31–46 179

Man to the deeds of a farmer, shepherd, and king equates to a correlation with a Messianic figure. That the king refers to "my Father" makes this more evident.[19]

The pericope of Matt 25:31–46 goes further than the parable of the sower of good seeds in Matt 13:24–30, 36–43, as the parable of the shepherd in Matt 25:32c–33 segues into a metaphor of the king (ὁ βασιλεύς 25:34). The sheep and goats then become the king's subjects under his jurisdiction, playing out an allegorical composition.[20] Parables and allegories are prevalent in traditional midrash. Thus, the allegory would expand upon the scriptural vision even further. While the parable has the reader contemplating on the shepherd separating the sheep from the goats, the allegory of the king utilizes the separation motif to structure the reading of the rest of the pericope in 25:34–45. While the parable of the sheep and goats highlights *how* the Son of Man judges, the allegory explains *why* those judged are being separated on the right and left: (1) 25:34–40 addresses the king's subjects on his right, and (2) 25:41–45 addresses

---

Brueggemann states, "the entire narrative of David's rise is staged from shepherd boy (1 Sam 16:11) to shepherd king.... It is Yahweh's overriding intention in the narrative that the shepherd boy should become the shepherd of Israel." See Walter Brueggemann, *First and Second Samuel* (Louisville: John Knox, 1990), 237–38. Though the title is never used, David is Israel's shepherd-king in Jewish literature. See also John Paul Heil, "Ezekiel 3 and the Narrative Strategy of the Shepherd and Sheep Metaphor in Matthew," *CBQ* 55 (1993): 698–708; Joel Willitts, *Matthew's Messianic Shepherd-King: In Search of "The Lost Sheep of the House of Israel"* (Berlin: de Gruyter, 2007).

19. John Nolland rightly asks, "Is the relationship of Jesus as Son to the Father being allowed to obtrude through the imagery?" (Nolland, *Gospel of Matthew*, 1027). I agree. However, Nolland, in my opinion, is too quick to suggest a correlation of Jesus with the Son of Man when he concludes, "The reference to the Father here is a quiet reminder that Jesus as the Son of Man exercises the functions of deity not independently but on behalf of his Father." I argue above that the shepherd and king metaphors remind the reader of Jesus's identity of the Son of God.

20. *Pace* John Nolland, who suggests that the metaphor of the king is not embedded in a story, "which at any level is the story of an earthly king" (Nolland, *Gospel of Matthew*, 1034). His reasoning is that the king is king "in virtue of being the Son of Man." This, however, is mixing the metaphors inappropriately. The king should metaphorically be understood first and foremost as an earthly king, albeit the throne already implies a divine king. But the king metaphor in 25:34 is presented more in sync with the shepherd metaphor as the shepherd-king than the Son of Man as a divine king.

180   Apocalyptic Sheep and Goats in Matthew and 1 Enoch

those on his left.[21] Moreover, the parable and the allegory are different expressions of judgment. Therefore, on the one hand, the directional indicators—right and left—of Matt 25:31–46 embody the motif of separation, which weaves together the eschatological vision, the parable, and allegory as expressions of judgment. On the other hand, the parable and allegory explain the scriptural vision through added details. Thus, meaning for the implied audience comes about conceptually through the metaphorical language and not literally through the dialogue.[22]

The composition of this three-part structure reveals temporal implications for our passage. First, the eschatological vision in Matt 25:31–32b gives indication for future time. Matthew employs a conditional construct, which has implications of the uncertain time of when this will happen in the future. In the protasis (25:31a), the time in which the parousia or the coming of the Son of the Man will ever occur is uncertain.[23] When

---

21. "[34]Then the king will say to those at his right hand, 'Come, you that are blessed by my Father, inherit the kingdom prepared for you from the foundation of the world; [35]for I was hungry and you gave me food, I was thirsty and you gave me something to drink, I was a stranger and you welcomed me, [36]I was naked and you gave me clothing, I was sick and you took care of me, I was in prison and you visited me.' [37]Then the righteous will answer him, 'Lord, when was it that we saw you hungry and gave you food, or thirsty and gave you something to drink? [38]And when was it that we saw you a stranger and welcomed you, or naked and gave you clothing? [39]And when was it that we saw you sick or in prison and visited you? [40]And the king will answer them, 'Truly I tell you, just as you did it to one of the least of these who are members of my family, you did it to me.'

"[41]Then he will say to those at his left hand, 'You that are accursed, depart from me into the eternal fire prepared for the devil and his angels; [42]for I was hungry and you gave me no food, I was thirsty and you gave me nothing to drink, [43]I was a stranger and you did not welcome me, naked and you did not give me clothing, sick and in prison and you did not visit me.' [44]Then they also will answer, 'Lord, when was it that we saw you hungry or thirsty or a stranger or naked or sick or in prison, and did not take care of you? [45]Then he will answer them, 'Truly I tell you, just as you did not do it to one of the least of these, you did not do it to me'" (Matt 25:34–45 NRSV).

22. The interpretation and implications of Matt 25:31–46 does not rest solely upon the literal narrative from which we may obviously see a dialogue. If that is the case, we would only conclude what is presented on the surface. For example, John P. Meier concludes, "Although the scene has parabolic elements (the comparison with a shepherd and his flock in verses 32–33), the body of the narrative is a straightforward depiction of what will take place on the last day." See Meier, *The Vision of Matthew*, 177. I feel this reading does no justice to the "parabolic elements" of the passage.

23. In the future-more-vivid construction. Ὅταν [subjunctive] … τότε [future

4. The Inner Textures of Matthew 25:31–46   181

that time does come, only then will the events it describes in the apodosis (25:31b) occur (future indicative): the Son of Man sitting upon his
throne, proclaiming judgment upon "all the nations," πάντα τὰ ἔθνη, and
separating them as a shepherd separates sheep from goats. Second, the
allegory reflects a speech act that aims to exhort Matthew's audience for
deeds in the here and now. As already mentioned in the beginning of this
study, scholars have explained the relations of future predictions and present deeds in terms of the imminent coming of the Son of Man. While I do
not deny the possibility of this belief among circles of Jesus followers in
the first century, I will argue throughout this study, rather, that the author
of the Gospel of Matthew, in Jesus, is not presenting but recontextualizing
future predictions by relating the future reality and present deeds in light
of the uncertain coming of the Son of Man. In this sense, the exhortation
for deeds is more in focus.

The uncertainty of the coming end is seen in the beginning of the
eschatological discourse on the Mount of Olives (24:3–8), where Jesus
informs his disciples that "not yet *is* the end." Matthew adds the copula
to be to his Markan source in order to emphasize this, making his version
different from Mark's (Mark 13:7) and Q's (cf. Luke 21:9). On the basis of
other passages (i.e., Matt 10:23; 16:28; 24:33), scholars have argued regarding the immediacy of Matthew's expectations of the parousia. However,
those passages speak indefinitely of time as well and highlight the assurance of the parousia's realization.

Matthew 10:23; 16:28; and 24:33 indicate for many that Matthew has
the imminence of the parousia in mind. However, these passages only
assure the future transition from Jesus on earth as the Son of God to his
identity in heaven at resurrection as the Son of Man without necessarily
insisting on the time of Jesus's return. In other words, the claims within
these passages are fulfilled in Jesus's resurrection as the Son of Man.
Matthew 10:23 and 16:28 refer to the Son of Man in terms of the Greek
deponent verb ἔρχομαι, which may mean "to come" or "to go."[24] In the

---

indicative]. See Herbert W. Smyth, *Greek Grammar* (Harvard: Harvard University
Press, 1984), 523–25. There is also the emotional-future condition, as the event of the
parousia is meant to be feared in order to give full force to its exhortation and rhetorical effect. Cf. Davies and Allison, *Matthew 19–28*, 323.

24. BDAG, s.v. "ἔρχομαι." In Matthew, the verb is often translated as "to come." It
also has the meaning of "to go" or "to proceed on a course, with destination in view"
(cf. 16:24; 21:19).

182   Apocalyptic Sheep and Goats in Matthew and 1 Enoch

context of exhorting his disciples in 10:23 and 16:28 in light of persecution and fear of discipleship, Jesus assures the glorious fate to which he must go and face (cf. Matt 9:15).[25] When he is resurrected, they will witness the Son of Man *go* into his heavenly kingdom. Witnessing Jesus going assures the disciples that the coming of the Son of Man (Matt 16:27), whenever that will be, indicates the return of the very person who went: Jesus. It speaks nothing of an imminent coming but only that Jesus's return is assured by virtue of the assured coming of the Son of Man. Likewise, in 25:31–46, the text does not ascertain the time of the coming Son of the Man, as also with more emphasis in 24:3–8; 24:36–25:30.[26] What is even more telling is the conflicting notion of an imminent coming with the commission to make disciples of all nations in 28:19. Therefore, Matt 25:31–46 should not be taken as a passage indicating an imminent arrival of the Son of Man but one of assurance that Jesus will return as the Son of Man, albeit in some unknown future, such that one's deeds in present time through his or her credence will not be in vain. The passage speaks more about deeds through the hope of assurance than the coercion of imminence.

The use of the Greek particle τότε (25:34, 37, 41, 44, 45) is the expansion of the above conditional construct as it dramatizes the apodosis. Therein lies the centrality of what is being communicated, as the particle introduces everything the allegory is saying. Just as the coming of the Son of Man is assured to take place as the returning Jesus at some uncertain time, the repetition of the temporal particle τότε emphatically assures the reality of the consequential actions that will take place. This reality is followed by the authoritative judgment evident in the formulaic saying of authority, ἀμὴν λέγω ὑμῖν, which ends each section of the allegory (25:40, 45).

---

25. Jesus going away has already been expressed in the narrative when Jesus answered the question posed by the disciples of John in Matt 9:14–17. In speaking of the new situation at hand, the presence of Jesus as the Son of God on earth, Jesus speaks metaphorically in terms of bridegroom, celebration, and fasting. Jesus says in Matt 9:15, "The wedding guests cannot mourn as long as the bridegroom is with them, can they? The days will come when the bridegroom is taken away from them, and then they will fast." Here, Jesus, who is the Son of God and bridegroom, will be taken away from the wedding guests.

26. Carter, *Matthew and the Margins*, 493. Contra Carter, who believes that, while 24:36–25:30 emphasizes the unknown time and delayed coming of Jesus the Son of Man, 25:31–46 places in focus the need to prepare now that the coming of judgment is described.

4. The Inner Textures of Matthew 25:31–46   183

Aside from its temporal elements, there are other significant literary elements that must be pointed out from the allegory. There is first the king's call to action that presupposes judgment upon those being judged. In 25:34, the judged are given the imperative "come," while 25:41 the imperative "depart." This is slightly different from the parable when the shepherd separates those judged to the right and left. The difference is more personal for the former. More so when the reason for the call begins with personal actions of the subjects toward the king (25:34–36, 41–43). This is indicated by the Greek postpositive γάρ in 25:35 and 25:42 that immediately follows. The personal actions toward the king become a reference to actions toward or in response to the ultimate authority, which may be likened to actions toward or in response to scriptural authority, insofar as we may understand Scripture to be the will of God. The accusations leave the subjects perplexed as they question the king (25:37–39, 44). The confusion lies in understanding how the accusations involving the king relate to them. For the blessed, there is a claim that they have performed righteous deeds. For the wicked, there is an accusation they have performed unrighteous deeds. The questioning by the subjects as to when they committed these deeds are ultimately questions of understanding the king and his judgment. This would also be likened to understanding Scripture, which is the challenge Jesus regularly has put to the Jewish authorities within the previous narrative. Such claims are explained further when it refers to a more experiential reference: actions done to "one of the least of these of my brothers and sisters" (25:40, 45). Thus, contrary to popular belief, the focus isn't really upon "the least of my brothers." The least of the king's brothers brings the subject's understanding of the king into context and realization. The primary focus of the allegory is on the subjects and their understanding of the king, those being judged and their understanding of the judge. We may be able to structure the allegory as follows:

25:34 Imperative to the Righteous Subjects: Come
    25:35–36 Give Authoritative Reason for the Imperative
        25:37–39 Questioning the Authoritative Reason
            25:40 Explain the Authoritative Reason Experientially
25:41 Imperative to the Unrighteous Subjects: Depart
    25:42–43 Give Authoritative Reason for the Imperative
        25:44 Questioning the Authoritative Reason
            25:45 Explain the Authoritative Reason Experientially

184   Apocalyptic Sheep and Goats in Matthew and 1 Enoch

Matthew 25:46 is not only a summary of the judgment made in the allegory (e.g., 25:34, 41) but also the end of the scriptural vision (25:31–32b), such that if we take away the parable and the allegory, 25:46 becomes the natural ending of the scriptural vision as such,

> [31]When the Son of Man comes in his glory, and all the angels with him, then he will sit on the throne of his glory. [32a]All the nations will be gathered before him, [32b]and he will separate people one from another.

> [46]And ... [the wicked] will go away into eternal punishment, but the righteous into eternal life.

The above reformulation resembles a straightforward prediction as seen in the vision of Matt 24:30–31. The parable and the allegory are enveloped within this scriptural vision of judgment, which strongly suggests a discourse beyond just a recitation of Scripture on eschatological judgment. It would suggest what Stephen O'Leary calls an "apocalyptic rhetoric." However, this study diverges from O'Leary on exactly what that consists of, namely, a rhetoric that isn't necessarily defined by eschatology and its aims of a possible ideology.[27] It is rather a rhetoric couched in heavenly communication for exhortation in the present with metaphorical language. It is a rhetoric undergirded more by hope that vindicates than anxiety that indicts.

I propose a simple structure for Matt 25:31–46 based on the structure of the allegory explained above:

A. Scriptural Vision of the Son of Man (Gathering for Judgment), 25:31–32b
    B. Parable of the Shepherd, 25:32c–33
        i. The Sheep at the Right, 25:33a
        ii. The Goats at the Left, 25:33b
    C. Allegory of the King, 25:34–45
        i. The Righteous Subjects, 25:34–40
        ii. The Unrighteous Subjects, 25:41–45
A'. Scriptural Vision of the Son of Man (Verdict), 25:46

---

27. See Stephen O'Leary, *Arguing the Apocalypse: A Theory of Millennial Rhetoric* (New York: Oxford University Press, 1994).

4. The Inner Textures of Matthew 25:31–46

Judgment via the motif of separation presupposes the duality of right and wrong that is marked by the subverdicts of 25:34 and 25:41, which are based on the deeds of the sheep (righteous) and goats (unrighteous), namely, how they treated "one of the least of these my brothers." The favorable deeds of the sheep become the measuring stick of righteousness. On the other hand, the shepherd-king would be the ultimate measuring stick, for it is he who has taken the least of these in as brothers. Thus, if Matthew, *through* Jesus, had to communicate anything of apocalyptic rhetoric with eschatological judgment, Matt 25:31–46 would be an ideal place to explore, as it involves a heavenly vision (re)explained in symbolic and metaphorical language.[28]

4.3. The Broader Narrative Context

The vision, parable, and allegory would evoke imageries of Jesus, namely, Jesus's identity as the Son of God and as the Son of Man. The audience would then harken back to significant sections of the broader narrative just told. The judgment imagery and the identity of Jesus as the Son of God would recall Jesus's first discourse in Matt 3:11–17. There, John the Baptist states in 3:11–12:

> [11]I baptize you with water for repentance, but one who is more powerful than I is coming after me; I am not worthy to carry his sandals. He will baptize you with the Holy Spirit and fire. [12]His winnowing fork is in his hand, and he will clear his threshing floor and *will gather his wheat* into the granary; but the chaff he will burn with unquenchable fire.

Like Matt 25:31–32b, gathering and separation become the actions of judgment and presuppose the end of the age. However, as I will show below, John seems to be confused as to who Jesus is and how this judgment will come about. More importantly, these passages identify Jesus explicitly as the Son of God. As hinted to above, there is also a significant and similar eschatological imagery in Matt 13:24–30, 36–43. Unlike Matt 3:11–17, Jesus seems to be identified more profoundly through the metaphor of the sower of good seed (13:24–30), as the Son of Man (13:36–43). The

---

28. Graham N. Stanton similarly states, "There is probably no better illustration of the evangelist's interest in apocalyptic than the apocalyptic vision in 25:31–46" (Stanton, *Gospel for a New People*, 163).

186 Apocalyptic Sheep and Goats in Matthew and 1 Enoch

juxtaposition of these two identities of Jesus, as I argue, is found in the correlation of the vision (Son of Man), parable and allegory (shepherd-king) in 25:31–46. Thus, the audience would have harkened back on sections of the narrative as inner textures. In fact, I argue that Matt 3:11–17 and 13:24–30, 36–43 are significant inner textures to the composition of Matt 25:31–46.

The juxtaposition of the Son of God with the Son of Man is not as old as the individual identities. The author of the Gospel of Matthew went to much length and effort in merging these two identities, as if the juxtaposition was not a well-known idea. The referent of the Son of Man, the shepherd, and king may be obvious and often taken for granted. I argue that Matt 25:31–46 is the culminating climax to the progression of Matthew's narrative of judgment imageries that begins in the two chapters before the Sermon on the Mount. The primary judgment narratives occur in Matt 3:1–4:17; 13:24–30, 36–43; 25:31–46, which means they occur strategically in the beginning, middle, and ending of Jesus's five discourses. This literary development draws attention to Matthew's Christology and to the ultimate significance of Matthew's apocalyptic discourse and juxtaposition in Matt 25:31–46.[29] I will show in what follows that the construct of Jesus's identities in Matt 25:31–46 is the result of a progressive development of Matthew's narrative. The persuasive force of the metaphors of sheep and goats hinges upon that development.

4.3.1. The Son of God: Matt 3:11–17

John's eschatological utterance in Matt 3:11–12 depicts Jesus as a political Messiah, baptizer, and reaper. It also depicts human subjects being judged as righteous and unrighteous, baptized with the Holy Spirit and fire, and reaped like wheat and chaff. These metaphors are placed side by side in such a way that one illuminates the other, adding clarity to the nature of the "one who is coming." One would envision a universal judgment from John's description, whereby righteous Israel (wheat) is the beneficiary, and gentiles and apostates (chaff) are condemned. The judgment is imminent,

---

29. Meyer, "Context," 69–72. Meyer recognizes the lack of attention of most interpreters to the context, namely, the "careful placement at the climax of Matthew's fifth and final large block of discourse material, i.e., at the end of Jesus's teaching just before the start of the Passion Narrative." He further states, "To ignore this placement is a major breach of simple exegetical and literary observation" (71).

4. The Inner Textures of Matthew 25:31–46   187

and options are scarce. However, these images are being challenged by what follows in 3:13–15.

[13a]Τότε παραγίνεται ὁ Ἰησοῦς ἀπὸ τῆς Γαλιλαίας ἐπὶ τὸν Ἰορδάνην πρὸς τὸν Ἰωάννην [b]τοῦ βαπτισθῆναι ὑπ' αὐτοῦ. [14a]ὁ δὲ Ἰωάννης διεκώλυεν αὐτὸν λέγων· [b]ἐγὼ χρείαν ἔχω ὑπὸ σοῦ βαπτισθῆναι, καὶ σὺ ἔρχῃ πρός με; [15a]ἀποκριθεὶς δὲ ὁ Ἰησοῦς εἶπεν πρὸς αὐτόν· ἄφες ἄρτι, [b]οὕτως γὰρ πρέπον ἐστὶν ἡμῖν πληρῶσαι πᾶσαν δικαιοσύνην. [c]τότε ἀφίησιν αὐτόν. (Matt 3:13–15) Then Jesus appeared from Galilee upon the Jordan to John in order to be baptized by him. But John prevented him saying, "I need to be baptized by you and you come to me?" But Jesus answered and says to him, "Let it be so now; for in this way, it is fitting for us to fulfill all righteousness." Then, he allowed it.

Matthew 3:13–15 acts as a bridge between John's eschatological expectation of Jesus and the heavenly vision in 3:16–17. Jesus's appearance becomes the pivotal point of the entire unit (τότε παραγίνεται [3:13]). The above verses are Matthew's addition.[30] He inserts these two verses to dramatize the appearance of Jesus and possibly cause conflict with John's expectations.[31] If Jesus is truly the superior authority, that would also provide a logical answer to obvious questions that would emerge from his sources of how it is that John is able to baptize Jesus.[32] The same logical conflict between expectations and comparisons of Jesus to a figure is seen in Jesus's question to the Pharisees in Matt 22:41–45:

---

30. W. D. Davies and Dale C. Allison, The Gospel according to Saint Matthew 1–7, ICC (New York: T&T Clark, 2004), 320. Matthew 3:14–15 tells us why Jesus has to be baptized (to fulfill all righteousness).

31. France, Gospel of Matthew, 117. France calls this a debate between John and Jesus and a paradox in light of previous passages where John speaks of Jesus's superiority.

32. It would also be at odds with some of the Pauline and other Christian communities who saw Jesus as sinless (2 Cor 5:21; Heb 4:15; John 8:46; 1 Pet 1:19; 2:22) and the forgiver of sins (e.g., 1 Cor 15:3; Rom 3:23–26). R. T. France rightly points out that sinlessness is not the issue raised here but "a matter of relative status and of the contrast between the two baptisms" (France, Gospel of Matthew, 118). This would not preclude the issue as a background in Matthew's attempt to bridge the two imageries through these verses. Generally speaking, sin has everything to do with righteousness, which is an important issue in these passages. See also notes by Ulrich Luz, Matthew 1–7, Hermeneia (Minneapolis: Fortress, 2007), 141.

188 Apocalyptic Sheep and Goats in Matthew and 1 Enoch

"What do you think of the Messiah? Whose son is he?" They said to him, "The son of David." He said to them, "How is it then that David by the Spirit calls him Lord, saying, 'The Lord said to my Lord, 'Sit at my right hand, until I put your enemies under your feet'? If David thus calls him Lord, how can he be his son?"

Here Jesus uses the classical rabbinic argument from lesser to greater. John in our passage also tries to reason using a similar logic. The schema below visualizes this more clearly and, in so doing, highlights an apparent conflict.

> Situation (Introducing Jesus): (3:13a) Then, Jesus appeared from Galilee upon the Jordan to John
> Rational Explanation of Situation: (3:13b) in order to be baptized by him.
> Evaluate Situation: (3:14a) But John prevented him saying,
> Rational Explanation of Evaluated Situation: (3:14b) "I need to be baptized by you, and you come to me?"
> Jesus's Exhortation: (3:15a) But having answered, Jesus says to him, "Let it be now,
> Rational Explanation of Exhortation: (3:15b) for in this way it is fitting for us to fulfill all righteousness."
> Reevaluate Situation: (3:15c) Then, he allowed it.

Matthew presents John as being perplexed about the appearance of Jesus to be baptized by him, "I need to be baptized by you, and do you come to me?"[33] To baptize Jesus would qualify Jesus as a subject rather than John's superior in baptism. John understands the coming of Jesus as implementing judgment rather than someone preparing for it.

Jesus insists upon his baptism and provides the reason, "for it is proper for us in this way to fulfill all righteousness." Instead of bringing justice and salvation through wrath and destruction, Jesus asks for baptism in order to fulfill "all righteousness." Matthew has Jesus modify what John initially expected of the "coming one." Why is it proper that Jesus be baptized in order for both John and Jesus to fulfill all righteousness? What

---

33. This section is a Matthean addition to his sources. Mark 1:9 and Luke 3:21 record Jesus being baptized like everyone else. Moreover, John does not recognize Jesus before being baptized.

4. The Inner Textures of Matthew 25:31–46   189

does "to fulfill all righteousness" mean? The answers to these questions underscore the missing premise. The reasoning becomes somehow logically valid as John reevaluates what Jesus says and allows it. I will return to these important questions shortly, but Jesus's statement transitions from John's eschatological expectations to the heavenly communication in Matt 3:16–17.

¹⁶βαπτισθεὶς δὲ ὁ Ἰησοῦς εὐθὺς ἀνέβη ἀπὸ τοῦ ὕδατος· ᵇκαὶ ἰδοὺ ἠνεῴχθησαν [αὐτῷ] οἱ οὐρανοί, καὶ εἶδεν [τὸ] πνεῦμα [τοῦ] θεοῦ καταβαῖνον ὡσεὶ περιστερὰν [καὶ] ἐρχόμενον ἐπ᾽ αὐτόν· ¹⁷καὶ ἰδοὺ φωνὴ ἐκ τῶν οὐρανῶν λέγουσα· οὗτός ἐστιν ὁ υἱός μου ὁ ἀγαπητός, ἐν ᾧ εὐδόκησα.³⁴

¹⁶*Having been baptized*, Jesus immediately rises *from* the water. ᵇAnd behold! *The heavens opened up* to him, and he saw the Spirit of God coming down just as a dove alighting upon him. And behold! ¹⁷a voice from the heavens said, "This is my beloved Son, in whom I am pleased."

Matthew returns to his sources but stays closer to Mark in these two passages as he narrates a vision experienced by Jesus. Matthew maintains the focus upon the baptism not as an act being performed but as a symbolic act.³⁵ Whereas Mark describes the heavens as being torn apart (Mark 1:10), Matthew opts for "the heavens opened up" (ἀνοίγω) in order to coincide with expressions of receiving revelations from the heavens.³⁶ The Matthean redaction from "heavens split" to "heavens opened" is telling. The difference in description is a distinction between an eschatological judgment vision and heavenly communication.³⁷ As it were, the baptism prompts

---

34. "¹⁶And when Jesus had been baptized, just as he came up from the water, ¹⁶ᵇsuddenly the heavens were opened to him and he saw the Spirit of God descending like a dove and alighting on him. ¹⁷And a voice from heaven said, 'This is my Son, the Beloved, with whom I am well pleased'" (Matt 3:16–17 NRSV).

35. Mark's use of the participle ἀναβαίνων and the preposition ἐκ as "immediately coming out of the water" (Mark 3:10) is descriptive and temporal as if telling a story for the first time. Matthew replaces the participle with an aorist active verb ἀνέβη and the preposition ἐκ with ἀπό in order to link the emergence from the water to the process of baptism (βαπτισθείς) as a unified event in a particular moment, hence the aorist. In other words, Matthew here is not concerned with minute details of going in and coming out and then, and so forth. Rather, Matthew means to link Jesus's baptism as a whole to what follows in 3:17.

36. Davies and Allison, *Matthew 1–7*, 329.

37. Davies and Allison, *Matthew 1–7*, 329. Davies and Allison state, "The splitting of the heavens in connexion with God's judgment was an eschatological expecta-

190   Apocalyptic Sheep and Goats in Matthew and 1 Enoch

the Spirit of God to descend and a voice to reveal Jesus as the Son of God (Matt 3:17). It is a heavenly communication of esoteric knowledge utilizing metaphorical language (also 16:16–17).[38] *Communication of esoteric knowledge between the heavenly and earthly realm is the essential element of what we mean when a discourse is said to be apocalyptic.* Thus, we may suggest that the revelation of Jesus as the Son of God in Matt 3:16–17 is an apocalyptic discourse in itself.

The epithet of the "Son of God" is an important concept in New Testament scholarship for obvious reasons. The sonship revealed in 3:17 is usually explained as echoing Ps 2:7, in which God addresses his anointed king, "You are my son; today I have begotten you." It may also echo Gen 22:2.[39] Throughout Matthew, the epithet refers to someone who obeys and does the will of God (4:3, 6) in his understanding of Scriptures, who has supernatural abilities on earth to control nature (14:33) and to interact against demonic forces (8:29), and who is an anointed Messiah (16:16; cf. 26:63) that parallels in meaning with servitude (cf. Isa 42:1).[40] Thus, a working definition can be as follows: Jesus as the Son of God is an anointed representative of God before humanity and on earth.

The voice uses a demonstrative to identify Jesus, rather than Mark's and Q's (Mark 1:11; Luke 3:22) second-person address, "This is my beloved Son, in whom I am pleased." It makes the communication more public.

---

tion.… But the pertinent texts for comparison [to Matt 3:16] are those in which Jewish or Christian seers receiving revelation see heaven opened." See also Adela Yarbro Collins, *Mark: A Commentary*, Hermeneia (Minneapolis: Fortress, 2007), 148. She states, "The verb 'to open' (ἀνοίγω) was more often used to express the idea of heaven(s) opening for … revelatory purposes." This is by no means an attempt to suggest that Matthew is making a distinction between apocalyptic and eschatology as defined in this study. It is only pointing out Matthew's implications in reconfiguring materials from his sources. Namely, that Jesus is not John's idea of the end-time figure, nor does Jesus bring the judgment he imagines.

38. "Simon Peter answered, 'You are the Messiah, the Son of the living God.' And Jesus answered him, 'Blessed are you, Simon son of Jonah! For flesh and blood has not revealed [ἀποκαλύπτω] this to you, but my Father in heaven'" (Matt 16:16–17 RSV).

39. Davies and Allison, *Matthew 1–7*, 336; France, *Gospel of Matthew*, 123; Mitch and Sri, *Gospel of Matthew*, 71. Scholars point out the similarities of the LXX wording of Gen 22:2, namely, ἀγαπητός and υἱός.

40. R. T. France sees the parallel in Isa 42:1 as strongly plausible. He states, "So that Matthew's readers would learn to see Jesus in the role of the 'servant of Yahweh' who would die for the sins of the people" (France, *Gospel of Matthew*, 123). See also Mitch and Sri, *Gospel of Matthew*, 70; Davies and Allison, *Matthew 1–7*, 337.

4. The Inner Textures of Matthew 25:31–46   191

However, in harkening back to Matt 3:15b (ἡμῖν, "for us"), it is natural that the dove and voice are known only to John and Jesus.[41] In taking this further, one is not only thinking back to the first-person plural pronoun in the dative (ἡμῖν, "for us") but also to the entire statement, "for us to fulfill all righteousness." With this in mind, the heavenly communication of Jesus's identity as Son of God is more than just a confirmation of identity; it is meant to be an integral part of fulfilling all righteousness, an aspect of the passage not found in Matthew's sources. Thus, it also becomes a confirmation of the role that involves saving his people from their sins (1:21).

The Greek verb πληρόω, "to fulfill," is almost always used in Matthew through Jesus's mouth within the context of fulfilling the words of the prophets or Scripture (Matt 1:22; 2:15, 17, 23; 4:14; 5:17; 8:17; 12:17; 13:35; 21:4; 26:54, 56; 27:9). However, it is not necessary to suggest that here, too, Jesus is speaking of Scripture when fulfilling all righteousness or when being baptized.[42] The term *righteousness* would not suggest that we should primarily be thinking of fulfilling prophetic predictions.[43] "To fulfill" has the primary transitive sense of "to make full or fill," as in fulfilling a task (cf. Acts 12:25, πληρώσαντες τὴν διακονίαν).[44] Given Jesus's identity as Son of God, the object of "to fulfill" in the above sense would be synonymous with fulfilling God's will, which is synonymous with the concept of righteousness. This is seen especially in Jesus's temptation in 4:1–11 that follows. Jesus as the Son of God does the will of his father in spite of the devil's attempts to lure him away.

Thus, the statement "for us to fulfill all righteousness" is closely related to Jesus's identity as the Son of God and has to do with setting out to make all righteousness full in light of his sonship, rather than his sonship or baptism fulfilling all righteousness. This is to say that Jesus is commissioned by God via the dove alighting upon him for a task. Matthew redacts his sources to present this section (3:16–17) as an apocalyptic communication between the heavens, John, and Jesus, with the possi-

---

41. Davies and Allison, *Matthew 1–7*, 325.

42. For this view, see Davies and Allison, *Matthew 1–7*, 326–27; John P. Meier, *Law and History in Matthew's Gospel*, AnBib 71 (Rome: Biblical Institute Press, 1976), 76–80.

43. Against Davies and Allison and Meier cited above, Ulrich Luz notes that the term *righteousness* (δικαιοσύνη) excludes the possibility of thinking primarily of the fulfillment of prophetic predictions (Luz, *Matthew 1–7*, 143 n. 24).

44. BDAG, s.v. "πληρόω," 1a.

192   Apocalyptic Sheep and Goats in Matthew and 1 Enoch

bility that the alighting of the dove upon Jesus is also an act of election for Jesus to fulfill all righteousness. It would explain why John approves the baptism, for baptism not only prepares one for judgment; it also prepares someone for a divine task. It makes no sense in the context of John's expectation that John approves of Jesus's baptism just so his baptism is to fulfill all righteousness. That would not have been what John expected. Moreover, it is doubtful that Matthew thought that John and Jesus had the same missionary task in mind (cf. Matt 11:2–3). Nevertheless, how does Jesus as the son of God "fulfill all righteousness"? What then constitutes this missionary task?

Scholars of Matthew seem divided as to what exactly "all righteousness" means. Some take the statement as referring to Old Testament predictions.[45] Others suggest that Jesus's life and teachings fulfill "all righteousness."[46] However, a growing consensus suggests that for Matthew, this abstract concept refers to God's demand upon human subjects.[47] It is this understanding that I assume in this study, with the exception that I interpret it to mean that Jesus becomes the agent in helping Israel to fulfill this demand.

From the Beatitudes (5:6, 10), we learn that righteousness is something to strive for and that it takes human will and action. The noun *righteousness* is a particular favorite of Matthew's, compared to the Synoptics.[48] The majority of instances are found in the Sermon on the Mount (Matt 5:6, 10, 20; 6:1, 33), where Jesus expounds upon the Torah and the Prophets (5:17; 7:12). There, it speaks of the righteousness of the kingdom of heaven.[49]

---

45. For example, Meier, *Law*, 76–80; Davies and Allison, *Matthew 1–7*, 326–27.

46. For example, Betz, *Sermon on the Mount*, 130–31; Luz, *Matthew 1–7*, 141.

47. This is well established in Benno Przybylski, *Righteousness in Matthew and His World of Thought*, SNTSMS 41 (Cambridge: Cambridge University Press, 1980). After the study of the seven occurrences of the term in Matthew (3:15; 5:6, 10, 20; 6:1, 33; 21:32), he states, "Righteousness is seen as God's demand upon man. Righteousness refers to proper conduct before God" (Przybylski, *Righteousness*, 99). See also France, *Gospel of Matthew*, 119–20. Eduard Schweizer suggests that "all righteousness" refers to the righteousness of God, which is equated with fulfilling the requirements of God's Law. See Eduard Schweizer, *The Good News according to Matthew*, trans. D. E. Green (Atlanta: John Knox, 1975), 55.

48. It occurs seven times in Matthew and once in Luke 1:75. It is missing in Mark. On an exposition of each, see Przybylski, *Righteousness*.

49. David Wenham, "The Rock on Which to Build: Some Mainly Pauline Observations about the Sermon on the Mount," in *Built upon the Rock: Studies in the Gospel*

The last use of the noun is found in Matt 21:32, "For John came to you in the way of righteousness, and you did not believe him." It seems to me that an initial understanding of the statement "for us to fulfill all righteousness" must begin in light of its immediate context, that is, in the context of John's baptism and the proclamation of the kingdom of heaven, for these are significant elements that structure the unit of which this statement is the center.

If the statement "for us to fulfill all righteousness" and the apocalyptic communications together imply an election for a mission, which is a modification of his sources, then it is likely that Matthew's redactions of this unit revolve around the comparisons between John and Jesus that begin back in 3:11–12. Ulrich Luz notes that Matt 3:15b are Jesus's first words. Up until then, Matthew's audience was familiar with the story of baptism without this statement and, according to Luz, "therefore [Matthew's implied audience] had to take special notice of it."[50] Davies and Allison suggest that the context for Jesus's baptism in 3:13–17 is the reader's knowledge of John the Baptist's christological statement about Jesus in 3:11–12.[51]

By having Jesus refer to both himself and John in 3:15b, the text harkens back to the comparison between John and Jesus as baptizers in 3:11, for both verses compare their roles. Significant is the fact that Matthew makes a distinction between the eschatological future in John's expectation and the present time: "Let it be so now."[52] The apparent incongruities make this retrospective reading more evident. It is also worth noting that Matthew's implied audience, as well as we, know that Jesus's appearance on earth as the political Messiah and eschatological reaper did not come to fruition. It would not be inappropriate to suggest that the metaphors of John and Jesus as baptizers linger beneath this statement in 3:15b, "Let it be so now, for it is proper *for us* to fulfill all righteousness."

Indeed, in antiquity John was known to be a baptist (ὁ βαπτιστής [Matt 16:14; Mark 8:28; Luke 9:19; cf. Josephus, *Ant.* 18.117]) or the baptizer

---

of Matthew, ed. Daniel M. Gurtner and John Nolland (Grand Rapids: Eerdmans, 2008), 199.

50. Luz, *Matthew 1–7*, 141.

51. Davies and Allison, *Matthew 1–7*, 311.

52. Daniel Patte, *The Gospel according to Matthew: A Structural Commentary on Matthew's Faith* (Philadelphia: Fortress, 1987), 50–51. Patte comments on the distinction that Matthew makes of the present and future eschatological judgment.

194   Apocalyptic Sheep and Goats in Matthew and 1 Enoch

(ὁ βαπτίζων [Mark 1:4; 6:14, 24]). The fact that the same verb is used to describe future tasks of Jesus (βαπτίζω [3:11d]) creates a metaphor in which Jesus is spoken of as a baptizer. John baptizes with water, but Jesus baptizes with the Holy Spirit and fire. The question then becomes, How is baptizing with the Holy Spirit and fire a cleansing action? How would these actions relate to fulfilling all righteousness in the here and now?

Robert L. Webb suggests that John through baptism of water cleanses for the purposes of repenting one's sins, which he calls "repentance-baptism." Webb uses as one of his prooftexts a contemporaneous text in Sib. Or. 4.162–170:

> Ah, wretched mortals, change these things, and do not lead the Great God to all sorts of anger, but abandon daggers and groanings, murders and outrages, and wash your whole bodies in perennial rivers. Stretch out your hands to heaven and ask forgiveness for your previous deeds and make propitiation for bitter impiety with words of praise; God will grant repentance and will not destroy. He will stop his wrath again if you all practice honorable piety in your hearts.[53]

The passage speaks to the reason for immersion. In this case, it is for the purification of the body in conjunction with the soul, while looking toward the future judgment.

However, Joan E. Taylor rightly finds Webb's premises problematic.[54] In arguing that Jews in antiquity did not distinguish between the body and heart, Webb believed that John's baptism in water would lead to the forgiveness of sins, as it symbolizes repentance. Taylor argues that Jews of the first century did distinguish between the inner and outer being of a person and thus cleansing the body with water does not mean also cleansing the

---

53. Robert Webb, *John the Baptizer and Prophet: A Socio-historical Study*, JSNT-Sup 62 (Sheffield: JSOT Press, 1991), 120–21. For the counter argument, see Joan E. Taylor, *The Immerser: John the Baptist within Second Temple Judaism* (Grand Rapids: Eerdmans, 1997), 91.

54. Arguing against Robert Webb, who believed that Jews in antiquity did not distinguish between the soul and body, Joan E. Taylor convincingly suggests the opposite and that purification includes independent cleansing of both the soul and body. It was understood that purity or impurity of one did not necessarily suggest the purity or impurity of the other. See Taylor, *Immerser*, esp. 88–100; and also Jacob Neusner, *The Idea of Purity in Ancient Judaism: With a Critique and a Commentary by Mary Douglas* (Leiden: Brill, 1973).

4. The Inner Textures of Matthew 25:31–46   195

soul. For Taylor, baptism with water does not result in the forgiveness of sins. She insists that they are two distinct entities: cleansing the body with water was experiential, and cleansing the heart was often associated with morality. Both were required for complete holiness. Taylor points out that "John's immersion was different [from other Jewish immersions] in that for him, no ritual for the purification of the body would have been acceptable to God, and thereby ineffective, unless one were repentant or righteous and kept God's Law."[55] In other words, cleansing of the heart preceded bodily purification and required keeping torah as a means of being righteous. Jacob Neusner recognizes that one would easily be confused for the other, since experiential cleansing was often used as a "metaphor of morality" in prophetic literature.[56]

In the Q passages of Matt 3:7–12, those who come out to John for baptism are expected to have borne fruit worthy of repentance (3:8), meaning that the inner being or the heart is assumed to be pure or well cared for. The rabbis saw good fruit as a metaphor of righteous deeds (Gen. Rab. 16.3), and deeds reflected the state of one's heart (Matt 7:15–20; 12:33–37). Matthew has John withholding bodily baptism from the Pharisees and Sadducees on the basis that they lack this inner cleansing (Matt 3:7). The fact that Matthew has John explicitly pointing out the shortcomings of the Pharisees and Sadducees in meeting this prerequisite suggests that they are not fit to be baptized and thus are at risk of God's imminent wrath, as it were. With the wrath at the threshold, imminent like an ax at the root of the trees (Matt 3:10),[57] and the one who brings it being right behind him (Matt 3:11), Matthew has John suggesting that the Pharisees and Sadducees will be condemned with no chance of or opportunity for repentance. In short, John's baptism in the desert is for the cleansing of the outer being or the body prior to eschatological judgment.

In Q, the call for repentance for the forgiveness of sins (Luke 3:3; Mark 1:4; cf. Acts 13:24; 19:4) is understood as John preparing Israel for the coming judgment. However, when Matthew instead redacts this to refer to

---

55. Taylor, *Immerser*, 94.

56. Neusner, *Idea of Purity*, 11; see also pp. 11–13, 36–38.

57. Nolland (*Gospel of Matthew*, 145) points out that felling of trees is a prophetic image of judgment in a number of Old Testament texts, citing Isa 6:13; 10:33–34 (cf. 10:15); 32:19; Ezek 31:12; Dan 4:14.

196   Apocalyptic Sheep and Goats in Matthew and 1 Enoch

repentance in light of the kingdom of heaven (Matt 3:2; 4:17),[58] he implies that the earthly Jesus is neither the political Messiah nor the eschatological reaper. As mentioned above, the same presupposition can be seen in the conflict that Matthew's statement of 3:15b (fulfilling all righteousness) makes with John's expectations. The news of the coming wrath is modified to refer to the news of the coming kingdom of heaven for both Matthew and his implied audience. It is not too far-fetched to assume that these two redactions by Matthew are closely and deliberately related.

In light of Matthew's redactions (i.e., kingdom of heaven, all righteousness, apocalyptic communication), the comparison of John and Jesus as baptizers—"I baptize you in water for repentance.... He will baptize you in the Holy Spirit and fire" (Matt 3:11)—should be taken as double in meaning. For John, it is based upon the metaphor JUDGMENT OF THE LORD IS BAPTISM,[59] where Jesus brings the wrath of the Lord through the metaphor of baptizing in the Holy Spirit and fire as in blessing and condemnation. For Matthew and his implied audience, this expectation didn't come to fruition. It is allegorized to fit the current situation, and this then modifies the eschatological metaphor to an apocalyptic metaphor in the here and now, RIGHTEOUSNESS OF THE LORD IS BAPTISM, where Jesus brings the righteousness of the Lord through the metaphor of baptizing in the Holy Spirit. Jesus cleansing Israel with fire takes on another meaning that lies in the future eschaton. As we find later, the Son of Man is the eschatological figure identified with Jesus (e.g., 13:36–43). Indeed, John understood Jesus in terms of eschatological judgment, informed by the image of a political Messiah. Nonetheless, if John's baptism cleanses the body, then Jesus's baptism cleanses souls in light of the future. Like John, Jesus becomes an

---

58. Jonathan T. Pennington gives three viable answers to the question of whether "kingdom of heaven" is Jesus's phrase. I side with the argument that "Jesus said kingdom of God and Matthew has changed (most of) these into kingdom of heaven, while also adding several occurrences of [the kingdom of heaven]." However, this does not preclude the other option scholars argue for--that Jesus could have had used both "kingdom of heaven" and "kingdom of God." Pennington favors the latter option. The third option is the idea that Jesus used only "kingdom of heaven" and that the other Synoptics changed them to "kingdom of God" to accommodate for gentile believers for whom the former phrase would make no sense. For a discussion on scholarly views, see Jonathan T. Pennington, *Heaven and Earth in the Gospel of Matthew* (Grand Rapids: Baker Academic, 2009), 300–302.

59. It is now conventional in cognitive linguistics to use capital letters to indicate names of frames, and capitalization of whole words to express metaphors.

4. The Inner Textures of Matthew 25:31–46   197

agent of righteousness.[60] In other words, Jesus, in his mission to fulfill all righteousness, sets out to cleanse the hearts of Israel as the son of God on earth in the here and now.

In rabbinic fashion, Matthew utilizes his sources and recontextualizes it to fit the current situation. He recontextualizes by way of apocalyptic communication. The political Messiah that John had imagined is then nullified in lieu of the son of God (a Messiah of moral and salvific authority on earth).[61] In Matt 22:41–45, Jesus rhetorically asks the Pharisees, "How is it then that David by the Spirit calls him Lord, saying, 'The Lord said to my Lord, "Sit at my right hand, until I put your enemies under your feet"?" I do not suggest that Matthew denies Jesus's genealogical ties to David but that Matthew undermines Davidic implications of a political figure to God's election of Jesus.[62]

---

60. Stanton, *Gospel for a New People*, 81. Stanton observes that like Jesus, John also came to Israel "in the way of righteousness" and was welcomed by tax collectors and sinners but not by "this generation" (11:19 and 21:32).

61. On Jesus's authority of teaching and healing, see, for example, Matt 7:29; 9:8. The latter is a result of the former. For example, instead of using divine authority for political reasons such as to kill (implied in the political Son of God), divine authority is used to heal. The interplay of divine authority and healing are reflected in this passage of Matt 9:2–8 in the interplay between the authority of the Son of Man to forgive sins and the authority of Jesus as the Son of God to heal. I am not denying that Jesus's messiahship resists the empire by suggesting the nullification of the political Messiah. I only mean to point out that the idea of a Davidic Messiah that comes to wage war and bring the wrath of God as expected on the day of the Lord is being denied in Matthew. See, e.g., Anthony J. Saldarini, *Matthew's Christian-Jewish Community* (Chicago: University of Chicago Press, 1994), 168. Saldarini states, "Jesus is not adequately identified as the Messiah only, but must be recognized as Son of God."

62. The idea of a healing Son of David is also vague. Such notions seem to be redefined in Matthew. Matthew 22:41–45 reads, "Now while the Pharisees were gathered together, Jesus asked them this question: 'What do you think of the Messiah? Whose son is he?' They said to him, 'The son of David.' He said to them, 'How is it then that David by the Spirit calls him Lord, saying, "The Lord said to my Lord, Sit at my right hand, until I put your enemies under your feet."'" When the two blind men call out to Jesus in 9:27–31 as Son of David, Jesus doesn't reply to their calls in a positive tone. He ignores them while they are still following. Apparently, they followed him all the way to the house. In fact, they entered the house. Only then did Jesus give them his attention. But when he responded, he asked them one thing, "Do you believe that I am able to do this?" They were healed according to their faith that Jesus is capable and not necessarily because he was the son of David. In the healing of the Canaanite woman, the woman also calls out to Jesus as Son of David. But it is said that Jesus "did

198 Apocalyptic Sheep and Goats in Matthew and 1 Enoch

Jesus cleansing the hearts of Israel speaks metaphorically to bringing God's righteousness on earth. The cleansing of the heart is a common expression of repentance, as in Ps 51:10, "Create in me a clean heart. O God, and put a new and right spirit within me." Here, David refers to a clean heart (לב טהור) as a new and right spirit (רוח) that purifies (טהור) the inner person. Similarly, in Ezekiel, we read, "I will give you a new heart and place a new spirit within you.... I will put my spirit within you and make you live by my statutes, careful to observe my decrees" (Ezek 36:25–27). This describes the upright as enjoying close relations with God (Ps 73:1–28). A clean and pure heart therefore by implication opposes sin and wickedness (Prov 20:9; Jer 4:14). The idea that a right spirit may reside in the inner person for the purposes of purification is an important one, for it underscores what I am describing as baptizing in the Holy Spirit.[63]

The occurrence of the term Holy Spirit in the Old Testament seems to describe God's charisma and presence (Isa 63:10, 11; Ps 50:13, LXX τὸ πνεῦμα τὸ ἅγιον; MT רוח קדש). This presence of God can give power and strength (Pss. Sol. 17.37). However, in apocalyptic literature, a different sense of the Holy Spirit replaces this sense of power and strength. The book of 4 Ezra states at 14.22, "If then I have found favor before you, send the *holy spirit* to me, and I will write everything that has happened in the world from the beginning, the things which were written in your Law, that men may be able to find the path, and that those who wish to live in the last days may live." Here, the Holy Spirit is the spirit of wisdom and understanding that enables the scribe to write down not only events of history but also the interpretation of the Law so that many will find the path and find salvation. This is clearly seen in texts such as Wis 9:13–18:

> [13]For who can learn the counsel of God? Or who can discern what the Lord wills? [14]For the reasoning of mortals is worthless, and our designs are likely to fail; [15]for a perishable body weighs down the soul, and this

---

not answer her at all" (15:23). In fact, the disciples attempted to throw her out. Again, like the blind men, her daughter was healed for her faith. I suspect that their faith is of a more spiritual variety that sees more in Jesus than a mere belief that Jesus is the son of David.

63. As stated above, Matthew is closer to Mark. As he does in other places, so here Matthew adds the Spirit of God (cf. 10:20; 12:18, 28), though this has no parallels in other gospels. It seems he does so to emphasize Jesus's election and distinguish it from the metaphorical reference to baptizing with the Holy Spirit. Jesus's election may be of the same Spirit, but the distinction has to do with function.

earthly tent burdens the thoughtful mind. [16]We can hardly guess at what is on earth, and what is at hand we find with labor; but who has traced out what is in the heavens? [17]Who has learned your counsel, unless you have given *wisdom* and sent your *holy spirit* from on high? [18]And thus the paths of those on earth were set right, and people were taught what pleases you and were saved by *wisdom*."

In Wis 9:17, "wisdom" (σοφία) and "holy spirit" (τὸ ἅγιόν σου πνεῦμα) are synonymous. Here, we are to understand the metaphorical expression of baptizing in the Holy Spirit in Matt 3:11 to be synonymous with wisdom and understanding. In Matt 11:2–19, John and Jesus reappear on the scene. John asks about the deeds of the Messiah, for apparently what he heard in prison is not what he expected (11:2–3): "Are you the one who is to come, or are we to wait for another?" Jesus answers him via his disciples with deeds of healing and proclamation (11:5). At the end of this pericope, those deeds are set in parallel with deeds of Wisdom— Matt 11:19 "the Son of Man came eating and drinking, and they say, 'Look, a glutton and a drunkard, a friend of tax collectors and sinners.' Yet Wisdom is vindicated by her deeds." As such, Jesus's role as Son of God in Matthew is identified with the figure of Wisdom herself;[64] Jesus aims to correct the paths of Israel through wisdom and the teachings of the law (Matt 13:54), which elevates him to a status greater than the wisdom of Solomon (Matt 12:42). The wisdom of God through his son can cleanse the hearts of Israel.

Scholars have long debated the issue of the law in Matthew: Does Matthew present a new torah? Does Matthew abrogate the law in the Sermon on the Mount (what scholars have labeled as the antitheses)? Does Matthew consider the law to be valid?[65] Matthew and his congregation did not abrogate the law. Nor did they consider themselves to be outside of Israelite beliefs and convictions in relation to torah and God.[66] Matthew does understand the law as completely valid (5:17–20) and could not under-

---

64. W. D. Davies and Dale C. Allison, *The Gospel according to Saint Matthew 8–18*, ICC (New York: T&T Clark, 2004), 264.

65. For an overview of these issues and more with regard to Matthew and law, see the essay by Klyne Snodgrass, "Matthew and the Law," in Bauer and Powell, *Treasures New and Old*, 99–128.

66. I side with those who see Matthew's congregation as still within Judaism, though a deviant minority of those who believe in what Jesus taught. See Saldarini, *Matthew's Christian-Jewish Community*, 125–64; J. Andrew Overman, *Matthew's*

200   Apocalyptic Sheep and Goats in Matthew and 1 Enoch

stand the Torah without the Prophets (5:17; 7:12; 22:40).[67] For Matthew, the torah and the prophets can generally be fulfilled and understood in terms of the love command and the demand for mercy.[68]

In a recent article, Eugene E. Park discusses the great commandment passage in Matt 22:34–40 and states that it provides "a hermeneutical principle for interpreting the rest of the Torah."[69] In these passages, two kinds of laws are presented: "You shall love the Lord your God with all your heart, and with all your soul, and with all your mind" and "you shall love your neighbor as yourself" (Matt 22:37, 39). Park argues that the second kind of law is a metaphorical analogy of the first through the adjective ὅμοιος. He suggests that the analogy is between what is divine and what is human and that perhaps one could say that the second is the first.[70] I could not agree more. Moreover, Park points out that these two laws represent the whole Torah and the Prophets. The phrase "the entire Law … and the Prophets" (22:40) harkens back to 5:17 and 7:20, where it brackets Jesus's teachings of the Sermon on the Mount.[71] In 5:17–20, the entire Torah and the Prophets are deemed to be salvifically binding. Here we have another example that seems to be peculiarly Matthean in style: he reformulates Q to clarify something previously inserted. In this instance, the double commandment of love in 22:34–40 becomes representative of the entire law and prophets, which is binding in accordance with 5:17–20 and thus functions to clarify salvation for Israel. Agreeing with Ulrich Luz, Park affirms that the subject is "the will of God that is proclaimed in both the Torah and the Prophets and fulfilled by obedience."

A strong case is also made for a possible anti-Paulinism that is found in 7:21–23.[72] This teaching of Jesus found in Q (cf. Luke 6:46; 13:26–27)

Gospel and Formative Judaism: The Social World of the Matthean Community (Minneapolis: Fortress, 1990), esp. 23–30.

67. See Gunther Bornkamm, "End-Expectation and Church in Matthew," in Bornkamm, Barth, and Held, *Tradition and Interpretation in Matthew*; Snodgrass, "Matthew and the Law," 107.

68. Snodgrass, "Matthew and the Law," 111.

69. Eugene Eung-Chun Park, "A Soteriological Reading of the Great Commandment in Matthew 22:34–40," *BR* 54 (2009): 61–78.

70. Park, "Soteriological Reading," 67–68. Park lists other texts as well that juxtapose these two commandments of loving the neighbor and loving God (e.g., T. Isaac 5.2; 7.5; T. Dan 5.3).

71. Park, "Soteriological Reading," 69.

72. Park, "Soteriological Reading," 72–73; David C. Sim, "Matthew 7:21–23: Fur-

polemically denies the idea that a Torah-free faith nonetheless can lead to salvation. It highlights obedience to God's will in the Torah and the Prophets. It is this passage that Park sees as pivotal, in that it harkens back to 7:12 and anticipates 22:34–40. It is much like what I claim Matthew does here in chapter 3, where he inserts 3:15 as significant while circling back to 3:11 and anticipating 3:17. In tracing the soteriological trajectory of Matthew's narrative, Park points out that it all culminates in Matt 25:31–46. There, he concludes that Jesus's teaching to love "the least" refers to needy people in general.[73]

Since Matt 3 closely links cleansing the hearts of Israel with John's baptism, all righteousness, and the kingdom of heaven, Jesus's mission ultimately deals with the salvation of Israel. Building on Park's insightful analysis about salvation, I suggest that the salvation of Israel is articulated in terms of humanity, which adds depth to Matthew's πᾶσαν δικαιοσύνην (3:15b), which is a rabbinic modification of John's expectation. What's more, the implication of Jesus as baptizer may in fact act as midrash to the Isaiah Scriptures that enclose this passage. In these cited Scriptures, the way (ὁδός, 3:3; 4:15) of the Lord gives a great light for those who are in the shadow of death (4:16). In other words, baptizing in the Holy Spirit and cleansing the hearts of Israel involves Jesus as Son of God teaching Israel the essence of the Torah, that includes performing acts of love to all fellow human beings, as Park puts it, "regardless of confessional stance or religious affiliation."[74] This would not suggest salvation of gentiles qua gentiles, because Matthew's teaching of salvation is founded upon the Torah and doing God's will.[75] Instead, it has everything to do with the judgment (salvation and condemnation) of Israel. As seen in Matt 25:31–46, it is not "the least" who are judged in the eschaton but those who show compassion to the least. This is not to suggest that the least are not judged at all but that the imagery focuses upon the judgment of Israel. Jesus as a Son of God means to point this out, for Israel will be held accountable by the Son of

---

ther Evidence of Its Anti-Pauline Perspective," *NTS* 53 (2007): 325–43. For an opposing view, see J. Willitts, "The Friendship of Matthew and Paul: A Response to a Recent Trend in the Interpretation of Matthew's Gospel," *HTSTSt* 65 (2009): https://doi.org/10.4102/hts.v65i1.151.

73. Park, "Soteriological Reading," 75.

74. Park, "Soteriological Reading," 77.

75. Here I follow David C. Sim, *Gospel of Matthew and Christian Judaism* (Edinburgh: T&T Clark, 1998), 216–17.

202 Apocalyptic Sheep and Goats in Matthew and 1 Enoch

Man. Therefore, notions of eschatology referenced in the five discourses of Jesus can be traced back to this very moment of apocalyptic communication (Matt 3:11–17), making the story of Jesus's proclamation apocalyptic through and through as it enacts what has been communicated here.

4.3.2. Son of Man: Matt 13:24–30, 36–43

As seen in the previous section, the proclamation of the kingdom of heaven is interconnected with the apocalyptic communication in 3:16–17 and the implications for Jesus as baptizer to fulfill all righteousness by cleansing the hearts of Israel through his teachings of the Torah. As such, the apocalyptic discourse recontextualizes and reconfigures what he receives from his sources to resituate Jesus as the confirmed and elected Son of God with moral and salvific authority who proclaims the nearness of the kingdom of heaven.[76]

On the other hand, the image of the Son of Man takes on a more majestic identity as seen in Matt 25:31. Whenever the Son of Man is mentioned with the phrase "in his glory," it takes on a serious tone in the first century. The Greek term δόξα carried much cultural weight as it does in Matt 25:31–33. The phrase "in his glory" would have a believer understand that the Son of Man comes from the heavens with his angels. It would also have one envision the Son of Man sitting upon a throne, where the divine would pass judgment.

As a significant inner texture to Matt 25:31–46 with reference to the Son of Man identity, I now turn to yet another similar eschatological imagery in Matt 13:24–30, 36–43.

> [24]He had told them another parable, saying, "The kingdom of heaven had been compared to a person sowing good seed in his field. [25]When the men were sleeping, his enemy came and sowed weeds in the midst of the wheat and went away. [26]And when the plant sprouted and bore fruit, then weeds appeared as well. [27]And having gone out, the slaves of the householder said to him, 'Lord, did you not sow good seed in your field? How then are there weeds?' [28]But he said to them, 'The human enemy did this.' The slaves asked him, 'Do you wish then going out that we may gather them?' [29]But he said, 'No, never gather the weeds, you would uproot together with them the seed. [30]Allow them to grow together until

---

76. On Jesus as Son of God with moral and salvific authority, see chapter 5 below.

4. The Inner Textures of Matthew 25:31–46

the harvest, and in that time of the harvest, I will say to the reapers, 'Gather first the weeds and bind them into bundles for them to be burnt. But regarding the seed, gather them into my barn.'" (13:24–30)

[36]When the crowds were permitting, [Jesus] went into the house. And his disciples came to him saying, "Explain to us the parable of the weeds of the field." [37]And in reply he says, "The one sowing the good seed is the Son of Man. [38]The field is the world, and the good seed, they are the sons of the kingdom, and the weeds are the sons of the evil one. [39]The enemy who sowed them is the devil, and the harvest is the culminating end of the ages, and the reapers are angels. [40]Therefore, just as the weeds are gathered and burned in fire, so also it will be in the culminating of the end. [41]The Son of Man will send his angels, and they will gather out of his kingdom all those causing stumbling and the doers of lawlessness. [42]They will throw them into the furnace of fire, where there will be weeping and the gnashing of teeth. [43]Then the righteous will shine out like the sun in the kingdom of their father. Let those who have ears hear. (13:36–43)

Among the parables in chapter 13, the double parables involve visions of judgment at the end of the age, as the above passages show: 13:24–30 and 13:47–50.[77] In Matt 13:36–43, we are conveniently given an explanation to the parable of the weeds in Matt 13:24–30, but the imageries from both are generally not the same. The latter concerns the present circumstances on earth and is being told to the public, the former concerns the future circumstances on earth (cf. Matt 13:43) and is being told only to the disciples (cf. Mark 4:33–34).[78] These are juxtaposed to amplify Jesus's teachings of the Torah for the present in light of the future judgment.

The metaphors in the above parable are about sowing, growing, and harvesting—parts of the same process. Matthew 13:24–25 speaks of sowing, 13:26–29 speaks of growing, and 13:30 speaks of harvesting. These correlate with the past, present, and future.[79] Interpreters indicate Mark 4:26–29 as the partial source of this parable. Too many similarities prevent one from ruling this out as a real possibility, at least for the parable itself.[80]

---

77. Jeremias has these two parables listed as one of many "double parables" of Matthew. See Joachim Jeremias, *Rediscovering the Parables* (New York: Charles Scribner's Sons, 1966), 72.

78. The reference to the field in 13:24 and its interpretation in 13:38 make the setting obvious.

79. Ulrich Luz, *Matthew 8–20*, Hermeneia (Minneapolis: Fortress, 2001), 252.

80. M. D. Goulder, *Midrash and Lection in Matthew* (Eugene, OR: Wipf & Stock,

204   Apocalyptic Sheep and Goats in Matthew and 1 Enoch

In both Matthew and Mark, the parable succeeds the parable of the sower, and all three expressions of sowing, growing, and harvesting are present in the parable.[81]

The introductory formula in Matt 13:24 presents a thesis: "The kingdom of heaven may be compared to a person sowing good seed in his field." The kingdom of heaven here is a metonymy,[82] though it may stand in for many other things.[83] For this particular parable, the kingdom of heaven is compared to a sower (cf. 13:18, σπείραντος) of good seeds.[84] It could also be compared to the action of the person sowing good seed in his field (13:24b, ἀνθρώπῳ σπείραντι καλὸν σπέρμα ἐν τῷ ἀγρῷ αὐτοῦ) insofar as actions identify the person.[85] But it may not be that simple.

2004). See also Luz, *Matthew 8–20*, 253–54. R. T. France sees the possibility of references to agricultural sabotage by the Romans. See France, *Gospel of Matthew*, 525.

81. There are significant differences as well. In Mark, no weeds are planted, and there is no contrast between the seeds scattered. Mark focuses solely on the harvest. If Matthew replaces Mark's parable, he redacts it substantially. His editions include adding the sowing of weeds (13:25–29) and an interpretation, thus making it a partial allegory. Related to this is the edition of Mark's kingdom of God for the kingdom of heaven. In this sense, Matthew goes beyond just the harvest. Despite these differences, it does not preclude the possibility that Matthew reworks Mark's parable as he does with much of Mark's other material.

82. Barbara Dancygier and Eve Sweetser define metonymy as "the use of some entity A to stand for another entity B with which A is correlated." See Barbara Dancygier and Eve Sweetser, *Figurative Language*, Cambridge Textbooks in Linguistics (Cambridge: Cambridge University Press, 2014), 100. Dancygier and Sweetser speak of two general types: categorial and frame. The former describes the relationship between the larger category and a smaller subcategory where one stands in for the other. Frame metonymy includes part-whole relationships where the part can stand in for the whole or vice versa.

83. These include a place one enters (5:19, 20; 7:21; 8:12; cf. 11:11; 16:19; 18:3; 19:23–24; 23:13), thing to possess (5:3, 10; 19:14), a person and its actions (who suffers, 11:12; who sows, 13:24; a merchant, 13:45; a king, 18:23; 22:2; landowner, 20:1; bridesmaid, 25:1), knowledge (13:11), and materials (seed, 13:31; yeast, 13:33; treasure, 13:44; net, 13:47).

84. J. D. Kingsbury, *The Parables of Jesus in Matthew 13: A Study in Redaction-Criticism* (London: SPCK, 1969), 67.

85. So also France, who sees the comparison made between the kingdom of heaven and the action that results from the person and not the person himself (France, *Gospel of Matthew*, 525).

4. The Inner Textures of Matthew 25:31–46   205

A field of wheat maps well onto the kingdom of God (on earth),[86] which can be a metonymy that stands in for a kingdom of subjects under the rule of God on earth. Subjects under the rule of God on earth are subjects who enact the will of God (cf. 7:21–23). In Matthew, actions and words are products of the heart, for out of the abundance of the heart, the mouth speaks (12:34) and a person acts (e.g., 5:28). Evil and righteousness come from the heart. Hence, enacting the will of God comes from the heart. In the parables of Matt 13, these aspects of the relationship between God and Israel are metaphorically spoken of in terms of soil, fields, seeds, wheat, and weeds.

For one to enact the will of God, subjects must know how to act in accordance with the will of God and thus are given knowledge to do so. Transferring knowledge from one person to another involves teaching. The knowledge that prototypically reflects the will of God for Israel is the torah. Building the kingdom of God on earth is comparable to teaching Israel the wisdom of the torah—that is, how to understand and practice the torah. Thus, we may have the conceptual metaphors: THE WILL OF GOD IS TORAH, BUILDING THE KINGDOM OF GOD IS TEACHING TORAH, AND THE KINGDOM OF GOD IS FOLLOWERS OF TORAH.

We find expressions of these conceptual metaphors in Matthew. For example, arguably we have "the good news of the kingdom" (4:23; 9:35; 10:7; 24:14), "whoever breaks one of the least of *these commandments*, and teaches others to do the same, will be called *least in the kingdom of heaven*" (5:19), "*strive* first for the *kingdom of God*" (6:33), "Not everyone who says to me, Lord Lord, will *enter the kingdom of heaven*, but only the one who *does the will* of my Father in heaven" (7:21), and expressions like "word of the kingdom" (13:19). Likewise, words of the prayer in 6:10 state, "Your *kingdom* come. Your *will be done*, on earth as it is in heaven," which could be formulations of the above conceptual metaphors. The association of torah with the teaching of the will of God has the torah closely linked to Wisdom, whereby the former may be a manifestation of Wisdom. Related expressions from entailments of such metaphorical association may be exemplified in the expression, "Everyone then who *hears these words* of mine and *acts* on

---

86. For instance, a seed is planted. If the seed grows well, depending upon the soil (13:1–9, 18–23), it will bear good fruit (cf. Matt 3:8, 10; 7:16–20; 12:33; 13:8, 23, 26; 21:19, 34, 41, 43) and yield a field of fruit bearing wheat. Sowing good seed is a process that has an end goal, a field of good fruits. Such also is the building of the kingdom of God on earth.

206   Apocalyptic Sheep and Goats in Matthew and 1 Enoch

them will be like *a wise man* who built his house on rock" (7:24). Learning the torah includes understanding and acting upon it, which is likened to a wise man. Hearing the word and not acting are actions of a fool (7:26).

The above metaphorical formulations can be spoken of in terms of agriculture, such as sowing good seed in a field of wheat that bears grain. It then follows that the kingdom of God on earth can be a metonymy for those who teach, learn, and follow the torah and can be compared to a person sowing good seed in his field. Thus, we have the conceptual metaphor, TEACHING TORAH IS SOWING GOOD SEED, from which we get metaphorical expressions such as,

> When anyone hears *the word of the kingdom* and does not understand it, the evil one comes and snatches away what is *sown* in the heart. (Matt 13:19)

The "kingdom" could be said to be taught through "the word," which can be spoken of as being "sown." From an apocalyptic context, such are also the metaphorical expressions as follows:

> But though our fathers received the law, they did not keep it, and did not observe the statutes; yet *the fruit of the law* did not perish—for it could not, because it was yours. Yet those who received it perished, because they did not keep what had been *sown* in them. (4 Ezra 9.32–33)

Actions as products of learning "the law" can be spoken of as "fruits," which are consequences of seed being "sown." This points toward another conceptual metaphor, THE KINGDOM OF GOD IS A FIELD OF WHEAT. From this we get expressions such as "the fruits of the kingdom" (Matt 21:43), or, more abstract expressions such as "give us this day our daily bread" (6:11). Just as bread is made of wheat and feeds the body, so also the word may feed the soul (e.g., 4:4, "One does not live by bread alone, but by every word that comes from the mouth of God").

A contrast to the above metaphors follows in Matt 13:25: "but when the men were sleeping, his enemy came and sowed weeds in the midst of the wheat and went away." In 13:26, we are told that "the plant sprouted and bore fruit, then weeds appeared as well." The wheat and weeds grew together and filled the field. Weeds here refer to darnel, a type of plant that looks like wheat, but its fruit is poisonous.[87] The dialogue that ensues between the master and his servants in 13:27–29 discusses two issues: where the weeds come from and what is to be done with them. When the master—identified in the parable as the sower and as a householder (13:24, 27)—answers that an enemy has planted the weeds, the slaves inquire if they should pull the weeds out. The master-sower-householder responds that they should not pull the weeds out but let them grow together until the harvest.

The householder and his slaves in these verses (Matt 13:25–29) seem to have a relationship to Jesus and his disciples (cf. 10:24–25, Jesus's household).[88] This parable also has ignited discussions among scholars about a mixed church.[89] To be sure, the theme of a mixed church is important in Matthew, but it doesn't seem to be the aim of the parable.[90] In the context of an apocalyptic discourse, it makes sense that the issue of evil and wickedness in the world is the primary issue,[91] because it is such a common issue in apocalyptic and wisdom literature. Yet, once again, one should not read too much into this problem of evil. For evil is, after all, a well-known reality of humanity on earth. Evil is the antagonist to wisdom and the will of God.[92] As a character in the story, evil serves a particular purpose. It harkens back again to Jesus's temptation (4:1–11), and, thus, this parable deals largely, as it did in Matt 3:11–17, with the identity of Jesus.

Matthew 13:30 reminds the reader of John's eschatological image of Jesus's appearance. Since that same agricultural imagery is being used here

---

87. Joachim Jeremias, *The Parables of Jesus* (London: SCM, 1963), 224–25; France, *Gospel of Matthew*, 525–26.

88. Warren Carter and John Paul Heil, *Matthew's Parable: Audience-Oriented Perspectives*, CBQMS 30 (Washington, DC: Catholic Biblical Association of America, 1998), 78. Carter and Heil imply that the change of the name from sower to householder (οἰκοδεσπότης) reflects the close relationship between the slaves, that is, between Jesus and his disciples.

89. For example, Sim, *Apocalyptic Eschatology*, 210–11. Sim sees the reference to "his kingdom" as a reference to the church rather than to the world.

90. France, *Gospel of Matthew*, 533.

91. Davies and Allison, *Matthew 8–18*, 408. Davies and Allison recognize that both the parable of the sower (13:1–23) and the parable of the weeds (13:24–30) address the issue of evil, "which is the failure of the gospel to win the hearts of all, and both answer in a similar fashion."

92. Nolland, *Gospel of Matthew*, 547. In Jewish literature, *enemy* often refers to Satan (e.g., LAE 2.4; 7.2; 25.4; 28.3; 3 Bar. 13.2; T. Dan 6.3; T. Job 47.10).

208 Apocalyptic Sheep and Goats in Matthew and 1 Enoch

in an eschatological context, it further affirms Matthew's attempts to modify John's image of Jesus as the political Son of God for the day of the Lord. The metaphor from 3:12 still applies here in 13:30, JUDGMENT OF THE LORD IS REAPING, as a conceptual metaphor in the formulation of the metaphorical language. Given the allegorical explanation of the parable that follows (13:36–43), 13:24 looks forward in anticipation to 13:30, and 13:25–29 acts as a bridge, since everything is being compared to the kingdom of heaven.

The kingdom of heaven is often understood as a reverential circumlocution of the kingdom of God.[93] Jonathan Pennington's studies on "the heaven and earth" themes in Matthew show that the beloved circumlocution argument rests on very slim evidence and should be reconsidered. He argues convincingly that "there is a better solution within Matthew's own usage."[94] Whether his solutions are persuasive or the only solutions must be the subject of another study.[95] Regardless, Pennington shows that the kingdom of heaven and heavenly language are distinctively spatial, that is, they reference the heavens as opposed to the earth.[96] He states,

---

93. An understanding that is traced to Gustaf Dalman, *The Words of Jesus*, trans. D. M. Kay (Edinburgh: T&T Clark, 1902). See Pennington, *Heaven and Earth*, 16–17.

94. Pennington, *Heaven and Earth*, 14. Pennington's work has so far withstood critics. In fact, Dale C. Allison, Richard Bauckham, and Daniel Gurtner provide positive reviews to the degree that they have been persuaded by Pennington's work. For example, Allison wrote, "When I began to read this book, I was sure that the main thesis was wrong. When I finished, I was sure it was right. This is a significant contribution that corrects much we have mistakenly taken for granted." Pennington points out that Matthew's heaven language manifests in four ways: (1) the plural οὐρανοί, (2) the heaven and earth pair, (3) the phrases Father in heaven and heavenly Father, and (4) kingdom of heaven. See Pennington, *Heaven and Earth*, 35, 340.

95. Pennington, *Heaven and Earth*, 343–48. Having surveyed the Old Testament and Second Temple literature, he concludes that Matthew's idiolectic use of heaven language (1) emphasizes the universality of God's dominion, (2) makes a biblical-theological connection with the Old Testament, (3) serves to strengthen the christological claims of the gospel, (4) undergirds the radical nature of the ethics and teachings of Jesus, and (5) legitimates and encourages Matthew's readers that they are the true people of God.

96. Pennington, *Heaven and Earth*, 297. He states, "It made perfect sense for Matthew to emphasize the heavenly nature of the one when stating the same for the other. That is, as Matthew emphasizes that God the Father is heavenly/in heaven, so too it is appropriate to depict God's kingdom as a heavenly one/from heaven. We may also recall the fact that [the kingdom of heaven] inevitably uses the plural form of οὐρανός. According to my findings ... these forms point to a reference to the divine realm as distinct from the earth."

4. The Inner Textures of Matthew 25:31–46

It is best … to think in terms of denotation and connotation. Each of the many kingdom expressions in Matthew (including kingdom of God and kingdom of heaven) *denote* God's kingdom, having been inaugurated and yet to come eschatologically, but the forms of the expressions have different *connotations*; they perform slightly different functions literarily and theologically.[97]

Pennington suggests that when Matthew speaks of the kingdom of heaven he does so for rhetorical and theological reasons, that is, "to contrast heaven (God's realm) with earth (humanity's realm)."[98] Pennington both argues for a spatial difference and strongly implies a temporal distinction between the kingdom of God and kingdom of Heaven. Many find the notion of a temporal difference quite convincing as well.[99]

In relation to the heavenly setting of 13:36–43 (cf. esp. 13:43, ὡς ὁ ἥλιος ἐν τῇ βασιλείᾳ τοῦ πατρὸς αὐτῶν, "as the sun in the kingdom of their Father"), it is safe to assume that the kingdom of heaven is, in the first instance, to be taken literally as being in the heavens. However, to take the kingdom of heaven as being only in the heavens can be problematic. The letter of the torah and its teachings, which is allegorically represented as the good seed (13:24, καλὸν σπέρμα), apply only to the realm of creation where humans live until all is accomplished (cf. 5:18).[100] Second, as the parable of the sower suggests (13:1–9, 18–23), not all do the will of God on earth as they do in heaven, for the hearts of Israel and humanity often

---

97. Pennington, *Heaven and Earth*, 309–10.

98. Pennington, *Heaven and Earth*, 37.

99. The temporal difference between kingdom of heaven and kingdom of God have been already proposed by W. C. Allen, *A Critical and Exegetical Commentary on the Gospel according to Saint Matthew*, 3rd ed., ICC (Edinburgh: T&T Clark, 1912), lxvii–lxviii, and Margaret Pamment, "The Kingdom of Heaven according to the First Gospel," *NTS* 27 (1981): 211–32. Pamment sees the sayings involving the kingdom of God as representing a present kingdom. Albright and Mann also argue for a temporal difference between the two concepts. In commenting upon 12:28, they state, " 'Kingdom of God' in the Matthean tradition is applied to the Father's reign after the judgment of the End, and 'Kingdom of heaven' to the continuing community of the Son of Man, lasting up to the time of the judgment." See W. F. Albright and C. S. Mann, *Matthew*, AB 26 (New York: Doubleday, 1971), 155.

100. Cf. Matt 5:18: "For truly I tell you, until heaven and earth pass away, not one letter, not one stroke of a letter, will pass from the law until all is accomplished." Here, we can safely say that the law is valid in the realm of history and humanity. The heaven here in the singular would mean the cosmos.

210   Apocalyptic Sheep and Goats in Matthew and 1 Enoch

go astray.[101] Metaphorical expressions of a field of wheat *without weeds* would make more sense for an ideal setting such as the heavens. As the above comparison stands, the images are incompatible if we are to take the kingdom of heaven as in heaven alone. The problem is amplified even more when the disciples themselves are baffled (Matt 13:36)!

In short, there is no reason why we should distinguish between the kingdom of heaven and the kingdom of God, for they mean the same thing in terms of who reigns and who makes up the kingdom. The only difference is in Matthew's presentation of "the one who is to come" (Matt 3:3, 11) or the sower of good seed, which is associated with the coming of the kingdom of heaven. In this light, the kingdom of heaven is not a circumlocution of the kingdom of God but rather the indication that the kingdom of God as it is in heaven has begun on earth and in the here and now in the presence of Jesus, the Son of God. This means that the kingdom of heaven is partially realized on earth.[102] This reading falls in line more naturally with the comparison of the kingdom of heaven to the sower of good seed. As we will see below, the explanation of the parable (13:36–43) expands the comparison by taking the kingdom of heaven beyond just the sower of good seed in making the connection to the Son of Man.

---

101. In antiquity, the earth as opposed to the heavens seems to be the dwelling of those who disobey God's will. In the Book of the Watchers (1 En. 1–37), those angels who disobeyed God came from the heavens and lived among humans on earth.

102. The four sayings of the kingdom of God seem to refer to the earth in the present. This coincides with Jesus's identity as the Son of God. An example can be seen in the triple tradition found in Matt 8:28–33 (Mark 5:1–20; Luke 8:26–39), when Jesus casts out two demons into a herd of swine. There, the demoniacs retaliate against Jesus. Matthew redacts his sources by referring to Jesus only as the Son of God rather than the Son of the Most High God (cf. Mark 5:7; Luke 8:28) and adding the detail that Jesus torments the demons "before the time" (Matt 8:29). The reference to "the time" (καιρός) could only be the future appointed καιρός of the eschatological judgment (cf. 13:30, ἐν καιρῷ τοῦ θερισμοῦ). Jesus then says later in Matt 12:28 to the Pharisees, "But if it is by the Spirit of God that I cast out demons, then the kingdom of God has come to you." Again, the phrase "by the Spirit of God" refers back to 3:16–17, discussed earlier, where Jesus is affirmed and elected as the Son of God by "the Spirit of God." As such, these related passages strongly suggest that Jesus's earthly existence as the Son of God labors in making realized the kingdom of God on earth through his teachings, which in Matthew includes his deeds. In the parable of the two sons (Matt 21:28–32), the kingdom of God is spoken of in the context of doing the will of God (Matt 21:31; cf. 19:24; 21:43). In these contexts, actions point toward doing the will of God on earth.

4. The Inner Textures of Matthew 25:31–46 211

In comparison to Mark 4:26–29, Matthew indeed makes this parable of Matt 13:36–43 into an apocalyptic discourse. The interpretation, which is peculiar to Matthew, vividly paints an image of the Son of Man, who, just as a reaper gathers the wheat into the barn and burns the weeds in a field,

> will send his angels, and they will collect out of his kingdom all causes of sin and all evildoers, and they will throw them into the furnace of fire, where there will be weeping and gnashing of teeth. Then the righteous will shine like the sun in the kingdom of their Father. Let anyone with ears listen!

The vision in the parable's explanation comes from Matthew's scriptural sources on the figure of the Son of Man. Its vision and judgment reference Dan 7. It also resembles what seems to be a citation from his Markan source in 24:29–31 (Mark 13:24–27; cf. Luke 21:25–28). It is a vision reapplied allegorically to the parable, which is common to rabbinic hermeneutics in which the parable provides clarity to the vision. What is then presented is a hidden message of the kingdom of heaven. The message in this parable isn't what the Son of Man will do, for it may have been known already through cultural traditions and the book of Daniel. It is rather the proposition that the sower is the Son of Man (13:37). Matthew's implied audience would imagine the vivid imagery of a sower reaping what he sows (cf. 25:24–27).

The earthly Jesus as the Son of Man is often taken for granted in modern scholarship and has become a bit of a cliché. But to Matthew's implied audience, it may have come across as astonishing that Jesus, the Son of God, could also be the Son of Man. Only the Similitudes (1 En. 37–71) and 4 Ezra juxtapose the figures of the Messiah (1 En. 48.10; 4 Ezra 12.32) and the Son of Man (1 En. 46.2; 62.5, 7; 71.14; 4 Ezra 13.1–4, 32) somewhat vaguely.[103] However, in Matthew, it seems that not even Jesus's disciples in the time of Jesus knew this (cf. 16:13).[104] Certainly the elite of Israel considered it appalling (26:64–66). From the agricultural metaphors

---

103. For an overview of messianic figures within apocalyptic and nonapocalyptic texts in Second Temple Judaism, see James C. VanderKam, "Messianism and Apocalypticism," in McGinn, Collins, and Stein *The Continuum History of Apocalypticism*, 112–38.

104. Matt 16:13: " 'Who do people say that the Son of Man is?' And they said, 'Some say John the Baptist, but others Elijah, and still others Jeremiah or one of the prophets.' "

of judgment in Matt 3:1–4:17, his implied audience is able to deduce that Jesus here in Matt 13:37 is referring to himself as the sower and the Son of Man.[105] The sower and the baptizer are synonymous metaphors insofar as sowing the seed and cleansing the heart speak of the same thing.

The Son of Man epithet, like the Son of God, is also an important concept in biblical scholarship of the New Testament in conjunction with Jewish apocalyptic literature. Space prevents a full analysis of scholarship on these two massive concepts. But like the Son of God, it suffices to suggest a working definition. In Matthew, Son of Man stands in distinction to the Son of God epithet, which we define generally above as the anointed representative of God before humanity and on earth. In seeing this distinction, one may refer to Matt 10:32: "Everyone therefore who acknowledges me before others [on earth], I also will acknowledge before my Father in heaven; but whoever denies me before others [on earth], I also will deny before my Father in heaven." Within this lies clues to the reader on the difference between the Son of God and the Son of Man, where the Son of Man becomes the representative of righteous humanity before God in heaven. As such, the Son of Man is the template of judgment. In Matt 7:23, Jesus tells of the last days of judgment when he has assumed the throne in heaven. At that time, he declares as the Son of Man (so also 25:31–46), "I never knew you; go away from me, you evildoers." The notion of a template for judgment is expressed in Jesus's reply to Peter's question, "Look, we have left everything and followed you. What then will we have?" Jesus replies, "Truly I tell you, at the renewal of all things, when the Son of Man is seated on the throne of his glory, *you who have followed me* will also sit on twelve thrones, judging the twelve tribes of Israel" (Matt 19:27–28). Thus, we may generally suggest as a working definition that Jesus as *the Son of Man is the representative of righteous humanity before God in heaven.* This concept of the divine Son of Man can only be an allusion to the Son of Man in Dan 7.

The link Matthew makes here between the Son of Man and the sower links the Son of Man with Jesus as the Son of God for his implied audience. This links the Son of Man with the teachings of the Son of God who aims to cleanse the hearts of Israel. The allegorical vision doesn't merely tell of what will happen in the future, but, more importantly, it gives the highest

---

105. Stern, *Parables in Midrash*, 5: "The *mashal* is a narrative that actively elicits from its audience the solution of its meaning, or what we could call its interpretations."

4. The Inner Textures of Matthew 25:31–46   213

authority to Jesus's teachings of the torah. Those who follow will be judged accordingly (Matt 19:28). For at the end, as it were,

> The Son of Man will send his angels, and they will collect out of his kingdom all causes of sin and all evildoers, and they will throw them into the furnace of fire, where there will be weeping and gnashing of teeth. Then the righteous will shine like the sun in the kingdom of their Father. Let anyone with ears listen! (13:41–43)

Thus, one is able to say that the kingdom built by the Son of God on earth could also be the kingdom of the Son of Man metaphorically, for in reality, the latter kingdom remains as eschatological hope. What is apocalyptic is the way in which the revelatory imagery forges metaphorical connections that bridge the heavenly realm and the earthly realm via the tasks and identity of Jesus. This knowledge is presented esoterically to Jesus's disciples as the parable is given to the crowd, and its meaning is made known only to the disciples.

Likewise, the kingdom of heaven can be compared to Jesus's teachings of the torah, for it will be Jesus, the Son of Man, who judges Israel at the end of the age (13:40) based on those teachings. In other words, the kingdom of heaven in this parable stands in as a metonymy for the values that encapsulate the essence of God's will that Israel so cherishes. A person obedient to the will of God may earn eternal life in the kingdom of heaven when the Son of Man takes his throne and becomes judge. And who knows the father better than his son? It is in this sense that we are to understand the nearness of the kingdom of heaven according to Matthew, through the teachings of the Son of God. Therefore, judgment of the Son of Man can be perceived to begin in the here and now, through what is created by the Son of God. It would then follow that the kingdom of heaven also begins in the here and now. Just as significant, the apocalyptic occasion allows the above renderings to occur. In other words, the apocalyptic discourse of visions and metaphorical language in Matt 13:24–30, 36–43 function to bridge the gap between heaven and earth via Jesus and the kingdom of heaven.

4.4. The Immediate Literary Context

We have discussed thus far the inner textures of the judging Son of Man and the shepherd-king in their broader Matthean context by tracing the narrative progression of the identities of Jesus from throughout the five

214   Apocalyptic Sheep and Goats in Matthew and 1 Enoch

discourses of Matthew via similar judgment images and what this may mean for the one identified as the judge in our text. As the narrative arrives in Matt 25:31–46, the Son of Man and the shepherd-king are two seemingly contradictory identities: the heavenly and future Son of Man and the earthly and present Son of God. As already mentioned above, Matt 25:31–46 serves like a midrash to Matthew's sources (Q in John the Baptist, Dan 7, and Matthew's own sources), a midrash that presents an interpretation of the eschatological vision. The interpretation of the vision includes juxtaposing and identifying the Son of God (3:11–17) with the Son of Man (13:24–30, 36–43).

4.4.1. Son of Man and Shepherd-King: Matt 25:31–46

Matthew 25:31–46 is a third key text unique to Matthew that juxtaposes the identities of the Son of God and the Son of Man in the person Jesus. Again the text presents Jesus's teaching from his visions for his implied audience. Such juxtaposition is a common way scribes settle seeming contradictions of texts in rabbinic hermeneutics, a way to adapt the torah, the Jewish rule of life, to changing and new conditions. Such reconfiguration and recontextualization are common features of apocalyptic discourses. Moreover, these hermeneutical practices are often controlled by certain rules called middot: the seven rules of Hillel, thirteen of Ishmael, and thirty-two of Rabbi Eliezer (ben Yose ha-Gelili).[106]

The thirteen middot attributed to Ishmael are essentially expanded versions of Hillel's seven middot. In one of them, the rule states,

> "Two verses of Scripture contradict each other until the third verse comes and decides between them." In the Talmud, an example is given in the Mek Pisha 4 (L.I.32): Aqiba points out that according to Deut 16.2 the Passover sacrifice is to be of flocks (sheep or goats) and herds (cattle), whereas in Exod 12.5 it is of sheep or goats. "How can these two passages be maintained? Say: this is a rule in the (interpretation of) Torah—two passages contradict each other. They remain in their place until the third verse comes and decides between them." Exod 12.21 mentions only flocks; thus it is clear that only flocks and not herds are suitable for the Passover sacrifice.[107]

---

106. H. L. Strack and Günter Stemberger, *Introduction to the Talmud and Midrash*, trans. Markus Bockmuehl (Minneapolis: Fortress, 1992), 15.

107. Cited by Strack and Stemberger, *Introduction*, 21.

In similar fashion, Matthew recognizes Jesus's earthly identity as the Son of God elected by the Spirit of God from his sources. From the explanation of the parable of the weeds (Matt 13:36–43) and Dan 7, Jesus is also the divine figure of the Son of Man. That Jesus is the Messiah and the Son of Man would have caused confusion and consternation.

Anxieties about Jesus's identity are evident in examples such as John's question to his disciples in Matt 11:3, the scribes and Pharisees regarding a sign from Jesus (12:38–42), and Jesus's question to his disciples, "Who do people say that the Son of Man is?" (Matt 16:13). In 25:31–46, the imagery vividly reveals that Jesus is both Son of Man and Son of God. He is the Son of Man who comes at the end of the age to judge. He is also the Son of God who has come to teach the torah. These two identities together give meaning to the statement in 1:23: "they will call his name Emmanuel (God is with us)."[108] The combination of these two figures in their roles and deeds culminates in the belief that Jesus's teachings of the torah save Israel from their sins. This is significant, as Matthew now paints a vivid image of how Israel may gain righteousness, not as a doctrine but as a way that recontextualizes Scriptures and its teaching in the identities of Jesus in light of a particular issue of great significance to the Gospel of Matthew: the demand for a greater righteousness.

---

108. Scholars have read the name *Emmanuel* (God with us) as Jesus being God's shepherd to save Israel from their sins. In other words, Jesus is a representative of God via Jesus's messiahship. See, for example, John Paul Heil, "Ezekiel 34 and the Narrative Strategy of the Shepherd and Sheep Metaphor in Matthew," *CBQ* 55 (1993): 698–708, esp. 700. See also B. B. Scott, "The Birth of the Reader," *Semeia* 52 (1991): 93: "I would suggest that Emmanuel is the presiding image or metaphor of the narrative and the function of the Gospel narrative is to form a consistency or gestalt in which Jesus is the presence of God with us. To fill in this gap is the way in which the implied reader will make sense (form a consistency) of the narrative." John Nolland rightly asks whether there is the possibility that the phrase μεθ᾽ ἡμῶν ὁ θεός— God with us—points toward the divine identity of Jesus. He asks, "Should we translate μεθ᾽ ἡμῶν ὁ θεός as 'God with us' and understand that Matthew intends to make the equation 'Jesus = God'?" This would include perceiving Jesus as a Godlike figure and that Jesus's presence as in 18:20; 28:20 is of a spiritual kind befitting a divine Jesus (Nolland, *Gospel of Matthew*, 101–2). Davies and Allison also provide the two options with which one may argue. Like Nolland, Davies and Allison choose to perceive *Emmanuel* to mean that God works in Jesus rather than seeing a divine aspect of Jesus. The divine aspect of Jesus is the way in which God works within Jesus, who represents God (Davies and Allison, *Matthew 1–7*, 217–18). I would not go as far as suggesting that Jesus equates with God. Rather, I would argue Jesus's divine being by virtue of being identified as the Son of Man.

216 Apocalyptic Sheep and Goats in Matthew and 1 Enoch

4.4.2. Sheep, Goats, and the King's Subjects: Matt 25:32c–45

Let us now turn to those who are being judged as the sheep, goats, and the king's subjects. The metaphors of sheep and goats in the parable have the reader recall the designation of "all the nations" in 25:31 and force Matthew's audience to compartmentalize humanity into two general categories. The audience would have reasoned naturally that if "all the nations" were either sheep or goats at the end of the age during judgment, then the mandate for righteousness requires all to become sheep and not goats. The original intent may have been lost, as the debates in the history of interpretation about the metaphors of the sheep and goats reveal. Ulrich Luz lays out in summary three main interpretive models without a clear consensus: universal, classical, and exclusive.[109] The universal model has all humanity being judged, and caring for the suffering humanity of the earth becomes the basis of judgment. For the classical model, according to Luz, all humanity stands in judgment, and caring for needy Christians becomes the basis of judgment. Finally, the exclusive model has all non-Christians being judged, and caring for Christians becomes the basis of judgment. These models are informed by the rhetorical force that Matt 25:31–46 has had on Christians and interpreters.[110] However, for the first century, I propose a variation of the exclusive model from the perspective that Matthew and his audience are still within Judaism.[111] I'll first state the obvious and propose a metaphorical reading of the text.

---

109. "The Universal Interpretive Model. 'When the Son of Man comes, he will judge all the nations. The judgment will be determined by the deeds of love and mercy shown to the marginal, the poor, and the suffering persons of the world, the least among Jesus's brothers and sisters.' *Accordingly, the brothers and sisters of the Son of Man are all the suffering persons of the earth, both non-Christians as well as Christians.... The classical interpretive model ... viewed 'the least of my brothers' as the members of the Christian church.... The exclusive interpretive model ... understands* panta ta ethne *not as 'all the nations' but rather as all the pagans.* Thus, it is only the non-Christians who stand before the heavenly judge; the Christians, to whom the heavenly judge makes special reference ('these' brothers!), stand to one side and are not judged. Here the 'least of the brothers' are for the most part Christians, occasionally also only the Christian apostles and missionaries" (Luz, "Final Judgment," 274–85, emphasis added).

110. Luz, "Final Judgment," 274–86. Cortés-Fuentes summarizes the debate in identifying "the least of these my brothers" (Cortés-Fuentes, "Least of These My Brothers," 107).

111. See, for example, Overman, *Matthew's Gospel*; Saldarini, *Matthew's Chris-*

4. The Inner Textures of Matthew 25:31–46   217

What is obviously portrayed by the vision, parable, and allegory is an image of eschatological judgment. The natural reading of "all the nations" refers to all of humanity who are being judged at the end of the age. The scriptural vision (25:1–32b) provides an authoritative proof, which is part of Matthew's inventions. When this is followed by a parable and an allegory, we have in 25:32c–45 a hermeneutical application that aims to give handles to the vision. Matthew's Jewish audience would have seen it this way. As both parable and allegory imply and are informed by the eschatological judgment set by the vision, comparisons of judgment imageries and contexts between the vision, parable, and allegory are sure to occur among Matthew's audience. I will return shortly to the implications, but interpretation is dependent primarily on the comparisons between the scriptural vision, parable, and allegory, highlighting the metaphorical and evocative language.

When one conceptually perceives the three judgment frames provided by the scriptural vision, parable, and the allegory mentioned above, "all the nations," sheep and goats, and blessed and cursed subjects map well between spaces under a generic space of judgment. In the interpretive process, the scriptural vision is now more intersubjectively accessible, while the parable and the allegory are less intersubjectively accessible for the latter functions to explain.[112] Each of the above three are their own mental space placed together by Matthew for the audience to make the connections.[113] Thus, the conceptual blend is yet to be created and emerges from within the minds of Matthew's audience as part of the rhe-

---

tian-Jewish Community.

112. Eve Sweetser describes mappings between the more concrete domain as the less intersubjectively accessible domain while the more abstract domain as the more intersubjectively accessible domain. See, for example, Eve Sweetser and Mary Therese DesCamp, "Motivating Biblical Metaphors for God," in *Cognitive Linguistic Explorations in Biblical Studies*, ed. Bonnie Howe and Joel B. Green (Berlin: de Gruyter, 2014), 10. While Scriptures would rhetorically suggest a less subjectively accessible state as proof for the informed reader, it changes in the interpretation of Scriptures when using parables and allegories. For the latter are meant to provide more concrete experience to bring about meaning to the scriptural vision. In other words, the intent involves defining the vision in more details. Thus, scripture becomes more intersubjectively accessible in this instance.

113. This of course is not to suggest that the author of the Gospel of Matthew was educated in modern metaphor theory but that the author, an expert exegete of Scripture, knew the importance of the comparative nature in metaphorical language and

218   Apocalyptic Sheep and Goats in Matthew and 1 Enoch

torical situation.[114] What I will show below is a possible implied blend and emergent structure.[115]

> Generic Space: Judgment
>   Judge
>   Judged
>   Punishment
>   Reward
>   Rule of Judgment

> Input 1 (Scriptural Vision; Matt 25:31–32b, 46) Judgment of the Son of Man:
>   Judge: Son of Man
>   Judged: All the Nations
>   Punishment: Demand the Wicked to Stand on the Left
>   Reward: Demand the Righteous to Stand on the Right
>   Rule of Judgment (Inferred): Fulfill the Will of the Father (Love *God* and *Neighbor*)

> Input 2 (Parable; Matt 25:32c–33) Judgment of the Shepherd:
>   Judge: the Shepherd
>   Judged: Sheep and Goats
>   Punishment: Separate the Goats to the Left
>   Reward: Separate the Sheep to the Right
>   Rule of Judgment (Inferred): Follow *the Path* of the Shepherd

---

imageries as taught and used by rhetors of antiquity. See above discussion of metaphors in antiquity.

114. The actual "running of the blend," according to Fauconnier and Turner takes place imaginatively. Using the example of the traveling monk who ascends a mountain and descends it at different times is blended in the mind such that one imagines two monks traveling at opposite directions along the same path and meeting at some point on the mountain. It is with this same idea that I argue for in Matthew's placing of the vision, parable, and allegory side by side. So that, the informed audience imaginatively blends the provided spaces. This same approach will be used again in chapter 5 below. See Gilles Fauconnier and Mark Turner, *The Way We Think: Conceptual Blending and the Mind's Hidden Complexities* (New York: Basic Books, 2002), chapter 3, esp. p. 44.

115. I will return to this approach to conceptual blending in chapter 5 below..

4. The Inner Textures of Matthew 25:31–46   219

Input 3 (Allegory; Matt 25:34–45) Judgment of the King:
    Judge: the King
    Judged: the Subjects of the King
    Punishment: the Cursed Subjects Burn in Everlasting Fire
    Reward: the Blessed Subjects Inherit the Kingdom
    Rule of Judgment: Caring for *the Least* of the King's Family

Possible Judgment Blend of the Son of Man/Son of God
    Judge: SON OF MAN IS THE MESSIANIC JESUS
    Judged: all the Nations/Sheep and Goats/Blessed and Cursed
      Subjects
    Punishment: Wicked **Goats** Stand to the Left and Are Burnt
    Reward: Righteous **Sheep** Stand to the Right and Inherit the King-
      dom
    Rule of Judgment: Caring for the Least of **King's Family**/Love for
      the Neighbor/Follow the Ways of the Shepherd

As already mentioned, the motif of separation weaves all three frames together. All three judges separate those being judged into two groups, the blessed and the cursed. The sheep and goats map well onto all of the nations (humanity) if we take sheep and goats as categories of the righteous and wicked humanity. Goats here would seem to be placed in a negative light. The common features of all of these groups imply authority. Sheep and goats are domestic animals led by the shepherd, just as the Son of Man determines the fate of humanity, and the king may claim royal authority over his subjects. Thus, those judged are humans who have asymmetrical and authoritative relations with the judge, as each group recognizes the authority of the latter.

All three figures, the Son of Man, the shepherd, and the king, enact deeds of a judge by deciding and labeling in order to separate two groups. As we run the blend, one realizes that the Son of Man, who sits on his throne of glory, is viewed anew. It is worth noting that the shepherd and king mapping onto the Son of Man could occur only when there was a time that the divine Son of Man was on earth to divide as a shepherd and declare as a king in order to make known what needed to be done before making a judgment of fate at the end of the age. This, of course, would be realized from the narrative. Thus, two important details emerge. First, the parable and allegory as explained above maps the shepherd and king onto the Son of Man well if the Son of Man is also the Son of God on earth,

220 Apocalyptic Sheep and Goats in Matthew and 1 Enoch

the Messiah. In the blend, the Son of Man is the earthly Jesus.[116] Second, judgment consequently begins with Jesus in the here and now through his teachings of the torah (cf. Matt 11:21–24; 25:14–30).

The structure of Matt 25:31–46 progresses from vision to allegory, which creates two main shifts of context in the narrative. First is a shift of spatial context, a shift from a general universal judgment to a specific earthly context. "All the nations," as in all humanity being judged, funnels down to only a segment of humanity who are sheep and goats/subjects of the king. The shift of context is especially obvious when we realize that the allegory becomes a more personal and experiential engagement between the king and his subjects. Moreover, "the least of these my brothers" (25:40, 45) are not being judged. In other words, there is a segment of human-ity that isn't directly involved in being judged. The context shifts from a divine judgment at the end of the ages, where only two sets of humanity are judged, to the judgment of earthly deeds in the here and now in the mode of the allegory where there are multiple groups of humanity.

The shift of context highlights the allegory, and, consequently, the spotlight is on the treatment of "the least" of Jesus's family. Thus, "all the nations," as all of humanity being judged, is secondary if not negligible in the blend, which is what often happens in metaphorical comparisons.[117] Second, the shift of temporal context also occurs. There is a shift from some unknown future time of judgment implied in the vision onto the present time of judgment implied in the allegory, which illuminates the specifics of the here and now within the blend and makes future time, whether distance or imminent, secondary.

The emergence of a third party in the least of the king's family wouldn't necessarily deem the scriptural vision (25:31–32b) incompatible in this respect. The love for God and neighbor as the scriptural rule of judgment for righteousness within the vision (cf. Jas 2:8) presumes God and the neighbor as the inferred third party and corresponds to the least indicated in the allegory. In Q, the love for God and neighbor is the greatest com-mandment of the law and the prophets (Matt 22:36–40; Mark 12:28–34; Luke 10:25–37). The Greek term for neighbor, τὸν πλησίον, is spatial and often means someone near in direct proximity or within a general area.

---

116. It is often recognized that Jesus proclaims himself as the Son of Man (cf. Matt 8:20; 9:6; 10:23; 11:19; 12:8, 40; 13:37; 16:28; 17:9, 12, 22; 18:11; 19:28; 20:18, 28; 26:2, 24, 45, 64).

117. In other words, not all elements of the frames transfer over into the blend.

4. The Inner Textures of Matthew 25:31–46   221

The term also connotes intimate space that speaks of nearness in terms of affection and would associate neighbor with kin or friend.[118] However, in Matthew and Q, *neighbor* is widened to include someone located afar and potentially hostile (Matt 5:43; cf. the Samaritan in Luke 10:25–37), whereby close affection associated with kin or friend is to be shown to the enemy.[119] Hence, in Matthew and for his audience by virtue of the teachings of the torah and prophets, neighbor may be expanded to refer to fellow humans, regardless of the distance or how hostile they may be. In other words, the entitlement of the neighbor ranges from a kin or friend to an enemy, which then maps onto the rest of society or humanity. The ideal and general rule for judgment as per cultural traditions then fall upon righteous deeds of loving God and neighbor/humanity (both near and far). By implication or entailments, therefore, the vision has God and the neighbor/humanity in purview as a third party. Thus, the least may be viewed within the blend as the neighbor. The correlation between God and neighbor in this instance is such that deeds done to the neighbor/humanity can also be seen as done to God (cf. Matt 22:34–40). This view would be culturally informed and seen compatible with the allegory. It may have even been the frame by which the allegory was created. The parable, on the other hand, would contain a similar frame of compatibility, where the least may be understood as the neighbor or fellow human being within the blend. This involves probing into further cultural intertexts that we have already explored in the previous chapter. How, then, is the least related to those being judged?

Least, as in the Greek adjective ἐλαχύς, is a relational term. It is used to refer to Bethlehem (Matt 2:6), which rhetorically points to Bethlehem's importance rather than its insignificance. Relational concepts in Matthew are often challenged, as seen in the use of first and last (Matt 3:9; 19:30). Matthew's use of this adjective plays with dichotomies to elevate the less

---

118. INTIMACY IS CLOSENESS and AFFECTION IS WARMTH are the Primary Metaphors. Sweetser and DesCamp state that these are "based on deep, early Primary Scenes of correlation between physical and social experience" (Sweetser and DesCamp, "Motivating Biblical Metaphors," 13).

119. While the Primary Metaphors INTIMACY IS CLOSENESS and AFFECTION IS WARMTH are the first and deepest experience of a positive power-assymetric relationship, Scriptures in Jewish culture may alter such natural perception, resulting in a differing categorization that is more in tune to the centrality of its cultural and religious teachings. See George Lakoff, *Women, Fire, and Dangerous Things: What Categories Reveal about the Mind* (Chicago: University of Chicago Press, 1987).

222   Apocalyptic Sheep and Goats in Matthew and 1 Enoch

fortunate or less popular. Like the Greek noun for neighbor, τὸν πλησίον, the Greek superlative in the genitive plural τῶν ἐλαχίστων connotes social implications and, like the concept neighbor, spatial relations. The adjective presupposes "the greatest," which is deemed *a fortiori* to be the opposite. *Least* describes those who break the commandments and teach others to do the same (Matt 5:19, ἐλάχιστος) and, thus, are often seen as outcasts lying at the fringe of Jewish society. Gentiles would be considered the least on these terms (cf., e.g., 5:47; 6:7, ἐθνικός; 6:32; 12:21, ἔθνος).

If the greatest among the nations would then mean the opposite of breaking the commandments and teaching others to do the same, then it follows that the least among the nations means those farthest away from proclaiming and doing the will of the Father, which often means doing righteousness. The superlatives are relational and presuppose certain degrees of righteousness (Matt 3:9) just as the elect presuppose a certain degree of righteousness. Among the nations, Israel would consider themselves as the greatest on these terms. That the least become the standard for judgment in the allegory suggests that they are being elevated to the status that determines the fate of the greatest. That the least also have familial ties with Jesus, these factors add another dimension to the least that prevents a simple analysis.

In a more universal setting, the scriptural vision itself would perceive all of humanity in some familial relation with the Son of Man, as in Dan 7. The idea is sapiential in nature, which finds root in wisdom and Jewish apocalyptic literature where God's domain of creation involves all of humanity. This was discussed in the previous chapter, and in that setting the greatest were viewed as the elect, which means that the elect are the ones being judged, while the least as the nonelect become the rule or standard. In Matthew, the concept of the elect is being (re)defined. This is seen in Matt 18:1–5. It reads as follows:

> [1] At that time the disciples came to Jesus and asked, "Who is the greatest in the kingdom of heaven?" [2] He called a child, whom he put among them, [3] and said, "Truly I tell you, unless you change and become like children, you will never enter the kingdom of heaven. [4] Whoever becomes humble like this child is the greatest in the kingdom of heaven. [5] Whoever welcomes one such child in my name welcomes me. (Matt 18:1–5 NRSV)

Jesus takes another opportunity to teach the disciples. The phrase "truly I tell you" indicates an authoritative statement, from which Jesus utters two

4. The Inner Textures of Matthew 25:31–46   223

important details about being "the greatest" (μείζων) in the kingdom of heaven. A child is known to be the least in the society of the first century. Such humble status predisposes one to being humble naturally. Based on the authoritative statement by Jesus, the greatest must be humble. This principle of humility can be seen in Jesus's statement of the first being last (Matt 19:30).

A second detail follows from the principle of humility above. The superlatives together presuppose a general categorization of social status in Jewish society. According to the allegory, the greatest must welcome with humility the least, for to do so welcomes Jesus. If this is indeed the case, which this study argues, what determines the social status as per traditions is hinted at by the parable of the laborers in the vineyard (Matt 20:1–16), which is also peculiar to Matthew. There, the greatest is paralleled with the first and the least with the last, attributing to the greatest, and thus the least, a temporal aspect. However, as seen in the parable of the laborers, importance is placed not as much upon the longevity of commitment as upon the substance, that is, upon the very commitment itself toward the kingdom of heaven, whether one begins in the first hour or the last. This then becomes a challenge to traditions of the first century that would (re)define the concept of elect.

Therefore, I conclude that the superlatives in Matt 25:31–46 should be understood as traditionally characterizing that part of humanity in terms of the temporal aspects of commitment to the torah. This is to suggest that those of the least are the nonelect. This also means to suggest that those being judged in the blend are supposed to be the elect. What is at stake is righteous commitment to the torah, that is, doing the will of the Father, which relates to the fact that the reward is referred to as an inheritance (Matt 25:34), such that those being rewarded are considered the elect. This does not suggest that Matt 25:31–46 means to point out who the elect are but that it sets out to challenge those considered to be the elect traditionally, with the least becoming the rule of judgment. A key intertext to this understanding is the metaphor of the sheep and goats.

The act of caring for "one of these least of my brothers" (ἑνὶ τούτων τῶν ἀδελφῶν μου τῶν ἐλαχίστων, Matt 25:40; cf. 25:45) includes giving food, water, and shelter (25:35) and providing clothes, care, and company (25:36). The demonstrative τούτων highlights the object of the act. Moreover, it places Jesus as the shepherd-king in the center of this salvific judgment. In other words, the speech act points toward salvation for Israel through Jesus. This is buttressed by the preceding formula ἀμὴν λέγω ὑμῖν

(Matt 25:40, 45) that was directed by the series of τότε (Matt 25:34, 37, 41, 44, 45) and the following questions of real time, πότε (Matt 25:37, 38, 39, 44). All of this directs the reader's attention toward present time and moments of reflection. In the blend, being caretakers of the least maps onto loving neighbor/humanity, which points to deeds that reflect following the law and the prophets as sheep.[120] The intent of saving Israel from their sins with Jesus at the center of that intention is prevalent throughout the Gospel of Matthew (e.g., Matt 1:21). Therefore, it would only make sense if the least is referring to gentiles who have acquired faith in God through Jesus's teachings and deeds, for whoever does the will of the Father is declared to be one of Jesus's family (Matt 12:50; cf. 8:5–13; 15:22–28). These would include gentile disciples.[121] Nevertheless, those being judged in the implied blend would then be Israel.

Israel's status of being the elect among the nations, as it were, is put to the test and therefore challenged by this Matthean discourse on whether they are in fact doing the will of the Father and reflecting righteousness. The unbelieving humans are included in this Matthean composition of judgment as part of those labeled the least. It is for this reason that we find an element of surprise in the allegory, for the faithfully committed are surprised at the consideration given even to that part of humanity farthest away from God, in other words, those gentiles who do not know the Father. This is indicative of the rhetoric evident in this Matthean composition, which is exhortative in nature, as already hinted above, and involves a mission toward the least. I argue that it is here at this juncture that the mission to the lost sheep of Israel (Matt 10:5–6) transitions into a mission to all of the nations of the world (Matt 28:19–20). At this point, however, nothing suggests a missional intent more than what the metaphor of the

---

120. As already indicated above, the metaphors present in the parable and allegory are key in making meaning of the mappings. The metaphors of the king (judge) and its subjects (judged—allegory) add on to the interpretive aims of the parable by providing a conceptual frame that goes beyond sheep following the ways of the shepherd. It provides actions that sheep or goats (judged—parable) are not naturally able to do. As a result, the sheep or goats in Matt 25:31–46 don't just follow as do herds of animals, but they are expected to provide care to the least of the king's family. In other words, through the allegory, the sheep and goats are personified.

121. Cortés-Fuentes, "Least of These My Brothers," 107. Hagner points out that the phrase "the little ones," of which "the least" is the superlative, refers often in Matthew to disciples. See D. A. Hagner, Matthew 14–28, WBC 33B (Nashville: Nelson, 1995), 744–45.

4. The Inner Textures of Matthew 25:31–46   225

sheep in the parable evokes as cultural intertexture. But, first, what does the pairing of sheep and goats say of Israel? In answering this question, we will begin probing within the intertextures of the sheep metaphor.

The judgment seems to place goats in a negative light. What lies behind the difference between the sheep and the goats? Why would caring for the least cause one to be labeled a sheep, and not caring for the least a goat? Kathleen Weber, in her astute reading of our passage, has rightly recognized the significance of the image of sheep and goats. She suggests two factors by which the image must play a larger role.[122] One factor refers to the immediate context, namely, "the reification of the defendants as sheep and goats" in 25:33 that would make the previous mention of sheep and goats more than just a mere comparison in 25:32c. The other factor refers to the "correlations between the image of sheep and goats and the broader Matthean literary context."[123]

Weber points out that there are two most likely candidates in determining the correlation between the image of sheep and goats. The first can be found in the series of offensive mixtures of wheat and chaff (3:12), wheat and weeds (13:24–30), and good and useless fish (13:47–50). The second can be found in the series of surprising reactions to judgment in the three judgment stories in Matt 25. These are the parable of the wise and foolish virgins (25:1–13), the parable of the talents (25:14–30), and our passage (25:31–46). Weber points out that each of the judgment stories in chapter 25 reflects the element of surprise by their characters as part of their reactions to the eschatological verdict, and, compared to the other two parables, our passage (25:31–46) shows the strongest element of surprise by the characters. She then proceeds to explore sociohistorical evidence from the Mediterranean world and concludes that the evidence does not support a widespread negative image of the goat. She concludes thus, "the author of the Gospel according to Matthew expects his audience to have a basically positive attitude toward goats that will make the absolute condemnation of Matt 24:31–46 surprising."[124]

Weber makes an enticing argument that rightly places a focus upon the correlation of sheep and goats, which plays a functional role in highlighting the fulfillment of righteousness. She also makes a clear case that

---

122. See the history of interpretation of this passage in Gray, *Least of My Brothers*.

123. Kathleen Weber, "The Image of Sheep and Goats in Matthew 25:31–46," *CBQ* 59 (1997): 657–78. So also Cope, "Matthew XXV:31–46," 32–44, esp. 33.

124. Weber, "Image of Sheep and Goats," 673.

explains the obvious element of surprise among the culprits who are rhetorically identified as the goats in the allegorized discourse. However, her conclusion that the goats are the complacent, self-proclaimed righteous Christians who failed to meet the requirements of righteousness seems wrong. For one, it overlooks Matthew's desire to persuade Jews to become believers, thereby neglecting a majority of the author's audience. Second, Weber's conclusion raises significant questions as to the referents of "the least of my brothers." Weber explains this by suggesting that the correlation of the sheep and goats has no relevance to the task of identifying who the least are, which is quite surprising, as the least are the important components of the verdict. The sheep and goats are what they are because of their attitude toward the least. Furthermore, these labels are mutually exclusive.

While Weber rightly points out key elements of the discourse in Matt 25:31–46, namely, the nonnegative image of the goats hinted at by the obvious elements of surprise and sociohistorical evidence, her conclusions should be revised by first observing the sheep fully in light of the context of Matthew. Weber suggested this in the series of offensive mixtures mentioned above but decided not to take it on in more detail. In fact, this route would have revealed more, and I would now like to expound upon these mixtures as supplementary inner textures to the correlations of sheep and goats.

The correlations of separation in the metaphors of wheat and chaff (3:12), wheat and weeds (13:24–30), and good and useless fish (13:47–50) must be understood in their immediate literary context, for their context determines the proper metaphor. As already discussed, John the Baptist introduced the wheat and chaff in his fiery judgment, where chaff is meant to be separated during harvest and burned. The metaphors of wheat and weeds are understood in the context of sowing seed and their respective fruit. The weeds are undesired and need to be pulled out, because good seed yields good fruit, while bad seed yields bad fruit. Judgment is made accordingly. Thus, wheat refers to those following the teachings of the Son of God who is revealed to be the Son of Man, while the weeds are those following false teachings by false teachers.

Humanity as fish in the parable of the net (13:47–50), on the other hand, must also be understood in light of its immediate literary context, which includes the two verses (13:51–52) that follow as part of the same literary unit. The preposition plus the demonstrative (διὰ τοῦτο, "because of this") in 13:52 attaches these two verses to the parable of the net, which

4. The Inner Textures of Matthew 25:31–46   227

then acts as further commentary, as Jesus continues to explain the images to his disciples. Matthew 13:52 indicates the context from which we are to understand the parable of the net by referring to scribes in teaching the kingdom of heaven. Thus, we are still within the context of teaching brought forth from teaching the word, as in the good seed in the parable of the wheat and weeds of the same chapter. The fish represent those who have been drawn in through the teachings of the kingdom of heaven, referred to as the net. One is reminded of Jesus's proposition to Peter and Andrew that he will make them fish for people (Matt 4:19). And "because of this"—pointing toward the judgment that would befall upon humanity or fish—in 13:52 stresses the importance of new ways of teaching by scribes.

Therefore, the literary correlation of Matt 25:31–46 to the similar eschatological scenes discussed already above suggests the reason why the correlation of sheep and goats would be seen in a similar context of teaching the kingdom of heaven, which is tied to the teachings of the torah. Moreover, it is widely known that in the context of the whole of Matthew, the teachings of the kingdom are never just teachings; they require actions as well. In the immediate context of Matt 25:31–46, those who are sheep who have been placed on the king's right side are identified as the elect (cf. 24:31) by implication, using language of election (25:34, "your inheritance"). Thus, we may then suggest that the sheep refer to those who teach and do the will of God to the least (gentiles/nonelect), while goats suffer a "minor blemish," a description used by Weber. The goats are those of the elect who fell short of the task by denying care for the least.

In the Gospel of Matthew, the twelve disciples are commissioned with the task of teaching and doing (Matt 10:1). The disciples gathered by Jesus in the narrative seem all to be Israelites (10:2–4). They were to go nowhere among the gentiles or Samaritans but to the lost sheep of Israel (10:5–6; also 10:16). In another passage found only in Matthew, Jesus confirms that he was sent only to the lost sheep of the house of Israel, when confronted by the Canaanite woman (15:24). Here, we have clear references to Israelites as sheep. In 9:36, Matthew uses his sources from Mark (Mark 6:34) where he has Jesus compare the crowd to sheep in need of a shepherd. In the context of Jesus healing Israel (Matt 8–9) and going to teach in "their synagogues" (9:35), it is highly likely that the crowd here are also Israelites.[125]

---

125. Luz, *Matthew 8–20*, 64

Inner textual evidence seems to suggest that sheep in Matt 25:31–46, in the overall context of the narrative, is referring more to Israelites than gentiles. Even in Matt 26:31, where Matthew adapts Mark 14:27, the disciples are compared to the scattered sheep. While the metaphor of the sheep as Israel is prevalent in Old Testament texts (e.g., Ezekiel), the mandate for Israel as sheep to teach gentiles the torah is found only rarely.

In the corpus of the New Testament, sheep (πρόβατον) is used thirty-nine times. The Gospel of John uses the term most often, and out of twenty occurrences of the Greek term there, fifteen are found in chapter 10, all of which connote following and being led, which is the typical use of the Greek noun elsewhere (cf. Luke 17:7; Rom 8:36; 1 Pet 2:25; Heb 13:20). The sacrificial lamb (ἀμνός)—as in John (also Acts 8:32; 1 Pet 1:19) and the lamb (ἀρνίον) of God throughout Revelation that brings judgment and wrath—all refer to Jesus. It is only in Matt 25:32–33 that the Greek term for sheep (πρόβατον) is used in an apocalyptic discourse to refer to subjects of judgment. The only other place outside of the New Testament and Hebrew Bible that the metaphor sheep is used prominently and programmatically in an apocalyptic context is the Book of Dreams.

5

The Apocalyptic Discourse of Matthew 25:31–46

5.1. Introduction

In chapter 3, the analysis of the Book of Dreams (1 En. 83–90; Animal Apocalypse of 1 En. 85–90) reveals a cultural and rich tradition involving the extensive use of sheep as a metaphor to retell the story of Israel that includes the present and future. At the ending of chapter 4 of this study, inner-textual evidence points to the hypothesis that the sheep and goats in Matt 25:31–46 refers to Israel both as the elect and as those being judged. The blessed subjects of the shepherd-king are found righteous, and the cursed subjects are found to have missed the mark. I propose that the metaphor of the sheep in Matt 25:31–46 evokes the cultural frame of the sheep in the Animal Apocalypse. As shown, the Animal Apocalypse refers to sheep as not just Israel as elect but also defines further what that constitutes: those who are faced with the obligation of teaching the world of gentiles the torah and the will of God, which in turn becomes a key element of the elect's own salvation and the renewal of creation. I conclude in this final chapter how Matt 25:31–46 would conceive of this intertexture via metaphorical language and what implications that conception would have for the interpretation of Matt 25:31–46 as an apocalyptic discourse.

5.2. A Metaphorical Reading

Scholars have rightly questioned how written texts evoke traditions and memories. Hays and Robbins have used the concept of echoes as a reply. To be sure, intertextuality and echoes involve processes of cognition where cultural traditions and memory are evoked via utterances of the written text. Comparisons of familiar conceptual frames are triggered, especially when aims of rhetoric are meant to be achieved. These

230   Apocalyptic Sheep and Goats in Matthew and 1 Enoch

cognitive processes of evocation and comparison are precisely what metaphorical language does through conceptual blending popularized by cognitive linguists.[1]

Conceptual blending may explain how certain words and phrases come to exist from the comparative process of merging experiential frames of knowledge. When considering rhetorical discourses, the same processes occur also in the interaction between the implied author and the implied audience via the written text. In other words, authors via texts induce this process through the images created by metaphorical language. This can be seen in poetic language, of which George Lakoff and Mark Turner ask,

> How do we understand so easily and naturally that the sequence of things the speaker mentions refers to [for example] the sequence of life-stages, to childhood, maturity, old age, death? The answer, in part, is that we know unconsciously and automatically many basic metaphors for understanding life, and [the author] relies on our knowledge of these metaphors to lead us to connect the sequence [the author] gives to the sequence of life-stages.[2]

In a culture that centers itself around the written word, authoritative texts become themselves potential input of knowledge for the audience.[3] The acquisition of knowledge would be dependent upon the engagement of the audience and author via texts.

The way in which Matt 25:31–46 is written may be the means of creating contextual interpretations through metaphorical language, with the hopes of depending upon the audience's thinking metaphorically upon known traditions. It is an occasion of creating new thought to adapt to the ever-changing world. Blending can then be induced by the implied author,

---

1. For an authoritative text on conceptual blending, see Fauconnier and Turner, *The Way We Think*.

2. George Lakoff and Mark Turner, *More Than Cool Reason: Field Guide to Poetic Metaphor* (Chicago: University of Chicago Press, 1989), 5.

3. This does not necessarily mean a Platonic realism that separates mind from body, as discussed in the beginning of this study, for those texts are born out of the experience of and can be verified by that culture. Moreover, texts are constantly being contextualized through interpretations. As seen in later talmudic literature of rabbinic Judaism, the interpretations of Scripture were dependent upon context and contemporary experience. Thus, the attempts of interpreting Scripture are founded on experience. The canonical Gospels were in many ways (re)interpretations of Scripture when they were written in the first century.

creating meaning within the minds of the implied audience through rhetorical discourse. Thus, we may then speak of an implied blend if meaning is meant to be realized by the implied audience. If we are to understand Matt 25:31–46 as the conceptual blend already written in ink, ready to be memorized by the audience as knowledge, then we are ignoring the persuasive intention and scribal creativity that are evident in the ambiguity and multivalence of the language. But if we are to understand that the conceptual blend has yet to be created, just as meaning has yet to be realized, then the parable and allegory within Matt 25:31–46 contribute to the cognitive process when the author presents it orally or written to the audience. In this light, Matt 25:31–46 as presented becomes a provided framework for Matthew's implied audience that induces the cognitive comparison of judgment scenes and inner textures of the language in the audience's effort to unravel the ambiguity and multivalence of the language and discern its discursive meaning. We have already begun this exercise in the previous chapter when placing the vision, parable, and allegory in comparison as provided by the text.

As shown in the judgment scenes of Matt 25:31–46, they are not just presented as a future prediction or for the sake of educating the audience of eschatological events. Each of these scenes projected by the vision, parable, and allegory provides important communicative assertions about the identity and roles of the characters within these scenes and about what acts of righteousness that are required of the elect. Moreover, together with the Animal Apocalypse via the sheep metaphor, the communicative assertions convey salvation and exhort the means to achieve that salvation while also dictating a course of action in the here and now. Such are the aims of the apocalyptic discourse in Matt 25:31–46.

The Matthean narrative, as explained in chapter 4, provides a developed image of Jesus's identity and role. The Animal Apocalypse is important for identifying further whom the sheep in Matt 25:31–46 evoke and what the expected roles would be. The scriptural status of 1 Enoch makes for credible proof, governing the perspective of the sheep. All of these provide conceptual inputs and are part of the rhetor's invention, using what is more familiar and credible. This is to say that the audience will conceptually create the implied blend whereby the audience is reminded of its role and identity as the elect if the intentions of the implied author are successful.

To recap the analysis in chapter 3, the final form of the Book of Dreams consists of two dream visions, with the Animal Apocalypse

(1 En. 85–90) constituting the second and larger part (1 En. 83–90).[4] A historical portrayal of Israel's journey from Genesis to 2 Kgs 25 and possibly Ezra-Nehemiah is retold in an allegory. Humanity, including Israel, in the allegory is represented by animals.[5] Sheep represent Israel, predators and animals are everyone else, and white cattle are righteous humanity.

A rhetorical and narrative reading of the Animal Apocalypse results in recognizing three key sections of the allegory.[6] The third key section of the allegory (1 En. 90.6–41) narrates the time of the Maccabees, which is the time of composition and our focus for the structure of input space 1. There, implications for the present may be perceived in the encounter between the sheep and animals. Also, a visual projection for a future scenario may also be perceived when the sheep and animals all turn into white cattle. The transformation from sheep/animals to white cattle becomes, as it were, a transition from one age to another, and it appears to be brought on by the emergence of a messianic-like figure, who is born of the earth, a white bull with large horns (1 En. 90.37).[7]

The allegorist narrates Enoch's vision as such (1 En. 90.19):

---

4. First Enoch 83.1 closely parallels the wording of 1 En. 85.1. See George W. E. Nickelsburg, *1 Enoch 1*, Hermeneia (Minneapolis: Fortress, 2001), 370. The first person speech in 1 En. 85.1 links it also to the first person account in 1 En. 83.1. As Tiller points out, "The An. Apoc. is a third person narrative of an account of a dream, enclosed within a first person narrative." See Patrick A. Tiller, *A Commentary on the Animal Apocalypse of 1 Enoch*, EJL 4 (Atlanta: Scholars Press, 1993), 225.

5. Animal and color depictions are based on Jewish morals for behavior and character of humans. For example, in the allegory, white cattle are those who are righteous, whereas black cattle are those who are violent and wicked. Sheep are those who are obedient and represent Israel. Predators and other animals depict those individuals encountering Israel. White and black cattle emerge presumably after being cast from the garden of Eden. The metaphors then shift from cattle onto sheep and other animals after the flood. Sheep and other animals dominate the characters of the narrative to the end, while centralizing on the former.

6. The first section is before the flood, the second is after the flood, and third is present time and future.

7. The figure may resemble the one like the Son of Man in Dan 7 who has all of humanity wholly in its purview, administering judgment upon all the nations. However, the figure in Daniel is not born but appears in the heavens and, thus, divine. It is likely that these are two different figures, one divine and the other human but with great authority, one godlike and the other a messianic-like human, respectively.

5. The Apocalyptic Discourse of Matthew 25:31–46 233

¹⁹And I saw until a large sword was given to those sheep, and the sheep went out against all the wild beasts to kill them, and all the beasts and the birds of heaven fled before them.

The Lord of the sheep—God—issues for the sheep a sword, with which the sheep retaliate against the animals of the earth. Then, the Lord of the sheep makes judgment (1 En. 90.20–27) upon the strayed sheep, predatory animals, and disobedient angels as they are cast into fire.[8] The rest simply remain on earth. The judgment was done in Jerusalem as described in Enoch's vision (1 En. 90.20). Enoch then sees what the remaining sheep and animals do:

³⁰And I saw all the sheep that remained. And all the animals on the earth and all the birds of heaven were falling down and worshiping those sheep and making petition to them and *obeying them in every word.* ³¹After that, those three who were clothed in white and who had taken hold of me by my hand, who had previously brought me up (with the hand of that ram also taking hold of me), set me down among those sheep *before the judgment took place.* ³²And all those sheep were white, and their wool was thick and pure. ³³And all that had been destroyed and dispersed <by> all the wild beasts and all the birds of heaven were gathered in that house. *And the Lord of the sheep rejoiced greatly because they were all good and had returned to that house.* ³⁴And I saw *until they laid down*

---

8. "²⁰And I saw until a throne was constructed in the pleasant land and the Lord of the sheep sat upon it, and he took all the sealed books and opened those books before the Lord of the sheep. ²¹And the Lord summoned those first seven white men, and he commanded them to bring before him beginning with the first star that had preceded those stars whose organs were like the organs of horses, and they brought all of them before him. ²²And he said to the man who had been writing before him—who was one of those seven white ones—he said to him, 'Bring those seventy shepherds to whom I delivered the sheep and who took and killed more than I commanded them.' ²³And look, I saw all of them bound, and they all stood before him. ²⁴And judgment was exacted first on the stars, and they were judged and found to be sinners. And they went to the place of judgment, and they threw them into an abyss; and it was full of fire, and it was burning and was full of pillars of fire. ²⁵And those seventy shepherds were judged and found to be sinners, and they were thrown into that fiery abyss. ²⁶And I saw at that time that an abyss like it was opened in the middle of the earth, which was full of fire. And they brought those blinded sheep, and they were all judged and found to be sinners. And they were thrown into that fiery abyss, and they burned. And that abyss was to the south of that house. ²⁷And I saw those sheep burning and their bones burning" (1 En. 90.20–27).

234 Apocalyptic Sheep and Goats in Matthew and 1 Enoch

that sword that had been given to the sheep; they brought it back to his house and sealed it up in the presence of the Lord. And all the sheep were enclosed in that house, but it did not contain them. [35]*And the eyes of all were opened*, and they saw good things; and there was none among them that did not see. [36]And I saw how that house was large and broad and very full.[9] (1 En. 90.30–36)

After the description of the judgment, the sword is returned. From the time the sword is issued to the time it is returned, it makes for a period of contemporary time such that the sword symbolizes some present injunction for Israel to fulfill before the emergence of the messianic-like figure. During this period of contemporary time, it is said that predators obey the sheep "in every word." In the allegory, this correlates with the sheep knowing the path, that is, knowing the ways of the Lord via the torah. As a result, all were good and returned to the house of the Lord where "the eyes of all were opened." That "the eyes of all were opened" suggests that the various animals are taught the ways of the Lord by the sheep, causing the animals to gather in the house of the Lord.[10]

The image in this third section of the allegory strongly implies a universally oriented task of teaching the torah, which was given to the sheep on Mount Sinai in the second section of the allegory (1 En. 89.28–36). The idea that a universal task is set before them correlates with Enoch's petition in the beginning of the Book of Dreams, where he asks God for a remnant in order to save humanity and creation as a whole from complete annihilation.[11] From among the cattle that survived the flood and the animals

---

9. Nickelsburg and VanderKam, *1 Enoch*, 134–35, emphasis added.

10. In the Animal Apocalypse, sheep gathering in the fold equates with Israel gathering in the tabernacle. It is in the fold that the path of the Lord of the sheep is made known to the sheep (cf. 1 En. 89.35–36). In other words, the tabernacle becomes a place where the torah is taught. As the narrative develops, the tabernacle becomes the temple, and Jerusalem becomes the house of the Lord (cf. 1 En. 89.50). Gathering in these places presupposes the teaching of the torah. Scholars take the final form of the Animal Apocalypse to have been written after the Maccabean revolt, which suggests that *the opening of eyes* would have been an agenda by the newly established state under the Maccabees, with the white bull as a priestly messiah, probably having the high priest Jonathan in sight.

11. "And now, my son, arise and make supplication to the Lord of glory, since you are faithful, that a remnant may remain upon the earth, and that he may not obliterate the whole earth" (1 En. 83.8).

5. The Apocalyptic Discourse of Matthew 25:31–46 235

that later emerged from the earth, Israel, depicted as the sheep, became the remnant and was elected to be given the torah.

The election, as it were, is not to be understood as one *apart* from the many but rather one *among* the many. In consideration of Enoch's petition, they were elected among humanity for the sake of humanity. This view of the elect is seen especially in wisdom traditions, as it is evident in Sirach. The sage, Ben Sira, uses a concept of the elect that does not stand in opposition to the nonelect but rather in correlation.[12] In this sapiential tradition, the elect is imparted special wisdom for the benefit of humanity. Thus, the sheep or Israel, as being the elect, are faced with the task of teaching the torah to the rest of humanity so that all may gather and become righteous in the presence of the Lord. In this way, the concerns of both Enoch and God, as implied in the beginning of Enoch's dream, are met: humanity is saved, and creation has returned to righteousness.

What becomes apparent in this third section of the allegory is a cultural and conceptual frame for the salvation of humanity and creation that centers on the image of the sheep, as it plays an instrumental role. The sheep, which represent Israel as the elect, gather the nations to the house of the Lord and teach them the torah. The messianic-like figure initiates a new age by sustaining the righteousness of all humanity as it was from the beginning at creation, hence the transformation of all animals back into one kind, white cattle. This cultural frame can be seen to be evoked in Matt 25:31–46 in its use of metaphorical textures of the sheep, an allusion to the concept of election, and the implied role they are to play in light of Jesus, the Son of God and the Son of Man. We begin our analysis with the way in which the Animal Apocalypse contributes to the conceptual blend that occurs with the vision, parable, and allegory of Matt 25:31–46. Utilizing the generic frame from chapter 3, we have the following domain and their respective elements of comparisons:

Intertextual Input: Animal Apocalypse (1 En. 89–90)
Judge: Lord of the sheep
Judged: sheep, shepherd, and animals
Punishment: the unrighteous sheep, shepherd and violent animals are
   condemned into the fiery abyss

---

12. See the discussion of the elect in connection to wisdom traditions in chapter 3 above.

236   Apocalyptic Sheep and Goats in Matthew and 1 Enoch

Reward: the righteous sheep and animals transform into white cattle
(1 En. 90.30)
Rule of Judgment: follow the path of the Lord of the sheep

The above would add conceptually to the parable of the sheep and goats (Matt 25:32c–33). The domain for the parable is as follows:

Judge: the shepherd
Judged: sheep and goats
Punishment: separate the goats to the left
Reward: separate the sheep to the right
Rule of Judgment (inferred): follow *the path* of the shepherd

Certainly the judge in the Animal Apocalypse is God himself as the Lord of the sheep. The judge in Matt 25:31–46 would be someone of divine authority, namely, the Son of Man and, as argued above, the shepherd-king or Jesus. That the judge shifts from God to the Son of Man at the end of ages is most likely the result of developments of the Son of Man traditions mainly among Jewish apocalyptic literature (i.e., Dan 7 and 1 Enoch).[13] The shift onto Jesus as the Son of Man would of course be a further development by Jesus followers of the first century. Nevertheless, the ultimate judge is God insofar as the Son of Man, who was Jesus on earth, judges on the basis of the Father's will in Matthew. Second, there is no explicit act of separation evident in the Animal Apocalypse. However, the act of judgment done in the Animal Apocalypse already indicates separation as only those unrighteous are judged or, rather, condemned. With regard to all the rest of the elements, we find that they map conceptually well across domains. What the intertexture of the Animal Apocalypse offers further brings to light other aspects of Matt 25:31–46, as they would map over well when considering the literary context of the above passage. One may infer from the Animal Apocalypse the following entailments:

---

13. See the works by Daniel Boyarin, "Beyond Judaisms: Metatron and the Divine Polymorphy of Ancient Judaism," *JSJ* 41 (2010): 323–65; Boyarin, "Daniel 7, Intertextuality, and the History of Israel's Cult," *HTR* 105 (2012): 139–62. See also Andrei Orlov, *The Enoch-Metatron Tradition*, TSAJ (Tübingen: Mohr Siebeck, 2005); Orlov, *The Glory of the Invisible God: Two Powers in Heaven Traditions and Early Christology*, Jewish and Christian Texts in Context and Related Studies (New York: T&T Clark, 2019).

5. The Apocalyptic Discourse of Matthew 25:31–46   237

The elect of humanity: sheep (1 En. 89–90)
The nonelect of humanity: the other animals
The mandate of the elect: teach humanity the torah
Messianic-like figure: firstborn of the white bull with horns (1 En. 90.37–38)
Righteous humanity: white cattle
Righteous creation: renewed creation free of wickedness, violence, and bloodshed

All of these entailments can be shown to be found in Matt 25:31–46, if not the entire narrative of Matthew up to this point, attesting to the use of the Animal Apocalypse and adding to the persuasiveness of this judgment imagery.

General descriptions of the righteous are refined when they point toward the elect, for the elect was traditionally understood to have divine inheritance (Matt 25:34). Furthermore, a similar version of Dan 7 is stated in Matt 24:31, which states, "And he will send out his angels with a loud trumpet call, and they will gather his *elect* from the four winds, from one end of heaven to the other." Therefore, those gathered and considered righteous are the elect.

The Greek postpositive conjunction γάρ (25:35, "for") introduces criteria by which God's elect, the sheep, were bestowed the inheritance of the kingdom.

> [35]*for* I was hungry and you gave me food, I was thirsty and you gave me something to drink, I was a stranger and you welcomed me, [36]I was naked and you gave me clothing, I was sick and you took care of me, I was in prison and you visited me. (Matt 25:35–36 NRSV)

As the elect, they were expected to become a light to the world and reveal in words and deeds the ways of the Lord via the torah so that all may open their eyes and see (Matt 5:13–16). The parable portrays an image of nurturing and caring, which are synonymous with shepherding and leading. The elect are depicted as sheep as they exemplify the sheep in the vision of Enoch and as the disciples who are to lead and gather others to righteousness in Matthew. On the contrary, the ones deemed wicked become instead stubborn as goats, not helping humanity toward righteousness by not nurturing and caring in ways becoming of the elect.

The concept of the elect discussed is associated with obedience to the instructions and commands of the torah. Along with the meaning

238   Apocalyptic Sheep and Goats in Matthew and 1 Enoch

of *elect* from the Hebrew Bible, it is for the above reasons that the Greek equivalent, ἐκλεκτός, is used, for it relates etymologically to the verb *to call*, καλέω, as someone being called. Here it would have the notion of being called to obedience. In Matthew, this same notion is evident in the parable of the wedding banquet (Matt 22:1–14). There, the person without a wedding garment was deemed disobedient, albeit was called. In the beginning of that parable, those called twice were the house of Israel but yielded negative responses. In the third summoning, the slave was ordered to call anyone on the streets. Thus, election in Matthew is fulfilled in and defined by obedience (cf. 3:7–9; 7:21).[14] The teachings of Jesus in Matthew, which are rooted in the law and the prophets (e.g., 5:18; 7:12; 11:13; 22:40), convey the will of God (e.g., 5:2–20). These teachings are the object of the obedience (cf. 21:28–31).

Righteousness as good fruits (e.g., 7:17; 21:43) results from this obedience. The term δίκαιος ("righteous") is associated with those who do the will of the Father (e.g., 1:19; 5:45; 10:41; 13:17, 43, 49; 23:28, 29, 35). Jesus in Matt 4–25 teaches righteous deeds that are expected of the elect. The elect is the house of Israel (cf. 10:5–6; 15:24), for it is assumed that they follow the ways of the Lord via the torah and the prophets. We may include "the crowd" as part of this elect group insofar as we may say that the crowd is composed of Israelites. Moreover, Jesus as the Son of God, the earthly king, is of the elect. In Matthew, he is the elect par excellence (cf. Matt 12:15–21).

The rest of humanity are the least of these who are members of the king's family. In the larger context of Matthew, they are not of the house of Israel. They are the gentiles, Samaritans, and the Canaanites. They are the little ones or the children in Matthew. They are the ones deemed as sinners. They are the lost. They are that part of humanity that has become Jesus's family through their faithful response to Jesus as the Son of God. The allegory (Matt 25:34–45) expands Dan 7 to show reasons for the judgment that is more in context with Matthew's narrative of Jesus. At the same time, it says something of those who have been cast out or considered nonelect. However, they are family largely by doing the will of God. They are family by virtue of faith.

[37]Then the righteous will answer him, "Lord, when was it that we saw you hungry and gave you food, or thirsty and gave you something to

---

14. So also Gottlob Schrenk, "ἐκλεκτός," *TDNT* 4:187.

5. The Apocalyptic Discourse of Matthew 25:31–46   239

drink? [38]And when was it that we saw you a stranger and welcomed you, or naked and gave you clothing? [39]And when was it that we saw you sick or in prison and visited you?" [40]And the king will answer them, "Truly I tell you, just as you did it to one of the least of these who are members of my family, you did it to me." (Matt 25:37–40 NRSV)

They are the ones who have been given food and water while listening faithfully to Jesus's teachings (cf. Matt 14:13–21; 15:32–39). They are the strangers (cf. Matt 15:21–28) who have been accepted and the sick who have been healed (cf. Matt 8:5–13) due to their unmatched faith in Jesus's teachings. They are the slaves imprisoned by wickedness (cf. Matt 18:23–35) for their loyalty. They are the faithful who, knowing of divine providence, first strive for "the kingdom of God and his righteousness" (Matt 6:25–33). Thus, in light of the intertexture of the sheep in its apocalyptic traditions, the mandate to care isn't just caring in the sense of meeting certain needs. It is caring on the basis of the faith in God's will in history. It is both caring for gentiles who have committed themselves in following the ways of righteousness and caring for gentiles in order to teach them the ways of righteousness. As hinted above in previous chapters of this study, Matt 25:31–46 serves as the pivotal point in the narrative that transitions from the earlier narrative of Jesus on to the passion narrative. Moreover, the Enochic mandate evoked by the metaphor of the sheep in Matt 25:32c–33 enables the pericope to act also as a bridge between the exclusive mission of the disciples in chapter 10 to the inclusive mission of chapter 28.

Righteous humanity are the sheep, those who have followed in words and deeds the teachings of the torah as described in 25:32–33. The righteous humanity is both those who were faithful in their duties as the elect and those who have come back into the fold in faith as the nonelect. Both inherit, as it were, that "kingdom created from the foundation of the world" (Matt 25:34), that world when wickedness is in nonexistence, where all of creation bleed righteousness. Throughout Matthew, this is presented as the kingdom of heaven, where the righteous will shine like the sun (13:43).

The mandate of the elect as seen in the Animal Apocalypse, therefore, maps across well when considering the requirements or rule of judgment implied by the allegory: caring for the least. In the Animal Apocalypse, this would be teaching the gentiles the torah that would lead to the ultimate care of showing the way to God's shade of salvation. This is seen especially in the healing stories of the centurion in Matt 8:5–13 and the Canaanite woman in Matt 15:21–28. In Matthew, the elect are called to become a light to the world and reveal in words and deeds the ways of the Lord (Matt 5:13–16). The metaphors of profit and good fruit are prominent in Matthew for expressing this expectation, as seen in parables. The parable of wicked tenants (21:33–41) is one such example in Matthew, where tenants were expected to create produce from the vineyard of the owner. The parable of the talents expresses a similar notion (25:14–30) when the servant failed to make a profit from the portion given to him. Consequently, the one talent was taken away upon the return of the owner.

We are now in the position of drawing a conclusion to this study by positing an implied blend. From what was begun in chapter 4, and in light of chapter 3, we have the following:

Generic space: judgment
>Judge
>Judged
>Punishment
>Reward
>Rule of Judgment

Input 1 (scriptural vision Matt 25:31–32b, 46) Judgment of the Son of Man:
>Judge: Son of Man
>Judged: all the nations
>Punishment: demand the wicked to stand on the left
>Reward: demand the righteous to stand on the right
>Rule of judgment (inferred): fulfill the will of the Father (love *God* and *neighbor*)

Input 2 (parable Matt 25:32c–33) judgment of the shepherd:
>Judge: the shepherd
>Judged: sheep and goats
>Punishment: separate the goats to the left
>Reward: separate the sheep to the right
>Rule of judgment (inferred): follow *the path* of the shepherd
>Intertextual input: Animal Apocalypse
>>Judge: Lord of the sheep
>>Judged: sheep, shepherd, and animals

5. The Apocalyptic Discourse of Matthew 25:31–46 241

Punishment: the unrighteous sheep, shepherd, and violent animals are condemned into the fiery abyss
Reward: the righteous sheep and animals transform into white cattle (1 En. 90.30)
Rule of judgment: follow the path of the Lord of the sheep

Input 3 (allegory Matt 25:34–45) judgment of the king:
Judge: the king
Judged: the subjects of the king
Punishment: the cursed subjects burn in everlasting fire
Reward: the blessed subjects inherit the kingdom
Rule of judgment: caring for *the least* of the king's family

The entailments that accompany the judgment of the sheep or the elect drawn from the Animal Apocalypse would add further to the possible blend.

The elect of humanity: sheep (1 En. 89–90)
The nonelect of humanity: the other animals
The mandate of the elect: teach humanity the torah
Messianic-like figure: firstborn of the white bull with horns (1 En. 90.37–38)
Righteous humanity: white cattle
Righteous creation: renewed creation free of wickedness, violence, and bloodshed

Implied blend: judgment of the Son of Man/shepherd-king/Son of God
Judge: SON OF MAN IS THE MESSIANIC JESUS
Judged: sheep and goats/blessed and cursed subjects/the elect Israel
Punishment: wicked goats stand to the left and are burnt/sheep going astray
Reward: righteous sheep stand to the right and inherit the kingdom/renewed and righteous humanity and creation
Rule of judgment: caring for the least of the king's family/love for the neighbor/teach humanity the torah—the way of righteousness

Matthew's apocalyptic discourse in Matt 25:31–46 aims to provide an identity link between heaven and earth through the person Jesus. The blend of present realities and known apocalyptic traditions creates conceptual structures that weren't there before. Jesus is the Son of God, but also the Son of Man; Jesus is the human king, but also the divine king. Jesus and the Son of Man are one and the same in the metaphor of the shepherd-king.

The use of the sheep metaphor by Matthew in Matt 25:31–46 contextualizes Dan 7 as it evokes known apocalyptic traditions, namely, the Animal Apocalypse. In the Gospel of Matthew, sheep correlate with an agenda that goes beyond a passive identity of a people *to be saved* and to an active identity of a people that were elected *to save*. In Matthew, the implied blend suggests that Israel as the elect are to save humanity and creation by teaching humanity the way of righteousness, which also becomes a formula for their own salvation.[15] In other words, the nonelect, the nations, become part of the vision. Thus, the proclamation of the kingdom of heaven involves an agenda for saving creation whereby creation is renewed alongside the resurrection of the righteous. This is expressed in the allegory of our text (Matt 25:34–45). The primary focus of the allegory is the subjects and the elect. Their understanding of the king and his will are challenged such that they are rhetorically being called to care for the least of this world.

The messianic-like figure and the divine figure of judgment now become one conceptual frame in ways not seen before. The inference created from this emergence is that the criteria of the judgment by the latter are, at the least, related to the contents taught by the former (cf. John 12:48). This is compatible with how Matthew portrayed Jesus in the narrative; one who taught and performed deeds of righteousness to all. Likewise, it is expected of the elect (Matt 25:31–46) and of his disciples (Matt 28:16–20). The span of time includes this life and the next. It would allow Matthew to speak of the present judgment as well as the future judgment of the kingdom of heaven. In other words, judgment would begin in the here and now, making the need in following the teachings of Jesus all the more alluring.

---

15. This, of course, is not to suggest that the concept of salvation is altogether the same in the Animal Apocalypse and Matthew. For instance, the concept of the resurrection is not evident in the Animal Apocalypse. I only mean to show that in both places Israel is both sheep and the means of achieving salvation from divine condemnation.

5.3. Conclusion

From the working definition of apocalyptic at the beginning of this study, the Gospel of Matthew certainly contains discourses that can be characterized as apocalyptic. The discourses we have examined and defined as such include the topos or images of eschatological judgment. However, the employment of such eschatological tradition does not necessarily make Matthew's discourses apocalyptic. It is the literary communication of esoteric knowledge through heavenly revelation and metaphors—which may take the form of dreams, visions, or angelic pronouncements—that characterizes the discourses of Matthew as apocalyptic. Common topical features found in Jewish apocalyptic literature, such as eschatological judgment, could substantiate even further the use of apocalyptic discourse in the Gospel of Matthew, but as Davies suggests, "If we need to explain the introduction of eschatology between ben Sira and Daniel (a gap of forty years), the events in Judah are sufficient. The Antiochean crisis did provoke the creation of the book of Daniel, and of one or two of the Enochic apocalypses. But it did not create 'apocalyptic.'"[16]

Defining apocalyptic as primarily a literary and scribal phenomenon allows the employment of sociorhetorical and metaphorical approaches to Matthew's apocalyptic discourses. These approaches examine the literary contents as a narrative and in conjunction with its cultural and historical intertexts. The use of metaphorical language in apocalyptic discourses reflects the literary and intellectual creativity of Jewish scribes. It is not just for poetic means but rhetorically and conceptually aids in the aims of apocalyptic discourse to convey knowledge between the heavens and earth. It breaks down seeming gaps between God and humanity by revealing a realism that perceives God as being among his people and creation. The metaphors we have discussed in this study are not far from the mundane realities of Matthew's implied audience as wheat, fruits, seeds, chaff, weeds, sheep, and goats, which express the close relations between God and humanity that is only separated through the lack of discernment. The metaphors illuminate a reality culturally conceived. These constitute skills and creativity of Jewish scribes that are normative and nothing less, which culturally appeal to the Jewish conception.

---

16. Davies, *On the Origins of Judaism*, 114.

244   Apocalyptic Sheep and Goats in Matthew and 1 Enoch

Chapter 3 explored the Book of Dreams as possible cultural intertexture to Matthew's use of the sheep metaphor and apocalyptic discourses. As argued, the metaphor of sheep takes on meaning clothed in cultural treasures of Jewish reality. Indeed, the apocalyptic narrative tells of a history in the form of Enoch's dream vision. Rather than a history focused solely on Israel, it is a history of Israel in light of God's creation of all things on earth. Though it is labeled as an historical apocalypse that linearly progresses forward in time toward a culminating end, our analysis shows that it cycles back to the Genesis stories of righteous creation and God's creation of humanity, in which Israel plays a pivotal role. We find that the focus of Jewish thinking and thus this apocalyptic narrative point toward the present, toward the here and now, which is a point in time that God has brought his people to a new experience and situation. Consequently, the narrative of the torah and the history of Israel is expanded and modified. It utilizes insights of wisdom and prophetic traditions to perceive Israel's election anew, that is, toward salvific relations between God, Israel, and the nations. There, the sheep as the elect and part of humanity assume an obligatory role that leads humanity and creation on earth to righteousness. The road map to this righteousness is the wisdom of the torah. All the above cultural treasures are part and parcel of the Book of Dreams's apocalyptic presentation, that is, the revelation of esoteric knowledge by God and the angels to Enoch and (the authors of) Enoch to Israel through visions and metaphorical language.

In chapter 4, I embarked upon an inner-texture analysis of Matt 25:31–46, whereby delineating its parameters and highlighting its reaches. We find that the three-part structure popularized by scholars may be maintained. However, instead of focusing on the dialogue within the narrative, we may see it as a presentation of interpretation where the implied author dialogues actively with the implied audience through a heavenly vision and metaphorical language.

The analysis of 3:11–17 and 13:24–30, 36–43 shows that 25:31–46 was possible only through the progressive developments of Jesus's identities and duties as both the Son of God and the Son of Man. This is also to say that these judgment imageries within the narrative of the Gospel of Matthew are in dialogue with each other. They technically function to recontextualize, reconfigure, and reaffirm previous texts. Through the metaphors of seeds and wheat, Jesus's teachings of the torah as the Son of God implied in 3:11–17 are confirmed. By doing so, it further substantiates with authority the identity and role of Jesus as the Son of God who

5. The Apocalyptic Discourse of Matthew 25:31–46

teaches the torah for the sake of Israel's salvation. Matthew 13:24–30, 36–43 expound more upon the kingdom of heaven in the parable of the weeds in the field. Through metaphorical language, Matthew likens the establishment of the kingdom of God on earth to the kingdom of heaven (kingdom of God in heaven). This is done through equating the sower of good seeds in a field to the Son of Man, suggesting implicitly the relationship between Jesus's earthly identity and role to his eschatological being. The parable serves to convey knowledge, namely, that Jesus is the Son of Man. It defers the eschatological judgment to the future that John expected of Jesus in his earthly presence. The image expresses the logic that what one sows he will reap.

In studying apocalyptic and eschatology within the Gospel of Matthew, I argue that the Animal Apocalypse lies in the background as a possible part of Matthew's Scriptures and sources to its apocalyptic discourses and metaphorical language. As such, it is not surprising that we find the use of the shepherd and sheep metaphors in one of Matthew's significant apocalyptic discourses in Matt 25:31–46. That the sheep are spoken of as righteous and in the language of election within an apocalyptic discourse and in the context of eschatological judgment is telling. Moreover, the sheep are judged from among humanity or "all the nations."

In Matt 25:31–46, a vision conveys the image of judgment in the end of the age. The image harkens back to the Son of Man vision presumably cited from Daniel in Matt 24:29–32 and the parable of the weeds in the field. The use of messianic metaphors of the king and shepherd alongside the figure of the Son of Man in Matt 25:31–33 links the coming Son of Man with Jesus, who was confirmed as Son of God in Matt 3:11–17. As such, *Jesus expresses the need for the sheep as the elect to embody the teachings of the torah by caring and teaching humanity on earth.* It is the belief of this study that this embodiment is the fulfillment of "all righteousness" that Jesus spoke of when he seemed to have corrected John the Baptist. This is to say that Matthew exhorts Israel so they may best prepare themselves in the here and now for judgment when the Son of Man returns.

The examination of the topos of eschatological judgment and the metaphors associated with it throughout Jesus's five discourses illuminates the difference between apocalyptic and eschatology. Apocalyptic discourses recontextualize, reconfigure, and reaffirm old texts to fit new situations. The situation may be a crisis such as the fall of the temple, but the situation may be much more ordinary than this. Whatever the situation, the discourses utilize eschatological material in a narrative of communication between the heaven and earth through Jesus. This highlights the fact that Matthew's apocalyptic discourse and metaphorical language involving eschatological judgment function to exhort Israel in the here and now to take up its role as God's elect in caring and teaching humanity for a better righteousness characterized by love for one's neighbor and obedience to the will of God, that is, the torah. The apocalyptic discourses examined in this study create a narrative in the life and teachings of Jesus that aims to provide for Israel a way to salvation, a way that prepares Israel and humanity for judgment to come, whenever that will be.

Appendix A
Aristotle and Topos

Amelie Oksenberg Rorty suggests, "It is time to reclaim the *Rhetoric* as a philosophic work."[1] In the same vein, Eugene Garver sees Aristotle's *Rhetoric* "as a piece of philosophic inquiry, and judged by philosophic standards."[2] This relatively recent emphasis upon classical rhetoric as philosophy or pursuit of knowledge contrasts with the traditional understanding that rhetoric and metaphor contribute nothing to knowledge. Carolyn Miller states with regard to the traditional view on rhetoric and topos: "The rhetor examines a preexisting inventory of 'stock arguments' and 'commonplaces' to select those that are most appropriate to the situation at hand."[3] Francis Bacon expresses the above traditional view with more detail when he states,

> The invention of speech or argument is not properly an invention: for to invent is to discover that [which] we know not, and not to recover or resummons that which we already know.... Nevertheless, because we do account it a chase as well of deer in an enclosed park as in a forest at large, and that it hath already obtained the name, let it be called invention: so as it be perceived and discerned, that the scope and end of this

---

1. Amelie Oksenberg Rorty, *Essays on Aristotle's Rhetoric* (Berkeley: University of California Press, 1996), ix.

2. Eugene Garver, *Aristotle's Rhetoric: An Art of Character* (Chicago: University of Chicago Press, 1994).

3. Carolyn R. Miller, "The Aristotelian Topos: Hunting for Novelty," in *Rereading Aristotle's Rhetoric*, ed. Alan G. Gross and Arthur E. Walzer (Carbondale: Southern Illinois University Press, 2000), 131. Miller disagrees with this static view of topos and argues instead for a venatic tradition evident within Aristotle where the rhetor utilizes topos with hunting instincts that search out knowledge and novelty.

248   Apocalyptic Sheep and Goats in Matthew and 1 Enoch

invention is readiness and present use of our knowledge, and not addition or amplification thereof.[4]

According to these views, as is also noted by Miller, Bacon suggests that "the invention of speech or argument"—rhetoric and topos—does not invent or create new knowledge but only "recover or resummons that which we already know." The view that rhetoric uses already existing proofs created by other means lies behind Bacon's reasoning. This echoes Plato's conviction that rhetoric does not produce knowledge of any sort. In the *Gorgias*, Plato replies to Polus that he thinks rhetoric is "a knack … for producing a certain gratification and pleasure" (Plato, *Gorg.* 462c).

I would argue, as I think Aristotle would have, that rhetoric is not just a knack but also an actual art in which knowledge is not only discovered *but also created*.[5] One of the earliest teachings and writings about oratory skills is Aristotle's *Rhetoric*, which contains three books that were composed in the latter part of the fourth century BCE.[6] Aristotle may be the first philosopher to have systematized rhetoric as a practical art (cf. *Rhet.* 1.2.7, 1356a20–35) and as a tool or method of argumentation (1.1.1, 1354a1–5). The treatise made an important contribution to rhetoric as an art. Of particular interest in this paper is Aristotle's implementation of topos. My goal is to explain the nature of Aristotle's concept of topos in general and to offer an interpretation that suggests that topos in the *Rhetoric* is generative in nature insofar as it is a "place" where the speaker interacts with the audience to discover and create knowledge through rhetorical demonstration (ἀπόδειξις).[7] In other words, topos is not simply a technical term

---

4. Francis Bacon, *Advancement of Learning*, vol. 30 of *Great Books of the Western World*, ed. Robert Maynard Hutchins (Chicago: Encyclopaedia Britannica, 1952), 13.1.6.

5. Whether Aristotle sees rhetoric as an art (*technē*) or merely a method is not clear. Kennedy suggests that Aristotle may have thought of rhetoric as a mixture (Kennedy, introduction to Aristotle, *On Rhetoric*, 16). I shall take a passive stance on this and live to fight another day. Nevertheless, any serious consideration given to rhetoric places Aristotle in contrast to Plato, who does not see rhetoric as anything but a knack for gratification and pleasure (Plato, *Gorg.* 462c). Yet, Plato seems later to have been more sympathetic in the *Phaedrus* as he hints by saying that until speech is systematized, it is not an art (Plato, *Phaedr.* 277b–d). Perhaps this is why Aristotle would have thought rhetoric to be art.

6. Aristotle, *On Rhetoric*, prooemion x.

7. Demonstration (ἀπόδειξις) as a philosophical process proceeded by strict

Appendix A: Aristotle and Topos

for "commonplaces" but rather points to a heuristic phenomenon within modern-day public lectures where knowledge is potentially discovered and created through the process of change and emergence.

Topos and Aristotle's *Topics*

It is well known that the first line of book 1 in Aristotle's *Rhetoric* asserts that rhetoric is an *antistrophos* to dialectic.[8] Like dialectic, rhetoric becomes a means of teaching knowledge through logic and, unlike dialectic, teaching through persuasion. Both depend upon topos for demonstration, and therefore topos functions as an integral, if not central, aspect of the art of rhetoric and dialectic. *Topos* literally means "place," and it seems that Aristotle uses the Greek term as a metaphor. However, pinpointing exactly what topos is a metaphor of is not exactly clear, though I hope to answer this to some extent in this essay. The lack of a direct definition warns anyone from making quick assumptions. To be sure, Aristotle does not explicitly define topos either in the *Rhetoric* or in the *Topics*, where topos is the central element for dialectic disputations. Nevertheless, Aristotle's *Topics* predates his *Rhetoric* and so can help inform our understanding of what Aristotle could have meant by topos as it relates to argumentation in general as well as in the *Physics* and *Metaphysics*, where topos is a key subject.[9] Let us begin with dialectic, the form of philosophical argumentation.

Aristotle speaks of the usefulness of dialectic in *Top.* 1.2, 101b:

---

deductive argument from premises that were themselves indemonstrable and was the primary way of acquiring scientific knowledge. See Geoffrey E. R. Lloyd, "Demonstration and the Idea of Science," in *Greek Thought: A Guide to Classical Knowledge*, ed. by Jacques Brunschwig and Geoffrey E. R. Lloyd (Cambridge: Belknap, 2000), 243–68. In the *Posterior Analytics*, where the central concept is demonstration, Aristotle defines *demonstration* as "a deduction that makes us know." The Greek noun ἀπόδειξις has the lexicon meanings of "showing forth, making known, exhibiting; deductive proof by syllogism" (LSJ, s.v. "ἀπόδειξις").

8. Aristotle, *Rhet.* 1.1.1, 1354a1–5. This study primarily understands the Greek term *antistrophos* as suggesting that rhetoric is a counterpart to dialectic.

9. It is known that the *Topics* was written at an early stage in Aristotle's thinking, when he was still heavily influenced by Plato. Thus, *Rhetoric* can be said to be a more mature work of Aristotle in which he develops more of his own thought. For a brief survey on scholarly dating of the *Topics* in relations to the *Rhetoric*, see Miller, "Aristotelian Topos," 144.

250   Apocalyptic Sheep and Goats in Matthew and 1 Enoch

What would follow the matters discussed is to say for how many and what [purpose] the study [on *dialectic*] should be useful. It is useful for three purposes: for mental training, for [serious] conversation, and for the sciences along philosophical lines. That it is useful for mental training is obvious in itself; for by having *a method we shall be able more easily to undertake discussion of any proposed question.* [It is useful] for conversation because after enumerating the opinions of the many we shall *engage in discussion with others on the basis of their own beliefs rather than that of others, restating whatever they seem to be saying to us when it is not well said.* [The study is useful] for the sciences along philosophical lines because if we are able to raise difficulties on both sides of the issue, *we shall more easily see in each case what is true and what false. Further, [it is useful] in regard to what things are primary in each science*; for it is impossible to say anything about them on the basis of the specific first principles of each proposed science, since the principles are primary in all cases, and it is necessary to discuss them on the basis of generally accepted opinions in each case. This is specific and most proper to dialectic; for since it is investigative, *it leads the way to the first principles of all methods.*[10]

Aristotle lists three possible uses of dialectic: (1) training in disputation (γυμνασία), (2) casual conversations (ἐντεύξεις), and (3) philosophical sciences and dialectical investigations.[11] It seems that Aristotle refers to dialectic as a method. What results from such a method is the ability to argue on both sides of a subject and to differentiate clearly what is true and false.[12] Indeed, the first two points essentially describe dialectic disputations. To the third point, it applies to Aristotle's philosophy and reinforces the importance of dialectic as being useful "in regard to what things are primary in each science" and "it leads the way to the first principles of all methods."[13] For Aristotle, primaries and first principles, which are made

---

10. Translation by Kennedy (Aristotle, *On Rhetoric*, 265–66, emphasis added). Unless otherwise indicated, all quotations of Aristotle are from the Kennedy translation.

11. What is being referred to here is primarily the list of topoi in the middle books. See Paul Slomkowski, *Aristotle's Topics* (Leiden: Brill, 1997), 11–12.

12. In arguments against a subject, Aristotle's *Sophistical Refutations* treats fallacious statements and serves as an appendix to *Topics*. The fallacious statements acquaint the speaker with what is false when arguing against a subject. See also *Rhet.* 2.24, 1400b34–1402a29.

13. The Greek term used is ἀρχή, which literally means beginning. In *Metaph.* 5.1.1–3, 1012b34–1013a23, Aristotle gives seven meanings of ἀρχή that point toward the

Appendix A: Aristotle and Topos 251

known through scientific demonstration (ἀπόδειξις) by way of deductive reasoning,[14] leads to an ἐπιστήμη (body of knowledge) specific to that science.[15] Dialectic can be deductive reasoning, and it reasons from generally accepted opinions (ἔνδοξα, endoxa).[16] Thus, truth and knowledge is attainable through what is perceived and through deductive reasoning because, for Aristotle, truth is rooted in nature.[17] Plato, on the other hand, perceives truth per se as unattainable because it dwells in the realm of forms. Thus, in addition to dialectic being a method used in disputation,[18] dialectic as such links intrinsically to the pursuit of possible truth and knowledge while dependent upon generally accepted opinions (endoxa).[19] I would like to stress Aristotle's emphasis upon endoxa in attaining truth as it contributes to the generative possibilities embodied within the topos, as posited here.

Aristotle lists about three hundred topoi in the Topics. The structure of the topos mainly consists of two parts: instruction and law. For instance, in Top. 2.2, 109a34–38, we have:

---

beginnings of something's existence or being or becoming known. This part of Aristotle's statement suggests that the first principles would not only be discussed but also be found (Slomkowski, Aristotle's Topics, 14).

14. Aristotle, An. post. 1.2, 71b9–72b4. Demonstration is "a deduction that makes us know." "By demonstration I mean a syllogism productive of scientific knowledge, a syllogism, that is, the grasp of which is eo ipso such knowledge. Assuming then that my thesis as to the nature of scientific knowing is correct, the premises of demonstrated knowledge must be true, primary, immediate, better known than and prior to the conclusion, which is further related to them as effect to cause. Unless these conditions are satisfied, the basic truths will not be 'appropriate' to the conclusion." Translations of Posterior Analytics follow those in Aristotle, "Posterior Analytics," trans. G. R. G. Mure, Internet Classics Archive, http://classics.mit.edu/Aristotle/posterior.html. See also Aristotle, Top. 1.1. "It is a 'demonstration', when the premises from which the reasoning starts are true and primary, or are such that our knowledge of them has originally come through premises which are primary and true." Translations of Topics follow those in Aristotle, "Topics," trans. W. A. Pickard-Cambridge, Internet Classics Archive, http://classics.mit.edu/Aristotle/topics.html.

15. Aristotle, An. post. 1.1, 71a1–71b8.

16. Aristotle, Top. 1.10–12, 104a3–105a19; Phys. 1.1, 184a10–25.

17. Aristotle, Phys. 1.1, 184a10–25.

18. In a dialectic disputation, the questioner (ὁ ἐρωτῶν) interacts with the answerer (ὁ ἀποκρινόμενος) much like what we see in the Socratic dialogues. The functions and roles of the questioner and answerer are spelled out in Top. 8.1–10, 156b23–161a15.

19. Aristotle Top. 1.1, 100b21–23; Rhet. 1.1.11, 1355a17–18.

252 Apocalyptic Sheep and Goats in Matthew and 1 Enoch

[Instruction:] Now one commonplace rule is to look and see if a man has ascribed as an accident what belongs in some other way.[20] This mistake is most commonly made in regard to the genera of things, e.g., if one were to say that white happens to be a colour—[law:] for being a colour does not happen by accident to white, but colour is its genus.[21]

In *Top.* 2.7, 113a20–23, we read:

[Instruction:] if the accident of a thing have a contrary, see whether it belongs to the subject to which the accident in question has been declared to belong: [law:] for if the latter belongs the former could not belong; for it is impossible that contrary predicates should belong at the same time to the same thing.

For the first example, the topos gives instruction to *observe* whether an accident rightly fits its subject. The instructions to observe permit the speaker to argue on the basis of the law of identity when an opposing speaker makes the mistake of attributing to a subject what in reality is a genus. In the second example, the topos gives instruction to observe what the contrary of the declared accident was. The law of noncontradiction can be used to argue for or against an opposing speaker based upon an accident and its contrary, for an accident and its contrary cannot be attributed to the same subject.[22] These rules and laws

---

20. An "accident" (συμβεβηκός) may be considered as an "attribute" (Slomkowski, *Aristotle's Topics*, 92). See Aristotle, *Top.* 1.5, 102b4–9. "An 'accident' is that which is none of these things—neither definition, nor property, nor genus—but still belongs to the thing. Also it is something which can belong and not belong to any one particular thing: for example, 'a sitting position' can belong or not belong to some one particular thing. This is likewise true of 'whiteness'; for there is nothing to prevent the same thing being at one time white and at another not white" (Pickard-Cambridge). For genus, property, and definition, see below nn. 22, 27, and 28.

21. "A 'genus' is what is predicated in the category of essence of a number of things exhibiting differences in kind ... for having argued that 'animal' is the genus of man, and likewise also of ox, we shall have argued that they are in the same genus; whereas if we show that it is the genus of the one but not of the other, we shall have argued that these things are not in the same genus" (Aristotle, *Top.* 1.5, 102a31–102b3 [Pickard-Cambridge]).

22. There are cases where one of the parts of the two-fold structure is implied and not mentioned: for example, with arguments from greater to lesser: "Here is another ... [(law:)] or, if the one that is less generally thought to belong does belong, so also does the other" (*Top.* 2.10, 115a8–11); with arguments of definition: "Another [topos]

Appendix A: Aristotle and Topos 253

are considered general principles, that is, as one and the same in all cases, obtained at all times and places in which the law's conditions are fulfilled. They are generally accepted truth and common in nature. They are distinct from primary or first principles insofar as they do not pertain to a particular science.

A principle provides the basis for a premise (protasis), which is the foundation for creating an argumentative scheme of logic in syllogisms and inductions. For the most part, these argumentative schemes take the form scholars call *modus ponens* and *tollens*.[23] A point of argument arises from a proposition (protasis) or problem.[24] The proposition predicates something about the ontological reality or "being" of a subject by expressing a definition (ὅρος),[25] genus (γένος), property (ἴδιον),[26] or accident (συμβεβηκός), and the speaker seeks whether the predicate befits its subject.[27] The above four predicables can facilitate the construction of an argument because the topos associated with them provides the logical

---

is [(instruction:)] to make definitions both of the accident and of that to which it belongs, either of both separately or one of them, and then see if anything untrue has been assumed as true in the definition" (*Top.* 2.2, 109a34–38).

23. Modus ponens: if P, then Q; P; hence Q. Modus tollens: if P, then Q; not Q; hence not P. See Slomkowski, *Aristotle's Topics*, 99; Sara Rubinelli, *Ars Topica: The Classical Technique of Constructing Arguments from Aristotle to Cicero*, Argumentation Library 15 (Dordrecht: Springer, 2009), 22.

24. Aristotle, *Top.* 1.4–5, 101b11–102b26. Protasis literally means "that which has been put forward," hence "proposition." In the context of logical reasoning, that is, an induction and a syllogism, it would take on the meaning of "premises." While protasis and problema are similar, Slomkowski suggests that Aristotle makes a distinction between protasis as proposition and problema as proposition, where the former serves as premises of the reasoning to refute or prove the latter and thus the latter had to be refuted or proved (Slomkowski, *Aristotle's Topics*, 16–17).

25. Aristotle, *Top.* 1.5, 101b38–102b26. A definition is a phrase signifying a thing's essence by means of its genus or differentia.

26. "A 'property' is a predicate which does not indicate the essence of a thing, but yet belongs to that thing alone, and is predicated convertibly of it. Thus it is a property of man to-be-capable of learning grammar: for if A be a man, then he is capable of learning grammar, and if he be capable of learning grammar, he is a man" (Aristotle, *Top.* 1.5, 101b38–102b26 [Pickard-Cambridge]).

27. Aristotle, *Top.* 1.4, 101b11–101b37. Here Aristotle gives an example of a topos from definition. A definition of a subject must apply to all its subspecies just as the definition of a human being must apply to all subspecies of human beings or all individual human beings.

254 Apocalyptic Sheep and Goats in Matthew and 1 Enoch

determinants for the attribution of predicates to subjects.[28] The questioner attempts to refute the thesis of the answerer by proving his own and by asking questions in the form of premises (protasis). For Aristotle, the significance of presenting propositions and problems is that through them we may come to know something else.[29]

Scholars observe that a topos can regularly be a source for a protasis both in content and form, which suggests that Aristotle's list of topoi is something of a sourcebook. Indeed, Aristotle organizes three hundred topoi into groups relevant in dealing with issues of accident (books 2 and 3), genus (book 4), properties (book 5), and definition (books 6 and 7). It is problematic, however, if the term *sourcebook* evokes a static notion for the function of a topos as merely a source for arguing a particular predicable. I would like to suggest that Aristotle implies a more dynamic function for a topos than he is often given credit for.

First, the topoi as shown above are presented with instructions, often with the injunction to *observe* the proposition brought forth. The speaker interacts conceptually with the topos insofar as the topos examines and investigates a proposition (protasis). The topos is not fixed upon any one predicable, but rather, it can be used to analyze a proposition pertaining to other predicables.[30] This is to say that the general principle contained within

---

28. The four attributions (definition, genus, property, and accident) are traditionally known by scholars to be predicables, which resulted from a reflection on what the predicates of propositions represent from a logical point of view. On this concept, see Slomkowski, *Aristotle's Topics*, chapter 3.

29. "A dialectical problem is a subject of inquiry that contributes either to choice and avoidance, or to truth and knowledge, and that either by itself, or as a help to the solution of some other such problem. It must, moreover, be something on which either people hold no opinion either way, or the masses hold a contrary opinion to the philosophers, or the philosophers to the masses, or each of them among themselves. For some problems it is useful to know with a view to choice or avoidance, e.g., whether pleasure is to be chosen or not, while some it is useful to know merely with a view to knowledge, e.g., whether the universe is eternal or not: others, again, are not useful in and by themselves for either of these purposes, but yet help us in regard to some such problems; for there are many things which we do not wish to know in and by themselves, but for the sake of other things, in order that through them we may come to know something else" (Aristotle, *Top.* 1.11, 104b1–12 [Pickard-Cambridge]).

30. Having reasoned the difference between the predicables, Rubinelli suggests that topoi particular to accidents can be used to refute all the others (Rubinelli, *Ars Topica*, 11). This and similar observations have led some scholars to suggest a more inclusive relationship between the predicables, positing that in this sense a definition

Appendix A: Aristotle and Topos 255

a topos can be used to analyze the possibilities of a proposition. Second, the consideration of combining more than one predicable to finalize a conclusion implies the creativity of knowledge. These two points perhaps lead William Grimaldi to understand topoi as not just a mere list of mechanical terms but also ways to think about the subject.[31] He states, "This was what was meant by saying that these particular topics are not mere mechanical lists of terms to be tried on a subject, no Procrustean bed to which the subject is fitted; rather we have here a method of analysis originating in the ontological reality of the subject."[32] Analyzing and contemplating about what is and what is not becomes the opportune possibility for discovery and novelty. This falls in line with Aristotle's use of syllogisms and inductions. He states in the beginning of *An. post.* 1.1, 71a5–9:

> and so are the two forms of dialectical reasoning, syllogistic and inductive; for each of these latter make use of old knowledge to impart new, the syllogism assuming an audience that accepts its premises, induction exhibiting the universal as implicit in the clearly known particular. (trans. Mure).

Third, and no less important, since the premises of a topos are rooted in commonly accepted opinions, the premises and the topoi themselves may also be subjected to scrutiny. This suggests a more indefinite nature of topos, for if a proposition successfully challenges the principles within the topos,

---

can be a genus or a property or an accident. That a topos is shared between predicables would not mean that one predicable can be interchangeably defined for another, for example, a definition can be also a genus or a property a genus, and so forth. On this scholarly debate, Slomkowski has rightly argued that this latter observation must be abandoned and that the predicables must remain exclusive, albeit a topos particular to one can be used by another (Slomkowski, *Aristotle's Topics*, 73–94). I believe that this underscores the general aspect of the common topos while highlighting its distinctiveness. See also Aristotle *Top.* 7.5, 151a3–14. "It is clear also that a definition is the easiest of all things to destroy; for, since it contains many assertions, the opportunities which it offers are very numerous, and the more abundant the material, the more quickly can reasoning set to work.… Moreover, it is possible also to attack a definition by means of the other attributes [i.e., genus, property and accident]; for if the description is not peculiar, or if that which is assigned is not the genus, or if something in the description does not belong, the definition is demolished."

31. William M. Grimaldi, "The Aristotelian Topics," in *Aristotle: The Classical Heritage of Rhetoric*, ed. Keith V. Erickson (Methuchen, NJ: Scarecrow, 1974), 185.

32. Grimaldi, "Aristotelian Topics," 185.

256   Apocalyptic Sheep and Goats in Matthew and 1 Enoch

then it may induce change, thereby creating new knowledge. Therefore, as Richard McKeon suggests, topos serves as a space for combination and recombination.[33] Both topoi and propositions, though readily and commonly accepted, are also meant to be carefully pondered.

Topos and Aristotle's Philosophy

We may understand the concept of topos further from Aristotle's philosophy of science, although I do not purport to present an in-depth study. In the *Physics*, Aristotle compares topos with a vessel and describes it as the boundary of a contained body or of what exists, that is, of form and matter.[34] Form and matter are conceptual insofar as they are not perceptible in themselves, even though they have perceptible attributes. In book 4 of the *Physics*, Aristotle's concept of topos is made to correspond with Plato's concept of spaces (χώρα). According to Plato, the process of becoming and perishing of substance occurs within these spaces.[35] In such places, nothing is completely determined, where uni-

---

33. Richard McKeon, "Creativity and the Common Place," in *Rhetoric: Essays in Invention and Discovery*, ed. Mark Backman (Woodbridge: Ox Bow, 1987), 31.

34. Aristotle, *Phys.* 4.2–4, 209a31–212a30. In speaking of sense perception, Aristotle distinguishes between form and matter, in *De an.* 2.12, 424a17–30: "By a 'sense' is meant what has the power of receiving into itself the sensible forms of things without the matter. This must be conceived of as taking place in the way in which a piece of wax takes on the impress of a signet-ring [form] without the iron or gold [matter]; we say that what produces the impression is a signet of bronze or gold, but its particular metallic constitution makes no difference: in a similar way the sense is affected by what is coloured or flavoured or sounding, but it is indifferent what in each case the substance is; what alone matters is what quality it has, i.e., in what ratio its constituents are combined" (translation by J. A. Smith at http://classics.mit.edu/Aristotle/soul.html).

35. Plato, *Tim.* 52a–c. In the *Physics*, Aristotle differs from Plato's concept of spaces in that Plato in *Timaeus* suggests place is coextensive with the object/matter occupying the place. For Aristotle, two bodies cannot be coextensive and so place is independent of the object yet it contains the object. Both form and matter occupy place where form is the intelligible, definable element in matter/substance. In Plato (*Tim.* 52a), the imprint of form and its copies are what enters the spaces of becoming, which is witnessed by the senses. See, for example, W. K. C. Guthrie, *The Later Plato and the Academy*, vol. 5 of *A History of Greek Philosophy* (Cambridge: Cambridge University Press, 1996), 262–70. See also Paul Natorp, *Plato's Theory of Ideas: An Introduction to Idealism* (Sankt Augustin: Academia, 2004), esp. chapter 12. See

Appendix A: Aristotle and Topos

versals, elements, and substances are unstable and constantly changing into one another, appearing and disappearing. Aristotle does not seem to disagree with this in particular, although he expresses his disagreement with Plato on other matters, that is, topos is separable from both form and matter while at the same time intrinsically part of them.[36] In the *Physics*, there are particular places (ἴδια) that are exclusively for a particular form and matter, and there are also general places (κοινά) that contain multiple forms and matters that are each in their own particular places, that is, place(s) within a place.[37]

In the *Metaphysics*, Aristotle suggests that universals and the general are common. These are important because without something universal and common, any becoming is inconceivable, for becoming presupposes something universal or ultimate that has not come to be.[38] Furthermore,

---

also Francisco J. Gonzalez, "Plato's Dialectic of Forms," in *Plato's Forms: Varieties of Interpretation*, ed. William Welton (Lanham, MD: Lexington Books, 2003), 46–47.

36. See above n. 35. Cf. Aristotle, *Phys.* 4.3–4, 210b25–211a7: "So much, then, is clear: that since the vessel is no part of its own content (for the primary and proper 'thing in the place' is other than the 'place the thing is in'), a thing's place can be neither its matter nor its form. It must be something other than either of these, for both matter and form are intrinsic to the 'content,' whereas its place is extrinsic to it....Well then, to begin with, we may safely assert—(1) That the place of a thing is no part or factor of the thing itself, but is that which embraces it; (2) that the immediate or 'proper' place of a thing is neither smaller nor greater than the thing itself; (3) that the place where the thing is can be quitted by it, and is therefore separable from it; and lastly, (4) that any and every place implies and involves the correlatives of 'above' and 'below' and that all the elemental substances have a natural tendency to move towards their own special places, or to rest in them when there—such movement being 'upward' or 'downward,' and such rest 'above' or 'below.'" Translation of *Physics* follows that in Aristotle, *Physics: Books I–IV*, Philip H. Wicksteed and Francis M. Cornford, LCL (Cambridge: Harvard University Press, 1957).

37. For example, Aristotle, *Phys.* 4.2, 209a–b: "We have seen that attributions are made directly, in virtue of their immediate applicability, or mediately, because, though not immediately applicable themselves, they include, involve, or imply something that is immediately applicable. And so, too, a 'place' may be assigned to an object either primarily because it is its special and exclusive place, or mediately because it is 'common' to it and other things, or is the universal place that includes the proper places of all things. I mean, for instance, that you, at this moment, are in the universe because you are in the air, which air is in the universe; and in the air because on the earth; and in like manner on the earth because on the special place which 'contains and circumscribes you, and no other body'" (trans. Wicksteed and Cornford).

38. Natorp, *Plato's Theory of Ideas*, 368.

258   Apocalyptic Sheep and Goats in Matthew and 1 Enoch

universals hold more items than one, unlike substances, which are exclusive and defined entities.[39] Matters may either be substances or have the powers or potentials (δυνάμεις) to become substances. Most are of the latter, being potentials.[40] Aristotle uses a box as an example of a substance: "A box is not earthen nor earth, but wooden; for wood is potentially a box and is the matter of a box." Wood here is matter, a potential substance. Box is substance and defined; it presents *differentia* as oppose to a wooden chair. The universals and common are closely linked to elements, for elements have derivative potentials. They cannot be substances because substances are more fundamental than things that are general, that is, actualized knowledge.[41] Such is the case of the "four elements" of earth and water and air and fire. Perhaps this is why Aristotle assigns elements to topos in *Rhetoric*,[42] where Aristotle may be referring to the nature of general principles contained in topos as potentials and does not make the distinction, for a topos is defined by what it contains, albeit a topos is separable from its contents.[43] The above possible associations suggest topos

---

39. Aristotle, *Metaph.* 7.13.2, 1038b8–12. "It is impossible that any universal term should be the name of a substance. For primary substances are those substances which are peculiar to an individual and which do not hold of anything else; but universals are common, since we call universal that which is of such a nature as to hold of more items than one." Translations of the *Metaphysics* follow those in Aristotle, *Metaphysics*, trans. Hugh Tredennick, LCL (Cambridge: Harvard University Press, 1933), https://tinyurl.com/SBLPress4827b1.

40. Aristotle, *Metaph.* 7.16.1, 1040b5–8. "It is obvious that even of those things which are thought to be substances the majority are potentialities; both the parts of living things (for none of them has a separate substantial existence; and when they are separated, although they still exist, they exist as matter), and earth, fire and air; for none of these is one thing—they are a mere aggregate before they are digested and some one thing is generated from them" (trans. Tredennick).

41. Scholars often refer to this as a response to Plato's theory of ideas, where ideas themselves are substances. Aristotle distinguishes what is conceptual and what is substance, what is general and what is individual. The substance is prior to intellect, for substances are individual identity and are not derivative. For Plato, the law of logic and things of intellect is prior to substance. See Natorp, *Plato's Theory of Ideas*, chapter 12.

42. Aristotle, *Rhet.* 2.22.13, 1396b20–23; 2.26.1, 1403a17–22.

43. Aristotle, *Phys.* 4.4, 210b32–211a11. Slomkowski believes that Aristotle's topoi are quite similar to Aristotle's highest principles, κοιναὶ ἀρχαί (Slomkowski, *Aristotle's Topics*, 49). Rubinelli suggests that the "elements" are not used by Aristotle to define topoi, but rather they are used as retrospectively identifying with the syllogisms within the topoi (Rubinelli, *Ars Topica*, 12–13).

Appendix A: Aristotle and Topos 259

as containing universals, the common, and elements that have derivative powers of potentiality.

Aristotle's use of particular and general places in the *Physics* is strikingly similar to Aristotle's use of *idia* and *koina* in the *Rhetoric*.[44] Furthermore, the discussions of topos centers on the common subjects of epistemology and being in these treatises. Therefore, mapping the concept of topos in Aristotle's philosophy onto *Topics* and *Rhetoric* metaphorically would be more revealing than problematic. This could suggest that topoi as described in argumentation are conceptual vessels containing universal principles of truth, possible and actual knowledge that is constantly changing and becoming.[45] In argumentation, topos becomes a place of interaction of all that takes part, as being parts of the whole,[46] in pursuing truth and actualizing knowledge. Whether particular or common, topos contains universals. They contain principles of possible knowledge that have the capacities ($\delta\upsilon\nu\acute{\alpha}\mu\varepsilon\iota\varsigma$) of potentialities.[47] Indeed, in this sense, topos

---

44. Aristotle, *Rhet.* 1.2.21, 1394a19–1395b19. Miller also makes this association between *Physics* and *Rhetoric* (Miller, "Aristotelian Topos," 135).

45. Aristotle indicates that both types of matter, possible/potential and actual/fulfillment, are in the same topos. Aristotle, *Phys.* 4.5, 212b33–213a11: "Nor is it without reason that each should remain naturally in its proper place. For this part has the same relation to its place, as a separable part to its whole, as when one moves a part of water or air: so, too, air is related to water, for the one is like matter, the other form—water is the matter of air, air as it were the actuality of water, for water is potentially air, while air is potentially water, though in another way. These distinctions will be drawn more carefully later. On the present occasion it was necessary to refer to them: what has now been stated obscurely will then be made more clear. If the matter and the fulfillment are the same thing (for water is both, the one potentially, the other completely), water will be related to air in a way as part to whole. That is why these have contact: it is organic union when both become actually one. This concludes my account of place—both of its existence and of its nature." Translations of the *Physics* follow those in Aristotle, "Physics," trans. R. P. Hardie and R. K. Gaye, Internet Classics Archive, http://classics.mit.edu/Aristotle/physics.html.

46. Aristotle *Phys.* 4.4, 211a29–211b5: "Again, when it is not separate it is described as a part in a whole, as the pupil in the eye or the hand in the body: when it is separate, as the water in the cask or the wine in the jar. For the hand is moved with the body and the water in the cask" (trans. Hardie and Gaye). Here, for Aristotle, being separate depends upon being in continuity. He sees the cask as surrounding the wine as not in "continuity" and thus water is in a place of itself and the cask is in another. It is also based on this distinction that he distinguishes between moving "with" and moving "in," as the case with the hand "with" body and water "in" the cask.

47. Aristotle, *Metaph.* 9.7.1–7, 1048b37–1049b3.

260 Apocalyptic Sheep and Goats in Matthew and 1 Enoch

has the capacity to discover and create knowledge. If common accepted opinions (*endoxa*) can serve to actualize possible knowledge perceived from argumentation based on universal principles, then *endoxa* may not only discover knowledge through the senses (as opinions comes about from what is perceived), but they could also have a reciprocal effect upon principles (as general accepted opinions, unless they are primary and first principles) insofar as common opinions may induce change through argumentation.[48] Aristotle intimates this in the beginning of *Top.* 1.1, 100a. He states, "Now reasoning is an argument in which, certain things being laid down, *something other than these* necessarily comes about through them" (emphasis added). Carolyn Miller suggests,

> Within it, new (or old) connections between audiences, terms, and propositions may (or may not) be found (or created). The *topos* is like a cauldron in which form and substance are brought together, where form and substance interact to create propositions shaped for argument and persuasion.[49]

Aristotle's philosophical perspectives enlighten our understanding as to the nature and potentials of topos in relation to the pursuit of truth and possible knowledge. As seen above, dialectic makes use of the concept by means of philosophical disputations in such a way that topos, as in the *Topics* and *Rhetoric*, is a metaphorical connection to the true existence of things and that disputation becomes a method in bringing into perception those things abstract or even unknown. Rhetoric, then, becomes a method that accelerates this epistemological process.

---

48. In the *Physics*, changes are described as motions where the new contents move in as the old elements are destroyed or moved out, thereby creating. Aristotle, *Phys.* 4.1, 208b1–8: "Where water now is, there in turn, when the water has gone out as from a vessel, air is present. When therefore another body occupies this same place, the place is thought to be different from all the bodies which come to be in it and replace one another. What now contains air formerly contained water, so that clearly the place or space into which and out of which they passed was something different from both" (trans. Hardie and Gaye).

49. Miller, "Aristotelian Topos," 136.

Appendix A: Aristotle and Topos   261

Topos and Aristotle's *Rhetoric*

That rhetoric is an *antistrophos* to dialectic suggests what applies to dialectic applies also to rhetoric. It would also suggest distinct differences, which include being of a different method of argumentation, one that is an offshoot of dialectic,[50] manifested through a crossbreed of tools used by philosophers and sophists.[51] Aristotle works between extremes and mediates the strong points of both.[52]

Like dialectic in *Topics*, Aristotle begins his treatise on *Rhetoric* by observing the usefulness of rhetoric. Aristotle states,

> But rhetoric is useful, because the true and the just are by nature stronger than their *opposites*, so that if judgments are not made in the right way are necessarily defeated. And this is worthy of censure. Further, even if we were to have the most exact knowledge, it would not be very easy for us in speaking to use it to persuade. Speech based on knowledge is teaching, *but teaching is impossible*; rather, it is necessary for *pisteis and speeches to be formed on the basis of common*, as we said in the Topics about communication with a crowd.[53]

Clearly, rhetoric is epistemologically useful for Aristotle, especially since truth is rooted in nature. As such, Aristotle differs both from Plato and the sophists.[54] It is also because of this conviction that Aristotle is more sympathetic to rhetoric. For Plato, truth rests beyond comprehension. On the other hand, for sophistry at its extreme, "man is the measure of all things: of things which are, that they are, and of things which are not, that they are not."[55] From Protagoras's dictum, knowledge perceived may be subjective and objective at the same time; it is subjective in the sense that possible truth and knowledge depends upon opinions; it is objective in the sense that truth and knowledge lie within nature, within the realms of the known, within the capacity of perceiving. Consequently, he certainly

---

50. Aristotle, *Rhet.* 1.2.7, 1356a25–27.

51. Aristotle, *Rhet.* 1.4.5, 1359b8–12.

52. E.g., Aristotle, *Rhet.* 1.5, 1360b4–1362a14.

53. Aristotle, *Rhet.* 1.1.12, 1355a20–29, emphasis added.

54. See Kennedy's n. 23 in Aristotle, *On Rhetoric*.

55. For example, Plato, *Theaet.* 152a. In his dialogue with Theaetetus, Socrates quotes Protagoras's famous saying, which Theaetetus seems to paraphrase.

262   Apocalyptic Sheep and Goats in Matthew and 1 Enoch

sees the importance of persuasion,[56] for rhetoric appeals more effectively to common opinions. With respect to the rhetor, the pursuit for attainable truth (as oppose to dialectic) becomes more vigorous and a broader audience requires more creativity. Rubinelli speaks of the distinction of rhetoric's domain. He states,

> It is confined to a particular class of probabilities, namely those things we deliberate about, which depend upon ourselves, and are in our own power to do or to abstain from. More generally, this is the class of human actions or those things immediately depending on them.

Gorgias hints at the ability of rhetoric when he says, "The thing [rhetoric] that is in actual fact the greatest good, Socrates. It is the source of freedom for humankind itself and at the same time it is for each person the source of rule over others in one's own city."[57] For Gorgias and the Sophists, rhetoric has superhuman powers and abilities to both liberate and enslave. As such, a doctor and a physical trainer become slaves to the orator, and a financial officer makes more money for others than for himself.[58] Moreover, rhetoric expands the efficacy of knowledge and truth and allows the freedom to judge what is true through the available means of persuasion.[59] In promoting civilized and free political communities, Aristotle sees the potentials of the power to persuade as beneficial for the rhetor and especially so for the citizens in political and democratic arenas. Orators of Athens have been praised for exercising such powers. The greatest of them include Pericles and Demosthenes, who were eloquent in empowering the

---

56. Aristotle, *Rhet.* 1.2.6, 1356a19–20. "Persuasion occurs through the arguments [*logoi*] when we show the truth or the apparent truth from whatever is persuasive in each case" (trans. Kennedy).

57. Plato, *Gorg.* 452d. Cf. *Phileb.* 58a, "On many occasions, Socrates, I have heard Gorgias insist that the art of persuasion is superior to all others because it enslaves all the rest, with their own consent, not by force." See also Gorgias, *Hel.* 8: "Speech is a powerful lord, which by means of the finest and most invisible body effects the divinest works: it can stop fear and banish grief and create joy and nurture pity" (trans. George A. Kennedy).

58. Plato, *Gorg.* 452d.

59. Aristotle, *Rhet.* 1.1.14, 1355b7–12; 1.2.1, 1355b26–27. Aristotle suggests that rhetoric does not essentially function to persuade "but to see the available means of persuasion in each case, as is true also in all the other arts." In 1.2.6, 1356a19–20, Aristotle states, "Persuasion occurs through the arguments when we show the truth or the apparent truth from whatever is persuasive in each case" (trans. Kennedy).

Appendix A: Aristotle and Topos

assembly and people.[60] What lies in the root of this power are common opinions (*endoxa*) and the ability of the speaker (*entechnic*) to activate them as he wills.

While the power of pure rhetoric is powerfully enticing, Aristotle's treatise on rhetoric ensures that logic and reason tame the seemingly unfettered aims of rhetoric. On the other hand, rhetoric provides docility, since teaching truth through logic would be impossible when communicating with a crowd.[61] One may suggest that for Aristotle, the multiplicity of perspectives creates a higher probability at attaining truth and knowledge that lies within nature. Furthermore, while the discovery of knowledge is significant, the generative quality of the topos is manifested in its ability to create changes through the perception of common opinions made submissive by the power of rhetoric.[62] This ability (or power) differentiates Aristotle from Plato, and rhetoric from dialectic. For the rest of this appendix, I would like to cover only two characteristics of rhetoric, which are closely related to topos, that hint at its ability to create change: *endoxa* and *entechnic*. The former is a feature of the audience, and the latter of the rhetor. Topos consists of how the rhetor draws in common opinion to make judgments, thereby creating change.

In *Rhetoric*, two types of topoi exist: common (*koinē*) and specific (*idia*) topoi.[63] The latter contains premises pertaining to the specific

---

60. Pericles's funeral oration is a well-known example of Pericles's skills. The funeral oration is preserved in the history of the Peloponnesian War, composed by his younger contemporary Thucydides. Examples of Demosthenes's orations include the *1–3 Philippic* orations.

61. Cf. Aristotle, *Rhet.* 1.1.6, 1354a26–31. "And further, it is clear that the opponents have no function except to show that something is or is not true or has happened or has not happened; whether it is important or trivial or just or unjust, in so far as the lawmaker has not provided a definition, the juror should somehow decide himself and not learn from the opponents" (trans. Kennedy).

62. Miller, "Aristotelian Topos," 137. Miller points out that Aristotle posits three kinds of ordinary change, or μεταβολή: alteration (change of quality), growth (change of size), and locomotion (change of place). Miller suggests that Aristotle posits in addition the change of substance. The change of substance leads to the change of place in the *Physics*. This type of change, according to Miller, is the only change that involves the creation of something new.

63. This does not mean that Aristotle fails to make a distinction in *Topics*. It only means that in *Rhetoric*, the distinction is made more explicit. While Aristotle does not refer to ἴδια as specific topoi, his discussion of "common" and "specifics" in *Rhet.* 1.2.21 implies both as topoi. Aristotle says, "I am saying that dialectical and rhetori-

264 Apocalyptic Sheep and Goats in Matthew and 1 Enoch

species and genus, and the former contains premises applicable to many different species.[64] Like dialectic, the general structure involves instructions and principles. Aristotle presents specific topoi in *Rhet.* 1.4–15, 29, common topoi in 2.23, and fallacious topoi in 2.24,[65] a far less extensive list from that of the *Topics*. However, the *Rhetoric* is filled with instructions and principles from common opinions and specifics from which topoi may be formulated in numbers far exceeding what is actually enumerated.

While general instructions in formulating an argument are typical of common topos, Aristotle provides contents that need arrangement only for specific topos.[66] Enthymemes (rhetorical syllogisms) and *paradeigmas* (rhetorical inductions) derive from commonly held opinions.[67] Like dialectic, the premises of enthymemes are attained from the principles contained in the topos. According to Aristotle, the premises of enthymemes come mostly from specific topos while only a few derive from the common topos. Aristotle seems to explain why in 2.22.1, suggesting that the speaker should reason with common among the educated and with specifics when

---

cal syllogisms are those in which we state topoi, and these are applicable in 'common' [κοινῇ] to questions of justice and physics and politics and many different species [of knowledge] ... but there are 'specifics' [ἴδια] that come from the premises of each species and genus [of knowledge]."

64. Aristotle, *Rhet.* 1.2.21, 1358a10–26.

65. This would not constitute a third type of topos, for the fallacious can be used both in specific and common situations.

66. Since specifics are closer to the primary principles of a particular science, specific topoi are more relevant to the subject at hand and closer to context. In a way, this falls in line with Aristotle's philosophy. The universals and common are general, conceptual, and derivative. Individuals and specifics are defined and closer to context and actualized knowledge, which may be perceived and easily understood. There exists a sense of dependence in terms of their relationship. Aristotle gives an example of the relationship between the two topoi in 2.22.12, 1396b12–20. He states: "By common I mean praising Achilles because he was a man and one of the demigods and because he went on the expedition against Ilium; for these facts apply to many others, so such remarks do not praise Achilles any more than Diomedes. Specific [*idia*] are what apply to no one other than Achilles; for example, his killing of Hector, the best of the Trojans, and of Cycnus, who prevented all from disembarking and was invulnerable, and praising Achilles because he was the youngest of those who went on the expedition and the one who had not sworn [to defend Menelaus's right to Helen], and anything else of this sort" (trans. Kennedy).

67. For example, Aristotle, *Rhet.* 1.2.8, 1356a35–1356b10; 2.25.2, 1402a32–34.

Appendix A: Aristotle and Topos   265

dealing with the uneducated. It should be noted that this would not be a statement of preference but rather speaks more to the importance of relevance in the enthymeme. I would argue that Aristotle means to use both, for the audiences that Aristotle has in mind consist of both the educated and the uneducated.

That persuasion comes through relevance is a significant aspect of enthymemes,[68] which is perhaps why enthymemes are "the 'body' of persuasion."[69] In other words, the premises contained in enthymemes should not be "external to the subject" just as things outside of the topos have no effect on the existence of the things inside it. They become ineffective if they do not apply to the subject at hand or if they have no relevance to the experiences of the audience. Together, common and specific make the argument logically persuasive, for without universals nothing is comprehensible, and without specifics nothing is defined and relevant. It seems that the topos permits the rhetor to engage in an interactive relationship with the audience through *endoxa*, where possible conflicting ideas and opinions are exchanged and compromised. To put it in other words, rhetoric highlights seeking truth *from within* existence, within the connections and associations of everyday life. This essentially suggests that the conceptual topos of disputation and rhetorical argumentation is a visualized place, a forum if you will, in which the audience exists as part of its constituents. This expands Aristotle's use of topos beyond logos, as the syllogism must now tailor toward ethos and pathos.[70] Aristotle's theory of invention then becomes crucial, for the speaker must be more creative in accommodating the various factors affecting the audience, for what is at stake is truth and knowledge.[71]

---

68. Aristotle, *Rhet.* 2.22.10, 1396a33–1396b6.

69. Cf. Aristotle, *Rhet.* 1.1.3, 1354a11–16. Kennedy notes, "Body is here contrasted with 'matters external'" (Aristotle, *On Rhetoric*, 31 n. 12).

70. John T. Gage, "An Adequate Epistemology for Composition: Classical and Modern Perspectives," in *Essays on Classical Rhetoric and Modern Discourse*, ed. Robert J. Connors, Lisa S. Ede, and Andrea A. Lunsford (Carbondale: Southern Illinois University Press, 1984), 157.

71. Eckart Schütrumpf and others have argued that the three species of rhetoric—argument, ethos, and pathos—in "invention" were not part of Aristotle's rhetorical theory and that it would be anachronistic to say so. See, for example, Eckart Schütrumpf, "Non-logical Means of Persuasion in Aristotle's Rhetoric and Cicero's *De Oratore*," in *Peripatetic Rhetoric after Aristotle*, ed. William W. Fortenbaugh and David C. Mirhady, Rutgers University Studies in Classical Humanities 6 (New Brunswick:

266   Apocalyptic Sheep and Goats in Matthew and 1 Enoch

The use of ethos and pathos certainly entices the audience in a persuasive attraction so as to achieve the ultimate goal (*telos*) of the three species of rhetoric—deliberative, judicial, and epideictic—concerning the possible and impossible.[72] In addition, style and arrangement are certainly no small endeavor, as all of these become the *entechnic* and *atechnic* arsenals of the rhetor to address the audience. Aristotle states,

> I call *atechnic* those that are not provided by "us" but are preexisting: for example, witnesses, testimony from torture, contracts, and such like; and *entechnic* whatever can be prepared by method and by "us"; thus one must use the former and invent the latter.[73]

The speaker creates his ethos in the speech so as to make himself or herself worthy of credence. For Aristotle, this becomes important in cases where there is not exact knowledge but room for doubt, for character is "the most authoritative form of persuasion."[74] Aristotle provides instructions in the *Rhetoric* on what the common opinions are for the types of character more suitable and morally pleasing.[75] Aristotle also suggests that the speaker must pay close attention to pathos, for there is also persuasion in what leads the audience "to feel emotion by the speech."[76] In book 3, Aristotle adds emphasis upon delivery (3.1.3–10), language (lexis and style—3.2–12), and arrangement (3.13–19), all of which the speaker must consider and invent as they are relevant to the audience and the subject at hand.

Aristotle places importance upon language in creating and actualizing truth. In his discussion of styles, Aristotle, in 3.10–11, sees words as creating knowledge to be pleasurable while understanding glosses as unintelligible. He places a cosmopolitan attribution to words that create knowledge and achieve a certain degree of sophistication, what he calls

---

Transaction, 1994), 101. However, Jakob Wisse and others disagree. See, for example, James M. May and Jakob Wisse, *Cicero: On the Ideal Orator* (Oxford: Oxford University Press, 2001), 30. This paper concurs with the latter.

72. Aristotle, *Rhet.* 1.3.7–9, 1359a6–29.

73. Aristotle, *Rhet.* 1.2.2, 1355b35–1356a1.

74. Aristotle, *Rhet.* 1.2.4, 1356a5–13; see also 1.8.6, 1366a8–16.

75. Aristotle, *Rhet.* 2.1.1–7, 1377b16–20; 2.12–17, 1388b31–1391b7. Aristotle states that there are three reasons why speakers themselves are persuasive; for there are three things we trust other than logical demonstration. These are practical wisdom and virtue and good will." See also Kennedy's n. 2 in Aristotle, *On Rhetoric*, 112.

76. Aristotle, *Rhet.* 1.2.5, 1356a14–15; 2.1–11, 1377b16–1388b30.

Appendix A: Aristotle and Topos 267

τὰ ἀστεῖα.[77] Kennedy notes that τὰ ἀστεῖα "came to mean good taste, wit, and elegant speech."[78] For Aristotle, τὰ ἀστεῖα is achieved through speech by "bringing before the eyes," πρὸ ὀμμάτων ποιεῖ (visualization). There are three things that a speaker must aim for to achieve such effect: metaphor, antithesis, actualization (ἐνεργείας).[79] Aristotle describes things before the eyes as personifying inanimate things as if they were alive, giving an example from Homer: "Then to the plain rolled the ruthless stone," or "the arrow flew ... eager to fly and ... they stood in the ground longing to take their fill of flesh."[80] Furthermore, antithesis and similes are among the rhetorical devices that can be used alongside the preferred metaphor to create actualization or vivification.

A large part of persuasion is dependent upon the rhetor's ability to express his arguments with clarity and creative language in order to "bring before the eyes" and have the audience actualize the possibilities, which means language is a crucial part of the rhetor's *entechnic*. Therefore, the rhetor uses all of his or her arsenals to invent topos and invites all who take part into the efficacy of the argumentation, topos, where the constituents of all that takes part in pursuing truth interact in the chemistry of changing and becoming, where knowledge and new knowledge may (or may not) be actualized, depending on whether the available means of persuasion has been demonstrated. We may see this in a speech, *3 Philippic*, given by Demosthenes, a contemporary of Aristotle.

Demosthenes delivers a deliberative speech to the men of Athens in 341 BCE. He attempts to persuade the men of Athens for future action, namely, to prepare for war against Philip, king of Macedon in northern Greece, who was conquering cities allied with Athens. In this speech, we witness rhetorical topoi and classical rhetoric in action to bring about something that does not exist among the Athenians. As far as Demosthenes is concerned, the Athenians live in a falsified state of reality. In relation to Philip, they dwell in a place of neutrality where "the forms and matters" of

---

77. The Greek term comes from the noun meaning "town." Thus τὰ ἀστεῖα are things of the town. Kennedy attributes a Latin term instead, "urbanity."

78. Aristotle, *On Rhetoric*, 218. On *asteia*, Kennedy references Dirk M. Schenkeveld, "Ta Asteia in Aristotle's Rhetoric," in *Peripatetic Rhetoric after Aristotle*, ed. William W. Fortenbaugh and David C. Mirhady, Rutgers University Studies in Classical Humanities 6 (New Brunswick: Transaction, 1994), 1–14.

79. Aristotle, *Rhet.* 3.10.6, 1410b31–36.

80. Aristotle, *Rhet.* 3.11.2, 1411b25–32.

268   Apocalyptic Sheep and Goats in Matthew and 1 Enoch

idled peace, so to speak, become the common topos of existence. Demosthenes, an Athenian himself, moves to create change by introducing war and resistance against Philip.[81] This is to say that Demosthenes aims to demonstrate Philip's true intentions.

At the outset of his speech, he sets out to establish his ethos. Demosthenes exploits speakers who speak to please rather than to say what is best for the future of Athens. He places these speakers in contrast to himself: "But if you want to hear without flattery what is in your best interests, I am ready to speak." Then, Demosthenes uses the argument "from definition" as he defines what peace is and what it is not in relation to the actions of Philip, thereby also arguing "from opposites."[82] He states:

> But if another person, holding weapons in his hands and having a large force behind him, holds out to you the name of peace but employs the deeds of war, what else is there to do but to resist? Though if you want to claim to be maintaining the Peace in the way he does, I don't disagree. But if anybody supposes this is peace, when that man will advance against us after capturing everything else, first of all such a person is out of his mind, and secondly he is talking about peace for him from you, not for you from him. What Philip buys with all the money he spends is for him to be at war with you but not to be warred on by you.[83]

Working on the principle that tyrants, armies, and weapons are affiliates of war, Demosthenes makes the proposition that Philip will bring war to Athens. From the common topos mentioned above, "from definition" and "from opposites," Demosthenes sets the general program, the common topos, of his argument. He sets out to gain the trust of Athens, by means of persuasive speech (*pisteis*), that it is in fact war and not peace in Philip that they must consider. This also becomes the specifics, for "war and peace" are one of the five things in which deliberative orators give advice.[84] All aspects of the speech must fall within the created topos for them to con-

---

81. "What then about us, Men of Athens? ... I shall tell you, by Zeus, and I will introduce a motion so that you may vote if you wish. I say we ourselves, first, should resist and make preparations with ships and money and soldiers; for even if all the others give way to slavery, we at least must fight for freedom" (trans. Kennedy).

82. Aristotle, *Rhet.* 2.23.1, 8, 1397a7–19, 1398a15–28.

83. Demosthenes, *3 Philip.* 9.8. Translation by Kennedy, in Aristotle, *On Rhetoric*, 281.

84. Aristotle, *Rhet.* 1.4.7, 1359b16–23. "The most important subjects on which people deliberate and on which deliberative orators give advice in public are mostly

Appendix A: Aristotle and Topos 269

tribute to the available means of persuasion, for to speak outside of the subject will be fruitless. History tells us that Demosthenes apparently succeeded as Athens changed and created for herself a new state of reality against King Philip of Macedon, the tyrant.

Conclusion

This section does not profess to unveil all there is about topos, nor does it aim to press forth an airtight argument as to what exactly Aristotle meant when he uses topos in the *Rhetoric*, for Aristotle does not explicitly define it. However, it is by that same reason one may be able to postulate within reason possible conjectures and interpretations. In its attempts to primarily elucidate the nature of Aristotle's topos, this appendix only hopes to offer an interpretation and burst the tightness that seems to have confined the concept of topos among modern scholars as static, which suggests that its sole purpose is to provide the tools for arguments and that it contributes nothing in the pursuit of truth and knowledge. I hope to have shown above that the rhetorical topos is a "place" indeed, and that it is a place not just to draw arguments from but also a place where the rhetor interacts with the audience in discovering and creating knowledge through rhetorical engagement.

Aristotle's concept of topos finds itself within the centerfold of rhetoric, having drawn from dialectic, as both of these aim toward the pursuit of truth and knowledge through argumentation, albeit in a distinct fashion. It certainly seems to have been a place from which arguments can be created, as Aristotle enumerates instructions and general principles in the *Topics* and *Rhetoric*. However, I think Aristotle goes beyond just a sourcebook, as he draws from a philosophical understanding of topos where truth and knowledge take place both in the realm of the abstract and the concrete, universals and substances, intellect and perception. I think topos is a place of interaction between universals and bodies of possible truth where indeterminate things come into being through actualization. As hinted at within Aristotle's philosophy, topoi are not just catalogs of prior knowledge and fixed clichés, but they are also places where the process of changing and becoming occurs in which knowledge is discovered and

---

five in number, and these are finances, war and peace, national defense, imports and exports, and the framing of laws" (trans. Kennedy).

created. Instructions and principles are only the beginning, and by themselves they mean nothing. However, as propositions and problems are introduced, topos begins to come alive and becomes a site of potentialities and possibilities for knowledge and truth, manifested in the interaction between the speaker and the opponent. As such, topos becomes a forum, a platform, a place of intellectual exchange.

While the above may be true for dialectic, it is more so for rhetoric as Aristotle amplifies the abilities of topos, as he takes advantage of the best of two worlds: philosophy and sophistry. In *Rhetoric*, argumentation takes on new parameters where topos is used in ways that exceeds its use in *Topics*. The audiences involved are not just the educated and intellectual but the wider public with its opinions based on the experiences of everyday life, which maximizes the use of *endoxa* that are closer to nature where truth is rooted. This is made possible as the rhetor engages more freely and actively in the interactions with the audience, as stipulated in Aristotle's invention, especially in his concept of *entechnic*. New connections are created between the rhetor and audience, and between terms and propositions, through rhetorical topos. Factors of logos, ethos, and pathos heighten the topos's ability to discover and create new principles and knowledge, an ability that depends upon whether the available means of persuasion is evident.

Appendix B
Cicero and Quintilian on Metaphors

Cicero, who was both an orator and philosopher, certainly was aware of the importance of incorporating the social and cultural context in both thought and speech in society.[1] Cicero states in *De or.* 2.68:[2]

> And I indeed believe that the orator should master everything that is relevant to the practices of citizens and the ways humans behave: all that is connected with normal life, the functioning of the State, our social order, as well as the way people usually think, human nature and character.[3]

This stands central to understanding the ideal orator as being the paradigmatic figure who safeguards and preserves the Roman culture and way of life.[4] For Cicero, culture and what is natural are the very sources of eloquence from which rhetoric, philosophy, and other arts emerge as offspring (*De or.* 1.146; cf. 1.193–194). Eloquence is not just rhetorical or philosophical, but rather both. In the *De oratore*, Cicero takes a more mature stance on rhetoric and philosophy as opposed to his earlier work, *De inventione rhetorica*.[5] The *De oratore* is generally considered Cicero's

---

1. On reading Cicero in social and cultural context, see James M. May, "Ciceronian Oratory in Context," in *Brill's Companion to Cicero: Oratory and Rhetoric*, ed. James M. May (Leiden: Brill, 2002), 49–70.

2. The authorship of *De oratore* is undoubtedly attributed to Cicero at the end of 55 BCE. See James M. May and Jakob Wisse, *Cicero: On the Ideal Orator* (Oxford: Oxford University Press, 2001), 3.

3. Translation from May and Jakob Wisse, *Cicero*, 49.

4. Cf. Cicero, *De or.* 1.34: "I assert that the leadership and wisdom of the perfect orator provide the chief basis, not only for his own dignity, but also for the safety of countless individuals and of the State at large."

5. Remarkably, *De inventione rhetorica* was written when Cicero was seventeen years old. This was an incomplete work on inventions of rhetoric in two books. In

272 Apocalyptic Sheep and Goats in Matthew and 1 Enoch

finest work on rhetoric.[6] His most important later works on rhetoric are *Brutus* and *De oratore*.

The extent to which Cicero is influenced by Aristotle's rhetorical and philosophical theories is not absolutely clear.[7] At the very least, we may conclude that Aristotle's works and those of his followers (i.e., Theophrastus) lie in the background, if not as actual sources for Cicero.[8] At the same time, Platonic (e.g., *De or.* 3.10) and Stoic thought (e.g., *Or. Brut.* 31.113) must be acknowledged as well. Though I will not address this question directly, I must say that Cicero emphasizes the eloquence of oratory in particular, while advocating the primacy of philosophy.[9] For Cicero, discerning logic and truth is not possible without philosophy. Moreover, without philosophy, ambiguities, consequences, and contradictories are incomprehensible (*Or. Brut.* 4.16).[10] Cicero draws from both rhetoric and philosophy without laying claim to either one.[11] His motivation stems from what is missing in the representatives of both arts: "the learned

---

the *De inventione rhetorica*, Cicero did not yet envisage a synthesis of oratory and philosophy. The vision of such a synthesis belongs to his mature works and dominates much of *De oratore*. See Jakob Wisse, "The Intellectual Background of Cicero's Rhetorical Works," in *Brill's Companion to Cicero: Oratory and Rhetoric*, ed. James M. May (Leiden: Brill, 2002), 361–62.

6. William W. Fortenbaugh, "Cicero as a Reporter of Aristotelian and Theophrastean Rhetorical Doctrine," *Journal of the History of Rhetorics* 23 (2005): 44.

7. See Fortenbaugh, "Cicero as a Reporter," 37–64. See also Eckart Schütrumpf, "Non-logical Means of Persuasion in Aristotle's Rhetoric and Cicero's *De Oratore*," in *Peripatetic Rhetoric after Aristotle*, Rutgers University Studies in Classical Humanities 6 (New Brunswick: Transaction, 1994), 95–110. Wisse believes that it is not improbable that Cicero read Aristotle's *Rhetoric* in the original (May and Wisse, *Cicero*, 39). The influence of Greek philosophy, however, must be qualified. On the one hand, some welcomed the Greeks and their philosophies, but, on the other, many had feelings of hostility against intellectuals and specifically Greeks. See Wisse, "Intellectual Background," 331–35, 339. Cicero's works show to be mixed and not clear, though some have argued his accounts of pro-Greek affiliations were fictional.

8. May and Wisse, *Cicero*, 38–39.

9. See Jakob Wisse, "*De Oratore*: Rhetoric, Philosophy, and the Making of the Ideal Orator," in *Brill's Companion to Cicero: Oratory and Rhetoric*, ed. James M. May (Leiden: Brill, 2002), 375–400, esp. 383.

10. *De or.* 4.16: "Surely without philosophical training we cannot distinguish the genus and species of anything, nor define it nor divide it into subordinate parts, nor separate truth from falsehood, nor recognize 'consequents,' distinguish 'contradictories' or analyse 'ambiguities.'"

11. Wisse, "*De Oratore*," 395–97.

Appendix B: Cicero and Quintilian on Metaphors 273

lacked an eloquence which appealed to the people, and the fluent speakers lacked the refinement of sound learning" (*De or.* 3.13). In other words, he embraces the idea of a perfect orator as one who employs metaphor frequently because of its shared commonalities in the language of cities and rural areas alike (*Or. Brut.* 24.81). At the very least, the perfect orator is both a philosopher and an eloquent speaker.

Cicero's rhetorical works, especially the *De oratore*, influenced Quintilian a century later, as evident in his *Institutio oratoria*. The close resemblance of their works leads some to question whether Quintilian made any novel contributions to rhetorical theory at all.[12] Yet, Quintilian has authored the most extensive rhetorical treatise (twelve books) surviving from antiquity. Some claim that Quintilian was less sympathetic to formal philosophical studies than Cicero was.[13] This cannot be ascertained by merely focusing on the surface level of Quintilian's work. Quintilian, as Cicero, places great importance on eloquence. It is chiefly in books 8–10 where he speaks of *elocutio*, or "diction/style," and expresses his thoughts on metaphor and the figurative.

For the term *metaphor*, Cicero and Quintilian alike use the Latin term *translatio* or the verb *transferre* and its cognates, to express the notions of transference (Cicero, *De or.* 1.155–165; *Or. Brut.* 26.92; Quintilian, *Inst.* 8.6.5). Cicero retains Aristotle's definition of transference, but, for him, metaphors are the migrations of words proper to other contexts (Cicero, *De or.* 3.149), which differs slightly from the notion of application (*epiphora*). With regard to a well-used metaphor, he states, "You would say it had not invaded into an alien place but had migrated into its own" (*Brut.* 274). Elsewhere, on the extended meaning of *fideliter* (faithfully), he states, "the word's proper home is in duty, but it has many migrations elsewhere" (*Fam.* 16.17.1). Metaphors are described as words in motion. The motive for metaphor is expressed in the simile, where everything that exists can be used in connection with other things through comparison (cf. *De or.* 1.157–158).[14] As such, Cicero defines metaphor as a form of simile. Quin-

---

12. George A. Kennedy, *Classical Rhetoric and Its Christian and Secular Tradition from Ancient to Modern Times*, 2nd ed. (Chapel Hill: University of North Carolina Press, 1999), 95, also 115–18.

13. Kennedy, *Classical Rhetoric*, 95.

14. Doreen Innes sees *De or.* 1.157 as offering a definition as a form of simile (Doreen Innes, "Cicero on Tropes," *Rhetorica: A Journal of the History of Rhetoric* 6 [1988]: 316).

274   Apocalyptic Sheep and Goats in Matthew and 1 Enoch

tilian shares this interpretation (*metaphora brevior est similitude* [*Inst.* 8.6.8]), but both would stand in contrast to Aristotle.[15]

For Aristotle, figurative language seems to fall under μεταφορά, similes included. For Cicero and Quintilian, metaphor is one among many tropes: metaphor, metonymy, antonomasia, metalepsis, synecdoche, catechresis, allegory, and hyperbole (Quintilian, *Inst.* 9.1.5), which may involve both things (*res*) and words (*verbus*). They distinguished between comparison (*comparatio*) in similes and substitution (*pro res*) in metaphor (Quintilian, *Inst.* 8.6.8) as the former is the genus. Cicero and Quintilian seem to have reduced metaphor to analogy. In other words, considering Aristotle's definition, it becomes less universal and abstract as it now deals more with particulars and primaries, to things closer to sense-perception.

The result of the movement of words in metaphors implies "substitution," which is a detail similar in essence to Aristotle's "application." Cicero states:

> When something that can scarcely be signified by a proper word is expressed by means of a metaphorical one, what happens is this: the meaning we want to convey is clarified by the resemblance between this thing and the thing [*res*] that we evoke by means of the metaphorical word [*alieno verbo*]. Therefore, such metaphors are borrowings, so to speak, since you take what you do not have from another source. (*De or.* 3.155–156; cf. *Or. Brut.* 26.92).

This refers especially to a thing that does not have a name, where a word from its own context would not suffice. A better word borrowed from another context stands in its stead, hence the modern translation of "substitution." The same can occur even if a thing already has a name. What seems to be left unstated is the notion of metaphor as predication and proposition, though it may be implied but hidden through emphasis and language, for Cicero states elsewhere the importance of these to the ideal orator.[16] The notion of substitution seems to imply the restriction

---

15. Cf. Aristotle, *Rhet.* 3.4.4, 1407a14–18; and 3.10.3, 1410b15–18. Aristotle sees simile as a lengthened metaphor.

16. *Or. Brut.* 32.115. Cicero exhorts, among other things, that one who is attracted by the glory of eloquence should be thoroughly trained either in the older logic of Aristotle, or the newer of Chrysippus, to know the different modes of predication and to know the method of distinguishing truth from falsity.

Appendix B: Cicero and Quintilian on Metaphors 275

of metaphor to a single word that stands in for a thing, that is, *pro re* (cf. Quintilian, *Inst.* 8.6.9).[17] However, more can be said.

The use of the Latin term *res* presents a crucial element in the relations of words and perceptions that illuminate the cognitive activities understood by both Cicero and Quintilian.[18] For them, the sole purpose of words is to represent *res*. The *res*—which can mean thing, property, matter, affair, activity, or situation—represents what is perceived by the senses from the outside world. It could also be what is already in the mind. For Cicero and Quintilian, *res* is perceived as true. The preposition *pro* may imply "an exchange" as in "in return for."

The reciprocal relationship of words and *res* is comparable to how words symbolize things perceived. The mind and soul take and gather the images of *res* and, when moved, transform them into what they have taken and gathered (Quintilian, *Inst.* 1.2.30). They become the *res*, that is, what one knows and says.[19] Edward Cranz speaks of *res* as also representing knowledge. Quintilian states, "Eloquence means to put forward and pass on to the listeners all which you have gathered by the mind" (*Inst.* 8, preface 15).[20] In a metaphor, *substitution* means that a word designates two *res*,

---

17. Innes, "Cicero on Tropes," 316. Quintilian, *Inst.* 8.6.9: *haec* [metaphor] *pro ipsa re dicitur ... cum in rebus animalibus aliud pro alio ponitur*. In translation: this substitute for the thing itself [lit., said instead of thing itself] ... the substitution of one animate thing for another [lit., placed instead of another animate thing].

18. See F. Edward Cranz, "Quintilian as Ancient Thinker," *Rhetorica: A Journal of the History of Rhetoric* 13 (1995): 219–30. Arguing against the medieval-modern categories emerging around the eleventh and beginning of the twelfth centuries (that Quintilian speaks of words representing both things and meaning), Kranz posits that for Quintilian (and Cicero) words represent only *res*, a dualism that Quintilian exhaustively deals with. According to Cranz, the category of meaning never existed. Quintilian's understanding of taking and gathering in the mind and soul differs from the medieval-modern understanding that the primary function of the mind is to create meanings in the mind so as to think about things outside the mind. For Quintilian, as per Cranz, *res* means more than just matter or thing. It connotes also what one sees and becomes.

19. Cranz, "Quintilian as Ancient Thinker," 228–29.

20. *Eloqui enim* [hoc] *est omnia quae mente conceperis promere atque ad audientis perferre*. Cranz sees the verbs *percipere* and *concipere* as referring to the process by which the whole or parts of the outside world are taken into the mind or by which what is already in the mind is gathered, distinguished, or combined. He states further that in both cases we may speak of *res*, whether of what is outside the mind or of what is in the mind (Cranz, "Quintilian as Ancient Thinker," 226).

276   Apocalyptic Sheep and Goats in Matthew and 1 Enoch

where two objects of understanding (whether of the outside world or of what is already in the mind) are superimposed within one's mind and soul. The images are gathered, distinguished, or combined; that is, the metaphor is applied. Thus, *pro res* does not merely mean substitution—that a word stands in for another—but rather that it refers to the cognitive process enacted through images of *rerum* interacting by the application of the metaphor. While the discussion of metaphor between Cicero and Quintilian seems to be predominantly in the context of oratory, this does not necessarily debunk philosophical aspects that may deliberately be placed in the background.

Like Aristotle, Cicero recognizes the special nature of metaphor as a mark of an innate ability to extend the listener's thought in a different but purposeful direction (*De or.* 3.160). However, Cicero (in character, Crassus) does not link this to an understanding of genus and species in the *De oratore*.[21] Quintilian neglects at the surface such theoretical categorization altogether and deems it rather for school boys (*Inst.* 8.6.13). To be sure, what is being neglected is not the ability of metaphors to convey reality or knowledge but the philosophical descriptions of theoretical divisions, in other words, philosophical language. The thrust of eloquence is the lack of need for technical explanations and jargons and has everything to do with what is natural and appropriate.[22] Cicero states, "After all, every aspect of our judicial and political speaking is variable and adapted to an ordinary and popular way of thinking" (*De or.* 1.108).

Cicero points to two basic uses of metaphor (*De or.* 3.155).[23] First, metaphors clarify (cf. Quintilian, *Inst.* 5.14.34–35), which he suspects may have been their original use (*De or.* 3.155). In addition to providing a name,

---

21. Innes, "Metaphor," 14.

22. Innes, "Cicero on Tropes," 307. "In the case of metaphor, which has the longest analysis, Crassus [Cicero] knows that his audience has no need to be given subdivisions (*De Oratore* 156), and he therefore omits discussion of the standard technical divisions according to genus and species or animate and inanimate. It is part of Cicero's general intention in *De Oratore* to avoid trite rules (*Fam.* 1.9.23), and therefore we cannot expect much interest in the technical apparatus of style or any sustained attempt to produce novel definitions or subdivisions."

23. Innes, "Cicero on Tropes," 314. Innes posits that Cicero speaks here of two types of metaphor: necessary metaphor and bold metaphors. However, Cicero iterates the usefulness or function of metaphor, and Cicero, as stated above, lists other uses of metaphors. Thus, it seems that Cicero emphasizes distinct functions that create a range or a spectrum based on a binary of use. I understand types as, for example,

Appendix B: Cicero and Quintilian on Metaphors 277

the function of clarifying includes using metaphor to define something obscure or unknown (cf. Quintilian, *Inst.* 7.3.13). As already suggested by Aristotle, this involves comparison. In *Top.* 32, Cicero explains, "Orators and poets often ... define by comparison, using metaphors with a pleasing effect." In quoting Aquilius, Cicero defines *shore* (*litus*) as "the place upon which the waves play." The defining function often goes hand in hand with logical disputation. Quintilian uses the same example that Cicero uses when defending the use of metaphor in argumentation (*Inst.* 5.14.34–35).[24] He admits that to be successful the metaphor itself must illuminate (*lucis adfert ipsa tralatio* [*Inst.* 5.14.34]) by improving the clarity of a term and should not obscure it.

Second, metaphor adds splendor to speeches. It is one of three forms of ornamentation, which also include archaisms and neologisms (*De or.* 3.152–153).[25] Metaphor is widely used (*De or.* 3.155; Quintilian, *Inst.* 8.6.4; also Aristotle, *Rhet.* 3.2.6, 1404b) and is the most important ornamentation of diction (*De or.* 3.166, 170). Although clarification may have been the original use of the metaphor, it evolved into a means of creating distinction and dignity, as it were, due to popularity (*De or.* 3.155).[26] Simply put, the natural use of metaphor developed into a form of art.[27]

Cicero expresses this in another way. When introducing splendor, the metaphor is bold and does not compensate for a shortage. The ordinary metaphor accommodates shortage by making matters more vivid and reveals

---

genus to species, species to genus, species to species, analogy, and so forth. Quintilian lists animate to inanimate, inanimate to animate, and so forth.

24. Quintilian, *Inst.* 5.14.34–35: "After all, even lawyers, who take great pains over the precise significance of words, venture to define the shoreline (*litus*) as the place where the wave 'plays itself out' (*eludit*)."

25. Archaism, neologism, and metaphor are known by scholars as the three standard categories of ornamentation (See, e.g., Innes, "Metaphor," 21). On the treatment of these three tropes, see Innes, "Cicero on Tropes."

26. Cicero uses the analogy of clothes: "just as clothes were first invented in order to ward off the cold, but later began to be used also for giving the body distinction and dignity, so metaphors were first established because of a shortage of words, but came to be used frequently because of their charm" (*De or.* 3.155).

27. Innes, "Cicero on Tropes," 314. In book 1 of *De oratore*, Crassus (Cicero) argues for the art of oratory over and against the philosophical definition given by Charmadas (1.92), which reduces the art of oratory to nonexistence (1.90). Crassus states that since oratory has been observed, recorded, defined, and clarified by division into classes and subclasses, then he does not see why oratory should not be called an art (1.109, 186).

278   Apocalyptic Sheep and Goats in Matthew and 1 Enoch

what is hidden. They also achieve brevity (*De or.* 3.158). In short, metaphors clarify, vivify, reveal, provide brevity, and adorn (*De or.* 3.155–158). Thus, for Cicero, the function of metaphors ultimately caters to the lack of signification of proper words, thereby contributing further to eloquent speech.

The function of metaphor, in clarifying something that is obscure, correlates with its functions of vivifying and revealing. These are integral components of what both Cicero and Quintilian designate as allegory, from the Greek ἀλληγορία, which is a style that comes about "when there is a continuous stream of metaphors" (*Or. Brut.* 27.94). Allegory derives from an ancient practice of poets and refers to an exegetical principle, employed for centuries by philosophers who saw deeper meanings in things (especially in texts) that appeared to be "saying something else."[28] They are found in the interpretative writings of early Jews in Alexandria (i.e., Philo), Babylonia, and Palestine (i.e., rabbinics), and later became popular among the early Christians (i.e., Origen).[29]

The power of metaphor to provide vivid visuals has been discussed since Aristotle and his contemporaries. This function of metaphor became especially important in personification (Aristotle, *Rhet.* 3.10.7, 1410b36–1411b23) as Aristotle refers to inanimate things brought "before the eyes," signifying *energeia*. Likewise, Cicero and Quintilian speak of ἐνάργεια (not ἐνεργεία), which is a vivid image or visualization (φαντάσια) painted in words, as in a simile when used as proof in argumentation (Quintilian, *Inst.* 8.3.72–82). The source of eloquent metaphors must originate in the activities of life and experience so that the mind may easily comprehend them (*Inst.* 8.3.72). Among the four classes of metaphor that Quintilian lists, personification falls within the fourth type, animating the inanimate. Citing *Aeneid* (2.307–308), "Sits ignorant the shepherd, from the tall rock's head catching the sound" (*Inst.* 8.6.10), he shows that personification produces a marvelous sublimity (*Inst.* 8.6.11).[30]

---

28. G. R. Boys-Stones, "Introduction," in Metaphor, Allegory, and the Classical Tradition, ed. G. R. Boys-Stones (Oxford: Oxford University Press, 2003), 2.

29. See Daniel Boyarin, "Origen as Theorist of Allegory: Alexandrian Contexts," in *The Cambridge Companion to Allegory*, ed. Rita Copeland and Peter T. Struck (Cambridge: Cambridge University Press, 2010); also R. P. C. Hanson, *Allegory and Event* (Richmond: John Knox, 1959). There is, however, a slight difference between creating allegory and perceiving something as allegory. The cognitive activities are reversed but the same.

30. The four classes are (1) the substitution of one animate thing for another, (2)

Appendix B: Cicero and Quintilian on Metaphors

In the *De oratore*, Cicero does not specify a particular preference for any one use of metaphors. He does, however, raise the question of why metaphorical words, including necessary metaphors, are even favored over proper words (*De or.* 3.159). He answers that this is essentially because they are pleasurable and goes on to ponder the delight aroused in (1) the natural talent of bringing something from afar, (2) having your thoughts led somewhere else in a purposeful direction, (3) evoking things and their similes, and (4) appealing to the senses. With respect to the senses, "the sense of sight is much more striking, putting what we cannot really see almost before our mind's eye" (3.159–161). This striking effect of sight is the greatest merit of metaphorical language (3.163).

As an extension of his musings, Cicero urges that "we should avoid baseness in the things to which the minds of our audience will be pulled by the resemblance" (*De or.* 3.163). As examples, he states, "I don't like people to say that by the death of Scipio, the State has been 'castrated'; I don't like Glaucia to be called 'the dung of the Senate House.'" Cicero suggests for the speaker to avoid the use of likenesses to things sordid and admonishes that resemblances should not be far-fetched. Furthermore, metaphor needs to be appropriate. It should not be stronger or weaker than the subject demands. Neither should it "be narrower in scope than the proper and literal word would have been" (3.164). It must seem natural and "appear to have been escorted there rather than to have burst in; it must seem to have come with permission, not by force" (3.165). If a metaphor seems too harsh, an introductory word should soften it. For example, leaving "the Senate an orphan" is harsh, while leaving "the Senate, so to speak, an orphan" softens the metaphor (3.165). In summary, metaphors should not be too vile, too frequent, or too far-fetched.[31]

Aristotle, Cicero, and Quintilian laid the foundation for the use of metaphor in centuries to come. Both the use and function of metaphor have been instrumental in the aims of rhetoric as well as philosophy. However, as often noted, metaphors took a more rhetorical route in subsequent centuries, perhaps due to the lack of attention to its inherent capabilities.

---

inanimate for inanimate, (3) inanimate for animate, and (4) animate for inanimate. See Quintilian, *Inst.* 8.6.10.

31. Innes, "Metaphor," 16–17.

Bibliography

Albrektson, Bertil. *History and the Gods: An Essay on the Idea of Historical Events as Divine Manifestations in the Ancient Near East and in Israel.* Lund: Gleerup, 1967.

Albright, W. F., and C. S. Mann. *Matthew.* AB 26. New York: Doubleday, 1971.

Allen, W. C. *A Critical and Exegetical Commentary on the Gospel according to Saint Matthew.* 3rd ed. ICC. Edinburgh: T&T Clark, 1912.

Allison, Dale C. *Studies in Matthew: Interpretation Past and Present.* Grand Rapids: Baker Academic, 2005.

Argall, Randall A. *1 Enoch and Sirach: A Comparative Literary and Conceptual Analysis of the Themes of Revelation, Creation and Judgment.* EJL 8. Atlanta: Scholars Press, 1995.

Aristotle. *Metaphysics.* Translated by Hugh Tredennick. LCL. Cambridge: Harvard University Press, 1933.

———. *On Rhetoric: A Theory of Civic Discourse.* Translated by George A. Kennedy. 2nd ed. Oxford: Oxford University Press, 2007.

———. "Physics." Translated by R. P. Hardie and R. K. Gaye. Internet Classics Archive. http://classics.mit.edu/Aristotle/physics.html.

———. *Physics: Books I–IV.* Translated by Philip H. Wicksteed and Francis M. Cornford. LCL. Cambridge: Harvard University Press, 1957.

———. "Posterior Analytics." Translated by G. R. G. Mure. Internet Classics Archive. http://classics.mit.edu/Aristotle/posterior.1.i.html.

———. "Topics." Translated by W. A. Pickard-Cambridge. Internet Classics Archive. http://classics.mit.edu/Aristotle/topics.2.ii.html.

Assefa, Daniel. *L'Apocalypse des animaux (1 Hen 85–90): Une propaganda militaire?* Leiden: Brill, 2007.

Austin, John L. *Philosophical Papers.* Oxford: Oxford University Press, 1961.

Avery-Peck, Alan J., Daniel Harrington, and Jacob Neusner, eds. *When Judaism and Christianity Began: Essays in Memory of Anthony J. Saldarini.* 2 vols. JSJSup 85. Leiden: Brill, 2004.

Backman, Mark. *Rhetoric: Essays in Invention and Discovery.* Woodbridge: Ox Bow, 1987.

Bacon, Francis. *Advancement of Learning.* Vol. 30 of *Great Books of the Western World.* Edited by Robert Maynard Hutchins. Chicago: Encylopaedia Britannica, 1952.

Bakhtin, Mikhail M. *The Dialogic Imagination: Four Essays.* Edited by Michael Holist. Translated by Caryl Emerson and Michael Holist. Austin: University of Texas Press, 1981.

Barr, James. *Biblical Words for Time.* 2nd ed. London: SCM, 1969.

Barth, Fredrik. "Introduction." Pages 9–38 in *Ethnic Groups and Boundaries: The Social Organization of Culture Difference.* Edited by Fredrik Barth. Boston: Little, Brown, 1969.

Barton, John. *Oracles of God: Perceptions of Ancient Prophecy in Israel after the Exile.* London: Darton, Longman & Todd, 1986.

Bauckham, Richard J. "The Delay of the Parousia." *TynBul* 31 (1980): 3–36.

Bedenbender, Andreas. "The Place of the Torah in the Early Enoch Literature." Pages 78–80 in *The Early Enoch Literature.* Edited by Gabriele Boccaccini and John J. Collins. Leiden: Brill, 2007.

Bendoraitis, Kristian. "Apocalypticism, Angels, and Matthew." Pages 31–52 in *The Jewish Apocalyptic Tradition and the Shaping of New Testament Thought.* Edited by Benjamin E. Reynolds and Loren T. Stuckenbruck. Minneapolis: Fortress, 2017.

Berg, Sandra Beth. "After the Exile: God and History in the Books of Chronicles and Esther." Pages 107–28 in *The Divine Helmsman: Studies on God's Control of Human Events, Presented to Lou H. Silberman.* Edited by James L. Crenshaw and Samuel Sandmel. New York: Ktav, 1980.

Betz, Hans Dieter. *Galatians: A Commentary on Paul's Letter to the Churches in Galatia.* Hermeneia. Philadelphia: Fortress, 1979.

———. "Literary Composition and Function of Paul's Letter to the Galatians." *NTS* 21 (1975): 353–79.

———. "On the Problem of the Religio-Historical Understanding of Apocalypticism." *JTC* 6 (1969): 134–54.

Birnbaum, Ellen. *The Place of Judaism in Philo's Thought: Israel, Jews, and Proselytes.* BJS 290. Atlanta: Scholars Press, 1996.

Black, C. Clifton. "Rhetorical Criticism." Pages 256–77 in *Hearing the New Testament: Strategies for Interpretation*. Edited by Joel B. Green. Grand Rapids: Eerdmans, 1995.

Black, C. Clifton, and Duane F. Watson, eds. *Words Well Spoken: George Kennedy's Rhetoric of the New Testament*. Waco, TX: Baylor University Press, 2008.

Black, Matthew, ed. *Apocalypsis Henochi Graece: Fragmenta pseudepigraphorum quae supersunt graeca una cum historicorum et auctorum judaeorum hellenistarum fragmentis collegit et ordinarit Albert-Marie Denis*. PVTG 3. Leiden: Brill, 1970.

———. *Book of Enoch or 1 Enoch: A New English Edition with Commentary and Textual Notes*. SVTP 7. Leiden: Brill, 1985.

Blenkinsopp, Joseph. *Isaiah 40–55*. AB 19A. New York: Doubleday, 2002.

———. *Wisdom and Law in the Old Testament*. New York: Oxford University Press, 1995.

Blocher, Henri. "The Fear of the Lord as the Principle of Wisdom." *TynBul* 28 (1977): 3–28.

Bloomquist, L. Gregory. "The Intertexture of Lukan Apocalyptic Discourse." Pages 45–68 in *The Intertexture of Apocalyptic Discourse in the New Testament*. Edited by Duane F. Watson. SBLSymS 14. Atlanta: Society of Biblical Literature, 2002.

———. "Methodological Criteria for Apocalyptic Rhetoric." Pages 181–203 in *Vision and Persuasion: Rhetorical Dimensions of Apocalyptic Discourse*. Edited by Greg Carey and L. Gregory Bloomquist. Saint Louis: Chalice, 1999.

Boccaccini, Gabriele. *Beyond the Essene Hypothesis: The Parting of the Ways between Qumran and Enochic Judaism*. Grand Rapids: Eerdmans, 1998.

———. "The Contribution of Italian Scholarship." Pages 33–50 in *Mysteries and Revelations: Apocalyptic Studies since the Uppsala Colloquium*. Edited by John J. Collins and James H. Charlesworth. Sheffield: Sheffield Academic, 1991.

———. "The Covenantal Theology of the Apocalyptic Book of Daniel." Pages 39–44 in *Enoch and Qumran Origins: New Light on a Forgotten Connection*. Edited by Gabriele Boccaccini. Grand Rapids: Eerdmans, 2005.

———. *Middle Judaism: Jewish Thought, 300 BCE to 200 CE*. Minneapolis: Fortress, 1991.

—. *Roots of Rabbinic Judaism: An Intellectual History, from Ezekiel to Daniel.* Grand Rapids: Eerdmans, 2002.

Boccaccini, Gabriele, and John J. Collins, eds. *The Early Enoch Literature.* Leiden: Brill, 2007.

Bornkamm, Gunther. "End-Expectation and Church in Matthew." Pages 15–51 in *Tradition and Interpretation in Matthew.* Edited by G. Bornkamm, G. Barth, and H. J. Held. London: SCM, 1963.

—. *Jesus of Nazareth.* New York: Harper & Row, 1960.

Boyarin, Daniel. "Beyond Judaisms: Metatron and the Divine Polymorphy of Ancient Judaism." *JSJ* 41 (2010): 323–65.

—. "Daniel 7, Intertextuality, and the History of Israel's Cult." *HTR* 105 (2012): 139–62.

—. *The Jewish Gospels: The Story of the Jewish Christ.* New York: New Press, 2012.

—. *Intertextuality and the Reading of Midrash.* Bloomington: Indiana University Press, 1990.

—. "Origen as Theorist of Allegory: Alexandrian Contexts." Pages 39–54 in *The Cambridge Companion to Allegory.* Edited by Rita Copeland and Peter T. Struck. Cambridge: Cambridge University Press, 2010.

—. *A Radical Jew: Paul and the Politics of Identity.* Berkeley: University of California Press, 1994.

—. "Rethinking Apocalypse; or, Apocalypse Then." Unpublished manuscript.

—. *Socrates and the Fat Rabbis.* Chicago: University of Chicago Press, 2009.

—. *A Traveling Homeland: The Babylonian Talmud as Diaspora.* Philadelphia: University of Pennsylvania Press, 2015.

Boys-Stones, G. R. "Introduction." Pages 1–5 in *Metaphor, Allegory, and the Classical Tradition.* Edited by G. R. Boys-Stones. Oxford: Oxford University Press, 2003.

Brueggemann, Walter. *First and Second Samuel.* Louisville: John Knox, 1990.

Brummett, Barry. *Contemporary Apocalyptic Rhetoric.* New York: Praeger, 1991.

—. "Premillennial Apocalyptic as a Rhetorical Genre." *Central States Speech Journal* 35 (1984): 84–93.

—. "Using Apocalyptic Discourse to Exploit Audience Commitments through Transfer." *Southern Communication Journal* 54 (1988): 58–73.

Bibliography 285

Bultmann, Rudolf. *History of the Synoptic Tradition*. New York: Harper & Row, 1963.

Burrows, Millar. "Ancient Israel." Pages 99–131 in *The Idea of History in the Ancient Near East*. Edited by Robert C. Dentan. New Haven: Yale University Press, 1955.

Bywater, Ingram. *Aristotle on the Art of Poetry: A Revised Text with Critical Introduction, Translation, and Commentary*. Oxford: Clarendon, 1909.

Campbell, Antony F. *1 Samuel*. FOTL 7. Grand Rapids: Eerdmans, 2003.

Carey, Greg. "Introduction." Pages 1–15 in *Vision and Persuasion: Rhetorical Dimensions of Apocalyptic Discourse*. Edited by Greg Carey and L. Gregory Bloomquist. Saint Louis: Chalice, 1999.

———. *Ultimate Things: An Introduction to Jewish and Christian Apocalyptic Literature*. Saint Louis: Chalice, 2005.

Carey, Greg, and L. Gregory Bloomquist, eds. *Vision and Persuasion: Rhetorical Dimensions of Apocalyptic Discourse*. Saint Louis: Chalice, 1999.

Carmignac, Jean. "Description du phenomene de l'Apocalyptique dans l'Ancient Testament." Pages 163–70 in *Apocalypticism in the Mediterranean World and the Near East: Proceedings of the International Colloquium on Apocalypticism Uppsala, August 12–17, 1979*. Edited by David Hellholm. 2nd ed. Tübingen: Mohr Siebeck, 1989.

Carter, Warren. *Matthew and the Margins: A Socio-political and Religious Reading*. New York: T&T Clark, 2000.

Carter, Warren, and John Paul Heil, *Matthew's Parable: Audience-Oriented Perspectives*. CBQMS 30. Washington, DC: Catholic Biblical Association of America, 1998.

Charette, Blaine. *The Theme of Recompense in Matthew's Gospel*. Sheffield: JSOT Press, 1992.

Charles, R. H., ed. *The Apocrypha and Pseudepigrapha of the Old Testament in English*. 2 vols. Oxford: Clarendon, 1913.

———. *The Book of Enoch or 1 Enoch*. Oxford: Clarendon, 1912.

Charlesworth, James H. "The Date and Provenience of the *Parables of Enoch*." Pages 37–57 in *Parables of Enoch: A Paradigm Shift*. Edited by Darrell L. Bock and James H. Charlesworth. London: Bloomsbury, 2013.

Clark, Donald L. *Rhetoric in Greco-Roman Education*. New York: Columbia University Press, 1957.

Clifford, Richard J., S.J. "The Roots of Apocalypticism in Near Eastern Myth." Pages 3–29 in *The Continuum History of Apocalypticism*. Edited by Bernard McGinn, John J. Collins, and Stephen J. Stein. New York: Continuum, 2003.

Clivaz, Claire, Andreas Dettwiler, Luc Devillers, and Enrico Norelli, eds. *Infancy Gospels: Stories and Identities*. Tübingen: Mohr Siebeck, 2011.

Cohen, Shaye J. D. *From the Maccabees to the Mishnah*. Philadelphia: Westminster, 1987.

Collins, A. C., S. E. Gathercole, and M. A. Conway, eds. *Theories of Memory*. London: Lawrence Erlbaum, 1993.

Collins, John J. *The Apocalyptic Imagination: An Introduction to Jewish Apocalyptic Literature*. 2nd ed. Grand Rapids: Eerdmans, 1998.

———. *The Apocalyptic Vision of the Book of Daniel*. HSM 16. Missoula, MT: Scholars Press, 1977.

———. "Genre, Ideology and Social Movements." Pages 19–20 in *Mysteries and Revelations: Apocalyptic Studies since the Uppsala Colloquium*. Edited by John J. Collins and James H. Charlesworth. Sheffield: Sheffield Academic, 1991.

———. "Introduction: Towards the Morphology of a Genre." *Semeia* 14 (1979): 1–20.

———. "The Jewish Apocalypses." *Semeia* 14 (1979): 21–59.

———. *Jewish Wisdom in the Hellenistic Age*. OTL. Louisville: Westminster John Knox, 1997.

———, ed. *The Oxford Handbook of Apocalyptic Literature*. Oxford: Oxford University Press, 2014.

———. *Seers, Sibyls and Sages in Hellenistic-Roman Judaism*. Leiden: Brill, 2001.

———. "The Symbolism of Transcendence in Jewish Apocalyptic." *BR* 19 (1974): 5–22.

Collins, John J., and J. H. Charlesworth. *Mysteries and Revelations: Apocalyptic Studies since the Uppsala Colloquium*. Sheffield: Sheffield Academic, 1991.

Collins, John J., and P. W. Flint, eds. *The Book of Daniel: Composition and Reception*. VTSup 83.1–2. Leiden: Brill, 2001.

Collins, John J., Gregory E. Sterling, and Ruth A. Clements, eds. *Sapiential Perspectives: Wisdom Literature in Light of the Dead Sea Scrolls*. STDJ 51. Leiden: Brill, 2004.

Cope, O. L. "Matthew XXV:31–46; 'The Sheep and the Goats' Reinterpreted." *NovT* 11 (1969): 32–44.

———. "'To the Close of the Age': The Role of Apocalyptic Thought in the Gospel of Matthew." Pages 113–24 in *Apocalyptic and the New Testa-

ment: Essays in Honour of J. Louis Martyn. Edited by J. Marcus and M. L. Soards. Sheffield: Sheffield University Press, 1989.

Cortés-Fuentes, David. "The Least of These My Brothers: Matthew 25:31–46." *Apuntes* 23 (2003): 100–109.

Court, J. M. "Right and Left: The Implications for Matthew 25:31–46." *NTS* 31 (1985): 223–33.

Cranz, F. Edward. "Quintilian as Ancient Thinker." *Rhetorica: A Journal of the History of Rhetoric* 13 (1995): 219–30.

Crenshaw, James L., and Samuel Sandmel. *The Divine Helmsman: Studies on God's Control of Human Events, Presented to Lou H. Silberman.* New York: Ktav, 1980.

Cross, Frank Moore, Werner E. LeMarke, and Patrick D. Miller, eds. *Magnalia Dei: The Mighty Acts of God; Essays on the Bible and Archaeology in Memory of G. Ernest Wright.* Garden City, NY: Doubleday, 1976.

Dalman, Gustaf. *The Words of Jesus.* Translated by D. M. Kay. Edinburgh: T&T Clark, 1902.

Dancygier, Barbara, and Eve Sweetser. *Figurative Language.* Cambridge Textbooks in Linguistics. Cambridge: Cambridge University Press, 2014.

Davies, Phillip R. *On the Origins of Judaism.* Bible World. Oakville, CT: Equinox, 2008.

Davies, W. D., and Dale C. Allison. *The Gospel according to Saint Matthew 1–7.* ICC. New York: T&T Clark, 2004.

———. *The Gospel according to Saint Matthew 8–18.* ICC. New York: T&T Clark, 2004.

———. *The Gospel according to Saint Matthew 19–28.* ICC. New York: T&T Clark, 2004.

Dentan, Robert C., ed. *The Idea of History in the Ancient Near East.* AOS 38. New Haven: Yale University Press, 1955.

Derrida, Jaques. *Margins of Philosophy.* Translated by Alan Bass. Chicago: University of Chicago Press, 1982.

deSilva, David A. "Rhetorical Criticism." *OEBI* 2:273–83.

Deutsch, Celia M. *Lady Wisdom, Jesus, and the Sages: Metaphor and Social Context in Matthew's Gospel.* Valley Forge, PA: Trinity Press International, 1996.

DeVries, Simon J. *Time and History in the Old Testament: Yesterday, Today and Tomorrow.* Grand Rapids: Eerdmans, 1975.

Dibley, Amy Genevive. "Abraham's Uncircumcised Children: The Enochic Precedent for Paul's Paradoxical Claim in Galatians 3:29." PhD diss.,

288 Apocalyptic Sheep and Goats in Matthew and 1 Enoch

Graduate Theological Union and University of California at Berkeley, 2013.

Dillman, August. *Das Buch Henoch übersetzt und erklärt.* Leipzig: Vogel, 1853.

Dimant, Devorah. "Jerusalem and the Temple in the Animal Apocalypse (1 Enoch 85–90) in Light of Qumran Sectarian Thought" [Hebrew]. *Shenaton* 5–6 (1981–1982): 177–93.

Dobschütz, Ernst von. "Matthew as Rabbi and Catechist." Pages 19–29 in *The Interpretation of Matthew.* Edited by Graham Stanton. Philadelphia: Fortress, 1983.

Dodd, C. H. *The Parables of the Kingdom.* London: Collins & Sons, 1978.

Donahue, John R. "The 'Parable' of the Sheep and the Goats: A Challenge to Christian Ethics." *TS* 47 (1986): 3–31.

Down, M. "Exegetical Note on Matthew 25:31–46: The Parable of the Sheep and the Goats." *ExpTim* 123 (2012): 587–89.

Dumery, Henry. *Phenomenology and Religion: Structures of the Christian Institution.* Berkeley: University of California Press, 1958.

Dunn, James D. G. "The Significance of Matthew's Eschatology for Biblical Theology." Pages 151–62 in *Society of Biblical Literature 1996 Seminar Papers.* SBLSP 35. Atlanta: Scholars Press, 1996.

Eco, Umberto. "Metaphor, Dictionary, and Encyclopedia." *New Literary History* 15 (1984): 255–71.

Eco, Umberto, Ursula Niklas, and Francis Edeline. "Metaphor." Pages 534–49 in *Encyclopedic Dictionary of Semiotics.* Edited by T. A. Sebeok. 2nd ed. Berlin: de Gruyter, 1994.

Emberling, Geoff. "Ethnicity in Complex Societies: Archaeological Perspectives." *Journal of Archaeological Research* 5 (1997): 295–344.

Erickson, Keith V. *Aristotle: The Classical Heritage of Rhetoric.* Methuchen, NJ: Scarecrow, 1974.

Eriksson, Anders. "Enthymemes in Pauline Argumentation: Reading between the Lines in 1 Corinthians." Pages 243–59 in *Rhetorical Argumentation in Biblical Texts.* Edited by Anders Eriksson, Thomas H. Olbricht, and Walter Übelacker. Harrisburg, PA: Trinity Press International, 2002.

Eriksson, Anders, Thomas H. Olbricht, and Walter Übelacker, eds. *Rhetorical Argumentation in Biblical Texts.* Harrisburg, PA: Trinity Press International, 2002.

Evans, Craig A. "Targumizing Tendencies in Matthean Redaction." Pages 93–116 in *When Judaism and Christianity Began: Essays in Memory of*

Anthony J. Saldarini. Vol. 1. Edited by Alan J. Avery-Peck, Daniel Harrington, and Jacob Neusner. JSJSup 85. Leiden: Brill, 2004.

Evans, Craig A., and James A. Sanders, eds. *Paul and the Scriptures of Israel.* Sheffield: JSOT Press, 1993.

Evans, Craig A., and H. Daniel Zacharias, eds. *Exegetical Studies.* Vol. 2 of *Early Christian Literature and Intertextuality.* New York: T&T Clark, 2009.

Evans, Craig A., and H. Daniel Zacharias, eds. *The Synoptic Gospels.* Vol. 1 of *'What Does the Scripture Say?' Studies in the Function of Scripture in Early Judaism and Christianity.* New York: T&T Clark, 2012.

Evans-Pritchard, E. *The Nuer.* Oxford: Clarendon, 1940.

Fauconnier, Gilles. *Mental Spaces.* Cambridge: Cambridge University Press, 1994.

Fauconnier, Gilles, and Mark Turner. *The Way We Think: Conceptual Blending and the Mind's Hidden Complexities.* New York: Basic Books, 2002.

Fillmore, Charles J. "Frame Semantics." Pages 111–37 in *Linguistics in the Morning Calm.* Edited by the Linguistic Society of Korea. Seoul: Hanshin, 1982.

———. "Frames and the Semantics of Understanding." *Quaderni di Semantica* 6 (1985): 222–53.

Flannery, Frances. "Dreams and Visions in Early Jewish and Early Christian Apocalypses and Apocalypticism." Pages 104–22 in *The Oxford Handbook of Apocalyptic Literature.* Edited by John J. Collins. Oxford: Oxford University Press, 2014.

Flesher, Leann S. "Rapid Change of Mood: Oracles of Salvation, Certainty of a Hearing, or Rhetorical Play." Pages 33–45 in *My Words Are Lovely: Studies in the Rhetoric of the Psalms.* Edited by Robert L. Foster and David M. Howard. New York: T&T Clark, 2008.

Fornberg, Tord, and David Hellholm, eds. *Texts and Contexts: Biblical Texts in Their Textual and Situational Contexts.* Oslo: Scandinavian University Press, 1995.

Fortenbaugh, William W. "Cicero as a Reporter of Aristotelian and Theophrastean Rhetorical Doctrine." *Journal of the History of Rhetorics* 23 (2005): 37–64.

Fortenbaugh, William W., and David C. Mirhady. *Peripatetic Rhetoric after Aristotle.* Vol. 6. Rutgers University Studies in Classical Humanities. New Brunswick: Transaction, 1994.

Foster, Robert L., and David M. Howard. *My Words Are Lovely: Studies in the Rhetoric of the Psalms*. New York: T&T Clark, 2008.

France, R. T. *The Gospel of Matthew*. NICNT. Grand Rapids: Eerdmans, 2007.

Fridrichsen, Anton, ed. *The Root of the Vine: Essays in Biblical Theology*. New York: Philosophical, 1953.

Gage, John T. "An Adequate Epistemology for Composition: Classical and Modern Perspectives." Pages 152–69 in *Essays on Classical Rhetoric and Modern Discourse*. Edited by Robert J. Connors, Lisa S. Ede, and Andrea A. Lunsford. Carbondale: Southern Illinois University Press, 1984.

Garver, Eugene. *Aristotle's Rhetoric: An Art of Character*. Chicago: University of Chicago Press, 1994.

Gell, A. *The Anthropology of Time: Cultural Constructions of Temporal Maps and Images*. Oxford: Berg, 1992.

Goering, Greg Schmidt. "Divine Sovereignty and the Election of Israel." Pages 144–69 in *The Call of Abraham: Essays on the Election of Israel in Honor of Jon D. Levenson*. Edited by Gary A. Anderson and Joel S. Kaminsky. Notre Dame: University of Notre Dame Press, 2013.

———. *Wisdom's Root Revealed: Ben Sira and the Election of Israel*. JSJSup 139. Leiden: Brill, 2009.

Goldstein, Jonathan A. *1 Maccabees: A New Translation*. AB 41. Garden City, NY: Doubleday, 1976.

Gonzalez, Francisco J. "Plato's Dialectic of Forms." Pages 31–83 in *Plato's Forms: Varieties of Interpretation*. Edited by William Welton. Lanham, MD: Lexington Books, 2003.

Goulder, Michael D. *Midrash and Lection in Matthew*. Eugene, OR: Wipf & Stock, 2004.

Grabbe, Lester L. *An Introduction to Second Temple Judaism: History and Religion of the Jews in the Time of Nehemiah, the Maccabees, Hillel and Jesus*. New York: T&T Clark, 2010.

Grabbe, Lester L., and Robert D. Haak, eds. *Knowing the End from the Beginning: The Prophetic, the Apocalyptic and Their Relationships*. New York: T&T Clark, 2003.

Gray, Sherman W. *The Least of My Brothers: Matthew 25:31–46; A History of Interpretation*. SBLDS 114. Atlanta: Scholars Press, 1989.

Green, Joel B. *Hearing the New Testament: Strategies for Interpretation*. Grand Rapids: Eerdmans, 1995.

Bibliography 291

Grimaldi, William M. "The Aristotelian Topics." Pages 176–93 in *Aristotle: The Classical Heritage of Rhetoric*. Edited by Keith V. Erickson. Methuchen, NJ: Scarecrow, 1974.

Grindheim, Sigurd. "Ignorance Is Bliss: Attitudinal Aspects of the Judgment according to Works in Matthew 25:31–46." *NovT* 50 (2008): 313–31.

Gruenwald, Ithamar. *Apocalyptic and Merkavah Mysticism*. Leiden: Brill, 1980.

———. *From Apocalypticism to Gnosticism: Studies in Apocalypticism, Merkavah Mysticism and Gnosticism*. New York: Lang, 1988.

Gundry, R. *Matthew: A Commentary on His Literary and Theological Art*. Grand Rapids: Eerdmans, 1982.

Gurtner, Daniel. "Interpreting Apocalyptic Symbolism in the Gospel of Matthew." *BBR* 22 (2012): 525–46.

Gurtner, Daniel M., and John Nolland, eds. *Built upon the Rock: Studies in the Gospel of Matthew*. Grand Rapids: Eerdmans, 2008.

Guthrie, W. K. C. *The Later Plato and the Academy*. Vol. 5 of *A History of Greek Philosophy*. Cambridge: Cambridge University Press, 1996.

Habel, Norman C., and Peter Trudinger. *Exploring Ecological Hermeneutics*. SBLSymS 46. Atlanta: Society of Biblical Literature, 2008.

Hadfield, P. "Matthew the Apocalyptic Editor." *London Quarterly & Holborn Review* 184 (1959): 128–32.

Hagner, Donald A. "Apocalyptic Motifs in the Gospel of Matthew: Continuity and Discontinuity." *HBT* 7 (1985): 53–82.

———. "Imminence and Parousia in the Gospel of Matthew." Pages 77–92 in *Texts and Contexts: Biblical Texts in Their Textual and Situational Contexts*. Edited by Tord Fornberg and David Hellholm. Oslo: Scandinavian University Press, 1995.

———. *Matthew 14–28*. WBC 33B. Nashville: Nelson, 1995.

———. "Realized Eschatology in the Gospel of Matthew." Pages 163–80 in *Society of Biblical Literature 1996 Seminar Papers*. SBLSP 35. Atlanta: Scholars Press, 1996.

Halbertal, Moshe. *People of the Book: Canon, Meaning, and Authority*. Cambridge: Harvard University Press, 1997.

Hallo, William W., ed. *Canonical Compositions from the Biblical World*. Vol. 1 of *The Context of Scriptures*. Leiden: Brill, 2003.

Hamilton, Catherine Sider. "Blood and Secrets: The Re-telling of Genesis 1–6 in 1 Enoch 6–11 and Its Echoes in Susanna and the Gospel of Matthew." Pages 90–141 in *The Synoptic Gospels*. Vol. 1 of 'What Does the

Scripture Say?' Studies in the Function of Scripture in Early Judaism and Christianity. Edited by Craig A. Evans and H. Daniel Zacharias. New York: T&T Clark, 2012.

Hanson, Paul D. "Apocalypses and Apocalypticism." *ABD* 1:279–82.

———. "Apocalypticism," *IDBSup.*

———. *The Dawn of the Apocalyptic: The Historical and Sociological Roots of Early Jewish Apocalyptic Eschatology.* Philadelphia: Fortress, 1979.

———. *Old Testament Apocalyptic.* IBT. Nashville: Abingdon, 1987.

———. *Visionaries and Their Apocalypses.* Philadelphia: Fortress, 1983.

Hanson, R. P. C. *Allegory and Event.* Richmond: John Knox, 1959.

Hartman, Lars. *Asking for a Meaning: A Study of 1 Enoch 1–5.* ConBNT 12. Lund: Gleerup, 1979.

———. "Survey of the Problem of Apocalyptic Genre." Pages 329–44 in *Apocalypticism in the Mediterranean World and the Near East: Proceedings of the International Colloquium on Apocalypticism Uppsala, August 12–17, 1979.* Edited by David Hellholm. 2nd ed. Tübingen: Mohr Siebeck, 1989.

Hays, Richard B. *Echoes of Scripture in the Letters of Paul.* New Haven: Yale University Press, 1989.

Heath, Malcolm. "Cognition in Aristotle's Poetics." *Mnemosyne* 62 (2009): 51–75.

Heil, John Paul. "The Double Meaning of the Narrative of Universal Judgment in Matthew 25:31–46." *JSNT* 69 (1998): 3–14.

———. "Ezekiel 34 and the Narrative Strategy of the Shepherd and Sheep Metaphor in Matthew." *CBQ* 55 (1993): 698–708.

Hellholm, David. "Apocalypse: Form and Genre." *RPP* 1:297–98.

———, ed. *Apocalypticism in the Mediterranean World and the Near East: Proceedings of the International Colloquium on Apocalypticism Uppsala, August 12–17, 1979.* 2nd ed. Tübingen: Mohr Siebeck, 1989.

———. "Methodological Reflections on the Problem of Definition of Generic Texts." Pages 135–63 in *Mysteries and Revelations: Apocalyptic Studies since the Uppsala Colloquium.* Edited by John J. Collins and James H. Charlesworth. Sheffield: Sheffield Academic, 1991.

Helmut, Koester. *Ancient Christian Gospels: Their History and Development.* Philadelphia: Trinity Press International, 1990.

Hengel, Martin. *Judaism and Hellenism: Studies in Their Encounter in Palestine during the Early Hellenistic Period.* Translated by John Bowden. 2 vols. Minneapolis: Fortress, 1991.

Bibliography 293

Hennecke, E., and W. Schneemelcher, eds. *New Testament Apocrypha.* Vol. 2. Philadelphia: Lutterworth, 1965.

Henze, Matthias. "Enoch's Dream Visions and the Visions of Daniel Reexamined." Pages 17–22 in *Enoch and Qumran Origins: New Light on a Forgotten Connection.* Edited by Gabriele Boccaccini. Grand Rapids: Eerdmans, 2005.

Hermann, V. "Anmerkungen zum Verständnis einiger Paralleltexte zu Matt 25:31ff. aus der altägyptischen Religion." *BibNot* 59 (1991): 17–22.

Heschel, Abraham J. *God in Search of Man: A Philosophy of Judaism.* Philadelphia: Jewish Publication Society, 1955.

Himmelfarb, Martha. *Between Temple and Torah.* Tübingen: Mohr Siebeck, 2013.

Holist, Michael. *The Dialogic Imagination: Four Essays.* Translated by Caryl Emerson and Michael Holist. Austin: University of Texas Press, 1981.

Horner, Winifred. *The Present State of Scholarship in Historical and Contemporary Rhetoric.* Columbia: University of Missouri Press, 1990.

Horsley, Richard A. *Revolt of the Scribes: Resistance and Apocalyptic Origins.* Minneapolis: Fortress, 2010.

House, P. *Beyond Form Criticism: Essays in Old Testament Literary Criticism.* SBTS. Winona Lake, IN: Eisenbrauns, 1992.

Hultgard, Anders. "Persian Apocalypticism." Pages 30–63 in *The Continuum History of Apocalypticism.* Edited by Bernard McGinn, John J. Collins, and Stephen J. Stein. New York: Continuum, 2003.

Humphries-Brooks, Stephenson. "Apocalyptic *Paraenesis* in Matthew 6:19–34." Pages 95–112 in *Apocalyptic and the New Testament: Essays in Honor of J. Louis Martyn.* Edited by Joel Marcus and Marion L. Soards. New York: Bloomsbury, 1989.

Hutter, M. "Matt 25:31–46 in der Deutung Manis." *NovT* 33 (1991): 276–82.

Innes, Doreen. "Cicero on Tropes." *Rhetorica: A Journal of the History of Rhetoric* 6 (1988): 307–25.

———. "Metaphor, Simile, and Allegory." Pages 7–27 in *Metaphor, Allegory and the Classical Tradition.* Edited by G. R. Boys-Stones. Oxford: Oxford University Press, 2003.

Jeremias, Joachim. *The Parables of Jesus.* London: SCM, 1963.

———. *Rediscovering the Parables.* New York: Charles Scribner's Sons, 1966.

Jones, Barrington. "Individuals in Aristotle's Categories." *Phronesis* 17 (1972): 107–23.

Joüon, Paul, and Takamitsu Muraoka. *A Grammar of Biblical Hebrew.* 2nd ed. Rome: Gregorian and Biblical Press, 2011.

Kaminsky, Joel. "Did Election Imply the Mistreatment of Non-Israelite?" *HTR* 96 (2003): 398.

———. *Yet I Loved Jacob: Reclaiming the Biblical Concept of Election.* Nashville: Abingdon, 2007.

Käsemann, Ernst. "The Beginnings of Christian Theology." *JTC* 6 (1969): 17–46.

———. "Die Anfänge christlicher Theologie." *ZTK* 57 (1960): 162–85.

Keller, Andrew, and Stephanie Russell. *Learn to Read Latin.* New Haven: Yale University Press, 2004.

Kennedy, George. *The Art of Persuasion in Greece.* Princeton: Princeton University Press, 1963.

———. *Classical Rhetoric and Its Christian and Secular Tradition from Ancient to Modern Times.* Chapel Hill: University of North Carolina Press, 1980.

———. *Comparative Rhetoric: An Historical and Cross-Cultural Introduction.* Oxford: Oxford University Press, 1998.

———. "Historical Survey of Rhetoric." Pages 3–42 in *Handbook of Classical Rhetoric in the Hellenistic Period 330 B.C.–A.D. 400.* Edited by Stanley Porter. Leiden: Brill, 1997.

———. *New Testament Interpretation through Rhetorical Criticism.* Chapel Hill: University of North Carolina Press, 1984.

Kingsbury, J. D. *The Parables of Jesus in Matthew 13: A Study in Redaction-Criticism.* London: SPCK, 1969.

Kirby, John T. "Aristotle on Metaphor." *American Journal of Philology* 118 (1997): 528–30.

Kister, Menahem. "Wisdom Literature and Its Relation to Other Genres: From Ben Sira to Mysteries." Pages 13–47 in *Sapiential Perspectives: Wisdom Literature in Light of the Dead Sea Scrolls.* Edited by John J. Collins, Gregory E. Sterling, and Ruth A. Clements. STDJ 51. Leiden: Brill, 2004.

Klein, Ralf. "Wer sind die 'geringsten Geschwister' in Matt 25?" *StZ* 237 (2019): 103–5.

Knibb, Michael A. "The Book of Enoch or Books of Enoch? The Textual Evidence for 1 Enoch." Pages 21–40 in *The Early Enoch Literature.* Edited by Gabriele Boccaccini and John J. Collins. Leiden: Brill, 2007.

———. *The Ethiopic Book of Enoch: A New Edition in the Light of the Aramaic Dead Sea Fragments.* 2 vols. Oxford: Clarendon, 1978.

Bibliography

Koch, Klaus. "The Astral Laws as the Basis of Time, Universal History, and the Eschatological Turn in the Astronomical Book and the Animal Apocalypse in 1 Enoch." Pages 119–37 in *The Early Enoch Literature*. Edited by Gabriele Boccaccini and John J. Collins. Leiden: Brill, 2007.

———. *The Rediscovery of Apocalyptic*. SBT 2/22. Naperville, IL: Allenson, 1972.

Konradt, Matthias. *Israel, Church, and the Gentiles in the Gospel of Matthew*. Translated by Kathleen Ess. Waco, TX: Baylor University Press, 2014.

Kosman, Aryeh. *The Activity of Being: An Essay on Aristotle's Ontology*. Cambridge: Harvard University Press, 2013.

Kovecses, Zoltan. *Language, Mind, and Culture: A Practical Introduction*. Oxford: Oxford University, 2006.

———. *Where Metaphors Come From: Reconsidering Context in Metaphor*. Oxford: Oxford University Press, 2015.

Kristeva, Julia. *Desire in Language: A Semiotic Approach to Language and Art*. Translated by Thomas Gora, Alice Jardine, and Leon S. Roudiez. Edited by Leon S. Roudiez. New York: Columbia University Press, 1980.

———. *The Kristeva Reader*. Edited by T. Moi. Oxford: Blackwell, 1986.

———. *The Portable Kristeva*. Edited by Kelly Oliver. 2nd ed. New York: Columbia University Press, 2002.

Kugel, James L. "Wisdom and the Anthological Temper." *Proof* 17 (1997): 9–32.

Kvanvig, Helge S. *Roots of Apocalyptic: The Mesopotamian Background of the Enoch Figure and of the Son of Man*. Neukirchen-Vluyn: Neukirchener Verlag, 1988.

LaCocque, André. "Allusions to Creation in Daniel 7." Pages 114–31 in vol. 1 of *The Book of Daniel: Composition and Reception*. Edited by J. J. Collins and P. W. Flint. VTSup 83. Leiden: Brill, 2001.

———. *The Book of Daniel*. Atlanta: John Knox, 1979.

Lakoff, George. *Women, Fire, and Dangerous Things: What Categories Reveal about the Mind*. Chicago: University of Chicago Press, 1987.

Lakoff, George, and Mark Johnson. *Metaphors We Live By*. Chicago: University of Chicago Press, 2003.

———. *More Than Cool Reason: Field Guide to Poetic Metaphor*. Chicago: University of Chicago Press, 1989.

———. *Philosophy in the Flesh: The Embodied Mind and Its Challenge to Western Thought*. New York: Basic Books, 1999.

Lambdin, Thomas O. *Introduction to Classical Ethiopic.* HSS 24. Missoula, MT: Scholars Press, 1978.

Lane, Nathan. "An Echo of Mercy: A Rereading of the Parable of the Good Samaritan." Pages 74–84 in *Exegetical* Studies. Vol. 2 of *Early Christian Literature and Intertextuality.* Edited by Craig A. Evans and H. Daniel Zacharias. New York: T&T Clark, 2009.

The Linguistic Society of Korea, ed. *Linguistics in the Morning Calm.* Seoul: Hanshin, 1982.

Lipschits, Oded, Gary N. Knoppers, and Manfred Oeming, eds. *Judah and the Judeans in the Achaemenid Period: Negotiating Identity in an International Context.* Winona Lake, IN: Eisenbrauns, 2011.

Lloyd, Geoffrey E. R. "Demonstration and the Idea of Science." Pages 243–68 in *Greek Thought: A Guide to Classical Knowledge.* Edited by Jacques Brunschwig and Geoffrey E. R. Lloyd. Cambridge: Belknap, 2000.

———. *The Revolutions of Wisdom: Studies in the Claims and Practice of Ancient Greek Science.* Berkeley: University of California Press, 1989.

Longenecker, Richard N., ed. *The Challenge of Jesus' Parables.* Grand Rapids: Eerdmans, 2000.

Luecke, Friedrich. *Versuch einer vollstaendigen Einleitung in die Offenbarung Johannis und in die gesammte apokalyptishe Literatur.* Bonn: Eduard Weber, 1832.

Luomanen, Petri, Ilkka Pyysiainen, and Risto Uro, eds. *Explaining Christian Origins and Early Judaism: Contributions from Cognitive and Social Science.* BibInt 89. Leiden: Brill, 2007.

Luz, Ulrich. "The Final Judgment (Matt 25:31–46): An Exercise in 'History of Influence' Exegesis." Pages 271–310 in *Treasures New and Old: Contributions to Matthean Studies.* Edited by David R. Bauer and Mark A. Powell. SBLSymS 1. Atlanta: Scholars Press, 1996.

———. *Matthew 1–7.* Hermeneia. Minneapolis: Fortress, 2007.

———. *Matthew 8–20.* Hermeneia. Minneapolis: Fortress, 2001.

———. *Matthew 21–28.* Hermeneia. Minneapolis: Fortress, 2005.

Mack, Burton L. *Rhetoric and the New Testament.* Minneapolis: Fortress, 1990.

Marcus, J., and M. L. Soards, eds. *Apocalyptic and the New Testament: Essays in Honour of J. Louis Martyn.* Sheffield: Sheffield University Press, 1989.

Marguerat, Daniel. *Le jugemant dans l'evangile de Matthieu.* Le Monde de la Bible. Geneva: Labor et Fides, 1981.

Bibliography

Martinez, Florentino G. "Qumran and Apocalyptic: Studies on the Aramaic Texts from Qumran." STDJ 9. Leiden: Brill, 1992.

———. *Wisdom and Apocalypticism in the Dead Sea Scrolls and in the Biblical Tradition*. Leuven: Leuven University Press, 2003.

Martinez, Florentino G., and Eibert J. C. Tigchelaar. *The Dead Sea Scrolls: Study Edition*. Vol. 1 (1Q1–4Q273). Grand Rapids: Eerdmans, 1997.

May, James M. "Ciceronian Oratory in Context." Pages 49–70 in *Brill's Companion to Cicero: Oratory and Rhetoric*. Edited by James M. May. Leiden: Brill, 2002.

May, James M., and Jakob Wisse. *Cicero: On the Ideal Orator*. Oxford: Oxford University Press, 2001.

Mayordomo, Moises. "Matthew 1–2 and the Problem of Intertextuality." Pages 257–79 in *Infancy Gospels: Stories and Identities*. Edited by C. Clivaz, A. Dettwiler, L. Devillers and E. Norelli. Tübingen: Mohr Siebeck, 2011.

McCall, Marsh H., Jr. *Ancient Rhetorical Theories of Simile and Comparison*. Cambridge: Harvard University Press, 1969.

McGinn, Bernard, John J. Collins, and Stephen J. Stein, eds. *The Continuum History of Apocalypticism*. New York: Continuum, 2003.

McKenzie, Steven, ed. *The Oxford Encyclopedia of Biblical Interpretation*. 2 vols. Oxford: Oxford University Press, 2013.

McKeon, Richard. "Creativity and the Commonplace." Pages 25–36 in *Rhetoric: Essays in Invention and Discovery*. Edited by Mark Backman. Woodbridge: Ox Bow, 1987.

Meier, John P. *Law and History in Matthew's Gospel*. AnBib 71. Rome: Biblical Institute Press, 1976.

———. *The Vision of Matthew: Christ, Church and Morality in the First Gospel*. New York: Paulist, 1979.

Meyer, Paul W. "Context as a Bearer of Meaning in Matthew." *USQR* 42 (1988): 69–72.

Milik, Jozef T. *The Books of Enoch: Aramaic Fragments of Qumran Cave 4*. Oxford: Clarendon, 1976.

Miller, Carolyn R. "The Aristotelian Topos: Hunting for Novelty." Pages 130–46 in *Rereading Aristotle's Rhetoric*. Edited by Alan G. Gross and Arthur E. Walzer. Carbondale: Southern Illinois University Press, 2000.

Miller, Patrick A., Paul D. Hanson, and S. Dean McBride, eds. *Ancient Israelite Wisdom: Essays in Honour of Frank Moore Cross*. Philadelphia: Fortress, 1987.

Mitch, Curtis, and Edward Sri. *The Gospel of Mathew*. Catholic Commentary on Sacred Scripture. Grand Rapids: Baker Academic, 2010.

Mitchell, Margaret. *Paul and the Rhetoric of Reconciliation: An Exegetical Investigation of the Language and Composition of 1 Corinthians*. Louisville: Westminster John Knox, 1993.

Möller, Karl. *A Prophet in Debate: The Rhetoric of Persuasion in the Book of Amos*. JSOTSup 372. Sheffield: Sheffield Academic, 2003.

Momigliano, A. *Essays in Ancient and Modern Historiography*. Oxford: Blackwell, 1977.

Moran, Richard. "Artifice and Persuasion: The Work of Metaphor in the Rhetoric." Pages 385–98 in *Essays on Aristotle's Rhetoric*. Edited by Amélie Oksenberg Rorty. Berkeley: University of California Press, 1996.

Muilenburg, James. "Form Criticism and Beyond." Pages 49–69 in *Beyond Form Criticism: Essays in Old Testament Literary Criticism*. Edited by P. House. SBTS. Winona Lake, IN: Eisenbrauns, 1992.

Müller, Reinhard. "The Blinded Eyes of the Wise: Sapiential Tradition and Mosaic Commandment in Deut 16:19–20." Pages 9–34 in *Wisdom and Torah: The Reception of 'Torah' in the Wisdom Literature of the Second Temple Period*. Edited by Bernd U. Schipper and D. Andrew Teeter. Leiden: Brill, 2013.

Murphy, Roland E. "Religious Dimensions of Israelite Wisdom." Pages 452–53 in *Ancient Israelite Wisdom: Essays in Honour of Frank Moore Cross*. Edited by Patrick Miller, Paul D. Hanson, and S. Dean McBride. Philadelphia: Fortress, 1987.

Najman, Hindy. Review of *Beyond the Essene Hypothesis*, by G. Boccaccini. *AJSR* 26 (2002): 352–54.

Najman, Hindy, and Judith H. Newman, eds. *The Idea of Biblical Interpretation: Essays in Honor of James L. Kugel*. Leiden: Brill, 2004.

Natorp, Paul. *Plato's Theory of Ideas: An Introduction to Idealism*. Sankt Augustin: Academia, 2004.

Neirynck, Frans, ed. *The Minor Agreements of Matthew and Luke against Mark with a Cumulative List*. BETL 37. Leuven: Leuven University Press, 1974.

Nestle-Aland, ed. *Novum Testamentum Graece*. 28th rev. ed. Stuttgart: Deutsche Bibelgesellschaft, 2012.

Neusner, Jacob. *Between Time and Eternity: The Essentials of Judaism*. Encino, CA: Dickenson, 1975.

———. *The Idea of Purity in Ancient Judaism: With a Critique and a Commentary by Mary Douglas*. Leiden: Brill, 1973.

Newsom, Carol A. "Enoch 83–90: The Historical Resume as Biblical Exegesis." Unpublished seminar paper. Harvard University, 1975.

Nickelsburg, George W. E. *1 Enoch 1*. Hermeneia. Minneapolis: Fortress, 2001.

———. "Enochic Wisdom and Its Relationship to the Mosaic Torah." Pages 81–94 in *The Early Enoch Literature*. Edited by Gabriele Boccaccini and John J. Collins. Leiden: Brill, 2007.

———. "Social Aspects of Palestinian Jewish Apocalypticism." Pages 641–54 in *Apocalypticism in the Mediterranean World and the Near East: Proceedings of the International Colloquium on Apocalypticism Uppsala, August 12–17, 1979*. Edited by David Hellholm. 2nd ed. Tübingen: Mohr Siebeck, 1983.

Nickelsburg, George W. E., and James C. VanderKam. *1 Enoch 2: A Commentary on the Book of 1 Enoch 37–82*. Minneapolis: Fortress, 2012.

———. *1 Enoch: The Hermeneia Translation*. Minneapolis: Fortress, 2012.

Nilsen, Tina D., and Anna Rebecca Solevag. "Expanding Ecological Hermeneutics: The Case for Ecolonialism." *JBL* 135 (2016): 665–83.

Nolland, John. *The Gospel of Matthew*. NIGTC. Grand Rapids: Eerdmans, 2005.

Nussbaum, Martha C., and Amélie Oksenberg Rorty, eds. *Essays on Aristotle's De Anima*. Oxford: Oxford University Press, 1992.

O'Leary, Stephen. *Arguing the Apocalypse: A Theory of Millennial Rhetoric*. New York: Oxford University Press, 1994.

———. "A Dramatistic Theory of Apocalyptic Rhetoric." *QJS* 79 (1993): 385–426.

Olson, Daniel C. *A New Reading of the Animal Apocalypse of 1 Enoch: All Nations Shall Be Blessed*. SVTP 24. Leiden: Brill, 2013.

Oppenheim, A. L. *The Interpretation of Dreams in the Ancient Near East, with a Translation of an Assyrian Dream-Book*. Philadelphia: American Philosophical Society, 1956.

Orlov, Andrei. *The Enoch-Metatron Tradition*. TSAJ. Tübingen: Mohr Siebeck, 2005.

———. *The Glory of the Invisible God: Two Powers in Heaven Traditions and Early Christology*. JCTCRS. New York: T&T Clark, 2019.

Orton, David E. *The Understanding Scribe: Matthew and the Apocalyptic Ideal*. JSNTSup 25. Sheffield: Sheffield Academic, 1989.

Overman, J. Andrew. *Matthew's Gospel and Formative Judaism: The Social World of the Matthean Community.* Minneapolis: Fortress, 1990.

Owen, G. E. L. "Inherence." *Phronesis* 10 (1965): 97–105.

Pamment, Margaret. "The Kingdom of Heaven according to the First Gospel." *NTS* 27 (1981): 211–32.

———. "Singleness and Matthew's Attitude to the Torah." *JSNT* 17 (1983): 73–86.

Park, Eugene E. C. *The Mission Discourse in Matthew's Interpretation.* Tübingen: Mohr Siebeck, 1995.

———. "A Soteriological Reading of the Great Commandment in Matthew 22:34–40." *BR* 54 (2009): 61–78.

Patrides, C. A. *The Grand Design of God: The Literary Form of the Christian View of History.* London: Routledge, 1972.

Patte, Daniel. *The Gospel according to Matthew: A Structural Commentary on Matthew's Faith.* Philadelphia: Fortress, 1987.

Pearson, Birger A., ed. *Religious Syncretism in Antiquity: Essays in Conversation with Geo Widengren.* Missoula, MT: Scholars Press, 1975.

Pennington, Jonathan T. *Heaven and Earth in the Gospel of Matthew.* Grand Rapids: Baker Academic, 2009.

Perrin, Norman. "Eschatology and Hermeneutics: Reflections on Method in the Interpretation of the New Testament." *JBL* 93 (1974): 3–14.

Petofi, Janos S. *Research in Text Theory (Untersuchungen zur Texttheorie).* New York: de Gruyter, 1991.

Plett, Heinrich F. "Intertextualities." Pages 3–29 in *Research in Text Theory (Untersuchungen zur Texttheorie).* Edited by Janos S. Petofi. New York: de Gruyter, 1991.

Popkes, Wiard. "Paraenesis in the New Testament: An Exercise in Conceptuality." Pages 13–46 in *Early Christian Paraenesis in Context.* Edited by James Starr and Troels Engberg-Pedersen. New York: de Gruyter, 2005.

Porter, Paul A. *Metaphors and Monsters: A Literary-Critical Study of Daniel 7 and 8.* ConBOT 20. Lund: CWK Gleerup, 1983.

Porter, Stanley, ed. *Handbook of Classical Rhetoric in the Hellenistic Period 330 B.C.–A.D. 400.* Leiden: Brill, 1997.

Porter-Young, Anathea E. *Apocalypse against Empire: Theologies of Resistance in Early Judaism.* Grand Rapids: Eerdmans, 2011.

Przybylski, Benno. *Righteousness in Matthew and His World of Thought.* SNTSMS 41. Cambridge: Cambridge University Press, 1980.

Bibliography

Putnam, Hillary. *Mind, Language, and Reality: Philosophical Papers*. Vol. 2. Cambridge: Cambridge University Press, 1975.

Rad, Gerhard von. *Old Testament Theology: The Theology of Israel's Prophetic Tradition*. Translated by D. Stalker. Vol. 2. New York: Harper & Row, 1965.

———. *Wisdom in Israel*. Translated by James D. Martin. London: SCM, 1972.

Reed, Annette Yoshiko. *Fallen Angels and the History of Judaism and Christianity: The Reception of Enochic Literature*. Cambridge: Cambridge University Press, 2005.

———. "'Revealed Literature' in the Second Century BCE: Jubilees, 1 Enoch, Qumran, and the Prehistory of the Biblical Canon." Pages 94–98 in *Enoch and Qumran Origins: New Light on a Forgotten Connection*. Edited by Gabriele Boccaccini. Grand Rapids: Eerdmans, 2005.

Reeves, John. "Sefer 'Uzza Wa-'Aza(z)el: Exploring Early Jewish Mythologies of Evil." https://tinyurl.com/SBL4827a.

Richter, Amy E. *Enoch and the Gospel of Matthew*. PTMS. Eugene, OR: Pickwick, 2012.

Ricoeur, Paul. Foreword to *The Book of Daniel*, by Andre Lacocque. Atlanta: John Knox, 1979.

———. *The Rule of Metaphor*. Toronto: University of Toronto Press, 1975.

Riniker, Christian. *Die Gerichtsverkündigung Jesus*. Bern: Lang, 1999.

Robbins, Vernon K. "Conceptual Blending and Early Christian Imagination." Pages 161–95 in *Explaining Christian Origins and Early Judaism: Contributions from Cognitive and Social Science*. Edited by Petri Luomanen, Ilkka Pyysiainen, and Risto Uro. BibInt 89. Leiden: Brill, 2007.

———. *Exploring the Texture of Texts: A Guide to Socio-Rhetorical Interpretation*. Valley Forge, PA: Trinity Press International, 1996.

———. "The Intertexture of Apocalyptic Discourse in the Gospel of Mark." Pages 11–44 in *The Intertexture of Apocalyptic Discourse in the New Testament*. Edited by Duane F. Watson. SBLSymS 14. Atlanta: Society of Biblical Literature, 2002.

———. *The Invention of Christian Discourse*. Vol. 1. Blandford Forum: Deo, 2009.

———. *The Tapestry of Early Christian Discourse: Rhetoric, Society and Ideology*. London: Routledge, 1996.

Robbins, Vernon K., Robert H. von Thaden Jr., and Bart B. Bruehler, eds. *Foundation for Sociorhetorical Exploration: A Rhetoric of Religious Antiquity Reader*. Atlanta: SBL Press, 2016.

Robinson, J. A. T. "The 'Parable' of the Sheep and the Goats." *NTS* 2 (1956): 225–37.

Rölver, Olaf. *Christliche Existenz zwischen den Gerichten Gottes*. Göttingen: V&R unipress, 2010.

Rorty, Amelie Oksenberg. *Essays on Aristotle's Rhetoric*. Berkeley: University of California Press, 1996.

Rosch, Eleanor. "Principles of Categorization." Pages 27–48 in *Cognition and Categorization*. Edited by Eleanor Rosch and B. B. Lloyd. Hillsdale, NJ: Lawrence Erlbaum, 1978.

Rosch, Eleanor, and B. B. Lloyd, eds. *Cognition and Categorization*. Hillsdale, NJ: Lawrence Erlbaum, 1978.

Rosch, Eleanor, and Carolyne Mervis. "Family Resemblances: Studies in the Internal Structure of Categories." *Cognitive Psychology* 7 (1975): 573–605.

Rowland, Christopher C. "Apocalyptic, the Poor, and the Gospel of Matthew." *JTS* 45 (1994): 504–18.

———. "The Eschatology of the New Testament Church." Pages 56–90 in *The Oxford Handbook of Eschatology*. Edited by Jerry L. Walls. Oxford: Oxford University Press, 2008.

———. *The Open Heaven: A Study of Apocalyptic in Judaism and Early Christianity*. New York: Crossroad, 1982.

Rowland, Christopher C., and John Barton, eds. *Apocalyptic in History and Tradition*. Sheffield: Sheffield Academic, 2002.

Rowley, H. H. *The Relevance of Apocalyptic: A Study of Jewish and Christian Apocalypses from Daniel to the Revelation*. London: Lutterworth, 1944.

Rubin, Nissan. *Time and Life Cycle in Talmud and Midrash: Socio-anthropological Perspectives*. Boston: Academic Studies, 2008.

Rubinelli, Sara. *Ars Topica: The Classical Technique of Constructing Arguments from Aristotle to Cicero*. Argumentation Library 15. Dordrecht: Springer, 2009.

Russell, D. S. *Apocalyptic: Ancient and Modern*. Philadelphia: Fortress, 1978.

Sabourin, Leopold. "Apocalyptic Traits in Matthew's Gospel." *Religious Studies Bulletin* 3 (1983): 19–36.

Sacchi, Paolo. *History of the Second Temple Period.* JSOTSup 285. Sheffield: Sheffield Academic, 2000.

———. *Jewish Apocalyptic and Its History.* Translation by William J. Short. Sheffield: Sheffield Academic, 1990.

Saldarini, Anthony J. *Matthew's Christian-Jewish Community.* Chicago: University of Chicago Press, 1994.

Sanders, E. P. "The Genre of Palestinian Jewish Apocalypses." Pages 447–460 in *Apocalypticism in the Mediterranean World and the Near East: Proceedings of the International Colloquium on Apocalypticism Uppsala, August 12–17, 1979.* Edited by David Hellholm. 2nd ed. Tübingen: Mohr Siebeck, 1989.

———. *Paul and Palestinian Judaism.* Philadelphia: Fortress, 1977.

Sanders, James A. *Torah and Canon.* Eugene, OR: Cascade, 2005.

Sauter, Gerhard. *Zukunft und Verheissung.* Zürich: Zwingli-Verlag, 1965.

Schaper, Joachim. "Torah and Identity in the Persian Period." Pages 27–38 in *Judah and the Judeans in the Achaemenid Period: Negotiating Identity in an International Context.* Edited by Oded Lipschits, Gary N. Knoppers, and Manfred Oeming. Winona Lake, IN: Eisenbrauns, 2011.

Schenkeveld, Dirk M. "Ta Asteia in Aristotle's Rhetoric." Pages 1–14 in *Peripatetic Rhetoric after Aristotle.* Edited by William W. Fortenbaugh and David C. Mirhady. Rutgers University Studies in Classical Humanities 6. New Brunswick: Transaction, 1994.

Schipper, Bernd U., and D. Andrew Teeter, eds. *Wisdom and Torah: The Reception of 'Torah' in the Wisdom Literature of the Second Temple Period.* Leiden: Brill, 2013.

Schofield, Malcolm. "Aristotle on the Imagination." Pages 249–78 in *Essays on Aristotle's De Anima.* Edited by Martha C. Nussbaum and Amélie Oksenberg Rorty. Oxford: Oxford University Press, 1992.

Schrenk, Gottlob. "ἐκλεκτός." *TDNT* 4:181–92.

Schüssler Fiorenza, Elisabeth. "The Phenomenon of Early Christian Apocalyptic: Some Reflections on Method." Pages 295–316 in *Apocalypticism in the Mediterranean World and the Near East: Proceedings of the International Colloquium on Apocalypticism, Uppsala, August 12–17, 1979.* Edited by David Hellholm. 2nd ed. Tübingen: Mohr Siebeck, 1989.

Schütrumpf, Eckart. "Non-logical Means of Persuasion in Aristotle's Rhetoric and Cicero's De Oratore." Pages 95–110 in *Peripatetic Rhetoric after Aristotle.* Edited by William W. Fortenbaugh and David C.

Mirhady. Rutgers University Studies in Classical Humanities 6. New Brunswick: Transaction, 1994.

Schweitzer, Albert. *The Quest of the Historical Jesus: A Critical Study of Its Progress from Reimarus to Wrede.* New York: Macmillan, 1968.

Schweizer, Eduard. *The Good News according to Matthew.* Translated by D. E. Green. Atlanta: John Knox, 1975.

Scott, B. B. "The Birth of the Reader." *Semeia* 52 (1991): 83–102.

Sim, David C. *Apocalyptic Eschatology in the Gospel of Matthew.* SNTSMS 88. Cambridge: Cambridge University Press, 1996.

———. *Gospel of Matthew and Christian Judaism.* Edinburgh: T&T Clark, 1998.

———. "Matthew 7:21–23: Further Evidence of Its Anti-Pauline Perspective." *NTS* 53 (2007): 325–43.

———. "Matthew 22:13a and 1 Enoch 10:4a: A Case of Literary Dependence." *JSNT* 47 (1992): 3–19.

Skehan, Patrick W., and Alexander A. Di Lella. *The Wisdom of Ben Sira.* AB 39. New York: Doubleday, 1987.

Slomkowski, Paul. *Aristotle's Topics.* Leiden: Brill, 1997.

Smith, A. D., and J. Hutchinson. *Ethnicity.* Oxford: Oxford University Press, 1996.

Smith, Jonathan Z. "Wisdom and Apocalyptic." Pages 131–56 in *Religious Syncretism in Antiquity: Essays in Conversation with Geo Widengren.* Edited by Birger A. Pearson. Missoula, MT: American Academy of Religion, 1975.

Smith, Morton. "On the History of ΑΠΟΚΑΛΥΠΤΩ and ΑΠΟΚΑΛΥΨΙΣ." Pages 9–20 in *Apocalypticism in the Mediterranean World and the Near East: Proceedings of the International Colloquium on Apocalypticism Uppsala, August 12–17, 1979.* Edited by David Hellholm. 2nd ed. Tübingen: Mohr Siebeck, 1983.

Smith, Robin. "Logic." Pages 27–65 in *The Cambridge Companion to Aristotle.* Cambridge: Cambridge University Press, 1995.

Smyth, Herbert W. *Greek Grammar.* Cambridge: Harvard University Press, 1984.

Snodgrass, Klyne. "Matthew and the Law." Pages 99–128 in *Treasures New and Old: Contributions to Matthean Studies.* Edited by David R. Bauer and Mark A. Powell. SBLSymS 1. Atlanta: Scholars Press, 1996.

Stanton, Graham N. *The Interpretation of Matthew.* Philadelphia: Fortress, 1983.

———. *A Gospel for a New People: Studies in Matthew.* Louisville: Westminster John Knox, 1992.

Starr, James, and Troels Engberg-Pedersen, eds. *Early Christian Paraenesis in Context.* New York: de Gruyter, 2005.

Stendahl, Krister. "The Called and the Chosen." Pages 63–80 in *The Root of the Vine: Essays in Biblical Theology.* Edited by Anton Fridrichsen. New York: Philosophical, 1953.

———. *The School of St. Matthew and Its Use of the Old Testament.* Philadelphia: Fortress, 1968.

Stern, David. *Parables in Midrash: Narrative and Exegesis in Rabbinic Literature.* Cambridge: Harvard University Press, 1991.

Stern, Sacha. *Time and Process in Ancient Judaism.* Oxford: Littman Library of Jewish Civilization, 2003.

Stone, Michael E. "Lists of Revealed Things in the Apocalyptic Literature." Pages 414–52 in *Magnalia Dei: The Mighty Acts of God; Essays on the Bible and Archaeology in Memory of G. Ernest Wright.* Edited by Frank Moore Cross, Werner E. LeMarke, and Patrick D. Miller. Garden City, NY: Doubleday, 1976.

Strack, H. L., and Günter Stemberger. *Introduction to the Talmud and Midrash.* Translated by Markus Bockmuehl. Minneapolis: Fortress, 1992.

Strecker, Georg. *Der Weg der Gerechtigkeit: Untersuchung zur Theologie des Matthäus.* 3rd ed. FRLANT 82. Göttingen: Vandenhoeck & Ruprecht, 1966.

Streeter, B. H. *The Four Gospels: A Study of Origins.* Rev. ed. London: Macmillan, 1930.

Stuckenbruck, Loren T. "The Early Traditions Related to 1 Enoch from the Dead Sea Scrolls: An Overview and Assessment." Pages 41–63 in *The Early Enoch Literature.* Edited by Gabriele Boccaccini and John J. Collins. Leiden: Brill, 2007.

Sturm, Richard E. "Defining the Word 'Apocalyptic.'" Pages 17–48 in *Apocalyptic and the New Testament: Essays in Honor of J. Louis Martyn.* Edited by Joel Marcus and Marion L. Soards. Sheffield: JSOT Press, 1989.

Suggs, M. Jack. *Wisdom, Christology, and Law in Matthew.* Cambridge: Harvard University Press, 1970.

Suh, J. S. "Das Weltgericht und die Matthäische Gemeinde." *NovT* 48 (2006): 217–32.

Sullivan, Karen. *Frames and Constructions in Metaphoric Language.* Philadelphia: John Benjamins, 2013.

Sweetser, Eve, and Mary Therese DesCamp. "Motivating Biblical Metaphors for God." Pages 7–23 in *Cognitive Linguistic Explorations in Biblical Studies.* Edited by Bonnie Howe and Joel B. Green. Berlin: de Gruyter, 2014.

Swiggers, Pierre. "Cognitive Aspects of Aristotle's Theory of Metaphor." *Glotta* 62 (1984): 40–45.

Taylor, Joan E. *The Immerser: John the Baptist within Second Temple Judaism.* Grand Rapids: Eerdmans, 1997.

Taylor, John R. *Linguistic Categorization.* Oxford: Clarendon, 1995.

Thaden, Robert H. von, Jr. "A Cognitive Turn: Conceptual Blending within a Sociorhetorical Framework." Pages 285–328 in *Foundations for Sociorhetorical Exploration: A Rhetoric of Religious Antiquity Reader.* Edited by Vernon K. Robbins, Robert H. von Thaden Jr., and Bart B. Bruehler. Atlanta: SBL Press, 2016.

Thomas, R. L. "Jesus' View of Eternal Punishment." *MSJ* 9 (1998): 147–67.

Tiller, Patrick A. *A Commentary on the Animal Apocalypse of 1 Enoch.* EJL 4. Atlanta: Scholars Press, 1993.

Trible, Phyllis. *Rhetorical Criticism: Context, Method, and the Book of Jonah.* Guides to Biblical Scholarship. Minneapolis: Fortress, 1994.

Trilling, Wolfgang. *Das Wahre Israel: Studien zur Theologie des Matthäusevangeliums.* 3rd ed. ETS 7. Munich: Kösel, 1964.

———. *The Gospel according to St. Matthew.* Translated by Kevin Smyth. London: Burns & Oates, 1969.

VanderKam, James C. *Enoch and the Growth of an Apocalyptic Tradition.* CBQMS 16. Washington, DC: Catholic Biblical Association of America, 1984.

———. *From Revelation to Canon: Studies in the Hebrew Bible and Second Temple Literature.* JSJSup 62. Leiden: Brill, 2000.

———. "Mapping Second Temple Judaism." Pages 1–20 in *The Early Enoch Literature.* Edited by Gabriele Boccaccini and John J. Collins. Leiden: Brill, 2007.

———. "Messianism and Apocalypticism." Pages 112–38 in *The Continuum History of Apocalypticism.* Edited by Bernard J. McGinn, John J. Collins, and Stephen J. Stein. New York: Continuum, 2003.

———. "Open and Closed Eyes in the Animal Apocalypse (1 Enoch 85–90)." Pages 279–92 in *The Idea of Biblical Interpretation: Essays in Honor of James L. Kugel.* Edited by Hindy Najman and Judith H. Newman. Leiden: Brill, 2004.

Vermes, Geza. *Scripture and Tradition in Judaism: Haggadic Studies.* Leiden: Brill, 1983.

Vielhauer, P. "Apocalypses and Related Subjects: Introduction." Pages 581–607 in *New Testament Apocrypha.* Vol. 2. Edited by E. Hennecke and W. Schneemelcher. Philadelphia: Lutterworth, 1965.

Walck, Leslie W. *The Son of Man in the Parables of Enoch and in Matthew.* Jewish and Christian Texts in Contexts and Related Studies. New York: T&T Clark, 2011.

Walls, Jerry L., ed. *The Oxford Handbook of Eschatology.* Oxford: Oxford University Press, 2008.

Watson, Duane F. "The Influence of George Kennedy on Rhetorical Criticism of the New Testament." Pages 41–62 in *Words Well Spoken: George Kennedy's Rhetoric of the New Testament.* Edited by C. Clifton Black and Duane F. Watson. Waco, TX: Baylor University Press, 2008.

———, ed. *The Intertexture of Apocalyptic Discourse in the New Testament.* SBLSymS 14. Atlanta: Society of Biblical Literature, 2002.

———. *The Rhetoric of the New Testament: A Bibliographic Survey.* Blandford Forum: Deo, 2006.

Webb, Robert. *John the Baptizer and Prophet: A Socio-Historical Study.* JSNTSup 62. Sheffield: JSOT Press, 1991.

Weber, Kathleen. "The Image of the Sheep and Goats in Matthew 25:31–46." *CBQ* 59 (1997): 657–78.

Weiss, Johannes. *Jesus' Proclamation of the Kingdom of God.* Translated by Richard Hyde Hiers and David Larrimore Holland. Philadelphia: Fortress, 1971.

Welton, William. *Plato's Forms: Varieties of Interpretation.* Lanham, MD: Lexington Books, 2003.

Wenham, David. "The Rock on Which to Build: Some Mainly Pauline Observations about the Sermon on the Mount." Pages 187–206 in *Built upon the Rock: Studies in the Gospel of Matthew.* Edited by Daniel M. Gurtner and John Nolland. Grand Rapids: Eerdmans, 2008.

Wilder, Amos N. *Early Christian Rhetoric: The Language of the Gospel.* Cambridge: Harvard University Press, 1964. Repr., 1976.

———. "The Rhetoric of Ancient and Modern Apocalyptic." *Int* 25 (1971): 436–53.

Willitts, J. "The Friendship of Matthew and Paul: A Response to a Recent Trend in the Interpretation of Matthew's Gospel." *HTSTSt* 65 (2009): https://doi.org/10.4102/hts.v65i1.151.

———. *Matthew's Messianic Shepherd-King: In Search of "The Lost Sheep of the House of Israel."* Berlin: de Gruyter, 2007.

Wills, Lawrence M. "Scribal Methods in Matthew and Mishnah Abot." *CBQ* 63 (2001): 258–64.

———. "Scribal Methods in Matthew and Mishnah Abot." Pages 183–97 in *The Gospel of Matthew.* Vol. 2 of *Biblical Interpretation in Early Christian Gospels.* Edited by Thomas R Hatina. LNTS 310. New York: T&T Clark, 2008.

Wilson, Alistair I. *When Will These Things Happen? A Study of Jesus as Judge in Matthew 21–25.* Waynesboro, GA: Paternoster, 2004.

Wisse, Jakob. "*De Oratore*: Rhetoric, Philosophy, and the Making of the Ideal Orator." Pages 375–400 in *Brill's Companion to Cicero: Oratory and Rhetoric.* Edited by James M. May. Leiden: Brill, 2002.

———. "The Intellectual Background of Cicero's Rhetorical Works." Pages 331–74 in *Brill's Companion to Cicero: Oratory and Rhetoric.* Edited by James M. May. Leiden: Brill, 2002.

Witherington, Ben, III. *New Testament Rhetoric: An Introductory Guide to the Art of Persuasion in and of the New Testament.* Eugene, OR: Wipf & Stock, 2009.

Wittgenstein, Ludwig. *Philosophical Investigation.* New York: Macmillan, 1953.

Wright, Benjamin G., III. "Torah and Sapiential Pedagogy in the Book of Ben Sira." Pages 157–86 in *Wisdom and Torah: The Reception of 'Torah' in the Wisdom Literature of the Second Temple Period.* Edited by Bernd U. Schipper and D. Andrew Teeter. JSJSup 163. Leiden: Brill, 2013.

Wuellner, Wilhelm. "Where Is Rhetorical Criticism Taking Us?" *CBQ* 49 (1987): 448–63.

Xeravits, G. G. "Wisdom Traits of the Eschatological Prophet." Pages 183–92 in *Wisdom and Apocalypticism in the Dead Sea Scrolls and in the Biblical Tradition.* Edited by F. Garcia Martinez. Leuven: Leuven University Press, 2003.

Yarbro Collins, Adela. *Mark: A Commentary.* Hermeneia. Minneapolis: Fortress, 2007.

Yerushalmi, Y. H. *Zakhor: Jewish History and Jewish Memory.* Seattle: University of Washington Press, 1982.

Ancient Sources Index

Hebrew Bible/Septuagint

Genesis	33–34, 83–84, 97, 100, 103–4, 114, 121–22, 124, 168, 232, 244
1	92, 97–98, 100, 110
1–3	100
1:20–21	113
2	97, 111
2:7	113
3	97–98, 100, 110
3:6	100, 162
3:7	162
4:2	112
4:4	100
4:7	100, 102
5–6	83
5:24	84, 139
8:6	131
9:9–10	113
9:20–27	160
21:27–34	113
22:2	190
29	112
29:31	131
30:22	131
30:32–33	112
30:32–42	112
32	117
32:22 LXX	117
37:12–46:4	114
41:56	131
45:5–8	114

Exodus	117, 124, 128, 132, 168
2:6	131

4:11	131
5:17	168
10:15	97
12:5	112
13:17–22	115
15	128, 168
15–40	122, 124, 126, 130–31
15:22–26	127
15:22–19:25	116
15:25–26	127, 131
17:1	127
17:8–16	160
18:20	134
19:3b–8	158
19:9	131
20:10	113
21:33	131
23:8	131
25:27	159
28:9	131
28:27	159
32	116
32:1–6	117
32:4	117
32:7	117
32:7 LXX	117
32:8	117
32:21	117
32:21–25	117
32:22	117
34:29–35	153
35–40	129

Leviticus	111
1:10	112

-309-

310 Apocalyptic Sheep and Goats in Matthew and 1 Enoch

Leviticus (cont.)	
4:32–35	112
9:3	112
20	113
22:19	112
22:27	112
Numbers	
16:32	131
19:15	131
31	160
Deuteronomy	127, 132, 160, 167
4:5–8	167
4:19	160
5:14	113
7:6–8	158
9:4–9	158
10:13–21	160
15:8	131
15:11	131
16:19	132
16:19–20	132
18:15–19	134
20:11	131
23:2–9	167
25:17–19	160
26:5–9	168
28:58	128
30:15	147
32:8	160
32:14	112
Joshua	168
Judges	111, 118
1 Samuel	
7	134
7:3–6	133
7:4	133
7:5	133
8–11	134
12:8	168
15	115, 160

15:9	112
16:11	179
17	112
2 Samuel	
24:17	113
2 Kings	111, 121–22
3:4	112–13
25	92, 232
Ezra	92, 111, 121–22, 232
10:2–3	166–67
Nehemiah	92, 111, 121–22, 232
Esther	148, 170
Job	6, 123
30:30	97
31:20	112
Psalms	135, 151
2:7	190
19:8	135
34:8	111
44	113
50:13 LXX	198
51:10	198
73:1–28	198
77:20	115
78	168
78:52	113, 115
100:3	110
119:18	137
Proverbs	123, 135
6:23	135
7:2	135
11:27	159
13:21	159
14:19	159
17:13	159
17:20	159
20:9	198

Ancient Sources Index

311

27:26	112	8	96
		12	21–22
Qoheleth	6, 123	12:6–7	21
7:14	159		
		Joel	
Isaiah	5, 154, 167–68, 201	3:1–3	36
6:13	195		
10:15	195	Amos	
10:33–34	195	1:1	112
14:1–2	158	3:12	154
32:19	195		
42:1	154, 190	Jonah	123
42:1 LXX	167		
42:4	167	Micah	
43:8–13	158	2:12	154
43:10	154	3:6	97
45:4	154	5:8	113
56:1–8	166–67		
63:10	198	Zephaniah	
63:11	198	3:11–13	154

Jeremiah			
4:14	198	**Deuterocanonical Books**	
25	149	Wisdom of Solomon	
27:5–7	119	9:13–18	198–99
51:40	113	9:17	199

Lamentations		Sirach	155, 157–58, 235
5:10	97	1:6	156
		1:9	156
Ezekiel	198, 228	1:9–10	156
34	113	1:10	156–57
34:11–31	112	1:20	156
36:25–27	198	1:26	156
40:18	159	2:16	128
42:7	159	17:17	160
44:6–9	167	19:20	135
		20:28	132
Daniel 6, 11–12, 14–15, 18, 21–22, 32–		24:6–7	160
33, 66, 86–87, 122–23, 149, 162, 165,		24:8	161
211, 232, 243, 245		24:12	161
4:14	195	24:23	157, 161
7 32, 36, 96, 176, 211–12, 214–15,		42–43	159
222, 232, 236–38, 242		42:24a	159
7–12	7, 65	44:17–19	161

Sirach (*cont.*)

49:16	100
50:27	155

Baruch	18

Susanna	33–34

1 Maccabees

3:5–6	164

2 Maccabees	90

Pseudepigrapha

Apocalypse of Moses

3.3–4	101

2 Baruch

	6–7
17.2–18.2	102
23.4	102
72–73	36

3 Baruch

13.2	207

1 Enoch

5–7, 18, 30–31, 33–35, 82, 84–85, 87, 90, 123–24, 170, 231, 236

1–5	105
1–36	31, 85, 87
1–37	210
6–11	29, 33–34
8.4	101
9.1–2	98
10.1–2	138
12.4	84
13	84
14.8–25	115
28–40	122
37–71	85, 211
46.2	211
48.10	211
62–63	36
62.5	211
67.2	153

71.14	211
72–82	85, 87
80–81	166
82.1	84
83–84	87, 92
83–90	14, 79, 85, 229, 232
83.1	92, 232
83.3–5	137
83.5	150
83.8	92, 137, 234
83.10	138
84.1–3	98
84.2	137
84.2–3	92
84.4	137, 150
84.5	137–38, 150
84.5–6	137
84.6	138, 140
85	103, 105
85.1	92, 232
85.1–2	96, 136
85.3	96, 98, 104
85.3–10	96, 104–106, 117
85.3–89.8	95
85.5	96
85.6	100–101
85.7	96, 101
85.9	96
85.10–86	87
85.53–54	106
85–90	79, 85, 87, 92, 96, 127, 153, 229, 232
86	102, 107, 136, 140, 152
86–88	103, 105
86.1	96, 146
86.1–3	87
86.1–4	103
86.1–87.1	139
86.2	96
86.3	96
86.4	105, 139
86.5	103, 105
86.6	103
87	139
87–88	139

Ancient Sources Index

87.1	96, 100, 103, 105, 136, 151
87.1–3	87
87.3	136, 138, 146
87.4	103, 105
88.1	96
88.1–3	103
89	102
89–90	235, 237, 241
89.1	103–4, 138–39, 152
89.1–8	102
89.9	99, 104
89.9–12	104–5
89.9–90.27	95
89.10	105
89.11	105
89.12	106, 111
89.13–14	111
89.14	113
89.15–16	100
89.16	100, 106, 111, 114–15, 136–37, 151
89.19	101
89.22	106, 115
89.24	106
89.28	106, 116, 126–31, 133
89.28–35	126
89.28–36	124–26, 134–35, 234
89.29–35	127, 130
89.30	128–30
89.32	106–7, 117, 128–30
89.33	128–30
89.35	106, 126, 134
89.35–36	129, 234
89.36	106, 126, 129, 134
89.38	152
89.39–40	106
89.41	133–34
89.41–42	118
89.42	106, 118
89.43	118
89.44	106
89.44–46	118
89.46	106
89.48	118
89.49	106

89.50	234
89.51	106, 134
89.52	153
89.53	106
89.54	134, 164
89.54–55	119
89.54–58	107
89.55–58	106
89.59	107, 119
89.59–60	140
89.60–61	119
89.61–64	107
89.65	120
89.65–68	107
89.68	120
89.69	120, 151
89.70–71	107
89.73	134, 163
89.74	107, 120
89.74–75	107
89.75	134
89.76	107, 151
90.1–4	120
90.3	100, 136, 139, 151
90.3–4	107
90.4	120, 139
90.6	101, 106, 146
90.6–9	88
90.6–18	89
90.6–19	87–89, 91, 106, 120, 130, 132
90.6–38	120
90.6–41	232
90.7	107
90.11	88, 139, 151
90.13	100, 139, 151
90.13–14	146
90.14	139
90.15	146
90.16	90, 163
90.16–18	89
90.17	107, 120
90.19	89–90, 106, 149, 163, 232–33
90.20	139, 233
90.20–27	88, 91, 95, 106, 139–40, 149–50, 164, 233

314   Apocalyptic Sheep and Goats in Matthew and 1 Enoch

1 Enoch (cont.)		23	7
90.20–42	150		
90.22	108	Life of Adam and Eve	
90.23	120	2.4	207
90.23–27	108	7.2	207
90.24–26	140	9–11	102
90.25	120	25.4	207
90.28	90, 108	28.3	207
90.28–29	108, 164		
90.28–36	91, 149	Psalms of Solomon	
90.28–38	95, 108, 140	17.37	198
90.28–42	150		
90.29	134	Sibylline Oracles	18
90.29–38	140	4.162–170	194
90.30	140, 151. 236, 241		
90.30–33	120	Testament of Abraham	
90.30–36	233–34	11–13	36
90.31	136, 149–50		
90.32	106, 108, 151	Testament of Dan	
90.33	95, 140–41, 151	5.3	200
90.34	91, 151, 163	6.3	207
90.35–36	129–30, 134		
90.37	98, 151, 162, 232	Testament of Isaac	
90.37–38	108, 120, 237, 241	5.2	200
90.38	95, 100, 151–52, 162	7.5	200
90.39–40	151		
90.52	137	Testament of Job	
90.54	129	47.10	207
90.58	137		
91	87	Dead Sea Scrolls	
92–105	14		
93	87	Damascus Covenant	
98.28–36	116	III, 18–20	100
4 Ezra	6–7, 11, 18, 198, 211	Rule of the Community	
7.31–44	36	IV, 23	100
9.32–33	206		
12.32	211	Thanksgiving Hymns	
13.1–4	211	XVII, 15–16	100
13.32	211		
14.22	198	Ancient Jewish Texts	
Jubilees	11, 18, 83, 86, 165	Babylonian Talmud	9
4.17	83, 165		
6.18	161	b. Pesachim 68b	147

Ancient Sources Index

315

Genesis Rabbah

16.3	195

Josephus, *Antiquities*

18.117	193

Philo, *On the Creation of the World*

136–150	100

New Testament

Matthew

1:1–2:23	31
3:1–12	18
3:1–4:17	78, 186, 212
3:11	63, 193–96, 199, 201, 204
3:11–12	37–39, 63, 78, 185–86, 193
3:11–17	79–80, 185–86, 202, 214, 244–45
3:13–15	187
3:15b	188, 191, 193, 196, 201
3:16–17	187, 189–91, 202, 210
4:4	76, 206
5:13–16	237, 240
5:18	209, 238
5:19	204–5, 222
7:21–23	37–38, 200, 205
7:23	212
7:24	206
8:28–33	210
9:15	182
10:23	32, 37–38, 181–82, 220
10:32	212
11:2–3	192, 199
11:19	197, 199, 220
12:15–21	238
12:21	167, 222
13:19	205–6
13:24	63, 203–4, 207–9
13:24–30	36–39, 63, 78–80, 178–79, 185–86, 202–3, 207, 213–14, 225–26, 244–45
13:25	63, 206
13:36–43	37, 39, 185, 196, 203, 208–11, 215

13:37	32, 211–12, 220
13:39	21
13:40	177, 213
13:41	35
13:41–43	178, 213
13:47–50	37–38, 203, 225–26
13:49	21, 35, 240
16:13	32, 211, 215
16:16–17	190
16:21	32
16:27	32, 35, 182
16:27–28	37–38
16:28	181–82, 220
18:1–5	222
19:27–28	212
19:27–30	37–38
19:28	32, 213, 220
21:32	192–93, 197
22:1–14	238
22:13	31
22:40	200, 238
22:41–45	187–88, 197
24:1	176
24:3	21
24:29–31	36, 38, 177, 211
24:30	35
24:30–31	32, 176–78, 184
24:31	227, 237
24:33	181
25:31	32, 35, 174, 180–81, 202, 216,
25:31–32b	176–77, 180, 184–85, 218, 220, 240
25:31–46	1, 19, 33, 35–40, 63, 72, 78–80, 82, 171–86, 201–2, 212, 214–16, 220, 223–28, 229–31, 235–37, 239, 242, 244–45
25:32c–33	177–79, 184, 218, 236, 239–40
25:34	63, 179, 182–85, 223–24, 227, 237, 239
25:34–45	179–80, 184, 219, 238, 241–42
25:35–36	183, 237
25:46	184
26:64–66	211

316   Apocalyptic Sheep and Goats in Matthew and 1 Enoch

Matthew (cont.)

27:24–25	33
27:51	30

Mark   21–22, 79, 181, 189–90, 192, 198, 204, 210–211, 227

1:4	194–95
1:9	188
1:10	189
1:11	190
3:10	189, 195
4:26–29	203, 211
4:33–34	203
5:1–20	210
5:7	210
6:14	194
6:34	227
8:28	193
12:28–34	220
13:7	181
13:24–27	36, 211
14:27	76, 228

Luke

1:75	192
3:3	195
3:16–17	37
3:21	188
3:22	190
6:46	200
8:26–39	210
8:28	210
9:19	193
10:25–37	220–21
13:26–27	200
17:7	228
19:46	76
21:9	181
21:25–28	36, 211

John   228

6:45	76
8:46	187
12:48	242

Acts

8:32	228
12:25	191
13:24	195
19:4	195

Romans

3:23–26	187
8:36	228

1 Corinthians

3	72
15:3	187

2 Corinthians

5:21	187

Hebrews

4:15	187
13:20	228

James

2:8	220

1 Peter

1:19	187, 228
2:3	111
2:22	187
2:25	228

Revelation   2, 10, 14, 23, 30, 176, 228

1:1	2–3
20	36

Early Christian Literature

Clement of Alexandria, *Paedagogus*

1.1	3

Eusebius of Caesarea, *Praeparatio evangelica*

9.17.2–9	84

Ancient Sources Index 317

Greco-Roman Literature

Aristophanes, *Equites*
864–867   46

Aristophanes, *Ranae*
905–906   46

Aristotle, *Analytica posteriora*
1.1, 71a1–71b8   251
1.1, 71a5–9   255
1.2, 71b9–72b4   251
2.19, 100a3–6   51

Aristotle, *Categoriae*
2, 1a16–19   49
4, 2a4–10   49
5, 3b10–24   51
6,4b26–27   50
7, 6b11   50
7, 7b15–8a12   50
8, 11a15   50

Aristotle, *De anima*
2.5, 417b21–3   53
2.12, 424a17–30   256
3, 428a12–15   52
3.3, 428b30–9a6   50

Aristotle, *De Interpretatione*
1, 16a1–5   51
1, 16a14–15   49
1, 16a15–19   49
1, 16a19   49
1–2, 16a1–34   51
3, 16b6–8   49

Aristotle, *De memoria et reminiscentia*
1, 449b30–451a17   51

Aristotle, *Historia animalium*
9.5, 611a15–30   50
9.7, 612b18–31   50
9.10, 614b18–30   50
9.39, 623a7–26   50

9.46, 630b18–21   50

Aristotle, *Metaphysica*
1.1–6, 980b26–981a13   51
1.5–6, 981a5–13   51
4.5.7–9, 1009a38–b9   52
4.5.23, 1010b1–4   52
5.1.1–3, 1012b34–1013a23   250
5.9.5, 1018a15-19   50
7.13.2, 1038b8–12   258
7.16.1, 1040b5–8   258
9.7.1–7, 1048b37–1049b3   259

Aristotle, *Physica*
1.1, 184a10–25   251
1.5, 189a5–8   53
4.1, 208b1–8   260
4.2, 209a–b   257
4.2, 209b29–34   53
4.2–4, 209a31–212a30   256
4.3–4, 210b25–211a7   257
4.4, 210b32–211a11   258
4.4, 211a29–211b5   259
4.5, 212b33–213a11   259

Aristotle, *Poetica*
19, 1456a34–b19   52
20, 1457a10–12   49
21, 1457b6–19   48
21, 1457b25–31   48
21–22, 1457a31–1459a16   52
22,1458a21–23   48

Aristotle, *Rhetorica*
1.1.1, 1354a1–5   249
1.1.3, 1354a11–16   265
1.1.6, 1354a26–31   263
1.1.11, 1355a17–18   251
1.1.12, 1355a20–29   261
1.1.14   52
1.1.14, 1355b7–12   262
1.2.1, 1355b8–11   52
1.2.1, 1355b26–27   262
1.2.2, 1355b35–1356a1   266
1.2.4, 1356a5–13   266

Aristotle, Rhetorica (cont.)

1.2.5, 1356a14–15	266
1.2.6, 1356a19–20	262
1.2.7, 1356a20–35	248
1.2.8, 1356a35–1356b10	264
1.2.21	264
1.2.21, 1358a10–26	264
1.2.21, 1394a19–1395b19	259
1.2.25–27	52
1.3.7–9, 1359a6–29	266
1.4–15, 29	264
1.4.5, 1359b8–12	261
1.4.7, 1359b16–23	268
1.5, 1360b4–1362a14	261
1.8.6, 1366a8–16	266
2.1.1–7, 1377b16–20	266
2.1–11, 1377b16–1388b30	266
2.12–17, 1388b31–1391b7	266
2.20.2, 1393a	54
2.22.10, 1396a33–1396b6	265
2.22.12, 1396b12–20	264
2.22.13, 1396b20–23	258
2.23	264
2.23.1, 1397a7–19	268
2.23.8, 1398a15–28	268
2.24	250
2.24, 1400b34–1402a29	250
2.25.2, 1402a32–34	264
2.26.1, 1403a17–22	258
3.1.2, 1403b16–17	45
3.1.8, 1404a21–22	51
3.2.6, 1404b	47, 277
3.2.7, 1405a3	49
3.2.13, 1405b	51
3.4.4, 1407a4	48
3.4.4, 1407a14–18	274
3.10, 1410b2	54
3.10, 1410b11	51
3.10.3, 1410b15–18	274
3.10.6, 1410b31–36	267
3.10.7, 1410b36–1411b23	278
3.11, 1412a6	55
3.11.2, 1411b25–32	267
3.11.6, 1412a26–28	54

Aristotle, Topica

1.1	251
1.1, 100a	260
1.1, 100b21–23	251
1.2, 101b	249
1.4, 101b11–101b37	253
1.4–5, 101b11–102b26	253
1.5, 101b38–102b26	253
1.5, 102a31–102b3	252
1.5, 102b4–9	252
1.10–12, 104a3–105a19	251
1.11, 104b1–12	254
1.18, 108b7–14	53
2.2, 109a34–38	251, 253
2.7, 113a20–23	254
2.10, 115a8–11	252
7.5, 151a3–14	255
8.1–10, 156b23–161a15	251
32	277

Cicero, Brutus

274	273

Cicero, De oratore

1.34	271
1.90	277
1.92	277
1.108	276
1.109	277
1.146	271
1.155–165	273
1.157	273
1.157–158	273
1.186	277
1.193–194	271
2.68	271
3.10	272
3.13	273
3.149	273
3.152–153	277
3.155	276–77
3.155–156	274
3.155–158	278
3.158	278
3.159	279

Ancient Sources Index

3.159–161	279	Plato, *Phaedrus*	
3.160	276	277b–d	248
3.163	279		
3.164	279	Plato, *Philebus*	
3.165	279	58a	262
3.166	277		
3.170	277	Plato, *Protagoras*	
4.16	272	352a	2

Cicero, *Epistulae ad familiares*		Plato, *Theaetetus*	
1.9.23	276	152a	261
16.17.1	273	152a–c	52

Cicero, *Orator ad M. Brutum*		Plato, *Timaeus*	
4.16	272	26c	47
24.81	273	52a–c	52–53, 256
26.92	273–74		
27.94	278	Quintilian, *Institutio oratoria*	273
31.113	272	1.2.30	275
32.115	274	5.11.5	54
		5.14.34–35	276–77
Demosthenes, *1–3 Philippic*	263	7.3.13	277
		8, preface 15	275
Demosthenes, *3 Philippic*		8.3.72–82	278
9.8	268	8.6.4	277
		8.6.5	273
Gorgias, *Helena*		8.6.8	274
8	262	8.6.9	275
		8.6.10	278–79
Isocrates, *Evagoras*		8.6.11	278
8–10	47	8.6.13	276
		9.1.5	49, 274
Plato, *Cratylus*			
430d	48	Rhetorica ad Herennium	
		4.45.59	50
Plato, *Gorgias*			
452d	262	Seneca, *Epistulae morales*	
455d	2	24.26	143
462c	248		

Plato, *Critias*	
113a	47

Plato, *Leges*	
944b	48

Modern Authors Index

Albrektson, Bertil 144
Albright, William F. 209
Allen, Willoughby C. 209
Allison, Dale C. 29, 36, 175–76, 181, 187, 189, 190, 191–93, 199, 207, 208, 215
Argall, Randall A. 158–59
Assefa, Daniel 91
Austin, John L. 58–59, 74
Backman, Mark 54, 258
Bacon, Francis 249–50
Bakhtin, Mikhail M. 73–74
Barr, James 144
Barth, Fredrik 169
Barton, John 8
Bauckham, Richard J. 25, 208
Bedenbender, Andreas 93, 122–23
Bendoraitis, Kristian 34–35
Berg, Sandra Beth 148
Betz, Hans Dieter 9, 68–69, 192
Birnbaum, Ellen 158
Black, C. Clifton 68–70
Black, Matthew 85, 87–88, 98, 150
Blenkinsopp, Joseph 157, 167
Blocher, Henri 130
Bloomquist, L. Gregory 42–43
Boccaccini, Gabriele 6–7, 122–24
Bornkamm, Gunther 18–19, 26–27, 200
Boyarin, Daniel 9, 10, 13, 32, 46, 64, 73, 236, 278
Boys-Stones, George R. 45–46, 278
Brueggemann, Walter 179
Brummett, Barry 41
Bultmann, Rudolf 174
Burrows, Millar 144

Bywater, Ingram 49
Campbell, Antony F. 134
Carey, Greg 14, 42
Carmignac, Jean 7–8, 12
Carter, Warren 76, 136, 176, 182, 207
Charette, Blaine 27
Charlesworth, James H. 6–7, 86, 114, 137, 141
Clark, Donald L. 68
Clifford, Richard J., S.J. 9
Cohen, Shaye J. D. 149, 163–64
Collins, John J. 4–9, 11–14, 23, 30, 65–66, 87, 93, 142, 157, 166
Cope, O. Lamar 16
Cortés-Fuentes, David 36, 176, 216, 224
Court, J. M. 36
Cranz, F. Edward 275
Crenshaw, James L. 148
Dalman, Gustaf 208
Dancygier, Barbara 56, 204
Davies, Phillip R. 10, 11, 12–13, 15, 25, 34, 164–65
Davies, William D. 36, 108, 175–77, 181, 187, 189–93, 199, 207, 215, 243
Derrida, Jacques 49, 52
DesCamp, Mary Therese 217, 221
deSilva, David A. 67
Deutsch, Celia M. 21, 28
DeVries, Simon J. 145, 147, 148
Di Lella, Alexander A. 135
Dibley, Amy Genevive 82
Dillman, August 90, 153
Dimant, Devorah 153
Dobschütz, Ernst von 64–65
Donahue, John R. 36, 174

-321-

Down, Martin 36
Dumery, Henry 144–45
Eco, Umberto 49
Edeline, Francis 49
Emberling, Geoff 169
Erickson, Keith V. 54, 255
Eriksson, Anders 69
Evans, Craig A. 29, 65, 76
Evans-Pritchard, E. 145
Fauconnier, Gilles 56, 61, 72, 218, 230
Fillmore, Charles J. 55, 62
Flannery, Frances 39, 135
Flesher, Leann S. 151
Fortenbaugh, William W. 45, 265, 267, 272
Foster, Robert L. 151
France, R. T. 36, 176, 187, 190, 192, 204, 207
Gage, John T. 265
Garver, Eugene 247
Gell, Alfred 145
Goering, Greg Schmidt 157–61
Goldstein, Jonathan A. 89, 164
Gonzalez, Francisco J. 54, 257
Goulder, Michael D. 64, 203
Grabbe, Lester L. 10, 149
Gray, Sherman W. 173, 225
Green, Joel B. 68, 217
Grimaldi, William M. 54, 255
Grindheim, Sigurd 36
Gruenwald, Ithamar 8
Günter Stemberger 214
Gurtner, Daniel 28–30, 34, 193, 208
Guthrie, William K. C. 53, 256
Habel, Norman C. 98
Hadfield, Percival 27
Hagner, Donald A. 15, 16, 19, 20–22, 25–26, 29, 30, 224
Halbertal, Moshe 170–71
Hamilton, Catherine Sider 29–30, 33–34
Hanson, Paul D. 5, 13–14, 16, 18, 20, 22–23, 25, 27, 29, 130
Hanson, Richard P. C. 278
Hartman, Lars. 8, 41, 43, 105
Hays, Richard B. 75–76, 78, 229

Heath, Malcolm 50, 52–53
Heil, John Paul 36, 179, 207, 215
Hellholm, David 2, 7–8, 16, 20, 41, 65
Hengel, Martin 9–10, 39
Henze, Matthias 123, 133
Hermann, V. 174
Heschel, Abraham J. 143–44, 147
Himmelfarb, Martha 111, 129, 165
Holist, Michael 74
Horner, Winifred 68
Horsley, Richard A. 142–43, 164
House, Paul R. 68
Howard, David M. 151
Hultgard, Anders 9
Humphries-Brooks, Stephenson 34
Hutchinson, John 169
Hutter, Manfred 36
Innes, Doreen 46, 48, 55, 273, 275–77, 279
Jeremias, Joachim 203, 207
Johnson, Mark 44, 55–57, 60–62
Joüon, Paul 148
Kaminsky, Joel 159–160
Käsemann, Ernst 1, 19
Keller, Andrew 148
Kennedy, George A. 48–49, 67–71, 73, 248, 250, 261–69, 273
Kingsbury, J. D. 204
Kirby, John T. 47–49, 51, 53
Kister, Menahem 157
Klein, Ralf 36
Knibb, Michael A. 85, 87, 114
Koch, Klaus 2, 3, 8, 22–23, 27, 153
Kovecses, Zoltan 56–59, 60, 62, 79, 73–75, 78
Kristeva, Julia 73–75, 78
Kugel, James L. 127, 154
Kvanvig, Helge S. 12
LaCocque, André 66, 98
Lakoff, George 44, 55–63, 221, 230
Lambdin, Thomas O. 131
Lane, Nathan 76
Lloyd, Geoffrey E. R. 46, 58, 249
Luecke, Friedrich 2
Luz, Ulrich 27, 36, 173, 175, 187, 191–93, 200, 203–4, 216, 227

Modern Authors Index

Mack, Burton L. 68
Mann, Christopher S. 209
Marguerat, Daniel 27
Martinez, Florentino G. 10, 97, 113, 129
May, James M. 45, 266, 271–72
Mayordomo, Moises 75–76
McCall, Marsh H. 46–47, 64
McKeon, Richard 54, 256
Meier, John P. 28, 34, 36, 180, 191–92
Mervis, Carolyne 58
Meyer, Paul W. 36, 186
Milik, Jozef T. 83, 85, 87–88, 98, 126, 152
Miller, Carolyn R. 247–49, 259–60, 263
Mirhady, David C. 45, 265, 267
Mitch, Curtis 176, 190
Mitchell, Margaret M. 69
Möller, Karl 70–71
Momigliano, A. 144
Moran, Richard 48
Muilenburg, James 68
Müller, Reinhard 132
Muraoka, Takamitsu 148
Murphy, Roland E. 130
Najman, Hindy 124, 127
Natorp, Paul 54, 258–60
Neusner, Jacob 65, 146, 194–95
Newsom, Carol A. 92, 94, 101
Nickelsburg, George W. E. 20, 66, 85, 88–89, 90, 92–95, 97, 99–104, 106–8, 111, 113, 120, 122, 125–27, 129, 130–32, 137–41, 150, 153, 163, 232, 234
Niklas, Ursula 49
Nilsen, Tina D. 98
Nolland, John 36, 176, 179, 193, 195, 207, 215
Olson, Daniel C. 82, 94, 98–101, 126, 128
Oppenheim, Allen L. 135
Orlov, Andrei 236
Orton, David E. 27, 34, 65
Overman, J. Andrew 199, 216
Pamment, Margaret 176, 209
Park, Eugene E. C. 37, 200–201
Patrides, Constantinos A. 143–44

Patte, Daniel 69, 193
Pennington, Jonathan T. 196, 208–9
Perrin, Norman 65, 93
Petofi, Janos S. 76
Plett, Heinrich F. 75
Popkes, Wiard 40
Porter, Paul A. 96, 113, 153
Porter-Young, Anathea E. 88, 91
Przybylski, Benno 192
Putnam, Hillary 56
Rad, Gerhard von 9, 66, 154, 157
Reed, Annette Yoshiko 13, 86
Reeves, John 31
Richter, Amy E. 29–32, 34
Ricoeur, Paul 47–49, 66–67
Riniker, Christian 15
Robbins, Vernon K. 35, 42–43, 69, 71–74, 76–78, 95, 110–11, 122, 229
Robinson, John A. T. 36, 173–74
Rölver, Olaf 15
Rorty, Amelie Oksenberg 48, 50, 249
Rosch, Eleanor 58–59
Rowland, Christopher C. 8, 11, 13–15, 23, 28–30, 34
Rowley, Harold H. 3
Rubin, Nissan 142, 145–46
Rubinelli, Sara 253–54, 258, 262
Russell, David S. 18
Russell, Stephanie 148
Sabourin, Leopold 15, 16, 18, 20, 22, 30
Sacchi, Paolo 6, 16, 25
Saldarini, Anthony J. 65, 197, 199, 216
Sanders, E. P. 7–8, 28, 157
Sanders, James A. 76, 168–69
Sandmel, Samuel 148
Sauter, Gerhard 26–27
Schaper, Joachim 166–67
Schenkeveld, Dirk M. 267
Schofield, Malcolm 50, 52
Schrenk, Gottlob 238
Schüssler Fiorenza, Elisabeth 65
Schütrumpf, Eckart 265, 272
Schweitzer, Albert 17, 26
Schweizer, Eduard 192
Scott, B. B. 215

Sim, David C. 1–2, 16–17, 19, 22–25, 29–31, 173–74, 200–201, 207
Skehan, Patrick W. 135
Slomkowski, Paul 250–55, 258
Smith, Anthony D. 169
Smith, Jonathan Z. 9, 10
Smith, Morton 2, 3
Smyth, Herbert W. 27, 148, 181
Snodgrass, Klyne 199–200
Solevag, Anna Rebecca 98
Sri, Edward 69, 176, 190
Stanton, Graham N. 16, 19, 20, 22, 25, 36, 65, 173, 176, 185, 197
Stendahl, Krister 28, 66
Stephen, O'Leary 41, 184
Stern, David 64, 212
Stern, Sacha 142, 145
Stone, Michael E. 9, 43, 131
Strack, Herman L. 214
Strecker, Georg 27
Streeter, Burnett H. 17, 20–22, 26
Stuckenbruck, Loren T. 35, 85
Sturm, Richard E. 3–4
Suggs, M. Jack 28
Suh, J. S. 36
Sullivan, Karen 44, 55
Sweetser, Eve 56, 204, 217, 221
Swiggers, Pierre 49
Taylor, Joan E. 194–95
Taylor, John R. 58
Thomas, R. L. 36
Tigchelaar, Eibert J. C. 113, 129
Tiller, Patrick A. 81, 87, 89–90, 92, 93–95, 99, 101, 104, 109, 111–14, 126, 129, 131–33, 136, 141, 150, 153, 164, 232
Trible, Phyllis 68
Trilling, Wolfgang 27
Trudinger, Peter 98
Turner, Mark 56, 61, 72, 218, 230
VanderKam, James C. 12, 66, 83–86, 88, 90, 92, 94, 104–5, 123, 127–28, 135, 165–66, 211, 234
Vermes, Geza 93
Vielhauer, P. 8

Thaden, Robert H. von, Jr. 69
Walck, Leslie W. 29, 30, 32, 34
Watson, Duane F. 42–43, 46, 68, 70–71
Webb, Robert 194
Weber, Kathleen 36, 225–27
Weiss, Johannes 17, 26
Wenham, David 192
Wilder, Amos N. 41, 45
Willitts, Joel 179, 201
Wills, Lawrence M. 28, 65
Wilson, Alistair I. 29
Wisse, Jakob 45, 266, 271, 272
Witherington, Ben, III 69
Wittgenstein, Ludwig 58
Wright, Benjamin G., III 156
Wuellner, Wilhelm 42, 70
Xeravits, Géza G. 10
Yarbo Collins, Adela 34, 190
Yerushalmi, Yosef H. 144

Subject Index

abstract, 47, 50, 55, 59–60, 217, 269
  in Aristotle's *topos*, 260, 274
  time, 145–47
abstraction, 60, 113
action(s), 40, 47, 71, 144, 146, 148, 169, 182–85, 192, 194
  and rhetoric, 262, 268
  as identity/fruits, 204–6, 210
aesthetics, 45, 68, 73, 95
alienation 19, 23
allegory, 81–83, 92–116, 122, 136, 142, 179–86, 204, 217–24, 231–42, 274, 278, 280
allusions, 14, 31–32, 34, 73, 84, 100, 103, 122, 124, 167
analogy, 48, 50, 55, 159, 200, 274, 277
angel(s), 4, 12, 13, 31, 35–38, 84, 88, 95, 98, 100, 102, 123, 136–38, 152–54, 161–62, 165, 176–78, 184, 202–3, 211, 213, 233, 237, 244
  as earthly rulers, 107–9, 119, 136, 140, 148, 150, 164
  as scribe, 100, 107, 139, 146
  as shepherd, 107–9, 119, 136, 140
angelus interpres, 12–14, 20, 35, 137, 139, 244
anthropology, 145
antiquity, 9, 45, 64, 68, 75, 84, 86, 143, 163–64, 193–94, 210, 217, 273
antithetical parallelism, 175
Apocalypse, 2–43, 64–67, 72, 81, 93
  historical, 23–24, 87, 141–43, 166, 244
apocalyptic, 1–40. *See also* rhetorolect
  communication, 135–36, 140, 154, 191, 193, 196–97, 202

apocalyptic (cont.)
  discourse, 1–2, 14–15, 19–21, 26–30, 34–36, 39–45, 64–67, 72–73, 78–81, 163, 167, 171, 175–77, 190, 202, 207, 211–14, 228–29, 231, 242–46
  eschatology, 1, 5, 14–18, 22–25, 30, 41, 173–74
  literature, 1–13, 16–18, 22, 25–28, 35, 39, 41–43, 65, 83–84, 121–24, 169, 198, 212, 222, 236, 243
  metaphor, 40–41, 44, 63, 66–67, 77–78, 93, 196
  phenomenon, 1, 4–7, 10–13, 16, 20, 24, 135–36, 175, 243
  rhetoric, 14, 41, 43, 184–85
  thought, 15, 18–20
apocalypticism, 2–10, 14–15, 23–24, 34
apodeixis, 251, 248
argumentation, 46, 52–53, 57, 69, 71, 248–49, 259–61, 265–70, 277–78
  deductive, 53–54, 248, 251
  inductive, 53–54, 253–255, 264
argumentative texture, 14, 42–43, 52, 73, 78, 95, 253
audience, 1, 28, 43–46, 55, 64, 67–69, 73, 180–81, 185–86, 193, 196, 211–12, 214, 216–21, 225–26, 230–31, 243–44, 248, 255, 260–70, 276, 279
author, 1, 17, 21–22, 40, 64, 66–67, 73, 76, 97, 181, 217, 230
authority (divine), 35, 183, 187, 197, 202, 219, 236, 244
  canon as, 86, 170–71, 183
  images of, 151–52, 162
  sayings/teachings of, 182, 213

-325-

background information, 11, 13, 164, 187, 245, 271–72, 276
baptism, 79, 187, 189, 191–96, 201
beatitudes, 192
beginning, middle, and end, 186. *See also* opening-middle-closing
behavior, 11, 26, 55, 113, 170, 232
belief, 14, 181, 183, 197, 199, 215, 250
believer, 14, 196, 226
beneficial exchange, 35, 99, 262
benefit, 41, 69, 160, 235
Bible, 8, 81, 100, 112–13, 131, 135, 159, 160, 226–27, 238
    as scriptural, 93–95, 115, 124, 145, 170
biblical studies, 68, 75
binary, 46, 46, 159–60, 276
blame, 113, 137
blending theory, 55, 61, 69, 72, 103, 230
body (human), 56, 59, 194–96, 198, 206, 230. *See also* embodiment
boundaries, 57–58, 86, 122, 169
brain, 51
canon/canonical, 86, 166–71
categories (philosophy), 50, 55–59, 62
    of intertexture, 76, 159–60, 216, 219, 277, 27
change, 47, 50, 54, 57, 145, 194, 249, 256, 260, 263, 269
character, 207, 232, 247, 266, 271
characters, 63, 93, 102, 165, 225, 231–32
childhood, 230
children, 31, 82–83, 103, 112, 165, 222, 238
Christ, 2, 71
Christianity, 19
Christology, 19, 186
church, 18, 207, 216
citizens, 262, 271
city, 126, 26
class, 2, 262
classicist, 68
clothing, 59, 112, 180, 237, 239
cognition, 50–52, 60, 77, 79, 229
cognitive
    frames, 4, 39, 44, 55, 57, 60–62, 72, 77, 109, 113, 196, 217, 219, 229–30

cognitive (cont.)
    linguistics, 39, 44, 55, 60, 62, 77, 196, 230
    models, 44, 50, 230–31, 275–76. *See also* Idealized Cognitive Models (ICMs)
    picturing, 44, 50–51, 55–57, 84, 176
    science, 77
    space, 53–56, 58, 61, 72–74, 109, 120, 217–18, 221, 232, 240, 256
    structures, 53, 56–62, 218, 232, 242
collective memory, 142
common topics, 256, 259, 264, 268
commonplaces, 54, 247–49, 252
communication, 10–14, 35, 41–45, 63, 69–73, 78, 135–37, 190, 243, 245
    divine, 12, 28, 35, 39, 43, 78, 135–37, 139–40, 143, 153–54, 184, 189–91, 196–97, 202
community, 19, 23–25, 29–30, 76, 132, 148, 170–71
comparative, 21, 93, 177, 217, 230
comparison, 46–47, 50, 54–55, 61, 85, 97, 113, 156, 187, 189, 193, 196, 204, 210–11, 217, 220, 229–31, 235, 273–74, 277
compression (of stories), 111, 113–15, 124, 168
conceptual
    blending. *See* blending theory
    domain, 60, 61, 77, 217, 235–36
    frame(work), 5, 39, 44, 55, 60, 94, 109, 112–13, 136, 224, 229, 235, 242
    map/mapping, 61, 205, 217, 219, 221, 224, 236, 239, 259
    metaphor, 60–63, 109, 205–8
    place/space. *See* cognitive, space
conceptuality/conceptualization, 50, 71, 77, 97, 112
conclusion (of an argument), 54, 80, 124–26, 175, 226, 240, 243–46, 251, 255, 269–70
confirmation, 191
confront/confrontation, 63, 227
conscious, 41, 52, 78, 232
construction, 130, 253

Subject Index

convention, 12, 17, 71–72, 77, 93, 196
cosmology, 87
cosmos, 83–84, 92, 108–10, 143, 209
court, 71
covenant, 82, 113, 122–24, 135, 144, 147, 157, 161
creation, 6, 81–82, 92, 97–98, 100–103, 108–10, 122, 137–38, 141, 151, 154, 156–58, 160–62, 166–67, 209, 222, 229, 234–35, 237, 239, 241–44
creativity, 72, 91, 264
   intellectual, 1, 9, 16, 54, 163, 243, 255
   literary/scribal, 10–11, 15, 231
creator, 98, 160
cross-space mapping. *See* conceptual, map/mapping
cultural
   categories, 76
   construction, 145
   context, 175, 271
   frames, 229, 235
   intertexture, 73, 77, 79, 122, 174, 223, 244
   knowledge, 13, 46
   memories, 78, 166, 171
   texture, 72
   tradition, 16, 34–35, 70–72, 79, 122, 174, 211, 221, 229
deliberative rhetoric, 266–68
denotation, 7, 17, 23, 47–48, 77, 99, 112, 114, 148, 158, 163, 209
diachronic, 75
dialectic, 46, 74, 249–51, 254–55, 260–64, 269–70
dialogue, 37, 74, 78, 173, 175, 180, 207, 244
dichotomy, 143, 163, 221
didactic, 46
disciples, 21–22, 30, 37, 39, 167, 181–82, 203, 207, 210–15, 222–26, 237–39, 242
diversity, 74
doctrine, 123, 158–59, 215
domestic, 178, 219
dualism, 23, 174, 275

dyadic personality, 159
ecclesiology, 19
echo, 73–77, 122, 190, 229
elaboration, 76
elect, 99, 101, 120, 133, 136, 140–51, 154–55, 158–62, 166–67, 177, 202, 210, 215, 222–24, 227, 229, 231, 235, 237–46
election, 78, 82, 94–95, 127, 133, 140–61, 192–93, 197–98, 227, 235, 238, 244–45
embodiment, 24, 55–56, 100, 122, 136, 155, 161, 166, 180, 245, 251
emergent structure, 61, 72, 175, 217, 218–20, 242
emotion, 55, 65, 266
empire, 88, 197
endoxa, 251, 260, 263, 265, 270
enthymeme, 42, 54, 69, 264–65
environment, 50, 145
epideictic rhetoric, 71, 266
epistēmē, 251
epistemology, 74, 259–60
epistles, 14, 68, 85–86
eschatology (definition), 14–15. *See also* apocalyptic, eschatology
eternity, 14, 37, 137–38, 146, 150, 180, 184, 213
ethics, 11, 18–19, 26, 40, 208
Ethiopia (language of), 85, 87, 94, 97, 101, 113–15, 128, 131, 133, 140–41
ethnicity, 155, 169
ethnocentrism, 154
ethos, 45, 265–70. *See also* character
etymology, 128, 238
evil, 31–32, 100, 102, 105, 109, 117, 122, 147, 152, 159–60, 180, 191, 203, 205–7, 211
exhortation, 7, 11, 20–21, 26, 34, 40, 180–81, 184, 188
eyes (in apocalyptic and wisdom context), 88, 106, 108, 116, 118–20, 125–40, 146, 150–52, 161–62, 234, 237, 259, 267, 278–79
faith, 144, 201, 224, 238–39

family, 59, 114, 139, 180, 219–20, 224, 238–39, 241
family resemblance, 58, 62
femininity, 100, 128, 156
flesh, 55, 72, 94, 137–38, 140–41, 150, 152, 156–57, 162
fluid, 86, 123, 169
forensic rhetoric. *See* judicial/forensic rhetoric
forgiveness, 194–95
formalism, 75
framing (in blending theory). *See* cognitive, frames; conceptual, frame(work)
friends, 199, 221
friendship, 200
genera, 48, 252
generic space, 61, 109, 120, 217–18, 240
genre, 3–8, 11–17, 23–24, 41, 64, 84, 135
gentiles, 40, 82, 90, 109, 149, 160, 164, 166–69, 186, 201, 222, 224, 227–29, 238–39
genus, 48, 54–55, 252–54, 264, 274, 276
gods, 2, 11, 117, 166
gospel, 5, 7, 14–15, 18, 24–26, 68, 72, 198, 208
grammar, 253
graphic images/pictures, 44, 51, 176. *See also* images; imagery; images/pictures; narrative, pictorial
Greco-Roman world, 68
Greece, 143, 267
Greek
  culture/society, 46, 143, 272
  language/literature, 2, 21, 33, 40, 46–49, 70, 81, 85, 87, 112, 114–15, 148, 159, 178, 181–83, 191, 202, 220–22, 228, 237–38, 249–50, 267, 278
guidelines, 68–69, 106, 120, 230, 248
  sociorhetorical, 71
guilt, 33
healing, 127, 197, 199, 227, 239
Hebrew
  Bible, 8, 81, 100, 112–13, 131, 135, 159–60, 168, 228, 238. *See also* Bible

Hebrew (cont.)
  language, 145
  prophets, 5, 82, 116, 121, 154, 163, 191–92, 200–201, 220–21, 224, 238
Hellenistic period, 9, 67, 85, 157, 170
Hellenistic-Roman
  culture, 84
  Judaism, 83
  language/literature, 11
  world, 4, 9
hermeneutics, 79, 93, 98, 211, 214
heteroglossia, 74
heuristic paradigm/framework/model, 4, 40, 44, 72, 173
hierarchy, 136, 147
historiography, 141–49
holiness, 195
holy nation, 127
Holy Spirit, 20, 32, 71, 185–86, 194–201
holy sword, 89
home, 38, 275
horns, 88, 90, 108, 120, 151–52, 162–63, 232, 237, 241
hostility, 19, 90, 99, 221, 272
household, 114, 202, 207
idealized cognitive models (ICM), 55
ideology, 1–2, 7, 10, 15–19, 25, 27, 41, 62, 122, 124, 143, 174–75, 184
idia, 259, 263–64
imagery, 39, 53, 55, 73, 115, 123, 128, 163, 176–78, 185, 187, 203, 211, 217. *See also* graphic
images, 18, 36, 50–54, 66, 275–76
  in Animal Apocalypse, 116, 120, 151
  in Matthew, 187, 210, 214, 227, 230
images/pictures
  agricultural, 207
  apocalyptic, 23, 90–91, 110, 140, 151–52, 213, 215
  eschatological, 1, 35, 78, 100, 178, 185, 202
  judgment, 2, 37–39, 44, 63, 67, 78, 150, 176, 185–86, 201, 214, 217, 237, 243–44

Subject Index

imagination, 65, 136, 160

imminent coming 1–2, 17, 21–26, 37, 41, 88, 173–74, 181–82, 186, 195. *See also* parousia

imperial, 91

implied author, 1, 76, 230–31, 244. *See also* author

implied reader/audience, 1, 180, 193, 196, 211–15, 228–29, 241–42

inner texture. *See* textures

input spaces, 61, 109, 120, 230

intention, 1, 61, 67, 224, 229, 266, 274

interpretive analytics, 33, 64, 66–67, 71, 76, 142, 216–17, 224

intertextuality, 32, 74–78, 229

intertexture. *See* textures

invention, 45–46, 69, 217, 229, 245–46, 263, 268–69

Israel, 40, 43, 64, 78–79, 81–83, 90–95, 109–50, 152–71

Jerusalem, 22, 126, 129, 163–65, 231–32

Jewish
    culture, 98, 142, 147, 171, 221
    literature, 17, 82, 100, 178, 207
    texts, 33, 69
    tradition, 177–78

Jews, 42–43, 68, 70, 84–86, 89, 122, 149, 158, 163–64, 169, 194, 277

Judaism, 40, 122–23, 142, 145, 216, 228, 234

Judea, 143

judge, 37, 133, 183, 214, 218, 235–36, 240, 262
    God, 42, 236
    heavenly, 36, 216
    king, 219, 224, 241
    shepherd, 63, 218–19, 236, 240
    Son of Man, 37, 213–19, 240–41

judged, 20, 33, 37, 57, 108, 141, 152, 177–79, 183, 186, 201, 213, 216–24, 229, 235–36, 240–41, 245, 247

judgment
    in Animal Apocalypse, 82, 88, 91, 95, 99, 101, 103–10, 119, 135–41, 149–54, 159, 164, 171

judgment (*cont.*)
    in Matthew, 1–5, 14–23, 33–44, 51, 63–67, 73, 78, 80, 174–78, 180–96, 201–3, 208–29, 231–45

judicial/forensic rhetoric, 71, 266, 276

kin, 105, 221

kingdom
    of God, 14, 26, 152, 165, 178, 180, 205–6, 208–11, 239, 241, 245
    of heaven, 182, 192–93, 196, 201–5, 208–11, 213, 219, 222–23, 227, 237, 239, 241–42, 245
    of priests (priestly kingdom), 127
    of the Son of Man, 213, 239

koine/koina, 261, 265. *See also* commonplaces

law court, 62, 71

law of Israel, 111, 124, 128, 130, 135, 167–68, 195, 198–200, 206, 220, 224, 238, 251

law of natural order, 105, 252

letter(s), 51, 196
    of the New Testament, 68, 72, 76
    of the torah, 209

light metaphor, 135, 201, 237, 240

linguistics, 58, 60, 204. *See also* cognitive linguistics

location, 8, 10, 128, 162–66, 221. *See also* social location

logic, 78, 101
    Greek, 60, 70, 249, 253, 258, 263, 274
    Greco-Roman, 272
    Jewish, 66, 135, 188, 245

logos, 41, 46, 265, 270

love, 26, 175, 200
    of God, 128, 156–57, 200, 218, 220, 240
    of neighbor, 26, 175, 200–201, 218–20, 240–41, 246

loyalty, 239

Macedonia, 267

mantic discourse, 11–12, 135, 166

marginalized, 5, 13, 19, 25, 216

mashal, 64, 212

material culture, 56, 73, 78, 115, 124, 143, 168

material culture (cont.)

apocalyptic, 1, 9, 17, 21–22, 24–27, 29–30, 35, 40, 114, 123

New Testament, 2, 186, 189, 204, 204

wisdom, 4

meaning effects, 40, 45–48, 54, 57, 60–63, 66, 72–74, 78–79, 94, 145, 180, 196, 212–17, 224, 231, 244, 275, 278

Mediterranean literature, 9

Mediterranean world, 2, 7, 83, 225

memory, 51, 53, 55, 142, 169, 229

mental images, 67. *See also* images; imagery

mental models, 250

mental spaces, 55, 61, 217

mercy, 15, 160, 200, 216

metaphor

apocalyptic, 40–41, 44, 63, 66–67, 77–78, 93, 196

conceptual, 60–63, 109, 205–8

definition, 14, 40, 44

light, 135, 201, 237, 240

primary/universal, 61, 221

source domain, 61–62

substitution theory of, 274–78

sheep, 79, 81–82, 113, 116, 122, 125, 135–37, 155, 161, 163, 166, 171, 178, 215, 225, 231, 242–45

synonymous concepts, 19, 29, 132, 147, 191, 199, 212, 237

theory, 44–55

classical, 46–55

modern, 55–63

universal, 61

values of, 34, 64, 67, 90, 106, 132

virtue of, 48, 50

metaphysics, 56, 249, 257–58

method of hermeneutics, 22, 40, 44, 54, 64–65, 69, 173, 177, 248, 250–51, 255, 260–61, 266. *See also* hermeneutics; rabbinic, hermeneutics

metonymy, 49, 55, 59, 204, 205–6, 213, 274

midrash, 21–22, 64–65, 73, 78, 177–79, 201, 214

mind, 53–56, 60, 70, 94, 200, 218, 231, 275–79

miracle, 30, 71.

modernism, 2, 45, 68, 69

modernist, 44, 83, 271

modernity, 45, 136, 145, 211, 217, 249, 275

monologue, 46, 74

moral

agents, 82

authority, 197, 202

behavior, 26, 232

character, 266

instructions, 26

models, 160

predispositions, 105

responsibility, 82

morality, 105, 195

multiplicity, 56, 62–63, 71, 74–79, 220, 257, 263

myth, 31–32, 66, 67, 101, 154, 169

mythology, 9, 31

narrative, 31–33, 39, 64, 74, 79, 92–95, 102–6, 109–10, 115–16, 124–26, 130, 167–68, 171, 174, 178, 185–86, 201, 215, 220, 227, 238, 245

apocalyptic, 4, 12, 29–31, 244

argumentative, 76–79, 219, 228, 232–34, 237, 242–46

birth/infancy, 20, 31

criticism, 32

crucifixion/passion, 20, 33–34, 186

judgment, 186

mashal, 64, 212

pictorial, 245. *See also* graphic images/pictures

progression/development, 213–14, 231, 234, 239

torah, 169, 244

nature, 190, 251, 261, 263, 270

neighbor, 26, 113, 175, 200, 218–24, 240–42, 246

networks, 77

neutrality, 74, 100, 267

New Rhetoric, 69

Subject Index

normative, 170, 243

novelty, 54, 249, 255

objectivity, 56–57, 62, 261

observation, 11–12, 50, 53, 68, 71, 94, 135

offspring, 99, 101–4, 271

Old Testament, 3, 70, 192, 195, 198, 208, 228. *See also* Bible; Hebrew Bible

ontology, 54–55, 253, 255

opening-middle-closing, 73. *See also* beginning, middle, and end

opposition, 46, 56, 100, 122, 158–59, 194, 218, 222, 235, 261, 269. *See also* binary

orators, 262, 268, 271, 274

perfect, 273

oratory, 248, 272–76

order, 11, 14, 20–21, 47, 83–85, 95, 105, 122, 127, 144, 152, 271

organization, 57, 148–49

organize, 62, 125, 149, 254

orientation, 62, 234

ornamentation, 44–46, 49–50, 277

otherworldly 4, 12, 87

pagan, 216

parable, 32, 37–39, 54, 64, 176–80, 183–86, 202–27, 231, 235–40, 245

paradox, 6, 82, 155, 158, 187

paradigm, 4, 8, 14, 40, 54, 64, 70

paraenesis 3, 9, 21, 40, 105, 147, 175

parallel, 9, 32–33, 64, 92, 130, 133, 146, 155, 159–61, 174, 190, 198–99, 223, 232

parallelism, 133, 175

parousia, 1–2, 16–17, 21–22, 25, 37, 180–81. *See also* imminent coming.

participation, 65, 150

passive, 51, 242, 248

pathos, 45–46, 265–66, 270

patriarchy, 83, 95, 168

patrilineage, 97

patron, 10

peace, 146, 268

perception, 27–28, 42–43, 50–53, 56, 63, 67, 94, 169, 256, 260, 263, 269, 274–75

periphery, 59–62

persecution, 4, 10, 17–19, 88, 148, 182

person (in speech), 92, 190–91, 233

as being, 159, 194, 198, 204, 215

personages, 77, 122

personification, 54, 156, 224, 267, 278

persuasion, 45–46, 67–68, 71–72, 102, 249, 260–62, 265–70

Pharisees, 187, 195–97, 210, 215

philosophy, 45, 49, 53–59, 71, 143–44, 163, 247–50, 255–79

physical, 73, 169, 221

physics, 53, 249, 256–59, 263–64

physiology, 135

pictures, 44, 51, 84, 176. *See also* graphic images/pictures

pisteis, 261, 268

place, 47, 53, 248–49, 253–57, 259–60, 263–70. *See also* commonplaces; space; *topos/topoi*

poet, 47–49, 52, 277–78

poetry, 46–49, 64, 230, 243

point of view, 147, 254

political assembly, 71

political Messiah/Son of God, 186, 193, 196–97, 208

politics, 10, 13, 66, 71, 91, 163–64, 170, 262, 276

polysemous nature of language, 48, 62–63, 66, 79, 128, 250

polyvalence, 63–67, 81

powers of potentiality, 258–59

powers of rhetoric, 262

praise, 40

of Athens, 262

of God, 98, 194

prayer, 133, 137–38, 146, 151, 205

precreation, 71

predication, 49–50, 55, 274

premises, 68, 194, 248, 251, 253–55, 263–65

presuppositions, 17, 44, 196

priest, 64, 90, 111, 122, 133, 164

high, 164–65

priestly, 71, 84, 122, 127, 234.

primary substances, 51, 250–53, 257–60, 264

primordial, 4
principles of science/classical philosophy, 54–62, 250, 253–55, 258–60, 264, 269–70
privilege, 138, 145, 149
proclamation, 193, 199, 202, 242
progressive texture, 73, 80, 105, 144, 186, 244
promise, 20, 34, 127
proof, 54, 248, 278
prophetic. *See* rhetorolect
prototype, 58–62, 77
pseudonym, 11, 83
public, 67, 190, 201, 270
    speaking, 249, 268
punishment, 23, 41, 119, 184, 218–19, 235–36, 240–41
pure, 151, 195, 198, 233
purity, 26, 99, 111, 154, 194
Qumran, 85–87, 98, 113–14, 170
rabbinic, 142, 175, 197, 201
    argumentation, 188
    hermeneutics, 64, 211, 214
    literature, 230, 278
race, 31, 99
radical rhetoric, 20, 208
rational argumentation, 163, 188
rationale, 53
realism, 56, 136, 232, 243
    embodied, 56
reality, 5, 16, 24, 44, 47–49, 54–57, 60–63, 97, 136, 145, 165, 181–82, 207, 213, 243–44, 252–55, 267–69, 276
    transcendent, 4, 136
reason, 28, 52–55, 77, 183, 188–89, 198, 216, 251, 255, 260, 263–64, 269
reciprocal, 262, 277
recitation, 76–77, 110, 168–69, 176, 184
recognition, 30, 34, 55, 131, 133
reconfiguration, 42, 76–77, 111, 214.
recontextualization, 76–77, 110, 214
reductionism, 65
referent, 65, 93, 186, 226
reformulation, 175, 184
reinterpretation, 175

rejection, 124, 134, 165
relational, 63, 221, 222
relativism, 56
relevance, 18, 26, 226, 254, 265–66, 271
religious response, 10, 65–67, 100, 138, 165, 183, 238
remnant, 92, 114, 127, 136–43, 149–55, 161–62, 234–35
repetition, 182
repetitive texture. *See* progressive texture
representation, 59, 73, 93–94, 154
res, 276–78
resemblance, 4, 18, 46–47, 58–62, 106, 177, 184, 211, 232, 273–74, 279
resistance, 88, 143, 233. *See also* religious response
resurrection, 4, 14, 28, 181, 242
revealed knowledge, 11, 39, 135–37, 149, 152–55
reversal, 32, 148
rhetography. *See* graphic images/pictures; narrative, pictorial
rhetor, 247, 262–70
Rhetoric of Religious Antiquity, 42, 69
rhetorical dialect, 72. *See* rhetorolect
rhetorical force, 216
rhetorical invention, 64, 68–69, 94. *See also* invention
rhetorolect, 71–72, 77
    apocalyptic, 14, 41–44, 98, 184–85
    early Christian texts, 71, 79
    prophetic, 4–5, 8–10, 71–72, 135, 154, 166, 191, 195, 244
    wisdom, 4–10, 12–13, 71, 77–79, 83, 98, 128, 131, 135, 152–66, 199, 205–7, 222, 235, 244
ritual, 146, 195
Roman culture, 143, 271
sacred. *See* textures
sacrifice, 112, 117, 214, 228
sage, 11, 64, 83–84, 142, 147, 158, 235
salvation, 4, 18–20, 38, 82–83, 111, 122, 136–38, 151, 154–55, 188, 198, 200–201, 223, 229–31, 235, 239, 242, 245–46

sanctuary. *See* temple
savior, 23, 174
schema, 23, 159–60, 188
scribal creativity, 10, 231
scribe, 1, 11–13, 27, 43, 64–65, 83–84, 123, 137, 155, 164, 198, 214–15, 227, 243
    angelic, 100, 107, 139, 146
science, 56, 58, 83, 165, 250–53, 256, 264. *See also* cognitive science
scientific, 15, 22, 83, 165, 248, 251
scripture, 82, 86, 109–15, 121, 124, 134, 166–71, 175–77, 183–84, 191, 201, 214–17, 230, 245
Second Temple, 21–22, 122, 134. *See also* temple
    ideology/tradition, 123
    Judaism, 123, 149, 211
    period, 15
sectarian, 13, 152
seer, 5, 189
seeing, 128, 130, 132
self, 142, 169
semantics, 60, 77
senses,
    bodily, 53, 256, 260, 275, 279
    interpretive, 53, 58–59
sensory-aesthetic texture, 73
Septuagint (LXX), 33, 112, 117, 167
sex, 31–32, 103, 105, 140
sheep metaphor, 79, 81–82, 113, 116, 122, 125, 135–37, 155, 161, 163, 166, 171, 178, 215, 225, 231, 242–45
shepherd, 63, 88, 107, 112, 116, 119–20, 136, 140, 150, 161, 164, 177–86, 213–15, 218–19, 227, 235–36, 240–41, 245
    angelic. *See* angel as shepherd
    shepherd-king, 178, 185–86, 213–14, 223, 229, 236, 241–42
sight, 55, 106, 116–18, 126–29, 134, 279
signification, 278
signs, 21, 51, 93, 177, 215
simile, 46, 50, 54–55, 64, 267, 273–74, 278–79
slaves, 202, 207, 239

slaves (cont.)
    to the orator, 262
social and cultural texture. *See* cultural, texture; textures
social environment, 145
social location, 72
social scientific criticism, 22, 72
society, 10, 19, 23, 70, 122, 142, 170, 221–23, 271
Society of Biblical Literature, 4, 42, 68, 98
sociology, 19, 29, 32
sociorhetorical
    criticism, 71–77
    guidelines, 71
    interpretation, 40–41, 43–44, 67–71, 173
Son of God, 30, 33, 39, 63, 78, 181–82, 185–86, 190–92, 197–202, 208, 210–15, 219–20, 226, 235, 238, 241–45
Son of Man, 16, 22, 32–37, 63, 78, 162, 176–86, 196, 199, 202–22, 226, 235–36, 240–45
sophistry, 261, 270
sound, 51, 273, 278
source criticism, 75
source domain (in metaphor theory), 61–62
space, 53–55, 61, 74, 109, 120, 217–18, 232, 240, 256. *See also* mental spaces; place
speaker, 67, 230, 248, 250–54, 263–70, 273, 279
species (classical rhetoric), 48, 69, 71, 253, 264–66, 276
    of animals, 106–8, 120
speech, 12, 17, 44–46, 50, 62, 70–71, 92, 110, 132, 232, 247–48, 261–62, 266–68, 271, 277–78. *See also pisteis*
    act/action, 149, 181, 223
spirit, 31, 32, 91, 147, 198
    of God, 188–90, 197–98, 210, 215. *See also* Holy Spirit
spiritual, 197, 215
    milk, 110
    turmoil, 3

status, 57, 86, 102–4, 138, 140, 149–54, 164, 170, 187, 199, 222–24, 231
stories, 30, 94, 113–15, 124, 168, 170, 225, 238, 244
style, 48, 69, 200, 266, 273, 278
substitution theory of metaphor, 274–78
subtexts, 119
surface, 44, 61–62, 95–97, 273
syllogism, 248, 251–55, 258, 264–65
symbolism, 3, 23, 30, 67, 93, 100, 117, 138, 154
symbols, 8, 12–13, 18, 28–30, 51, 65–67, 94, 135
synagogues, 227
synchronic, 75
synecdoche, 49–50, 55, 274
synonymous concepts/metaphor, 19, 29, 132, 147, 191, 199, 212, 237
Synoptics, 1, 174–76, 192, 196
target domain (in metaphor theory), 61
tax collector, 197, 199
techniques (rhetorical/argumentative), 52, 64, 70, 149, 253
temple, 21–22, 95, 122, 129, 134, 139, 149, 163–64, 170, 234
    cult, 163
textures, 72
    ideological, 6, 25, 62, 72, 123
    inner, 40, 78–79, 173–74, 186, 213, 226, 231
    intertexture, 40–42, 69, 72–80, 225, 229, 236, 239, 244
    sacred, 72
    social and cultural, 46, 71–79, 122, 174, 221, 225, 244, 271
theme, 14–15, 75
    Ben Sira, 156–58
    Enoch, 31, 34, 92, 111, 116–20, 126–27, 142, 154–56, 166
    Matthew, 18–19, 175–76, 207–8
theology, 1, 6, 9, 19, 29, 40, 158
thinking, 9–10, 44, 53, 57, 66, 71, 77–78, 84, 191, 230, 244, 249, 276
throne, 82, 108, 139, 176, 179–81, 184, 202, 212–13, 219, 233

time, 6, 13, 23, 40–42, 49, 66, 142–48, 180–82, 193, 203, 210, 220, 224, 232–34, 242–44
    end, 8, 14, 17, 23, 29–30, 63, 82, 122, 176–77, 181–82, 209
topical, 36, 243
topics, 42, 53–54, 249–51, 255, 259–61, 264, 269, 270. *See also topos/topoi*
topos/topoi, 54, 62, 247–49, 251–70. *See also* space
    apocalyptic, 43
    conceptual, 39. *See also* imagery; conceptual, frame/framework
    eschatological, 40, 64, 78–80, 243–45
Torah, 78, 122–25, 165–69, 199–201, 244
    as revealed knowledge, 137, 153–58, 161, 171, 192, 205, 234
    interpretation, 64, 200, 214. *See also* mashal, midrash
    Israel's relationship with, 79, 93, 141, 158–60, 163, 166–67, 170, 205, 223, 235, 246
    teachings of, 78, 82, 128, 131–37, 141, 158, 171, 195, 202–6, 209, 213–15, 220–21, 227–29, 234–41, 245
touch, 55
trade, 64
tradition, 6, 8–9, 31–33, 43, 45, 63, 71–72, 75, 77–79, 82, 89, 93–94, 98, 123–24, 150, 154–55, 169–70, 173, 223, 229, 231, 237, 247. *See also* cultural, tradition
    apocalyptic, 6–7, 19, 25–27, 65, 72, 83, 239, 242
    Davidic, 168–69
    eschatological, 40, 243
    esoteric, 94
    genealogical, 166
    historical, 66–67, 77
    Jewish, 177–78
    kingly, 72
    Matthean, 209
    Mosaic, 167–69
    oral, 93, 122
    prophetic, 3, 135, 166, 244

Subject Index

335

tradition (cont.)
  rabbinic/haggadic, 101, 175
  scribal, 34
  Son of Man, 238
  source, 168
  triple, 210
  wisdom, 6–9, 12–13, 77–79, 98, 130–32, 135, 155–61, 166, 235
  written, 110
transformation, 4, 20, 67, 74, 95, 104, 145, 151–54, 232, 235
transgressions, 31
tropes, 48, 274
typology, 31, 66, 98
universal, 50–53, 68, 70–71, 155, 158–59, 255–60, 265, 269
  interpretive model, 216
  judgment, 23, 36, 51, 186, 220
  metaphors, 61
  perspective, 83, 155, 160, 222
  purpose, 149, 155, 163, 234
universalism, 158, 160
universe, 28, 145, 254, 257
  symbolic, 23
unpacking, 66
urbanity, 267
utopian, 164
values, 112, 213
  in intertexture, 73
  of metaphor/symbol, 34, 64, 67, 90, 106, 132
venatic, 247
virgins, 225
virtue, 11, 266
  of metaphor, 48, 50
visual, 136
  texture, 94, 104, 232, 278
visualizations, 51, 188, 265–67, 278
voice, 51, 74–76, 79, 98, 115, 136, 189–91
Western thought, 98
wisdom, 10, 71, 83, 128, 149, 154–62, 166, 198–99, 205. *See also* rhetorolect
  divine, 152
  ethical, 11
  literature, 6, 123, 135, 207, 222

tradition, 3–4, 8–9, 12–13, 77–79, 98, 131, 135, 155–62, 166, 235, 244
  scribal, 9
world, 4, 13, 14, 21, 52, 56–57, 63, 73, 104–5, 109, 143–45, 198, 203, 207, 230, 237–40, 275–76
  ancient, 4, 9, 83–84, 134, 225
  as mysterious, 4
  end of, 26, 28, 30, 40
  other, 4–5, 12, 87
  scriptural, 33, 40, 72, 79
  symbolic, 23
worldview, 4–5, 10, 122, 142
worship, 31, 66, 108, 117, 120–21, 151, 233
writers, 5, 17, 20, 47, 68, 75, 91, 122, 162

CPSIA information can be obtained
at www.ICGtesting.com
Printed in the USA
JSHW020311170322
23744JS00003B/13